What Moves Man

SUNY series in Global Politics

James N. Rosenau, editor

What Moves Man

The Realist Theory of International Relations and Its Judgment of Human Nature

Annette Freyberg-Inan

State University of New York Press

Published by
State University of New York Press, Albany

Printed in the United States of America

For information, address State University of New York Press,
90 State Street, Suite 700, Albany, NY 12207

Production by Kelli Williams
Marketing by Michael Campochiaro

Library of Congress Cataloging-in-Publication Data

Freyberg-Inan, Annette.
What moves man : the realist theory of international relations and its judgment of human nature / Annette Freyberg-Inan.
p. cm. — (SUNY series in global politics)
Includes bibliographical references and index.
ISBN 0-7914-5827-X (alk. paper) — ISBN 0-7914-5828-8 (pbk. : alk. paper)
1. Political science. 2. Realism—Political aspects. 3. International relations. I. Title. II. Series.

JA66.F68 2003
327.1'01—dc21 2002045263

10 9 8 7 6 5 4 3 2 1

Contents

1

Introduction

Exploring the Realist Image of Man

This book discovers and examines important psychological assumptions and arguments that underlie the so-called realist approach to the study of international relations and foreign policy.[1] In these fields of study, the realist approach is considered "paradigmatic." A "paradigm" is "a larger frame of understanding, shared by a wider community of scientists, that organizes smaller-scale theories and inquiries."[2] One might say that a paradigm provides a "common sense" that informs those individual attempts at explanation which fall within its frame of understanding. These individual attempts at explanation are what we call "theories."

A theory may be described as a "deductively connected set of laws."[3] It consists of a number of related statements that link causes to effects to provide an explanation for, and sometimes a prediction of, a particular phenomenon.[4] For example, a theory that tries to explain why nations go to war might identify a number of possible reasons and argue that some of these are more important than others under specific conditions. By doing so, it would not only explain why war might break out but also give us some idea when it would be more and when it would be less likely to occur.

Being part of the same paradigm, all realist theories, no matter what they try to explain, share certain characteristics. However, it is not always fully clear what those shared characteristics are, and the nature of the paradigm as a whole is thus somewhat elusive. This book will examine a particular defining aspect of the realist paradigm: the realist psychology. More specifically, it will focus on realist views concerning human motivation, the psychological driving forces for action. To be able to examine these views, this book takes a closer look at a range of individual realist theories and makes explicit the psychological beliefs on which they are based.[5]

As Graham Allison has explained, "[T]he purpose in raising loose, implicit conceptual models to an explicit level is to reveal the basic logic of an analyst's activity."[6] When we examine a basic characteristic of the realist paradigm, we gain insight into the logic of realist theories, which share this characteristic. By identifying what individual realist theories have in common, we also learn something about realist theory in general and thus develop a clearer understanding of the nature of the paradigm as a whole. To identify those theories which help define the realist paradigm, we need to begin by explaining what we mean when we speak of realism.

As Cornelia Navari has put it, the term

> realism was first used in philosophical discourse to denote the doctrine that universals exist outside the mind. . . . In political theory, however, the term has come to be

> reserved for the theorists of raison d'état or Realpolitik. It denotes a school which holds that there are real forces operating in the world beyond our immediate perceptions of them, that these forces are revealed by the historical process and that the able political practitioner takes account of these forces and incorporates them into his political conceptions and his political acts.[7]

Political realism may be contrasted with a number of alternative worldviews or paradigms. As a political worldview, it is traditionally opposed to idealism. As a paradigm of international relations and foreign policy, it is more commonly contrasted today with liberalism or pluralism, with constructivism, or with globalism.[8] Compared with these other approaches, political realism is arguably the dominant paradigm in the fields of study of international relations and foreign policy today. According to Joseph Nye, "[T]he conventional wisdom in the professional study of international relations since 1945 has awarded the 'realists' a clear victory over the 'idealists,'"[9] particularly in the United States. Comparing realism with the main competing theoretical approaches, scholars in the field today frequently conclude with Stephen Walt that "realism remains the most compelling general framework for international relations."[10]

The realist paradigm has been evolving through the centuries, with roots as far back as the famous "Athenian thesis" presented in Thucydides' *History of the Peloponnesian War*.[11] There are different kinds of realist theories, and realists may even develop explanations and predictions that contradict one another. However, it is possible to identify core elements, the criteria that make an argument "realist," as opposed to something else. According to Benjamin Frankel, for example, "[T]he theories in the realist family . . . do have a common center of philosophical gravity: they are all grounded in an understanding of international relations, and politics more generally, as a constant struggle for, and conflict over, power and security."[12] This understanding is based on beliefs that are shared by realist theorists.

As John Vasquez has explained, when we speak of the "realist paradigm," we really speak of "the shared fundamental assumptions various realist theorists make about the world."[13] Assumptions can be defined as "postulates relied on as part of a theory's foundation, which the theory itself does not account for or explain."[14] A number of these postulates of realism are routinely acknowledged by realist theorists. Realists have, for example, traditionally claimed that nation-states are the relevant actors in the field of international relations. These nation-states are seen as unitary in the sense that the policies they produce may be regarded as the authoritative decisions of indivisible entities. Nation-states are also rational in the sense that their responses to international events are based "upon . . . cool and clearheaded means-end calculation[s]" designed to maximize their self-interest.[15]

An understanding of the motives of nation-states—that is, of their basic goals and of the underlying reasons for their decisions—requires the analyst to determine how the national self-interest may be defined in any given case. To avoid the need to actually examine the particular interests of individual states at different times, realist theories traditionally employ the strong simplifying assumption that one goal all states strive to maximize at all times is power. In defense of this assumption, realists commonly point out that power is a necessary means needed to achieve all other possible goals a state might have. In addition, a nation's power relative to other nations is considered crucial in the pursuit of the most basic and important of these goals. That goal is the survival of the nation–state as an independent entity.[16]

In the words of neorealist Kenneth Waltz, all states "at a minimum, seek their own preservation."[17] Offensive realist John Mearsheimer agrees that "the most basic motive driving states is survival."[18] He explains that this, however, makes it necessary for "states in the international system [to] aim to maximize their relative power positions over other states."[19] This is why states "at a maximum, drive for universal domination."[20] It appears thus that, even if a state possesses no desire to expand and no imperialistic ambitions—that is, even if it is motivated purely defensively, by a desire to survive as an independent nation—its rational strategy would be to attempt to become as powerful as possible. This is how it becomes reasonable to view power not merely as a means to other ends but rather as the end itself and thus the most important motive driving state behavior.

According to realists, this characterization of international relations as a constant struggle for power is supported by the observation of political reality. Its reliance on the rationality assumption allows realism to employ the so-called rational calculus to judge the preferences, or goals, of states based on their observed behavior: Whatever interest a state appears to be maximizing must be identical to what it has chosen as its goal.[21] Thus, behavior such as the participation in an arms race or an attack on another state is easily interpreted by realists to support the belief that states try to maximize power. However, it is not logically necessary to perceive such actions as part of a proactive strategy motivated by a lust for power and domination. It is, in fact, just as plausible to view them as part of a reactive strategy, as responses to a more basic motive, which is the emotion of fear. Whereas power, even if viewed as an end in itself, remains an attribute that is instrumental to the pursuit of other goals, the emotion of fear is the natural, perhaps inescapable response to threats to one's survival. In other words, fear is what drives actors to attempt to protect themselves; to accomplish this they strive to become powerful. A complete account of the motivational assumptions of realism requires us to pay attention not only to the rationality assumption and the motives of survival and power but also to the role played by the motive of fear, which has been a cornerstone concept in the works of important realist theorists such as Thomas Hobbes.[22]

This book will show that assumptions about the motives of political actors, which represent beliefs about individual psychology, form the ontological foundation of all realist theories, even those which, like the structural systemic realism of Waltz, attempt to avoid all concern with how individual actors come to make their policy choices.[23] The fact that realists have traditionally been primarily concerned with the behavior of nation–states rather than individual policy makers has served to obscure the role these beliefs play in supporting realist arguments.[24] In particular, the relationships between the central motivating forces of fear, self-interest, and the desire for power have not been systematically specified by realist theory. Neither has the degree of influence that the operation of these motives, as compared to that of constraints imposed by the environment, is expected to have on foreign policy decisions.[25]

The assumptions that characterize the realist paradigm include a particular view of human nature from which realist theorists develop expectations about the likely behavior of states. The assumption of rationality concerns the characteristics of the human thought process and thus may be called a "cognitive" assumption.[26] By comparison, motivational assumptions concern the forces that stimulate human action. Motives are commonly understood to be activators of behavior. In fact, in the words of psychologist K. B. Madsen, "[I]t is not possible to understand, explain or predict human behavior without some knowledge of 'motivation'—the 'driving force' behind behavior."[27]

There are many theories of motivation, and parts of many learning and other psychological theories also deal with the basic motives that underlie human behavior.[28] However, despite the diversity of views on motivation, we can identify a consensus on its basic characteristics. Motivation is commonly treated as a part of the human organism, or human nature. It interacts with environmental factors insofar as the environment can facilitate or restrict the operation of motives and insofar as it provides stimuli for what psychologists refer to as "motive arousal." Motives are aroused by internal or external stimuli, such as hunger or provocation, and determine how human beings will react to such stimuli. Motive arousal may be explained as a function of three main variables: motive dispositions, or needs, such as physical drives; characteristics of the incentive, that is, the opportunities that present themselves to fulfill these needs; and expectations of the attainability of goals, or the difficulty and likelihood of taking advantage of those opportunities. Thus, motives are related to, yet at least conceptually distinguishable from, needs, incentives, and goals. It is useful to conceptualize the process of motivation as has been suggested by Russell Geen: Actors are always simultaneously confronted with their own needs and with external situations that affect what is achievable.[29] Both need and situation determine which behavioral incentives the actor will perceive.[30] The actor then defines his goals accordingly and will take action to achieve these goals.

The assumptions that realism makes about the nature of human motivation are less easy to identify than some of the more commonly acknowledged postulates of the paradigm. Realist theories emphasize different aspects of the same realist view of human nature for different purposes, which allows them to achieve plausibility under a variety of circumstances.[31] They also frequently fail to spell out the specific psychological assumptions that underlie their individual arguments. As a consequence, the overall idea of the realist psychology that emerges from the literature is fragmented, incomplete, and may even contain contradictions. There exists no evidence for a scholarly consensus on a precise and comprehensive definition of the realist view of human nature, nor an analysis of its role.[32]

This is a surprising state of affairs, given the facts that realist motivational assumptions, if analyzed in their entirety, do form a coherent view of human nature, and that they have remained stable enough over many centuries to give realist thought the status of a coherent scientific paradigm. Even more puzzling is the widespread acceptance of the realists' choice to ignore other possibly relevant motives for state action than the ones emphasized by their paradigm. After all, as will be made clear in this book, realists attribute political decisions to a very narrow range of such motives. The assumption of one particular view of human nature as opposed to any other must be expected to have consequences for the resulting interpretations of human (and state) behavior. Especially given the degree of influence that the realist paradigm possesses in the real world, it seems necessary to ask what the consequences of the realist view of human nature may be. It is puzzling that such questions are only infrequently raised and even less frequently answered.

The specific questions I will address in this book arise out of the related puzzles I have just described. My central premise is that ideas have the power to shape human reality through affecting our interpretations of our observations and thereby influencing our reactions to them. My goal is to examine the nature, function, and effects of that particular set of ideas that is represented by the motivational assumptions of realism. To achieve this goal, I raise the following questions:

1. What is the *nature* of the motivational assumptions of realism?
2. What is the *function* of these assumptions in realist theory? What role do they play, and how are they used?
3. What are the *effects* of using these particular assumptions in this way on (a) the insights produced by realist scholarship and (b) the policies that are informed by realist scholarship?

Main Arguments

The central claim made in this book is that realist motivational assumptions function differently than is commonly argued by realists and that they have more sinister effects. Specifically, I take issue with the following view: Realists claim that the motivational assumptions which underlie their paradigm serve as basic building blocks for theories and models used to explain and predict political phenomena. In this way, these assumptions fulfill the necessary function of axioms on which realist arguments can come to rest. In addition, to call oneself a "realist," in the study of politics just as in common usage, is to make the claim that one sees the world as it really is, rather than through the rose-tinted glasses of idealism or through the distorting lens of an ideology.[33] It is to make the claim that one is "objective" in one's interpretation of observable phenomena. Thus, in the words of Steven Forde, "[D]rawing on analyses of human nature, on arguments about the necessary structure of international relations, and on laws of political behavior derived from both these sources, realists have quite frequently posed as the clear-eyed apostles of objective reason, confronting the deluded idealism or self-righteous moralism of their fellow men."[34]

Realists do not commonly claim that the assumptions they use to simplify and represent the complex reality of human motivation are 100 percent correct. However, they consider them to be a close enough approximation to this reality to provide their theories and models with a defensible axiomatic basis for the development of plausible explanations and reasonably accurate predictions. They do commonly claim that their view of human motivation is supported by observation of human behavior, and they frequently use cases of foreign or international policy making to illustrate the behavior that supposedly results from such motivation as well as the apparent ease with which such behavior can be explained by realist theories. When a particular realist study has delivered a widely accepted explanation or an accurate prediction of a political event, this is considered evidence for the accuracy of the assumptions it employs. Its explanatory and predictive power is commonly cited as the explanation of why realism is and deserves to be the dominant paradigm in the study and practice of international relations and foreign policy. It is also the reason why realist motivational assumptions are so seldom questioned.

The reason, then, why realism chooses to employ the particular motivational assumptions it does is supposedly that these assumptions sum up the reality of human motivation in a way that is at once an acceptable simplification of empirical reality and a sound axiomatic basis for theories that are logically coherent and possess explanatory and predictive power. Realists obviously do not believe their motivational assumptions to have a distorting effect on their interpretations of political phenomena. They naturally do not believe that policies developed based on realist arguments suffer from any harmful bias.[35] Nor do they believe that the realist paradigm fails to meet standard criteria for the proper conduct of science.

This book disputes the view of the function and effects of realist motivational assumptions that I have just sketched. I argue that instead of playing a scientifically defensible role in a quest for a more accurate understanding of reality realist motivational assumptions serve to justify realist arguments and to help solidify the dominant status of the paradigm in a scientifically "illegitimate" manner. The motivational assumptions employed by realists not only represent a simplification of reality; they are, in fact, biased in favor of the particular view of reality that corresponds to the ideological preferences shared by realist theorists and policy makers. It is true that these assumptions do, in fact, occasionally produce plausible explanations and accurate predictions, but they do so only in cases in which they perchance adequately capture the motivation of the particular actors observed.[36] This cannot legitimately be viewed as an indication for their general validity. In addition, it is quite likely that the interpretive bias introduced by realist motivational assumptions into scholarship may translate into a policy-making bias with potentially harmful effects.[37] This can happen in several ways: first, through the academic education of policy makers; second, through the active involvement of realist scholars in political decision making;[38] and, third, and most important, through the incorporation of paradigmatic assumptions and arguments into political "common sense."

I argue that realist motivational assumptions function as the axiomatic basis for an argumentative strategy that works backwards to set up a seductive circular logic: Realists share a particular view of how the world functions. They employ particular motivational assumptions because those assumptions support this view of the world. Using those assumptions as the basis for their explanations of international events, they derive interpretations of such events that confirm their initial views. This confirmation, in turn, is viewed to justify the use of their basic assumptions.

Such a tautology does not need to be consciously pursued by any scholar to characterize the paradigm, but it would have to be consciously countered to be overcome. The realist paradigm, by continually evolving through attempts to explain the international events observed at any given time, has achieved both a widespread acceptance of its core assumptions and a position of dominance in the study of international affairs. It has also arguably achieved the status of common sense in influential sectors of the policy-making establishments of many nations.[39] As Robert Keohane has observed, in the United States, "[F]or the most part, discussions of foreign policy have been carried on, since 1945, in the language of political realism—that is, the language of power and interests rather than ideals or norms."[40] This book will show that realism has not achieved this status by following the logic of science but rather by subverting it.[41]

I argue that realism functions as a self-fulfilling prophesy by favoring such interpretations of political events that serve to confirm the assumptions initially adopted. Thus, the empirical validity of realist assumptions becomes difficult to judge. Realist theory, caught up in this circularity, becomes irrefutable.[42] It is quite plausible that the paradigm may have become dominant by virtue of this lack of refutability, rather than by virtue of its superior "realism."

Realism has become the "normal science" of international relations and foreign policy.[43] Thus, if we follow Thomas Kuhn, its status could only be weakened by the discovery of facts that contradict its central hypotheses. According to Imre Lakatos, its theories can reign as the state of the art until replaced by others that are shown to possess superior explanatory power.[44] The problem here is the following: First, the existence of facts that contradict central hypotheses of realist theory may simply not be acknowledged by staunch realists.[45] Instead, they may be more likely to adopt ad hoc assumptions or adjust their own arguments in an ad hoc fashion to protect their theory from refutation.[46] They do so, in the words of Karl Popper, "only at the price of destroying, or at least lowering, its scientific status" by rendering it irrefutable.[47] Second, as a further consequence, it becomes virtually impossible for rival theories to demonstrate superior explanatory power. After all, realism seems to explain everything, or at the very least as much as any of its rivals could.[48]

The motivational assumptions of realism play a crucial role in this strategy: First, they are usually not made explicit, which makes possible their ad hoc modification and gives realist arguments increased flexibility and an unfair advantage over rival theories with explicit images of human nature. This is why it is important for the sake of progress in the discipline to establish a general and maximally consensual definition of what realist motivational assumptions actually are. Second, realist motivational assumptions contain a bias in favor of that particular view of human nature which is consistent with the realist worldview as a whole. As a consequence, they function to support realist arguments ex post facto by favoring such interpretations of political events that are consistent with the same bias. This is why it is important to analyze the role played by these assumptions in realist theory. Finally, the circularity of the realist logic serves to uphold the traditional choice and usage of realist motivational assumptions. The obvious entrenchment of these assumptions in the discipline, which is a consequence of this tendency, increases the necessity to examine the effects of this choice and usage.

Of course it is possible to defend the use of realism as a theoretical approach to the study of international relations; however, any such defense must include a recognition of the motivational assumptions employed, of the role they play in the theory, as well as of their consequences for the findings and recommendations that result from the study. Realists are justified in employing particular motivational assumptions to the extent to which they are able to defend them as empirically accurate.[49] While it is often said that descriptive accuracy is not the only criterion by which theoretical assumptions may be judged, if we attempt to judge the value of realist motivational assumptions instead by their scientific merit (that is, by the contribution they make to models and theories that serve to advance our knowledge of international politics), we run into the problem that the realist paradigm in its current vogue state is impossible to refute. The quality of its assumptions, embedded as they are in the logic of the paradigm, is difficult to assess in isolation. To achieve greater a priori explanatory and predictive power, realists would likely have to modify their motivational assumptions to make them more broadly representative of the actual panoply of human motives. Doing so would mean sacrificing parsimony. It might also in effect mean abandoning long-cherished paradigmatic confines. However, it would reduce the temptation experienced by realists to interpret events to fit their assumptions, and it could only improve the usefulness of their theories.

Approach and Layout of This Book

In this book I attempt to answer three questions. The first concerns the nature of realist motivational assumptions. The second concerns their function, that is, the role these assumptions play and the way they are used in realist theory. The third concerns the effects of realist motivational assumptions on both the insights produced by realist scholarship and the policies that are informed by such insights.

In the first part of this book, I take what might be called a historical–hermeneutic approach to answering these questions:[50] Tracing the evolution of the realist paradigm from the fifth century B.C. to the present day, I analyze the use of motivational assumptions by various paramount thinkers of the realist tradition, including Thucydides, Niccolo Machiavelli, Thomas Hobbes, Hans Morgenthau, and Kenneth Waltz. In so doing, I rely on my own analysis of primary texts as well as on a range of commentary and criticism. This in-depth analysis of the development of the realist psychology, summarized in Table 1.1, is necessary to develop comprehensive and

Table 1.1
The Evolution of the Realist Psychology

Theoretical variant	Author*	Works examined	Main contributions
Athenian justifications of power politics—first indications of the realist psychology	Thucydides	*History of the Peloponnesian War*	Realist interpretation of the three basic motives of fear, honor, and profit; stress on the needs for power and security; universalism; determinism; irrelevance of morality in interstate relations: *We have been forced to advance our dominion to what it is, out of the nature of the thing itself; as chiefly for fear, next for honour, and lastly for profit.* (70) . . . *We have therein done nothing to be wondered at nor beside the manner of men.* (70) . . . *Having computed the commodity, you now fall to allegation of equity; a thing which no man that had the occasion to achieve anything by strength, ever so far preferred as to divert him from his profit.* (70–71)
Classical Ideological Realism	Niccolo Machiavelli	*The Prince; Discourses on Livy*	Stress on the universal wickedness of human nature; advocacy of the manipulation of fear as a policy tool: *This can generally be said about men: that they are ungrateful, fickle, dissimulators, apt to flee peril, covetous of gain; . . . and men are less reticent to offend one who makes himself loved than one who makes himself feared.* (*The Prince*, 62)
Classical Paradigmatic Realism	Thomas Hobbes	*Leviathan; Behemoth; De Cive*	Resurrection of the realist interpretation of the three basic motives of fear, honor, and profit; fear as the primary motive; stress on the destructive irrationality of human nature and the amorality of human congress; prescription of rational fear and self-interest as political solutions: The state of nature is characterized by *continuall feare and danger of violent death* (*Leviathan*, 89); the cause of this fear *consists partly in the naturall equality of men* and *partly in their mutuall will of hurting* (*De Cive*, 45); *to this warre of every man against every man, this also is consequent; that nothing can be Unjust* (*Leviathan*, 90); *the Originall of all great, and lasting Societies, consisted not in the mutuall good will men had towards each other, but in the mutuall fear they had of each other (De Cive*, 44).
Classical Twentieth-Century Realism	Hans J. Morgenthau	*Scientific Man vs. Power Politics; Politics among Nations*	Traditional realist image of human nature as the axiomatic foundation for the development of realist policy prescriptions; anti-idealist pessimism; advocacy of a politics of prudence: *Politics . . . is governed by objective laws that have their roots in human nature* (*Politics among Nations*, 4); *the sinfulness of man is . . . not . . . an accidental disturbance of the world sure to be overcome by a gradual development toward the good but . . . an inescapable necessity* (*Scientific Man vs. Power Politics*, 204); *a tendency to dominate*, the *aspiration for power over man, is the essence of politics* (*Politics among Nations*, 31, and *Scientific Man*, 45).

(*continued*)

Table 1.1 (*continued*)
The Evolution of the Realist Psychology

Theoretical Variant	Author*	Works Examined	Main Contributions
Classical Twentieth-Century Realism	Reinhold Niebuhr	*Moral Man and Immoral Society; The Structure of Nations and Empires; Christian Realism*	Neo-Augustinian evil-in-man premises; the wickedness of human nature asserts itself especially in relations between groups; stress on the destructive power of the motives of irrational fear and pride.
Classical Twentieth-Century Realism	Edward H. Carr	*The Twenty Years' Crisis, 1919–1939*	Anti-utopian criticism of the idea of a *natural harmony of interests (89)*; critical view of normative approaches: *power goes far to create the morality convenient to itself* (236).
Neorealism	Kenneth Waltz	*Man, the State, and War; Theory of International Politics*	Traditional realist image of man as implicit first-image foundation for systemic international relations theory: *The root of all evil is man, and thus he is himself the root of the specific evil, war.* (*Man, the State,* and *War,* 3) . . . *Struggles for preference arise in competitive situations and force is introduced in the absence of an authority that can limit the means used by the competitors* (*Man, the State,* and *War,* 35).

* See Appendix for brief biographical information on the authors of classical realism studied in this book.

defensible answers to the three questions raised above. Such answers, in turn, are the necessary basis for the critique of realist motivational assumptions, which is the key purpose of this book.

The second chapter begins the historical analysis by examining the origins of the realist view of motivation through a close reading of Thucydides' *History of the Peloponnesian War*. It identifies the central tenets of the realist view of human nature, in general, and motivation, in particular, as they are presented by Thucydides. It then compares the elements of the realist psychology found in the *History* with elements of the alternative views that are also presented by the historian. This approach allows us to bring into focus those enduring motivational assumptions that have characterized the paradigm since the known beginnings of political theorizing.

The third chapter analyzes the highly influential contributions of Machiavelli and Hobbes to the further development of realist motivational assumptions. In so doing, it discusses the impact of modern rationalism and scientism on the realist psychology. It also examines the role played by the realist psychology in the development of modern views on the methodology of political science.[51]

The fourth chapter examines the work of representative realist scholars of the twentieth century to bring up to date the historical analysis of the development of the realist view of human nature. It includes treatments of both the "classical" realist and the structural, or neorealist, schools of international relations theory as well as of important contemporary developments in realist scholarship. It also briefly analyzes the impact of rational choice and game theory on the development of the realist psychology. The fifth chapter summarizes the conclusions of the historical analysis and provides answers to the three central questions raised above.

Based on these answers, the second part of the book presents a critique of the use of motivational assumptions in realist theory, relying also on a transdisciplinary survey of research into the nature of basic human motivation and into the effects of theoretical assumptions on decision-making processes as well as on a range of studies of realist policy-making biases. It argues, first, that realist motivational assumptions constitute an incomplete representation of the basic elements of human motivation and that they carry a bias in favor of a particular and pessimistic view of human nature. Second, it suggests that this bias has the potential of systematically affecting realist scholarly findings as well as policies in ways that we may find undesirable. Third, it claims that a necessary critical revision of realist motivational assumptions is impeded by the tendency of the realist paradigm to function as a self-fulfilling prophesy. It suggests ways in which the use of restrictive motivational assumptions may support the perpetuation of the pessimistic bias that pervades realist political theory and praxis and thus fulfill a crucial role in justifying the "politics of distrust," which realism presents and excuses as inevitable.

The first part of my critique, developed in chapter 6, involves the claim that realist motivational assumptions constitute an incomplete representation of the basic elements of human motivation and that they carry a bias in favor of a particular and highly pessimistic view of human nature. There is ample evidence in the psychological as well as political–psychological literature to the effect that realist motivational assumptions are in fact unrealistic, that is, that the actual range of motives underlying human behavior differs substantially from the realist image of man. Of particular relevance here are the findings of David McClelland on the elements and operation of motivation as well as studies by David Winter and others that attempt to link motivation to specific foreign policy decisions.[52] Those studies, alongside many others, show that to actually explain and predict political behavior a broader range of motives than those acknowledged by realism has to be taken into account. This broader range of motives may include, for example, the desire for affiliation or community as well as the operation of altruism.[53] Such motives have traditionally been disregarded by realism, which, as a consequence, has adopted a dim view of human nature and a pessimistic outlook on possibilities for international peace and cooperation.[54]

The second part of the critique involves the suggestion that the empirical bias contained in realist motivational assumptions has the potential of systematically affecting realist scholarly findings as well as policies in ways we may find undesirable. Chapter 7 explains how the bias in the psychological assumptions underlying realist theory can translate into a bias in the findings that result from the application of that theory. In short, biased assumptions translate into particular explanations and expectations. Both scientific hypotheses and policy recommendations are developed based on such expectations. Occurrence of the expected results is taken as proof of the correctness of the assumptions used, and even results that contradict the researcher's expectations can be "explained away," rather than lead to a revision of incorrect assumptions.

Chapter 7 further argues that the bias introduced into policy making as a result of the dominant status of the realist paradigm is potentially harmful in its real-world effects. Several case studies and comprehensive analyses of foreign policy making, such as the one conducted by Yaacov Vertzberger, have demonstrated and explained the harmful effects of motivational biases in international politics.[55] Other work, such as that of Ralph White, analyzes more directly the operation of some of the particular biases contained in realism, finding that the realist emphasis on the motives of fear and power at its worst supports "paranoid" tendencies in foreign policy decision making.[56] Scholars writing in this area commonly argue that biased general assumptions about the motives of other actors cause decision makers to make erroneous judgments about the reasons behind the particular decisions made by those actors. Such erroneous judgments may then lead to conflict-stimulating reactions that may have been avoided given fuller, more accurate information about the other actors' motives.

The third part of my critique, developed in chapter 8, involves the argument that a necessary critical revision of realist motivational assumptions is impeded by the tendency of the realist paradigm to function as a self-fulfilling prophesy. I suggest ways in which the use of restrictive motivational assumptions may support the perpetuation of the pessimistic bias that pervades realist political theory and praxis and thus fulfill a crucial role in justifying the "politics of distrust," which realism presents and excuses as inevitable. One body of literature relevant for this argument consists of critiques of the rationality assumption in particular. Representative here is Mark Petracca, who suspects that "public policy fashioned on the assumption of self-interested behavior may beget precisely such behavior when implemented."[57] In addition, a few scholars have levied similar criticism at the realist paradigm as a whole. Adopting a line of argument well established in European peace research since the 1960s, they fear with Ernst-Otto Czempiel that "realism as a strategy recommends a behavior, the implementation of which serves to confirm realism as a theory."[58]

I argue that it is the realist view of human nature, in general, and of motivation (and rationality), in particular, that supports the self-fulfilling tendency of the realist paradigm: It encourages distorted judgments of the motives of other actors and thereby creates incentives to respond to others' behavior in exactly the ways predicted by the paradigmatic worldview. The fact that realism functions as a self-fulfilling prophesy in the real world contributes to the ease with which the paradigm dodges scientific refutation: The more widely accepted realist arguments become, the less it appears necessary to question the ad hoc adjustments that are employed to save the theory (and its assumptions) from refutation. The less such adjustments are questioned, the more widely accepted the paradigm becomes. To explain how realism escapes from refutation, I rely on the arguments of Karl Popper and later theorists of science who have examined the process of scientific advancement.[59] (See table 1.2)

Table 1.2
Three Stages of Critique

Empirical Critique	The realist image of man is incomplete and biased in favor of divisive, competitive, and destructive aspects of human nature. Realism concentrates on the motive of fear and the goals of power and security and emphasizes rational self-interested behavior, neglecting other important motivational and cognitive elements of human psychology, in particular the motivational complexes revolving around the goals of achievement and affiliation, whose relevance is stressed by psychologists and political psychologists alike.
Political Critique	The bias contained in the realist image of man translates into a bias in realist scholarly findings which, in turn, negatively affects the real world of foreign policy making. The realist image of human nature diminishes chances for peaceful coexistence, international cooperation, and transnational institution building. At its worst, the realist emphasis on the motive of fear and the goal of power supports paranoid tendencies in foreign policy decision making, which increases the probability of international violence.
Epistemological Critique	A necessary critical revision of the realist psychology is impeded by the paradigm's tendency to function as a self-fulfilling prophesy. The use of restrictive motivational assumptions supports the perpetuation of the pessimistic bias that pervades realist political theory and praxis, and fulfills a crucial role in justifying the "politics of distrust," which realism presents and excuses as inevitable. Lack of explicitness and consistency in applying its psychological assumptions helps realist theory "dodge" refutation in ways that threaten the degeneration of its research programs.

The concluding chapter moves beyond the analysis and critique that constitute the bulk of this work to identify some of the wider implications of the arguments made in this book. It attempts to locate these implications within the context of major scholarly divisions in the field of international relations theory. First, it briefly discusses possible realist responses to the findings of this study and examines options for the future development of realist theory. Second, it explores how a transcendence of theoretical divisions might help to ameliorate the problem of biased motivational assumptions in the study and conduct of international affairs. A comparison of three major schools of international relations theory—realism, liberalism, and constructivism—reveals that each of these schools coheres around one of the three basic motive categories: power, achievement, and affiliation. It is suggested that new integrative frameworks for the study of international political behavior should incorporate all three of these motive categories to avoid the type of bias that has been identified in realist theory. Finally, the concluding chapter argues that the search for such new frameworks stands to gain from disregarding entrenched epistemological divisions in the discipline, which only serve to uphold theoretical biases. It closes with a number of related theoretical and methodological suggestions for the future development of international relations theory.

I conclude that the nature and use of its motivational assumptions diminish the value of the realist paradigm to the extent that it should be rejected as a complete and legitimate theoretical approach to the study of international relations and foreign policy. Both the psychological literature on human motivation and rival theoretical approaches to the study of international relations have made important contributions to a more appropriate understanding of motivation that could serve as the foundation for new theories. Specifically, I argue that the insights of both liberal and constructivist approaches should complement realist motivational assumptions to provide a more complete account of human motivation.[60] Such a revised account would serve to counter the potentially dangerous dominance of the realist paradigm in the study and practice of foreign policy and international relations.

Why Is This Study Important?

One needs only to be superficially familiar with the theory of international relations and foreign policy to realize that within both these subdisciplines of political science a vast body of literature dealing with various aspects of realism has accumulated over the years. Critiques of realism abound,[61] ranging from narrow and focused refutations of particular realist studies or their findings to sweeping rejections of the merit of the paradigm as a whole.[62] There also exists a vast array of realist defenses.[63]

It is difficult to divide this body of literature into subsections dealing with well-defined issues, such as the realist view of human nature or motivation. Rather, issue areas overlap, which makes it difficult to assess the proverbial "state of the discipline" with respect to any particular issue or to judge the progress achieved in its study. Contemporary scholarship seems far from achieving a consensus on many fundamental points, including the view of human motivation that informs various theories of international relations or foreign policy, not to mention the view of human motivation that should. This book makes an attempt to address these gaps in the literature. It is specifically designed to make the following contributions.

First, it aims to identify the nature of the motivational assumptions of realism. This is necessary because there exists no explicit consensus on the nature of these assumptions, either among realist scholars or outside the realist paradigm. This state of affairs has contributed to the abuse of such assumptions: The lack of clarity on what these assumptions should be and how they should be consistently employed allows realists too much flexibility in the formulation of their theories as well as in the interpretation of their findings. It also makes the ontological foundations of realism too difficult to criticize, contributing to the lack of refutability from which the paradigm suffers.

The second contribution this book makes is to show that rather than representing a harmless simplification of reality for the purposes of theory testing realist motivational assumptions contain a bias that translates into realist findings and policies. If it is true that this bias can affect policy making in undesirable ways, an awareness of the nature and operation of this bias becomes necessary as the first step toward its removal.

The third contribution of this book is to show that realist motivational assumptions, once again rather than being harmless axioms, function to uphold the elevated status of the paradigm in whose services they are employed. This explication of the role realist motivational assumptions truly play within realist theory is necessary for an understanding of the tendency of realist theory to function as a self-fulfilling prophesy. An awareness of this tendency, in turn, is necessary to understand why the problematic tendencies discussed here have been so difficult to fight.

Moving beyond investigation, this book also attempts to make a suggestion on how these problematic tendencies might be overcome. It does so by showing how a broader view of human motivation could serve to deliver more complete explanations of political behavior, while at the same time reducing the risk of biased interpretation. Reducing the risk of bias is necessary for the sake of scientific advancement. More important, given the nature of the realist bias, it is necessary for the sake of practical progress in the conduct of international affairs.

Part I

What Moves Man? An Analysis of the Realist Psychology

2

The Roots of Realism

This chapter examines the origins of the realist view of motivation by means of a close reading of Thucydides' *History of the Peloponnesian War*. It identifies the central tenets of the realist view of human nature, in general, and motivation, in particular, as they are presented by Thucydides. It then compares the elements of the realist psychology found in the *History* with elements of the alternative views also presented by the historian. This approach will bring into focus those enduring motivational assumptions that have characterized the realist paradigm since the known beginnings of political theorizing.

Introduction

Around the fifth century B.C., a particular worldview gained currency in ancient Greece.[1] This worldview combined a shift from religious to secular interpretations of historical events with an instrumental view of the knowledge to be gained from such interpretations. It supported what one might today call a "positivistic–scientific epistemology," that is, a particular approach to the acquisition of knowledge based on three major assumptions: First is the belief that phenomena exist independent of human observation. There are, in other words, facts of nature. Second is the belief that it is, in principle, possible to explain all facts of nature with reference to other facts of nature. Mythology or religion cannot contribute to a better understanding of the "real" world. Third is the belief in the power of human observation and interpretation to uncover the "real" nature of the phenomena observed. This belief is inspired by the hope that the knowledge gained through a scientific understanding of the real world may be actually useful to us in shaping this world according to human aspirations or in guiding us toward getting along more successfully in the world as it is.[2]

The historiographic work of the Athenian general Thucydides, who lived from ca. 460 B.C. to ca. 400 B.C., illustrates this newly emerging epistemology. His work is commonly contrasted with that of Herodotus of Halicarnassus, who recounted the Persian War in mythological terms.[3] The fact that Thucydides broke with the mythological tradition makes his work of particular interest to modern students of history, who consider him the first "scientific historian."[4] It is evident from Thucydides' own words that he was well aware of being unorthodox in his approach. He justifies the loss of entertainment value that results from turning history from storytelling into a science with gains in objective accuracy, or at least in falsifiability:

> Now he, that by the arguments here adduced, shall frame a judgment of the things past, and not believe rather they were such as the poets have sung, or prose-writers

> have composed, more delightful to the ear than conformably to the truth, as being things not to be disproved, and by the length of time turned for the most part into the nature of fables without credit; but shall think them here searched out by the most evident signs that can be, and sufficiently, too, considering their antiquity; he, I say, shall not err.[5]

Modern mainstream political science has borrowed from the discipline of "scientific" history the belief that political events can and should be described in a "detached" and value-neutral manner and that plausible explanations of such events may be developed inductively, from an observation of the facts. The discipline of history has traditionally ventured beyond the mere description of events to explain their causes and effects. However, historians tend to focus on what is unique about the particular events they study. Their explanations are "deep," unparsimonious, and therefore rarely applicable across cases. The discipline of political science, by contrast, attempts to develop general lessons, explanations of entire classes of events, which might enable us to predict and perhaps manipulate the affairs of the world.

At the time of the Peloponnesian War, a desire for knowledge of general "laws" of history and human behavior was spreading among Athenian statesmen and philosophers.[6] The work of Thucydides illustrates the "birth" of political science out of such an interest in establishing the "laws" that could explain political events.[7] In writing his *History of the Peloponnesian War*, Thucydides went beyond description in an effort not only to explain the causes of individual events but also to suggest some general patterns that characterize political affairs. Once again, he acknowledges that political theorizing makes for boring reading. Yet he justifies it with the potential benefits to be derived from an enhanced understanding of the rules of the political game: "To hear this history rehearsed, for that there be inserted in it no fables, shall be perhaps not delightful. But he that desires to look into the truth of things done, and which (according to the condition of humanity) may be done again, or at least their like, he shall find enough herein to make him think it profitable."[8]

It is clear that Thucydidean historiography is motivated by the hope that the past may be employed to generate lessons applicable in the future. Underlying this hope is the belief that there are fundamental facts and rules which constitute our reality and are unlikely to change over time. Still, as Michael Clark has pointed out, Thucydides does not present a "theory" of international relations in the modern sense of the word.[9] This judgment is supported by two crucial observations: First, Thucydides' presentation of the possible causes of the events of the *History* is entirely unparsimonious. He explores a wide range of facts which may have contributed to the outbreak or shaped the course of the war.[10] Owing to their speculative and exploratory nature, Thucydides' explanations of the events of the *History* have inspired research into the causes of war at all levels of analysis.[11] To mention but a few avenues of research that have received inspiration from his work, balance-of-power, power transition, and hegemonic war theorists have explored Thucydides' observations concerning the systemic causes of war;[12] students of the linkages between domestic politics and foreign policy have focused on his remarks concerning the effects of national character or domestic decision-making structures on foreign policy decisions;[13] and those interested in political psychology have closely read his descriptions of individual leadership styles.[14]

The second reason why Thucydides does not present a theory of international relations proper consists in the fact that he does not explicitly express his own judgments concerning the causes of relevant events. His work is written in the form of a descriptive history and contains no digressions in which he could openly present his own explanations for the events he observes. Instead, he reports historical speeches, in which central actors in the *History* argue their positions and explain the reasons for their individual decisions.

These speeches are of central importance for an understanding of the lessons of the *History*, and especially of its political psychological lessons.[15] As Luis Lord has put it, "[T]he most important purpose that the speeches serve is to indicate 'what was proper to the occasion,' that is, the motive from which the subsequent actions spring."[16] However, it causes problems for interpretation that only eight of the twenty-eight speeches presented in the *History* were probably witnessed by Thucydides himself.[17] Of the others Thucydides says: "But as any man seemed to me, that knew what was nearest to the sum of the truth of all that had been uttered, to speak most agreeably to the matter still in hand, so I have made it spoken here."[18] Thomas Hobbes explains in a marginal note to his translation of the *History*, "To the analogy and fitness of what was to be said; so that though he used not their words, yet he used the arguments that best might serve to the purpose which at any time was in hand."[19]

It is widely believed that Thucydides' rendering of the speeches should be considered historically accurate. According to Lord, "the words may not be those actually spoken, but the thoughts are those which fit each of the critical situations which these formal orations invariably mark."[20] Still, his practice certainly leaves room for the author to infuse the *History* with his own interpretation of the events, thus fueling disagreements over the extent to which Thucydides' own opinions are reflected in the speeches

As a consequence, in addition to spawning controversies over where to locate the causes of war, Thucydides has inspired political scientists to ask whether it may not be possible after all to read some kind of political theory between the lines of the *History*, and if so, what kind of political theory it may be. Specifically, scholars of international relations and foreign policy theory debate whether Thucydides should be considered a realist.[21] Those involved in this debate attempt to identify Thucydides' own opinions by looking at the way he presents the arguments and explains the actions of the subjects of his *History*.[22]

The claim that Thucydides was essentially a realist is based primarily on two elements in his work: first, his suggestions concerning the causes of the war and, second, Athenian views on human nature and the nature of interstate relations, as they are expressed in the speeches. Based on readings of the relevant passages, realists, along with some nonrealist scholars, have repeatedly traced the lineage of realism back to Thucydides, identifying him as the forefather or "founding father" of the paradigm.[23] International relations scholars as prominent as Hans Morgenthau, Joseph Nye, Robert Keohane, Kenneth Waltz, Robert Gilpin, Paul Viotti and Mark Kauppi, and Michael Doyle have claimed that the writings of Thucydides are in some way part of the realist tradition.[24] However, it should be noted that, among these scholars, views on just what kind of realist Thucydides actually was differ dramatically.[25] Moreover, contrary to the realist interpretation, Laurie Johnson Bagby, Paul Rahe, and others argue forcefully that many passages in the text contradict realist political philosophy and that, in the end, Thucydides presents the realism of the Athenian thesis as but one form of political rhetoric, "subject to practical as well as moral evaluation by the analyst."[26]

Such disagreements exist because, in the words of David Grene, "the supporting evidence from the *History* is only a series of hints, which are not susceptible of certain interpretation."[27] If this were not the case, it is unlikely that we would still be talking about Thucydides today. It is the very lack of theoretical parsimony in Thucydides' presentation of events which not only makes it difficult to label him a realist or, for that matter, a member of any other school of political thought but also makes his *History* such a rich and suggestive collection of historical data.

In the following pages, I will show how scholarly controversy over the proper interpretation of Thucydides' remarks concerning the impact of human nature on international politics contributes to a better understanding not only of Thucydides but also of modern international relations theory. Thucydides explores the role played by human motivation in international relations and the making of foreign policy.[28] Psychological explanations involving the motives behind particular strategies and decisions figure prominently in his attempts to shed light on the events of the *History*.[29] However, he does not deliver a coherent theory of human nature and its effects on international politics. Rather, he presents both realist as well as alternative claims. This chapter will support the view that Thucydides should not be viewed as a realist. However, the views of one ancient historian are ultimately of no relevance for the status of either realist theory or of its alternatives. The purpose of my participation in this debate is to identify the timeless basic elements of the realist view of human nature. By examining the evidence used to support the claim that Thucydides should be considered a realist, we can find out what political theorists today perceive to be the foundational elements of realism. On the other hand, by studying the arguments of those who claim that Thucydides should not be considered a realist, we can more clearly identify the traits that distinguish the realist psychology from its alternatives. In addition, reflected in Thucydides' critical presentation we encounter not only the defining characteristics of the realist view of human nature and its impact on international politics but also some of the problems that have been associated with this view throughout the ages. A close reading of the *History of the Peloponnesian War* thus serves as a useful introduction into a general assessment of the psychological foundations of the realist theory of international relations.

The Roots of Realism in the History of Thucydides

After having fought side by side in the Persian War, Athens and Sparta emerged as rivals for hegemony in Greece. Sparta possessed the strongest land army of all Greek cities and was the leader of an alliance of independent states that encompassed most of the major land powers of the Peloponnese and central Greece, as well as the sea power Corinth.[30] However, between 460 and 446 B.C., the Athenian alliance, which included most island and coastal states around the northern and eastern shores of the Aegean Sea, grew steadily in power by subduing or forming alliances with many cities in the regions formerly dominated by Sparta. The strongest naval power in Greece, Athens amassed considerable wealth in the form of tribute payments from her empire. Fighting erupted between the two rival cities, and, in 445, Athens was forced to give up most of her new gains in territory under the Thirty Years' Peace Treaty.[31] Hostility between the two cities reached critical levels again only twelve years later, in 433, when Athens allied herself with Corcyra, a strategically important colony of Corinth. Athenian violations of the peace treaty as well as entreaties by allies, most importantly by Corinth, eventually led Sparta to threaten war. Following the advice of her leader Pericles, Athens refused to give in to Spartan demands. In the spring of 431, Thebes, an ally of Sparta, attacked Plataea, an ally of Athens, and all-out war began.

Many students of history and politics have come to view Athens as the first secular empire and, for that very reason, the cradle of power politics. In the words of Grene, Athens has taught the world "to be aware of the creation of power in the name of nothing except itself and to consider the factor of the creation of power openly and rationally."[32] In fact, Thucydides states clearly that Athenian imperialism was an important cause of the war: "And the truest quarrel, though least in speech, I conceive to be the growth of the Athenian power; which putting the Lacedaemonians into fear necessitated the war."[33]

It is common to interpret this statement on the so-called real or truest cause to support the arguments of power transition or hegemonic war theory: Different rates in the growth of power among competing cities and alliances caused a shift in the balance of power in the Greek interstate system, eventually leading to an all-out war for hegemonic dominance.[34] However, the "truest cause" is more complex than that, in that it combines a systemic with a psychological explanation. Arnold Gomme explains: "The main cause of the war was Athenian imperialism and Spartan fear of her rival; for Athens only 'became great' through her empire. That is, the Athenians were the provocative cause; the Spartans were, however, animated by fear lest their own position should be weakened."[35]

Both Athenian expansionism and Spartan fear are presented as necessary conditions for the outbreak of the war. Either condition, by itself, presumably would not have been sufficient to trigger open conflict. In addition, some readers have pointed out that Thucydides in his statement perhaps also recognizes the relevance of national character in foreign policy making. It may have been because it was expansionism

Athens style that Athenian expansionism was so offensive to the Spartans. It may also have been due to particular cultural traits that Sparta "feared" Athens enough to resist the empire's expansion with military force.[36]

While Thucydides' summary of the "truest cause" of the Peloponnesian War is seductively concise, it is thus anything but easy to translate into the language of a political scientific thesis. Nonetheless, realist interpreters traditionally insist on reading this passage as a statement of historical necessity or the inevitability of the war. In this view, Sparta was forced to resist the growth of the Athenian empire with force to protect its own status and independence, while the Athenians in turn were forced to be imperialists. In search of an explanation for why Athens had no choice but to expand, it is common to turn to a passage in a speech given by an Athenian diplomatic delegation at Sparta before the outbreak of the war.

In this passage, the Athenians present a realist view of human nature and its impact on interstate politics, which is commonly referred to as the Athenian thesis, and whose basic message is repeated throughout the work. The Athenians are here to defend their breeches of the Thirty Years' Peace Treaty, which amount to a resumption of the imperialist policies of the period before the settlement. They claim that they have been "forced to advance [their] dominion to what it is, out of the nature of the thing itself; as chiefly for fear, next for honour, and lastly for profit."[37] The famous three motives of the Athenian thesis are not only presented as leading to an irreversible quest for power, they are also claimed to be universal, meaning that interstate relations must of necessity be characterized by constant power struggles between identically motivated states. The Athenians explain: "Though overcome by three the greatest things [*sic*], honour, fear, and profit, we have both accepted the dominion delivered us and refuse again to surrender it, we have therein done nothing to be wondered at nor beside the manner of men."[38]

The term used by the Athenians for the concept of fear, *deos*, indicates a lasting state of alarm as opposed to a sudden fright. It can also mean the possession of a reason to fear or of a means to inspire fear in others.[39] While the exact meaning of the term, as it is used by the Athenians, is debatable, one can safely say this much: Thucydides has the Athenians acknowledge that fear is one of the main psychological driving forces in relations among states. States try to protect themselves from others. They also try to inspire fear in others, so as to deter them from attacking.

The next important motive operating in relations among states, according to the Athenians, is the desire for profit. The term used by Thucydides, *heleia*, can mean as much as material profit or advantage as well as a source of gains, especially of gains made in war. However, and especially in Thucydidean usage, it also refers to material aid or support in war, meaning that, contrary to popular interpretation, the Athenians may have tried to say not that they were greedy for riches but that, by expanding their empire, they were trying to gather internal strength and allies so as to make themselves more secure.[40] This interpretation makes sense, given the fact that the purpose of the Athenian speech was to excuse Athenian expansionism in the eyes of her rivals. Clearly, defensive motivation must have been considered less objectionable than offensive motives for imperialistic policies. Once again, it is possible to establish an interpretive minimum consensus: The Athenians acknowledge the role played in interstate relations by the realization that security has an economic component. States need a minimum of resources simply to survive. Moreover, a limitless desire for security leads to a limitless desire for material advantage, since such advantage is a component of superior power.

The third motive acknowledged by the Athenians also poses some problems for interpretation. The term used for honor, *time*, has normative as well as material connotations.[41] In the normative sense, honor here can refer to the sense of pride or dignity acquired through service to the community. The Athenians may have tried to explain that giving up the possibility of strengthening their empire would have been a dishonorable thing to do according to commonly accepted norms of behavior. It might have made them look weak and discredited their community and its members in the eyes of the world. However, it is possible, given the double meaning of the word, that such a normative argument was not then commonly separated semantically from the idea that part of the reason for conquest are the honors it brings in the form of material recognition, such as rewards and honorary titles.

The role of the elusive motive of honor in Athenian politics is of particular relevance for a discussion of the roots of realism in the Athenian worldview. I have mentioned earlier that it is common to view Athens as the first secular empire. What this means in effect is that the justification used by the Athenians for their imperialistic policies rests not on religious or quasi-religious claims, such as fate or a calling, but instead on claims concerning the observable facts of human existence. One major problem with such arguments is that the secularism they encourage does not stop outside the city walls. An astute observer of Athenian domestic politics as well as interstate relations, Thucydides inarguably laments the breakdown of civic virtue in Athens that occurs during the time of the war. This breakdown of civic virtue involves a reconceptualization of the motive of honor from the quasi-religious aspiration to fulfill the superior fate of one's community to a pragmatic evaluation of "honors" purely in terms of material or other practical advantage. Thucydides witnesses how public officials value their personal careers over the long-term interest of the city; he witnesses political factions vying for power while endangering the commonwealth; and he quite clearly links the degeneration of civic virtue of which such events are symptomatic to the eventual tragic demise of the great Athenian empire.

The realist reading of the *History*, however, receives its inspiration not from the somber judgment of Thucydides; instead, realist interpreters listen more closely to the Athenians. Not only do they seem to accept at face value the self-justificatory rhetoric of the Athenian diplomats at Sparta, they also fail to associate the apparent rise of the Athenian thesis to the status of accepted wisdom with the decline of the city's domestic order and, ultimately, international status. Realism adopts from the Athenian thesis and the observation of Athenian political behavior an emphasis on the role of the motives of fear and profit. The concept of profit is reconceptualized as self-interest and thus broadened to include intangible advantages, of which honor is but one. The relevance of motives that are "unselfish," in the sense that they depend on the identification of the self with other actors, is implicitly denied. Thus, the realist interpretation of the *History* accepts as "natural" the lack of civic virtue and the corruption of the motive of honor that are lamented by Thucydides himself.

Their emphasis on motives which are self-referential in nature, exclusive in focus, and competitive in their effects leads realist interpretations (as well as it did Athens) into the trap of power politics. As Ashley Tellis writes, "[F]ear, honor, and interest thus conspire—as necessity—to create a pragmatic, amoral rationality of political action which seeks to preserve the empire at all costs."[42] Henry Immerwahr explains: "Power and war are intimately connected by the desire for security (phobos), the desire for expansion (pleonexia), and more generally by what Thucydides calls 'necessity' (ananke), which means that in power politics a mechanism develops in the relations between antagonists, which regularly, although not automatically, leads to war."[43] The fact that nations are inevitably motivated by fear and self-interest must lead them to pursue power, which leads them into conflict with one another, which is likely to end in war. The same sequence can be expected to develop in relations between individuals within nations, threatening civil war.

According to Steven Forde, "Thucydides' presentation of Athenian imperialism . . . represents a prototypical study of political psychology"—a political psychology based on an analysis of Athenian behavior in particular.[44] Imperialism is seen as based on certain traits inherent in human nature, which are judged to be universal.[45] "Egoistic individuals pursuing wealth and security" are thus viewed to "lie at the root of all political struggles for domination . . . ; power politics is ultimately rooted in a first-image explanation based on egoistic human nature."[46]

In the words of Clifford Orwin, the Athenians would make us believe "that all inclinations to empire are compulsory and irresistible simply because no society has ever known to resist them."[47] By presenting the motives for imperialism as "equally irresistible and so equally extenuating," the Athenians "erase the distinction between necessity and mere expediency."[48] A consequence of fundamental importance is that when the Athenians decided that the political world was ruled by necessity, rather than by the gods, they lost the possibility of moral choice.

"Owls hoot, olives ripen, Athenians harry their neighbors."[49] This becomes the argumentative strategy of the Athenian delegation at Sparta: "[Their] defense would plead an overwhelming internal compulsion, which, because overwhelming, exonerates the actor of all responsibility for what would otherwise be imputed as an injustice. So, in fact, these Athenian speakers do plead—with a remarkable twist. Not just as Athenians but as human beings are they congenitally unable to leave their neighbors in peace."[50]

The determinism of the Athenian thesis renders moot all consideration of the morality or justice of human action by explaining all such action solely with reference to laws of human behavior that follow logically from the psychological and ontological assumptions made by the observer. According to the Athenians at Sparta, one of those "laws" is that "it hath been ever a thing fixed, for the weaker to be kept under by the stronger."[51] The Athenian delegation makes reference to this alleged natural law as part of its rhetorical strategy designed to excuse or justify the rampant imperialism of its city.[52] Thucydides presents the Athenians to be combining this excuse for their own lack of moral restraint with an insulting attitude against the Spartans: "Having computed the commodity, you now fall to allegation of equity; a thing which no man that had the occasion to achieve anything by strength, ever so far preferred as to divert him from his profit."[53]

It is worthwhile restating this remark in simpler terms: If the Spartans are trying to argue normatively, they are in fact admitting to be inferior in power to the Athenians. How could the Spartans have reacted to such a challenge? Accused of being weak, many a self-respecting Spartan must have been ready to fight right then and there to prove the contrary. Arguing for restraint surely must not have seemed as attractive to the Spartan moderates once they risked being accused of being desperate or cowardly. Thucydides here clearly suggests that the argumentative strategy, the rhetorics used by the Athenians to justify themselves before their critics, might have helped to provoke the war.

The Athenians at Sparta know well that their policies are objectionable from a normative standpoint; otherwise they would not feel the need to make excuses in the first place. Rather than attempting to address these concerns, however, they choose the far more promising strategy of denying out of hand the relevance of normative arguments for the issue at stake. Once again, this strategy is based on a deterministic view of human behavior. As Grene points out, only "when an action can actually be consummated with the true possibility of choice—that is, when it proceeds from men's freedom of decision rather than the compulsion of necessity—a moral comment can be significant."[54] Such a possibility of choice does not exist, however, in the eyes of the Athenians, at least not as long as man's basic needs for security and power are not satisfied.

The Athenians do not argue that justice is always an irrelevant idea. However, they do claim that morality and justice are "luxuries," human inventions which are not necessary for survival and will therefore remain forever secondary to the pursuit of security and power. The concept of justice, for example, is understood solely as a voluntary restraint in the exercise of power. According to the Athenians, "those men are worthy of commendation, who following the natural inclination of man in desiring rule over others, are juster than for their own power they need."[55] We may certainly wonder whether the Athenians truly expect that morality and justice can ever play a role in international politics, given that it is unclear that the needs for security and power can ever be considered fully satisfied.

By denying their reality and relevance, the Athenians emerge unrestrained by the common norms of justice and morality that others may still want to respect. A belief in the superiority of intellectual independence from traditional norms, by this time, has been popularized through the teachings of the sophists.[56] Their amoral relativism would become another key ingredient of the realist philosophy.[57]

The Athenians obviously do not stand alone in their judgment of the rules of international politics. It is worth noting that the Corinthians, who argue against the Athenian defense to persuade Sparta to take action against Athens on their behalf, do not take issue with the Athenian thesis. Rather, they attempt to persuade Sparta to adopt an attitude identical to that of the Athenians. In the words of Laurie Johnson, "by blaming the Spartan's lack of initiative more than the Athenians' grasping for empire, the Corinthians sanction as natural both the endless pursuit of power and the defense against it."[58]

The consequences of such rhetorics for practical political decision making receive striking illustration in later speeches. Take the Mytilenean debate in 427 B.C.[59] After an attempted revolt by Mytilene, an independent ally of Athens, two Athenian leaders, the hard-liner Cleon and the more moderate Diodotus, argue over the proper punishment for the Mytilenean population. Although this debate is ostensibly concerned with justice, it is evident that the real question before the assembly is how Athens can best serve its strategic self-interest by deterring future revolts in the empire. More so than Cleon, who likely appears irrationally vengeful to many Athenian citizens, Diodotus argues purely from expediency. It is obvious that Diodotus's suggested course of action is more merciful and more just. However, he does not even attempt to use these facts to his advantage, admitting instead that "a great power must counter humans' natural compulsions with power, not with argument or judicial procedure."[60] While Antonios Rengakos has attempted to point out some differences between the stark realism of the war-hawk Cleon and the seemingly more moderate, Periclean position of Diodotus, it is by far more striking that, by this point, there is no true alternative in Athenian politics to arguments from expediency.[61] By foregoing appeals to mercy or justice while arguing purely from the standpoint of Athenian strategic self-interest, "Diodotus explains the full philosophical and practical consequences of the thesis first articulated by the Athenian envoys at Sparta before the war began."[62]

What makes the Athenian thesis "realistic" in the philosophical sense of the word is made clear by James Boyd White, who points out that the Athenians react to appeals to justice "by making other appeals of a more or less established kind: to human nature, to commonly accepted motives and values, to a sense of reciprocal benefits, and to the facts of the world."[63] It is at this point that it becomes understandable why realism as a political philosophy emerged in the context of the ontological revolution in fifth century B.C. Greece. We recall that the new worldview included the belief that what human beings experience through their senses are facts of nature, which can be explained through reference to other facts of nature. This belief does not allow for a questioning of reality, as it is defined by the observer. The Athenians do not refuse to justify themselves, but they will justify themselves only with respect to those aspects of their particular situations that they perceive to be real and relevant.[64] Their thesis has great force, not because it is logically compelling but because it is difficult to refute. It is based in essence on the simple assumption that if other observers claim not to share the same view of reality they must be either blind or lying.[65]

Alternatives to Realism in the History of Thucydides

A number of Thucydides scholars have countered the efforts of realist interpreters to claim the historian as one of their own. In his *Thukydides-Studien*, Hans Drexler explicitly denies the possibility of making Thucydides fit into the tradition of American political realism as exemplified in the works of Reinhold Niebuhr and Hans Morgenthau.[66] Christoph Schneider agrees that Thucydides should not be viewed as a determinist and a realist, Hobbesian style, but rather as a moral thinker who was highly critical of the reign of self-interest, especially as it affected the cohesion and well-being of the Athenian community.[67]

While admitting that Thucydides undoubtedly presents realist views in his *History*, scholars who attempt to reclaim Thucydides from realism identify fundamental inconsistencies between realist assumptions and arguments and the speculative exploration of human psychology as well as the normative judgment evident in Thucydides' presentation. They argue with Grene that evidence from the *History* "should . . . dispel the idea that there is no moral conviction behind Thucydides' observation of the facts."[68] Moreover, they interpret Thucydides to be critical of Athenian realism, claiming that he clearly saw how the political culture this philosophy supported contributed to the city–state's eventual downfall.

According to Schneider, to begin with, Thucydides does not view the Peloponnesian War as inevitable. It is true, on the one hand, that the expansion of the Athenian empire caused pressure on the Spartans and that this pressure, at a certain time, seemed too much for the Spartans to bear. On the other hand, this "true cause" for the war makes it neither inevitable "nor does it transfer its causes into the realm of 'historical necessity' and metaphysics."[69]

The fact that human beings are often selfish and act according to self-interested motives also does not mean that self-interest has to reign always and everywhere. On the contrary, Thucydides shows quite clearly that the free reign of particular interests is detrimental to the community as a whole and, therefore, in the long run, ill-conceived.[70] The selfish pursuit of power as exemplified in the careers of several Athenian statesmen is as dangerous to the well-being of the Athenian community as the unbridled imperialism of her city–states is to Hellas. Not only should power not be abused, it should also never be viewed as an end in itself. Drexler puts it bluntly: "To desire power for its own sake is worse than a crime: it is stupid and invariably leads to nemesis."[71] In the case of Athens, nemesis came as the ultimate total defeat in the war.

The motive of fear is presented by the Athenians at Sparta as one of the chief reasons for their imperialism. As Rengakos points out, the importance the Athenians place on the motive of fear parallels the primacy of fear in Hobbesian theory.[72] However, unlike Hobbes, Thucydides does not leap to the conclusion that fear should be relied on to discipline human action. According to Orwin, "Thucydides knows that men are readier to hope than to fear, and that we promptly forget even our best founded fears at the beckoning of groundless hopes. . . . If Hobbes stresses the solidity, Thucydides underscores the fragility of the floor furnished by fear, which is necessary but by no means sufficient for ensuring decent political restraint."[73]

For Thucydides, the motive of honor plays an important role in the proper conduct of politics, and it is readily apparent how different his views on this subject are from those of Hobbes. Frank Adcock makes a crucial observation when he says that, for Thucydides, "to be admired is a legitimate ambition, but as the spring of courage, the spur of action, in the public interest."[74] For Thucydides, the motive of honor is not necessarily destructive of order, as it is for Hobbes. Neither can it be subsumed under the category of self-interest. Instead, while self-interest is a purely self-referential motive, which will divide a society in times of crisis, honor has the community as its focus and, if properly cultivated, can support cohesion and enhance cultural evolution, as it did in Athens before the war.

For Thucydides, "the city comes first, the individual citizen second" and, "in great affairs of state, civic virtue—courage and devotion—is the one virtue that claims preeminence."[75] The motive to achieve this virtue must be distinguished from the motives acknowledged in realism. G. F. Abbott explains:

> Generally, self-interest is the mainspring of human conduct, and goodness a matter of condition. The average man, when well off, is comparatively good; but his virtue will not bear the stress of adversity. . . . Stronger than the religious conscience—though operating only in a few cases—is the sense of honour (literally of disgrace . . .): the sense which not only makes some men ashamed to do what is base, but even impels them to self-sacrifice.[76]

According to Thucydides, the decline of Athens was caused, at least in part, by the rise to power of inferior leaders, who, rather than setting an example of civic virtue for the citizens, used Athenian democracy to further their own selfish and shortsighted ambitions. Grene points out how, to Thucydides, good statesmanship seemed the most realistic means of transcending the deterministic tendencies of human nature and historical necessity.[77] The way for collectivities to overcome the selfish motives of their members, which do indeed often tend to be destructive of community, is to foster and follow an elite of statesmen who in some significant ways are different from, "better," than everybody else.

Thucydides does not claim human nature to be uniform. He does not attribute the same motives to a Pericles as he does to a Cleon, or an Alcibiades. It is, instead, striking how different the forms are that human nature takes in his presentation, if one compares, for example, the Athens of Pericles with that of the Sicilian expedition.[78] It is the very exceptionality of superior statesmen that helps them to overcome their own "base" motives and even to persuade the demos to weigh its motives differently. We may call Thucydides an educator because he believes that human beings can learn from good example (as well as from the reading of history).[79] We may call him an idealist because he does not reject the possibility that human beings can learn to wish to "adjust" their priorities in spite of their own initial inclinations. We may also call him an elitist, who, in the words of Leo Strauss, "never calls into question the intrinsic superiority of nobility to baseness."[80] According to John Finley, "the didactic purpose of the *History* rests on the assumption that, by knowing the natural tendencies of society, you can, if not change, at least guide them. Certainly nothing is more characteristic of Thucydides than his faith in the human mind or his admiration for able leaders."[81]

The one statesman who best exemplified the meaning of superior motivation for Thucydides was Pericles, of whom, in the words of Walter Lamb, "Thucydides has tried to explain how he held before the people of every class an Athenian ambition for a strong but generous leadership of Greece, and for an aesthetic and intellectual refinement at home."[82] Speaking of Pericles, Grene finds that

> the democracy whose dynamic was greed and fear and whose might was the offspring of that greed and fear was held in check by a single autocrat whose rule it accepted because he was not as other men were. In this voluntary acquiescence of the vulgar, in this submission to the statesman who neither flattered nor feared them but who put heart into them or made them tremble with the witchcraft of his own aloof certainty, Thucydides may have seen the transcendence of the materialism in which he believed.[83]

According to Rengakos, Thucydides throughout his work defends the Periclean virtues of morality, moderation, and reason.[84] His emphasis on morality and restraint becomes particularly clear in those passages in which Thucydides illustrates the effects of the disappearance of those virtues. In Book 2 of the *History*, he describes the effects of a plague which breaks out in Athens in 430 B.C. and leads to a breakdown of domestic order. In Book 3, he describes a shockingly brutal civil war in the city of Corcyra, fought between democratic and aristocratic factions.[85] He identifies as the cause of civil strife, or stasis, "the desire of rule, out of avarice and ambition; and the zeal of contention from the two preceding,"[86] and he observes how, under such conditions, "the nature of man, which is wont even against law to do evil, gotten now above the law, showed itself with delight to be too weak for passion, too strong for justice, and enemy to all superiority."[87]

Characterizing Thucydides as a defender of traditional morality and religion, Nanno Marinatos notes that "the phenomenon that most interested Thucydides in the plague and stasis passages is the disappearance of ordinary morality and the replacement of arete by selfishness."[88] Peter Pouncey agrees that, in particular, the portrayal of stasis shows Thucydides' horror of the reign of unbridled selfish interests without the intervention of morality and moderation.[89] The realist judgment of human motivation is presented as truly realistic in the abnormally horrifying context of a civil war, when "the motives behind all the partisan involvements are self-centered—individual ambition or individual fear determines the decisions."[90]

Thucydides' portrayals of stasis, the plague, and the decline of community values in Athens parallel Hobbes's description of the state of nature, which was, after all, modeled after such a civil war. However, while Hobbes presents the social dynamics of perpetual conflict to be "natural" in the absence of supreme disciplining force and views the motivating power of rational fear combined with the strict rule of the *Leviathan* as the only means to overcome it, Thucydides does not want to believe in the inevitability of a war of all against all in the absence of tyranny; neither does he agree with Hobbes's solution to the problem of passions.[91] In contrast to Hobbes, Thucydides does not view a state of violent disorder as natural in the sense of being inevitably brought about by the human condition, since he does not regard human nature to be constant and uniform. Instead, he quite obviously views such a state with horror as the result of the abdication of reason, moderation, and moral restraint to unbridled emotion and selfish impulses.[92]

As demonstrated by David Cohen in an analysis of the events at Corcyra and Mytilene, Thucydides does not completely avoid a normative judgment of foreign policy decisions, as the realist interpretation would have us believe. He is, in Cohen's words, not an "amoral realist."[93] Thucydides' account of the events at Melos in 416 B.C. illustrates with particular force his judgment of the horrors brought about by the abdication of moral restraint and moderation in relations among states. Athens has launched an attack on this neutral Lacedaemonian colony, an island near Athens to the east of the Peloponnese. The Melians reject the harsh terms of truce offered by the Athenians. They attempt to argue that, since they have taken no side in the war and pose no threat to the Athenians, they have a right to be left alone. The Athenians refuse to listen to the Melians' appeals for justice, claiming once again that "in human disputation justice is then only agreed on when the necessity is equal; whereas they that have odds of power exact as much as they can, and the weak yield to such conditions as they can get."[94] Once again they explain their attitude with reference to what they perceive to be the immutable facts of reality: "We think . . . of men, that for certain by necessity of nature they will every where reign over such as they be too strong for. Neither did we make this law, nor are we the first that use it made: but as we found it, and shall leave it to posterity for ever, so also we use it: knowing that you likewise, and others that should have the same power which we have, would do the same."[95] They ridicule the Melians' idealistic hopes that justice will prevail and that their allies will come to their rescue: "You are the only men, as it seemeth to us, . . . that think future things more certain than things seen; and behold things doubtful, through desire to have them true, as if they were already come to pass. As you attribute and trust the most unto the Lacedaemonians, and to fortune and hopes, so will you be the most deceived."[96] As if to fulfill their own prophesy, they lay siege to the city, starve its inhabitants into submission, and eventually put to death all the men of Melos and enslave all her women and children. This excessive cruelty on the part of the Athenians is made possible by a cool disregard for norms of justice and morality, for which Thucydides presents no excuses.

One year later, when the Athenians debate whether they should send a naval expedition to Sicily, Thucydides illustrates the effects of a lack of prudent moderation. The Athenian general Alcibiades is eager to lead this expedition himself and manages to sway the assembly in his favor. He admits openly that, by this point, Athens must continue to expand its empire to protect itself from internal destruction through stasis.[97] Undertaken as a diversion from domestic conflict and without proper consideration of the likelihood of its success, the Sicilian expedition is doomed to fail from the beginning. In addition, a crucial mistake removes all chances to beat the odds. In response to allegations of religious crimes brought forward by his political enemies, Alcibiades is forced to relinquish his command before the fleet even reaches its destination. This decision illustrates how the Athenian war effort is suffering by this time from the progressive degeneration of civic virtue at home, which is symptomized by political infighting as well as an extreme volatility of public opinion.

We can summarize with Tellis the main elements of realism that emerge from a reading of Thucydides' presentation of realist arguments and politics: "(i) Human nature is egoistic and pursues security, power, and material gain. (ii) The pursuit of such objectives creates a necessity to dominate and this, in turn, inevitably leads to disorder, violence, and decay. (iii) The disorder caused by the logic of domination cannot be avoided or subdued."[98] In contrast with this view, Thucydides, first, believes that power can be exercised with and controlled by reason and, second, shows how realist arguments contribute during the course of the war to the corruption of reason and to an excess of passion.[99] As has been forcefully argued by Orwin, Thucydides clearly sees how the Athenian thesis, with its "inherently corrosive effects on all traditional means of fostering citizenship, mutual trust, and virtue," contributes to the corruption of Athenian politics.[100] The cultivation of prudence and moderation, along with the preservation of a traditional sense of morality, might instead have made it possible for Athens to keep in check the more destructive aspects of human nature that doubtlessly operate as well.

In his critical analysis of selfish political motivation and the domestic effects of *Realpolitik*, Thucydides identifies himself as a defender of aristocratic ethics.[101] To him, reason, justice, and the good of the community possess a value of their own, which is too important to be placed in the service of self-interest and the rule of the stronger.[102] As Simon Hornblower points out, Thucydides' judgments can be understood as a reaction to the teachings of the sophists, "who denied the validity of any principle of morality but a short-sighted self interest."[103] To be sure, his generalizations "imply that although human behaviour changes according to changes in attendant circumstances, the 'nature of men' can be made the basis for predictions [and] the assumption behind all this is that people are rational and act according to their own interests."[104] However, an unreliable tendency toward rational and generally self-interested behavior, for Thucydides, does not eliminate the role of morality in politics, as exemplified by the pursuit of honor; if anything, it makes such morality more imperative. Neither does such a tendency remove the possibility of human choice of both intention and action. We may conclude with Laurie Johnson Bagby that Thucydides departs from realism by

> (1) emphasizing the importance of . . . "national character," (2) highlighting the influence of the moral and intellectual character of individual leaders, (3) showing the importance of political rhetoric for action and treating what we call realism as another argument in political rhetoric, not a theory that Thucydides thinks describes

the whole truth about political things, and (4) showing that, for him, moral judgments form an integral part of political analysis.[105]

Similar to Morgenthau after the Second World War, Thucydides has become aware, through personal experience, of the tragic tension between the values of justice and power,[106] between moral and political requirements,[107] and between choice and necessity.[108] However, unlike Morgenthau, he exhibits no desire to resolve that tension.[109] He is, after all, a historian, not a political scientist.

The lesson Thucydides nonetheless has to teach students of international relations may be summarized with Johnson Bagby as follows:

> To obtain and inculcate true political wisdom we may have to abjure the notion that any one theory or formula will accurately predict human behavior or solve human problems. In a sense this is only accepting what we already know: the price of celebrating our free will is lamenting the inability to easily explain and solve the problems of the human condition. Thucydides teaches us that even though internal passions and external forces may exceed much force, humans are in control of themselves and morally aware; they can blame only themselves for their failures.[110]

Summary and Conclusions

The original elements of the realist view of human motivation, as they are presented in Thucydides' *History of the Peloponnesian War*, can be summarized as follows: All human beings share certain basic motives. These motives are self-referential, meaning that they drive individuals to pursue their own individual goals. They are exclusive in the sense that they are not shared across actors but motivate individual actors to pursue their goals independent of their social contexts. They are also competitive, in the sense that they lead human beings to pursue interests that are likely to conflict with those of others. Fear and self-interest are the most important of these motives. The goals that follow from these motives are security and power. Human motivation is universal and stable. Insofar as basic motives are assumed to be universal, the realist philosophy is egalitarian. Insofar as they are assumed to be stable, it is static.

Human beings are compelled, by a combination of their motivational characteristics and a variety of external constraints, to act in particular ways. Laws of human behavior result, which are highly deterministic. As far as these laws apply, it is meaningless to speak of human choice or agency. As a consequence of this determinism, it usually makes no sense to question political behavior on moral grounds. Instead, normative arguments are commonly interpreted to be mere rhetorical devices, intended to distract the listener from the truly relevant aspects of a disagreement.

As a consequence especially of their pursuit of power, human beings are highly competitive in all social contexts. However, there is a difference between relations within and relations between nation-states. Relations between states are anarchical, since they are not governed by enforceable laws. International norms or diplomatic arrangements do not stop states from acting on their basic (and base) motives. They are, therefore, embroiled in constant power struggles, which regularly lead to war. Within states, on the other hand, relations among individuals and groups are governed through law, which can, under normal circumstances, keep competition in bounds and interaction civilized. However, human motivation as perceived in realism leads to problems in times of domestic crisis. A lack of motivation to identify or cooperate with others, or to act in the interest of the community against one's own narrow and short-term rationale, has the effect that, to the degree that domestic law enforcement is weakened, relations among individuals within states begin to resemble relations among states.[111]

This view of human nature and the social conditions faced by human beings emerged in the following context: In the fifth century B.C., a scientific–positivistic epistemology gained ground in ancient Greece, which was heavily influenced by Hippocratic medicine. This epistemology included the beliefs that objective facts exist, that we can observe them accurately, and that we can explain them with reference to other facts, through the operation of what we might call "laws of nature." It was supported by a secular and anthropocentric worldview, which sought explanations for observed events not through religious or mythical interpretation but through types of interpretation whose accuracy might be tested by means of human observation—in other words through the sciences as we know them today. Positivistic science attempts "detached" description and explanation as a means to minimize the impact of the interpreter's personality and preferences on the interpretations developed. It is nonnormative and, in this sense, amoral. It is also anti-moralistic, since it views attempts to introduce normative arguments into science as illegitimate, arguing that they can only do harm by encouraging subjectivism, inaccuracy, and wishful thinking.

The ultimate goal of all science is, of course, to enhance our understanding of the world we live in and, thus, to help us thrive in this world. Positivism incorporates an instrumental view of science, which perceives scientific knowledge as a set of tools, which can be used to control and manipulate various aspects of reality.[112] Inasmuch as there is room for human volition in this world, science can help us change it in accordance with our wishes. However, realism emerges from the worldview and epistemology discussed previously with an added twist: its pessimistic view of human nature and its static orientation. As a consequence, it seeks to describe and explain reality, not because it believes that this reality could be fundamentally changed if we found it to be wanting but because a knowledge of its laws can increase our ability to adapt successfully to what reality is and will always be. Realism incorporates crucial elements of the sophistic rhetorical tradition by arguing that while an objective reality exists, which realism alone seems to understand, normative conceptions are inherently subjective. It is impossible to persuade others through reasoned discourse that we, or they, are right or wrong, since such terms have no objective meaning. If we intend to change others' courses of action, then, manipulation or coercion are our only recourses.

We learn from Thucydides a crucial lesson on the functioning of realist rhetorics. Realism must logically, based on its deterministic view of human nature, claim that the impact of reasoned argument on human behavior is minimal. However, it is apparent that realism vitally depends on a particular and potentially manipulative rhetorical strategy for its defense against critics: The irrelevance of moral considerations in anarchic social settings is defended with reference to an assumed reality, supposedly objective characteristics of the human condition. Inasmuch as they can or should not be simply silenced, critics must be persuaded that this reality is, in fact, real. The realist reliance on arguments from expediency is part of this strategy of persuasion, which will be examined in greater detail in the following chapter.

3

Realism Goes Modern

The writings of Niccolo Machiavelli and Thomas Hobbes have had an important influence on the evolution of the realist paradigm. This chapter analyzes the contributions of these two thinkers to the historical development of realist assumptions about human nature. In so doing, it discusses the influence of early modern rationalism and scientism on the realist political psychology as well as the role played by that psychology in the development of the emerging epistemology of political science.

Introduction

Most historical treatments of realist thought jump from a discussion of Thucydides across nineteen hundred years to continue with a treatment of Machiavelli.[1] Of course it is not the case that not a word of relevance was written in the interceding years. For example, Michael Loriaux, Willis Glover, and Jim George have all pointed to the influence of the medieval tradition of Christian pessimism associated with St. Augustine on the realist view of human nature and its judgment of the possibilities of moral and political progress.[2] According to George, this tradition contributed to realist thought a religiously founded "'evil-in-man' premise as the fundamental characteristic of the international system and the major limitation upon any 'utopian' approach to ethics."[3] However, while the tradition of Christian pessimism would later find eloquent expression in the works of several twentieth-century realists, it was out of opposition to Christian political thought that the first paramount realist political scientist would make himself heard.

Machiavelli's *The Prince* ostensibly belongs to the "mirrors for princes" genre of political consultative literature, which was well established at the time.[4] However, Machiavelli makes a significant break with this tradition by not grounding his authority in references to older texts. He does so as part of a rhetorical strategy designed to minimize his apparent need for appeals to authority or tradition. Instead, he claims to base his arguments purely on observation of the facts of the world. Robert Hariman thus gathers from a reading of Machiavelli that "the realist style . . . requires the pose of the artless reporter: realists must minimize their use of explicit rhetorical form precisely because they ground their authority in a clear understanding of the 'real' world."[5]

Gregory Crane points out that the invigoration of scientific realism, which we find in both Machiavelli and Hobbes, is best explained in the context of the modernization of science that occurred in Renaissance western Europe. It has parallels in medicine, where anatomists began to rely on direct observation rather than the authority of Galen, and in the rediscovery of Euclidean geometry. Crane claims that, while "parallels to medicine might suggest that Machiavelli simply wished to replace textual authority with a pure empiricism," the mathematical model suggests movement in a different direction.[6] That different direction was deductive scientific theorizing, which we encounter in the work of Hobbes a century later. Hobbes writes in "Human Nature" that political philosophy and ethics, as opposed to the natural sciences, can legitimately proceed from a priori assumptions, like geometry.[7] They do not need to, and actually cannot sensibly, proceed inductively from a posteriori observation because their function is not to describe but to create objects of knowledge. What the mathematical model suggests is that in order to create such knowledge it is advisable to employ a technical language, which attempts to approximate as closely as possible the artificial "reality" that provides the elements and logic of the theorist's suggestions.

The status of both Machiavelli and Hobbes as political realists is almost entirely undisputed, among realists as well as their critics.[8] Most commentators would probably agree with E. H. Carr that Machiavelli is indeed the first important political realist.[9] Michael Doyle identifies Machiavellian realism as "fundamentalist," meaning that the most important contribution made by Machiavelli to the development of realist theory lies in his account of human nature, which provides a "first-image" foundation for realist arguments. The Florentine's views on human psychology can "provide the means and ends that so many critics of Realism fail to find in modern abstractions."[10] Thus, according to Markus Fischer, Machiavelli's thought can offer even neorealism, the most "abstract" of modern realist theories, its missing microfoundation in the form of a coherent theory of human nature:

> Machiavelli's thought offers neorealists a deductive argument to ground their concept of political unit in concrete assumptions on individuals; for he generates his propositions from a well-developed psychology, and his propositions on political order are broadly compatible with neorealist assumptions about the state. This grounding consists in the generation of political order from the state of licence and premises on human nature.[11]

We can identify some interesting parallels between the lives and works of Thucydides and Machiavelli. Like Thucydides, Machiavelli was an active politician and military leader as well as a historical and theoretical commentator on political life. Like Thucydides, he became a victim of the vagaries of that life, being forced into premature retirement, where he, just like the Athenian general, composed his greatest work. Like Thucydides, Machiavelli, who was by his own admission profoundly influenced by the writings of the ancient Greek and Roman historians and philosophers, writes inductively, attempting to gather general lessons about politics from an in-depth examination of historical facts. Unlike Thucydides, however, who presents the facts but keeps his explanations largely to himself, Machiavelli presents his lessons explicitly and sets out to corroborate them with evidence.[12] Clearly, his objective in his theoretical works is not to write history but to defend his theory of politics. This theory, in its essence, identifies the roots of violence, within as well as between states, in individual ambition, and informs us both about how a ruler may achieve power and glory and about how a republic may achieve order and security. It seeks to understand human nature and its consequences for political behavior, with the express purpose of stabilizing the state.

Hobbes shares Machiavelli's view of human nature as well as his ultimate purpose of stabilizing domestic politics. Yet he employs, in large part, a different epistemological strategy and some of his arguments as well as conclusions differ from those of the Florentine.[13] Hobbes was undoubtedly influenced in his thinking by Thucydides' *History*, which he translated in 1628.[14] However, Laurie Johnson's in-depth comparison of Thucydides and Hobbes concludes that, while Thucydides provides a comprehensive account of human nature and avoids restrictive psychological assumptions, Hobbes, and with him realist theory, embark on an argumentative strategy that relies heavily on such assumptions.[15] While indebted to Thucydides' presentation of realist arguments, Hobbes departs from his judgment. Instead of building his theory on conclusions drawn from the analysis of the historian, Hobbes adopts the realist position of the Athenians at Sparta and incorporates it into a larger theoretical framework with the explicit purpose of developing a coherent political theory of human nature and the nature of the state. By incorporating the Athenian thesis into his model of the "natural" state of human affairs, Hobbes sets the precedent for the realist interpretation of the *History*; by formulating his own theory based on such an interpretation, he contributes significantly to the further development of realism.[16]

A materialist and cautious believer in positivist epistemology, Hobbes presents in his *Leviathan* a mechanistic view of nature, in general, and man as well as his social organization, in particular.[17] He bases his theory on a view of how man "functions," a question he believes can, in principle, be answered through scientific observation. An insight into the rules of human behavior, thus obtained, can help to "adjust" such behavior through the manipulation of exterior conditions. Much like the addition of a set of proper eyeglasses may be expected to stop the shortsighted person from running into walls, the threat of death may be expected to stop men from purposely colliding with each other. It is not a coincidence that we find in the work of Hobbes what is apparently one of the earliest uses of the term *political science*,[18] as it is clear that Hobbes shares with Machiavelli the purpose of elucidating human affairs to make them more predictable and thereby more manipulable. Unlike Machiavelli, however, Hobbes proceeds to develop a deductive theory on the impact of human nature on politics, which is more general and abstract and therefore appears less contingent on historical circumstances and the evidence of the theorist's observations.

While Hobbes is usually characterized as an empiricist, he is at best a skeptical one.[19] As Quentin Skinner has shown, Hobbes begins his intellectual development at a time when the newly emerging culture of positivist science is struggling to free itself from humanist rationalism.[20] He reacts, especially in his early works, against the view, held by the Tudor rhetoricians, that the findings of reason require reinforcement through eloquence to be considered persuasive. He develops the belief that science should instead rely as much as possible on concrete evidence gathered through observation. Drawing on the pre-Socratics, he makes a distinction in "Human Nature" between "the 'mathematici'—those who start their reasoning from humble principles—and 'dogmatici'—those who hold maxims learned from authority or custom."[21] He clearly sees himself as a *mathematicus*, who attempts to build his theories on minimal assumptions that are strongly supported by empirical evidence.

On the other hand, Hobbes states clearly that the human powers of observation are limited. As Laurie Johnson Bagby has observed, Hobbes does not believe that human beings can easily know the world for what it is.[22] In addition, he holds that communicating scientific truths introduces additional risks of distortion. Thus, he is acutely aware of the power of rhetoric in communicating "truths" and of the difficulties faced by positivist science.[23] Indeed, as we will see, in moving from induction to deduction and from observation to prescription, Hobbes himself comes to rely heavily on strong maxims concerning human nature. His reconciliation of empiricism with rationalism, which finds its most powerful expression in the *Leviathan*, involves the employment of rhetorics in the service of science.[24] It makes him the first paradigmatic realist.

Niccolo Machiavelli

My examination of Machiavelli's political theory will concentrate on his chief theoretical works, *The Prince* and the *Discourses on the First Ten Books of Titus Livy*. Like Ernst Cassirer, Leo Strauss, Friedrich Meinecke, and, most recently, Ashley Tellis,[25] I read both works as contributing to the realist tradition, not only by "speaking essentially to the same power-political issue of how and why order is created and sustained,"[26] but also by giving complementary answers to those questions, which have survived at the core of realist theory.[27]

Machiavellian political theory rests, like the Athenian thesis, on a conception of human nature as stable and uniform. In fact, it is because we may legitimately make general assumptions about human motivation that we can explain the regularities of the sociopolitical world. Machiavelli explains:

> Prudent men are in the habit of saying, neither by chance or without reason, that anyone wishing to see what is to be must consider what has been: all the things of this world in every era have their counterparts in ancient times. This occurs since these actions are carried out by men who have and have always had the same passions, which, of necessity, must give rise to the same results.[28]

> Anyone who studies current and ancient affairs will easily recognize that the same desires and humours exist and have always existed in all cities and among all peoples. Thus, it is an easy matter for anyone who examines past events carefully to foresee future events in any republic and to apply the remedies that the ancients employed, or if old remedies cannot be found, to think of new ones based upon the similarity of circumstances. But since these considerations are ignored or misunderstood by those who read, or they are understood but are not recognized by those who govern, it always follows that the same conflicts arise in every era.[29]

As human nature is bound to remain what it has been, we may expect that the regularities we observe in the past will hold true in the future. In fact, in Machiavellian theory, an insight into these regularities is our best hope to avoid those disasters which arise from a lack of understanding of what is given. Thus, it is Machiavelli's "project" to provide such an understanding, clear and undiluted by wishful thinking, of the realities of political life.

At the core of the Machiavellian worldview lies a conception of man as an incorrigibly selfish, opportunistic, and deceitful being.[30] Machiavelli warns the prince that

> this can generally be said about men: that they are ungrateful, fickle, dissimulators, apt to flee peril, covetous of gain; and while you do them good, they are all yours, they offer you their blood, their things, their life, their children, . . . when need is far off; but when it draws near to you, they revolt. . . . And men are less reticent to offend one who makes himself loved than one who makes himself feared; because love is held by a bond of obligation which, since men are shabby, is broken for their own utility upon every occasion; but timorousness is secured by fear of punishment which never lets you go.[31]

Human beings are naturally possessive, rapacious, and imperious, greedy for both material riches and glory. Machiavelli observes that "to desire to acquire is truly something very natural and ordinary, and always, when men do it who can, they will be lauded, or not blamed."[32] It is quite unnatural for such beings to sacrifice their personal desires to get along with others. However, they are also motivated by a fear for their physical security, and their leader should not shy away from making use of scare tactics, intimidation, terror, and violence, if they become necessary to establish his power or to preserve his rule. Machiavelli identifies the ability to instill fear as the most important power resource. He also identifies fear as the motive that can be most easily employed by the powerful to manipulate the behavior of others, an observation that will play a central role in Hobbesian theory and the further development of the realist paradigm.

Like Hobbes, Machiavelli is primarily concerned with how, given the essential wickedness of human nature, political order can be established and maintained. He holds that it can be established, first, by the prince's "own arms and virtue [*virtu*]," or, second, "by means of the arms of others and fortune [*fortuna*]."[33] The Machiavellian concept of virtu is a complex one. According to Isaiah Berlin, it includes such diverse "virtues" as "courage, vigor, fortitude in adversity, public achievement, order, discipline, happiness, strength, justice, [and] above all [the] assertion of one's proper claims and the knowledge and power needed to secure their satisfaction."[34] *Virtu* combines all those qualities the Romans thought appropriate for a man, including, but not restricted to, the martial virtues. A leader who possesses *virtu* will be able, almost by definition, to conquer and maintain power. A leader who rises to power on the waves of fortune, on the other hand, needs solid advice in order not to get cut down on the first adverse occasion.

The Machiavellian concept of *fortuna* is one that, at first glance, seems at odds with the realist worldview. However, it is not really a metaphysical concept. Machiavelli has *fortuna* refer to those aspects of reality beyond our immediate control. If *virtu* promises mastery of agency, it is *fortuna* that provides the challenges with which the actor is faced. *Fortuna* is unpredictable, the "chance" factor that operates in everything man does not understand and cannot directly control, but she is not a goddess. She is not to be worshipped, but engaged in combat.

Machiavelli compares fortune to a river. He explains that the wise man builds levies and makes provisions for the time when the river might flood. This will help him survive the raging waters. He also compares fortune to his idea of woman, who, although known for her obstinate and destructive irrationality, can be "charmed" or "put down" by strength of will or sheer force, at least temporarily.[35] *Virtu* with respect to *fortuna* means knowing when and how to take advantage of her currents or moods. After all, "fortune is the arbiter of half our actions, but . . . she leaves the other half, or nearly, to be governed by us."[36] As Tellis has emphasized, "Machiavelli emphatically argues that *virtu* can in fact subjugate *fortuna*. What is required is a proper understanding of political reality as it actually is, and a willingness to act appropriately upon that understanding."[37] Machiavelli sets out to provide the first and encourage the second.

Machiavellian realism contains both structural and psychological elements. Structure constrains and psychology compels ordinary men. However, a better understanding of reality does allow for greater success in adapting to its conditions, and *virtu* allows for the strength to act on that understanding. The rules of the political game are knowable because they are grounded in both human nature and the structure of the environment in which political action occurs. In the absence of sovereign control, that structure is anarchic and characterized by constant conflict arising from human ambitions combined with natural scarcity.[38] A "realistic" judgment of such conditions, combined with *virtu*, can help the prince play the political "game" more successfully. According to Tellis, "[T]he Machiavellian version of political realism is thus a model of science in the service of political control—science as technology."[39]

Machiavelli claims that his superior understanding of the realities of political life enables him to explain how the new prince may best solidify his grasp on power. To control his subjects, the prince may have to use drastic means: "And let this be perceived, that a prince . . . cannot observe all those things by which men are considered good, it often being necessary to maintain the state, to operate against faith, against charity, against humaneness, against religion."[40] One of the most important lessons Machiavelli has to teach the prince is that it is much more important for a ruler to cultivate Roman *virtu* than to follow the dictates of Christian virtue: "Let him not care about incurring infamy for those vices without which he might hardly save the state; because, if one considers everything well, one will find that something that appears a virtue, if followed, would be his ruin, and that some other thing that appears a vice, if followed, results in his security and well-being."[41] In the *Discourses*, Machiavelli goes even further by quite openly attacking Christianity for "making the world prey to the wicked through its refusal to resist evil with evil."[42]

Machiavelli warns the prince that it is important to be "smart" about being unscrupulous. He counsels that cruel means to assert one's power have to be used "well," not halfheartedly, but thoroughly and without hesitation, so that they do not have to be reapplied.[43] In addition, *The Prince* contains teachings on an "economy of violence," for, while it is more important for the prince to be feared than to be loved, causing unnecessary resentment in the populace is dangerous. Machiavelli advises that the prince act like both a lion and a fox, relying on his strength when he must, and on cunning and deception when he can. A successful prince has to be able to control how reality appears to others. To this end, he must become a master actor and rhetorician. Where the lion suppresses opposition with violence, the fox manipulates appearances.

In the long term, a stable government relies on both "good arms" and "good laws." The first are a prerequisite to any stable order, since "there cannot be good laws where there are not good arms [but] where there are good arms there must be good laws."[44] Machiavelli argues in the *Discourses* for a republic, as opposed to a "princely" form of government. A republic, he claims, would be more stable in the long run because it would invite less domestic strife and because it could foster *virtu* among its citizens. A republican government is best able to foster *virtu* because it preserves liberty in relative equality, which is required for the development and exercise of civic virtue.[45] Having a "virtuous" citizenry, in turn, helps a state to thrive and to increases its international status.

In addition to strong government and domestic order, political survival in the long run also depends on expansion. Once again Machiavelli counsels the prince not to hesitate to use his power to increase it. He explains that war is always unavoidable in the long run, and that it is better to initiate war when one has the advantage than to wait to be attacked.[46] War must be fought for two main reasons besides self-defense: first, to fulfill man's innate desire for glory and, second, to stifle domestic opposition. According to Doyle, Machiavelli announces that

> we are lovers of glory . . . . We seek to rule or at least to avoid being oppressed. In either case we want more for ourselves and our states than just material welfare. Because other states with similar aims thereby threaten us, we prepare ourselves for expansion. Because our fellow citizens threaten us if we do not allow them to satisfy their ambition or to release their political energies through imperial expansion, we expand. In so doing, we create a state of war—insecurity abroad as a way of mitigating, but never successfully eliminating, insecurity at home.[47]

Given the risk of civil strife at home and the inevitable insecurity of the international realm, "establishing a republic fit for imperial expansion is . . . the best way to guarantee the survival of a state that can overawe domestic enemies and overcome foreign foes."[48]

The third ingredient needed for stable government is a kind of "civic religion," which can provide "the false consciousness required to motivate individuals to behave well and to sacrifice their lives for the state."[49] For Machiavelli, such a civic religion must include a "story" of the past that can instill civic pride and unity in the citizenry. Machiavelli's own historiography may be read as an attempt to recount history in such a way as to inculcate such pride and to provide inspiration in the service of the state. However, as Steven Forde has shown, Machiavelli, unlike Thucydides, does not perceive of domestic politics as a realm in which genuine moral concerns do and should play a role. Instead, "for Machiavelli, realism in the international arena is inseparable from moral skepticism that extends to the very foundations of political life."[50] His civic religion is a charade, not a vehicle for moral improvement, but a tool the prince can use to encourage voluntary submission.

John Pocock speaks of the "Machiavellian moment" as the moment in which human beings achieve secular self-consciousness, that quintessentially modern vision which entails the realization of the consequences of human commitment and responsibility for the world we inhabit.[51] Strauss has identified the realization that the world is what we make it as the primeval or original terror.[52] When Machiavelli is admired today, it is because he did not shy away from this terror. He did, by his own standards, possess the *virtu* necessary for a political leader, and, after all, he wrote a manual not on religion or family life, but on politics, which is, in his view at least, of necessity a "dirty business." When he is blamed today, on the other hand, it is because of the extent to which he was willing to grant moral absolution to ruthless rulers (and their opportunist advisers).

Albert Hirschman is perhaps being too idealistic when he suggests that genuine "concern for improving the quality of statecraft was at the origin of the quest for greater realism in the analysis of human behavior."[53] While such a concern is undoubtedly paramount for many writers of the realist tradition, a problem that has received more attention, at least since the 1940s, is the degree to which the Machiavellian concept of *ragione di stato* (reason of state) can be abused in the service of egoistic passions and even paranoid delusions. As Tellis has pointed out, Machiavelli "presents the realist argument in its complete and purest form: egoist competition engenders violence, contention, and brutality, and it cannot be resolved except through the logic of domination."[54] That "logic," however, deserves some healthy skepticism today if we are to have learned anything from the many forms of oppression that have clad their ideologies in its guise.

According to Tellis, "Machiavelli laid the foundations of modernity—and, by implication, for modern social science—by explicitly treating the nature of man and the consequences of that nature for the formation, maintenance, and growth of the state."[55] Leonardo Olschki has similarly identified Machiavelli as the first political scientist, claiming that, his "theoretical presuppositions and the inner logic of his doctrines led him to conceive of examples and imitation in a more scientific than didactic sense."[56] Machiavellian political science, more so than Thucydidean scientific history, "discloses the internal analogies of the historical events . . . considered typical, significant and decisive."[57] Thus, it is theory written to enable "political leaders [to] discover in the events of the past the similarities of the circumstances and conditions which may determine their initiatives and reveal their chances of success and failure."[58] Tellis identifies as another major contribution to the development of modern social science Machiavelli's view that politics should be grounded in fact rather than in value.[59] Political science, Machiavellian style, is born from his distinction, echoed in Benedict de Spinoza, between positive and normative thinking.

In his extraordinary work *The Passions and the Interests*, Hirschman explores the impact of early modern realist thought on the development of economic theory. He notes that, "in attempting to teach the prince how to achieve, maintain, and expand power, Machiavelli made his fundamental and celebrated distinction between 'the effective truth of things' and the 'imaginary republics and monarchies that have never been seen nor have been known to exist.'"[60] While moral and political philosophers had in the past talked much about utopias yet achieved little actual improvement, Machiavelli writes that "how one ought to live is so far removed from how one lives that he who lets go of what is done for that which one ought to do sooner learns ruin than his own preservation . . . . Because of this it is necessary to a prince, wanting to maintain himself, to learn how to be able to be not good and to use this and not use it according to necessity."[61] Machiavelli employs an anti-normative, positivistic–scientific approach to political affairs designed to provide guidance in the real world. In the real world of Machiavellian politics, genuine normative aspirations are simply madness, likely to endanger the survival of the regime.

Machiavelli sets the clear precedent for the realist separation of politics from the realm of morality, which has been foreshadowed in the Athenian thesis. He asserts, in the words of Doyle, that "politics has a moral logic of its own, an independent value in the common life of the citizens, separate from Christian moral teachings."[62] According to Tellis, "[T]his severance of politics from the pursuit of virtue is derived from an explicit assertion about the bestial nature of man and the imperative of security which flows from it. From such an assertion then emanates both Machiavelli's description of how states are formed and his prescriptions for how they can be maintained in greatness."[63]

In the realm of politics, the only valid ethics is one of pragmatic responsibility in which the end of state preservation justifies all means necessary to obtain it. In the words of Forde, for Machiavelli there exists only "one goal that is intrinsic to the political realm, and that is success measured as survival, longevity, or glory."[64] If a policy is successful at preserving the state, it is "good." If it is unsuccessful, it is "bad." Machiavelli claims of man that "it is truly appropriate that while the act accuses him, the result excuses him, and when the result is good . . . it will always excuse him."[65] As George has put it, realism gathers from this "recognizably modern rationale for an ethics of 'doing evil'" an attitude which "brings into clearer relief the modern agency of ethical detachment—the egoistic interests of the sovereign state."[66]

In typical realist fashion, Machiavelli equates the state with its ruler, with the current regime. Thus, *ragione di stato* is presented as identical with the needs of any present government to stay in power. Machiavelli employs the concepts of *interesse* (interest) and *ragione di stato* synonymously. They function, in the words of Hirschman, as a "declaration of independence from the moralizing precepts and rules that had been the mainstay of pre-Machiavellian political philosophy."[67] Their purpose is, according to Meinecke, to identify "a sophisticated, rational will, untroubled by passions and momentary impulses."[68] However, Machiavelli is not merely trying to make a statement, and his overriding goal is hardly a Nietzschean emancipation of the human mind.[69] Instead, Machiavelli writes always primarily as an advocate of the requirements of *Realpolitik*. He is a realist ideologue.

"Necessity" to Machiavelli means the necessity of political survival.[70] The end of *mantenere lo stato* (preserving the state) justifies all means, not because Machiavelli supports a particular ruler or class, but because the survival of the state depends on secure government, which, in turn, depends on the internal stability and the external security of the state. Tellis points out that, thus,

> for the first time since the Sophists, the *telos* of the earthly polity was openly defined in negative rather than in positive terms. No longer would it be considered as a progressive ascent toward the *agathon* (as in Plato), or as a communitarian search for *eudamonia* (as in Aristotle), or as a pilgrim's search for the *summum bonum* (as in Aquinas); instead it would be seen merely as an artificial device created purposely for avoiding the *summum malum*.[71]

The "*summum malum*," for Machiavelli as well as Hobbes, was political disorder.

Thomas Hobbes

The impact of Hobbesian thought on the development of realism is complex. As we will see, Hobbes proceeds both inductively, developing ideas about human nature and the inevitability of conflict from the observation of human behavior, and deductively, developing, based on the axioms inspired by his observations, a model theory of the state designed to counter the unfortunate tendencies he observes. His political theory as a whole thus combines strictly empirical with normative elements. The sheer complexity of his work has fueled scholarship on a wide variety of aspects of Hobbesian thought. It is common for Hobbes scholars to argue over which of those aspects should be stressed and which ignored, and such arguments are made more complicated by the fact that his work, much like that of Thucydides, has frequently been used to bolster the arguments of those who read it, rather than those of Hobbes himself. Among critics of realism, it is, as Christopher McDonald has written, common to impose "upon Hobbesian thought what are in essence the limitations and failures of contemporary realism."[72] To avoid this problem, I choose a new approach to reading Hobbes's work, which is designed to uncover an internal logic in his political oeuvre.

My analysis relies on an examination of three of Hobbes's major works. The rationale for choosing *Behemoth*, *De Cive*, and *Leviathan* to analyze Hobbesian thought in general is that, first, these three works are widely considered his most important political treatises and, second, they are representative of Hobbesian political philosophy in its complexity. A reading of these three works reveals an underlying logic in Hobbesian thought, which connects all three works, albeit not in a convenient chronological fashion. *Behemoth*, the last work of the three, illustrates the problem that primarily concerned the political philosopher: the problem of civil strife. *De Cive* and *Leviathan* together present suggestions toward the solution of that problem. Specifically, *De Cive* is primarily concerned with the exploration of possible institutional solutions, whereas *Leviathan* eloquently combines the mature vision of Hobbes's institutional solution with a normative theory that provides an ethical foundation for his theory of the state. Since *Leviathan* is the work that would prove to have the strongest impact on the development of the realist paradigm, it will be treated here in the most detail.

In *Behemoth or The Long Parliament*, Hobbes provides a descriptive and interpretive treatment of the civil war that devastated England between 1640 and 1660. In his introduction to a recent edition of the book, Stephen Holmes writes that "the general impression left by . . . [Hobbes's] dialogues on the civil war is that many human beings are, first of all, incapable of calculative reasoning and, second, stupidly indifferent to self-preservation."[73] In fact, *Behemoth* leaves no doubt that "civil war broke out because key actors were bewitched by irrational passions and tragically misled by doctrinal errors" (viii). Irrational motives and a psychological reliance on belief and norms are dangerous because they can lead human beings to place less value on their own survival. This in turn makes their behavior not only unpredictable but also uncontrollable by the authority of government, which relies ultimately on coercion in the form of the threat of physical harm.

Based on a close reading of *Behemoth*, Holmes can claim that to accuse Hobbes of motivational reductionism constitutes "one of the most common and persistent errors of Hobbes scholarship" (x). In fact, according to Holmes, *Behemoth* ably argues and illustrates that "human motivations are much too disorderly and perverse to be reduced to self-preservation or the rational pursuit of private advantage" (xi). Hobbes's treatment of the impact of factors such as norms and passions on human behavior contains important lessons concerning the functioning and the limits of self-interested motivation. Specifically, according to Holmes, Hobbes finds that "motives that remain irreducible to self-interest are especially powerful in complex choice situations where considerations of advantage do not clearly privilege one decision over another" (xx). In sum, Hobbes illustrates in *Behemoth* what he perceives to be the major problem underlying political disorder: the limits of rationality and the reign of passions. He identifies ideologies, most notably religious ones, and irrational motives that lead to the neglect of caution and prudence, such as, most notably, pride, as the causes of violent conflict among human beings and the breakdown of domestic order.

De Cive was the first of Hobbes's political philosophical works to actually be published. It examines the possibilities of the commonwealth to control the destructive aspects of human nature that are illustrated in *Behemoth*. Hobbes criticizes the classical Greek view of man as a *zoon politikon* (political animal), as represented in the works of Aristotle, for falsely claiming that "Man is a Creature . . . born fit for society."[74] Instead, Hobbes holds that even though human beings may desire the company of others, that does not mean that they are by nature fit for it. After all, "it is one thing to desire, another to be in capacity fit for what we desire (44–45). According to Hobbes, it is important to realize that human beings desire company "not . . . for its own sake, but that we may receive some Honour or Profit from it" (42). He claims that, in fact, "all free congress ariseth either from mutual poverty, or from vain glory" and "all Society therefore is either for Gain, or for Glory; not so much for love of our Fellowes, as for love of our Selves" (43).

The danger in this state of affairs lies in the fact that "no society can be great, or lasting, which begins from Vain Glory" (43–44) because, as will be stressed in *Leviathan*, vainglory, or pride, is an eternal source of conflict. Moreover, man's desire for gain, while leading him to associate with others for his own advantage, is even more likely to lead him to seek their domination. The logic of the following passage is seductive:

> Though the benefits of this life may be much farthered by mutuall help, since yet those may be better attain'd to by Dominion, then by the society of others: I hope no body will doubt but that men would much more greedily be carryed by Nature, if all fear were removed, to obtain Dominion, then to gaine Society. We must therefore resolve, that the Originall of all great, and lasting Societies, consisted not in the mutuall good will men had towards each other, but in the mutuall fear they had of each other. (44)

Hobbes stresses that the mutual fear which motivates human beings to live in civil contract has nothing to do with hysterical fear, or panic, which would leave man with but the two alternatives of fight or flight. He explains: While others "believe, that to fear is nothing else then to be affrighted: I comprehend in this word Fear, a certain foresight of future evill; neither do I conceive flight the sole property of fear, but to distrust, suspect, take heed, provide so that they may not fear, is also incident to the fearfull" (45). The elements of this "rational" fear, which is the central motivating force in Hobbesian contract theory, are prudence, caution, and an insight into the necessity of making provisions for one's security.

Hobbes suggests two complementary strategies for overcoming the natural lack of security experienced by human beings: one institutional, the other ethical. Both rely primarily on the motive of fear. First, "security is the end wherefore men submit themselves to others."[75] The institution of the state exists to protect human beings from one another's hurtful designs. To do so, it must possess absolute power of coercion, since "consent, or contracted society, without some common power whereby particular men may be ruled through feare of punishment, doth not suffice to make up that security which is requisite to the exercise of naturall justice."[76] Second, Hobbes designs, in *Leviathan*, ethical rules, "Articles of Peace,"[77] which can not only guide man in his pursuit of safety but which also serve to support the Hobbesian theory of the absolutist state. Those "laws of nature" are presented as following logically from what Hobbes calls the "right of nature," which is the prerogative of self-defense.

The parallels between Athenian realism as portrayed by Thucydides and the thought of Hobbes are especially apparent in *Leviathan*, which, as the first general theory of politics published in the English language, represents Hobbes's mature views on the impact of human nature on politics. Here, the three motives of the Athenian thesis are mirrored in Hobbes's statement about the "three principall causes of quarrell. First, Competition; Secondly, Diffidence; Thirdly, Glory."[78] Moreover, Hobbes's portrayal of the state of nature, a hypothetical state of complete anarchy, is strikingly similar to Athenian views on power politics and the irrelevance of justice and morality in interstate relations: "To this warre of every man against every man, this also is consequent; that nothing can be Unjust. The notions of Right and Wrong, Justice and Injustice have there no place."[79] However, *Leviathan* is obviously more than a mere restatement of Athenian ideology. Instead, it is, in fact, one of the most influential works in the history of political thought and contains an account of human nature that has served as the foundation of realist as well as liberal political theory.

Hirschman points out that, by the time Hobbes was writing his Leviathan,

> advances of mathematics and celestial mechanics held out the hope that laws of motion might be discovered for men's actions, just as for falling bodies and planets. Thus Hobbes, who based his theory of human nature on Galileo, devotes the first ten chapters of *Leviathan* to a mechanistic description of the nature of man before proceeding to that of the commonwealth.[80]

Hobbes portrays human beings as driven by a range of passions. As compared to lifeless bodies, which can only be moved through the application of force from the outside, human beings can be moved from within as well, through the workings of these passions, which, in contrast to the individual ends toward which they are directed, are commonly shared by all human beings.[81] These passions, which Hobbes lists in the sixth chapter of *Leviathan*, are also called "animal" or "voluntary" motions. In contrast to the vital motions, as for example the beating of the heart, voluntary motions can be directed toward diverse ends, which is why not all human beings share the same passions toward the same objects. However, all individuals are alike in that they are motivated, in principle, by the same range of passions. Thus, Hobbes, just like the Athenian realists, views human nature as essentially stable and human action as governed by certain immutable motives.[82]

Most of these motives are causes of conflict, making the state of nature a war of "every man, against every man"[83] in which life is "solitary, poore, nasty, brutish, and short."[84] According to Hobbes, the three principal causes of quarrel are the competition that arises out of every man's desire for personal gain and power, diffidence, which arises from fear, and glory, which is derived from the motive of pride or arrogance. Conflict, then, arises not from particular situations but from the very nature of man, which is composed of both his internal characteristics, the "motions," and his natural vulnerability.[85]

The constant conflict arising in the state of nature, however, is not consistent with the "right of nature" and man's primary goal of self-preservation. A correct understanding of the primacy of self-preservation should instead lead rational man to follow the nineteen "laws of nature," which, according to Hobbes, follow logically from this right. These laws of nature are ethical guidelines, which comprise the practical normative foundation for Hobbes's political theory.[86] The only way for man to properly institutionalize the laws of nature and thereby to ensure his safety is to be ruled by an all-powerful authority, the *Leviathan*, "king over all the children of pride,"[87] which would be strong enough to suppress all domestic dissent as well as to defend the state against threats from abroad.

Hobbes's account of the passions is of great importance for his general account of human nature and his theory of the state, because he regards those commonly shared motives not merely as what moves all human beings from within, but also as the sole sources of our ends and goals in life. In contrast to so-called philosophers of reason like Immanuel Kant,[88] who believe that what is good and right can be understood through the use of the faculties of mind, Hobbes declares that "the felicity of this life, consisteth not in the repose of a mind satisfied. For there is no such Finis ultimus, (utmost ayme,) nor Summum Bonum, (greatest Good,) as is spoken of in the Books of the old Morall Philosophers."[89] Instead, human happiness consists in the pursuit of self-interest, a "continuall progresse of the desire, from one object to another; the attaining of the former, being still but the way to the latter."[90] According to Hobbes, man is led in his endeavor to achieve happiness by nothing but his passions, which determine his ends and move him to attain them. Cornelia Navari holds that "it is not ideas that constrain him but the passions within himself which produce his desires and aversions. He is directed by them alone. His problem is that he is not alone; he lives with others of his own kind, desiring the same things, forming ideas of good and bad in the same solipsist's fashion."[91] The usefulness of reason consists in its potential to help man achieve the ends dictated by his passions through rational planning, while avoiding destructive conflict with others around him. Reason is thus purely instrumental.[92] So, by extension, is science. Hobbes cannot aspire to change what is objective reality, as viewed by a disillusioned pessimist. He remains, in spite of all his criticism of man, a genuine realist.

According to Hirschman, Hobbes became one of the main thinkers involved in the modern demolition of heroic ideals. These ideals, among them the quest for public honor, had reasserted themselves during the Renaissance, "as the influence of the Church receded and the advocates of aristocratic ideals were able to draw on the plentiful Greek and Roman texts celebrating the pursuit of glory."[93] However, the arguments of early modern realists, among them both Machiavelli and Hobbes, did not "restore the equality in ignominy that Augustine had meant to bestow on love of money and lust for power and glory."[94] Instead, they contributed in various ways to the development of the "principle of countervailing passion."[95] This principle, also articulated in the works of Benedict de Spinoza and Francis Bacon, pitted such ostensibly "safe" passions as the private pursuit of wealth against those passions which were deemed unsafe in a commonwealth.[96]

In the words of Hirschman, "[T]he Hobbesian Covenant . . . is concluded only because the 'Desires, and other Passions of men,' such as the aggressive pursuit of riches, glory, and dominion, are overcome by those other 'passions that incline men to Peace,' which are 'Fear of Death; Desire of such things as are necessary to commodious living; and a Hope by their industry to obtain them."[97]

While Hobbes thus does not fail to acknowledge that, on an empirical level, a rich variety of motives for human behavior exists, he builds his model theory on the primacy of the motive of self-preservation or the fear of violent death.[98] Fear haunts man in the state of nature, which is characterized by "continuall feare and danger of violent death,"[99] which is "the chiefest of naturall evills."[100] The cause of this fear "consists partly in the naturall equality of men" and "partly in their mutuall will of hurting: whence it comes to passe that we can neither expect from others, nor promise to our selves the least security."[101] Fear is also what induces man to enter civil society: "The original of all great and lasting societies consisted not in the mutual good will men had toward each other, but in the mutual fear they had of each other."[102] Fear, then, is "at once the principal cause of war and the principal means to peace, fear is the basis both of man's most urgent plight and of his only possible escape."[103]

Using fear, Hobbes "reintroduces an element of constraint into a system in which the analysis of human nature has justified or even exalted the unlimited use of power for self-aggrandizement."[104] If the motive of fear is not strong enough, human beings with their "perpetuall and restlesse desire of Power after power"[105] will not be restrained from doing anything at all to increase their "present means to obtain some future apparent Good."[106] However, if it is, human beings can be persuaded to follow the laws of nature, which are designed to minimize conflict as well as to provide a normative "superstructure" for the rule of the *Leviathan*.

While building his theory on the axiomatic primacy of the motive of rational fear, Hobbes views the motive of pride, or the desire for honor, as the chief obstacle to such sensible caution.[107] This "social passion" is not only identified as one of the three principal causes of conflict but also as the main source of madness. Whereas the motives of "profit" and fear lead men to fight, perhaps understandably, for gain and for safety, pride leads to the use of violence "for trifles, as a word, a smile, a different opinion, and any other signe of undervalue, either direct in their Persons, or by reflexion in their Kindred, their Friends, their Nation, their Profession, or their Name."[108] Hobbes views pride, in direct disagreement with Thucydides, as an entirely destructive motive. Not only does he recommend as an institutional remedy that all public display of honor be focused on the absolute ruler, he also designs three different laws of nature for the express purpose of suppressing the motive of pride.[109]

The other main obstacle to the workings of rational fear is the human quest for power, which is motivated by both the search for honor and the need for gain, or profit. As human beings cannot know what the future holds in store, they also never know how much power they will need to survive and prosper. The effect of this insecurity is that there are no limits to the human desire for power. This must necessarily lead to competition, first, because power is viewed as a relative good, so that one person's gain will always be another's loss and, second, because a limitless desire for power will inevitably lead human beings to attempt to wrestle power from others. Hobbes identifies the desire for power as a passion that can be useful, because it provides an incentive for man to educate himself and thus further the development of reason and science. However, the competition caused by the human drive for power also poses a major risk of conflict unless this competition is kept in check through limits that are set by the *Leviathan*.

Hobbes builds his political theory on parsimonious assumptions about the motives that drive human behavior. He portrays human beings as being primarily motivated by fear, greed, and pride—the motives of the Athenian thesis. He argues that these motives lead human beings into an eternal quest for power, possessions, and status, which brings them into conflict with one another. While he views the motive of pride as entirely destructive, parting company with Machiavelli, he believes that the motive of greed and the drive to power should be harnessed for the advancement of science and general progress. However, these passions can only be made safe by the absolute primacy of the motive of fear, properly exploited in a repressive political system and made to directly inform human behavior through rational insight.

Holmes attempts to answer the question, What made Hobbes "flirt with [such a] motivational reductionism, even though . . . his portrait of the human psyche is actually rich and unparsimonious"?[110] He comes up with several possible explanations: First, motivational reductionism might have been attractive to Hobbes because it "helped him pillory his political foes."[111] Second, it may be further explained through a normative bias against certain passions and norms, which Hobbes, due to his personal experience, considered particularly dangerous. Finally, both of these concerns relate to Hobbes's desire to stifle the ambitions of political elites. It may be said that Hobbes was "universalizing . . . the morality of the common man. His disproportionate emphasis on self-preservation was profoundly egalitarian or majoritarian."[112] Whereas, traditionally, political theory had divided humankind into two groups, a majority of the instinctually selfish and an idealistic and self-sacrificing elite, Hobbes holds that such a distinction is itself ideologically motivated and misleading, and that all human beings, in principle, share similar goals.[113]

While once again acknowledging the complexity of Hobbesian political theory, it is thus essential to note that Hobbes does lay important foundations for the motivational reductionism of later realist thought. He does so not by asserting the empirical accuracy of the realist view of motivation but rather by its normative defense through his deductive theory of the state. Hobbes's frequently bitingly cynical treatment of the role of passions, norms, and conventions in human conduct in *Behemoth* does little to dispel the impression that he views rational, self-interested motivation as a sign of superior intellect. The fact that Hobbes also realizes that such motivation is not at the same time a sign of superior virtue has been neglected in scholarship, at least partly due to the fact that Hobbes presents himself not as a moral philosopher but as a political scientist. Thus, while Hobbes in fact acknowledges the empirical complexity of human motivation and laments the real-life unpredictability of human behavior, his theoretical and normative aspirations combined lay the groundwork for a reductionist political psychology.

In the following, I will attempt to draw those lessons from the Hobbesian logic that are most relevant for the further development of the realist paradigm. While the power of motivational assumptions in structuring our explanations and expectations of political behavior becomes apparent in the *History* of Thucydides as well as in the work of Machiavelli, it is Hobbes who uses the motivational assumptions underlying the Athenian thesis as the basis for a comprehensive theory of human nature, the state, and relations among human beings as well as states. In his analysis of *The Logic of Leviathan*, David Gauthier finds that "from statements about motives, Hobbes derives statements about behavior" and that, to be valid, Hobbes's conclusions "must be formally inferred from his account of human nature—that is, primarily from his account of human motivation."[114]

I will use the insightful work of Gauthier to explain the Hobbesian logic of inference. For Hobbes, man's primary motive is the fear of violent death and, thus, his primary desire is to preserve himself. Every action aimed at self-preservation is therefore a means to man's highest end and in accordance with human nature. In Gauthier's words: "From premises of the form 'X is a necessary means to self-preservation,' Hobbes can derive conclusions of the form 'a man must do X to secure what he wants'" (21). Hobbes also defines reasonable or rational actions as those which represent the best means to achieve a given end. This means that "we can then derive from 'a man must do X to secure what he wants,' the further conclusion 'a man, if rational, will do X'" (ibid.). Man, not being fully rational and tending to misjudge his own ends as well as the most rational means to achieve them, will however not always do X. Therefore, "from the claim 'a man, if rational, will do X,' it seems possible to derive the imperative of advice 'Do X!' For any man has sufficient reason to do whatever he would do, were he fully rational, and what he has sufficient reason to do is what he is best advised to do" (ibid.). The advice "Do X!" cannot be derived logically from the previous statement. However, it may be justified through it, because it is plausible "that a man who accepts the statement is behaving irrationally if he rejects the imperative" (22).

We can see how Hobbes's theory not only rests on restrictive assumptions concerning the motives for human behavior but also relies heavily on an assumption of rationality. In fact, "Hobbes's account of man as rational provides the key link between his psychological doctrines and his moral and political conclusions. . . . In characterizing man as rational, Hobbes provides for the derivation of judgments which describe how an ideal man would behave, but prescribe how actual men should behave" (22–23). Hobbes's derivation of normative moral and political conclusions from empirical psychological premises thereby escapes accusations of logical fallacy. He does not in fact contradict his own determinism, as Laurie Johnson has claimed.[115] The real problems afflicting Hobbes's argument lie, rather, with his assumptions themselves. As Gauthier points out, it is often possible to "explain a particular action of a particular person in terms of a particular motive."[116] It is also often possible to make general motivational statements that "explain many actions of many persons in terms of a certain type of motive" (ibid.). The mistake Hobbes makes is to attempt to explain all actions of all rational persons in terms of a single primary motive. In fact he predicts that "a normal person in normal physiological and psychological condition . . . must act in a certain way because he must be motivated by [the desire for self-preservation]" (ibid.). This position is empirically indefensible, as Hobbes himself recognizes.

Hobbes follows the Athenians' lead in attempting to establish fixed laws of human behavior from restrictive assumptions about the motives for human action. In contrast, as Gauthier rightly points out, any tenable theory of motivation can "show us only what a man in normal circumstances may do, not what he must do"(24). Thus, we can certainly say that self-preservation is a very important motive, but not that it determines all human behavior at all times. This means that "from the premise 'X is a necessary means to self-preservation' we can derive only the conclusion 'a man must do X to secure what, very probably, he wants.' Hobbes's psychological theory will still support his normative conclusions, but the support will be substantially weakened" (ibid.).

A second problem affecting Hobbes's reasoning is his premise of instrumental rationality, which, as we have seen, is necessary to support his theoretical conclusions. This premise is restrictive because it leaves no room for behavior that does not accord with his account of rationality, but might still be called reasonable or even "normal." Moral action, for example, "is often thought to conduce not to a man's ends, but to the ends of other men, or society, or of God; yet moral action is not thought to be against reason" (25). Such a view of morality does not have to be correct, "but it cannot be ruled out of court simply by an alleged factual claim that reasonable actions are those which conduce to a man's ends. This claim embodies a fundamental normative contention" (ibid.).

In light of these considerations, we might modify the Hobbesian rationality assumption to read "'actions which conduce to the agent's ends are, in this respect, reasonable,' leaving open that other factors as well may bear on the reasonableness of action, and may in some cases override a man's own ends" (ibid.). While this statement involves a normative claim as well, this claim seems more difficult to dispute. We can now deduce from the statement "'a man must do X to secure what, very probably, he wants'" the finding that "'a man very probably has some reason to do X.' This will still provide some reason, though by no means always sufficient reason, for the imperative 'Do X!'" (ibid.).

The normative advice given by Hobbes is simply that man should follow the laws of nature, which, ideally, would simultaneously also be the dictates of the *Leviathan*. As Forde has pointed out, Hobbes's laws of nature "differ fundamentally from more traditional systems of natural law in that their foundation is self-interest."[117] Hobbesian morality exhausts itself in prescribing certain rules that man should follow in the pursuit of his egoistic desires. Leslie Mulholland has argued that Hobbes establishes norms to lead man from "act egoism, [that is,] the egoism of a person who aims to maximize utilities without limits," to "rule egoism, [that is,] the egoism of a person who aims to maximize utilities through constrained cooperation with others."[118] Similarly, according to Dana Chabot, Hobbes endeavors to show that "reasoning scientifically, each [person] can see that to struggle alone for self-preservation is a futile undertaking and that the end we all seek (i.e., our safety and comfort) is more likely to be achieved by compromise than by combat."[119] The cooperation prescribed by this insight, however, has to be incorporated into laws and convention to have the desired effect. R. E. Ewin explains that "Hobbes believed that even those parts of morality that were not conventional required a background of convention and, in an important way, depended on public judgment's being given precedence over private judgment."[120] Public judgment and laws are needed to ensure that the "act egoists" of the state of nature will actually submit to the limits of "rule egoism." After all, as Hobbes writes in *De Cive*, "[C]ivill Societies are not meer meetings, but Bonds, to the making whereof, Faith and Compacts are necessary."[121] In the words of Gregory Kavka, "[B]asic moral rules are natural, in the sense of being derivable by reason from the universal common interest in social peace. But their effectiveness as means to security and well-being depends on their authoritative interpretation and enforcement by the legal apparatus of the State."[122]

Forde has pointed out that "we might paradoxically say, therefore, that Hobbes accepts a universal code of ethics, but it is one that no [person or] state is morally bound to follow."[123] In the end, Hobbes remains unable to show why man as he portrays him would ever willingly do anything that would not further his own self-interest. As Laurence Thomas has argued, egoistic motivations alone cannot sustain a commitment to morality; for such a commitment, nonegoistic motivations are necessary.[124] Such nonegoistic motivations, however, are not recognized in Hobbesian theory. Hobbes, just like Machiavelli, emerges as a moral skeptic, who, as argued by Navari, "holds morality to be a social construct, a series of ideas thought up by priests and moralists, indeed, by political theorists, which guide, constrain, or fog us, and from which his freely deliberating man constantly escapes."[125] The *Leviathan* leaves us with an image of man as described by John Mitchell:

> Inherently selfish he is a cunning creature whose bonds of loyalty are limited by his own physical needs and become expanded to the needs of his primary group only because obviously he can survive more effectively in a collective than in isolation. . . . Man's first obligation is to himself; his second to others who are directly involved in his personal welfare. . . . Man's sense of Morality is imposed on him by fear of punishment or reprimand, and in their absence he has moral fiber of no greater quality than any other social animal.[126]

The best we can hope for with respect to this creature is the realization that good and bad are merely subjective attributes, projected onto the facts of the world by human beings with ulterior, and invariably selfish, motives. Such a realization might lead one to the judgment that ideas of good and bad are not worth losing one's life over. While it cannot free man completely from the influence of moral and other irrational passions, such a view of the world will at least foster that rational skepticism and prudent constraint in his interaction with others which can keep open conflict in bounds.

The mainstream view of Hobbes's impact on international relations theory is reflected in the following statement by Paul Viotti and Mark Kauppi: "Hobbes's impact upon the realist view of international relations stems from his image of individuals in a mythical state of nature. His description is equally applicable to relations among states because in the state of nature as well as in international politics there is no *Leviathan* or superordinate power to impose order."[127] The pervasive sense of insecurity nations experience under conditions of anarchy forces them to pursue power to make themselves less vulnerable. As one state becomes more powerful, however, it appears more threatening to the others. This so-called security dilemma creates persistent and unavoidable conflict in the international system.[128]

To be sure, care must be taken when equating Hobbes's model state of nature with the realities of international politics. The so-called English school of international relations theory, of which authors such as John Vincent and Hedley Bull are representatives, argues that Hobbes does not view international relations as analogous to the state of nature but instead takes a "Grotian" perspective on world politics.[129] However, it is not necessary to agree with this view to recognize a crucial difference between Hobbes's portrayal of the state of nature and the international realm. This difference consists in the absence of equality among nation–states.[130] While a rough equality of power among individuals is a fundamental premise of Hobbes's state of nature, not all nation–states in the international system are equally threatened by all others. Moreover, nations are not likely to experience the same level of fear that individuals do in the state of nature. It has generally been much easier for one person to kill another than for one nation (or even several) to eliminate another. Besides, individuals inhabiting a state are less immediately threatened by interstate conflict than they would be in a true state of nature. Instead, they may even thrive on such conflict. Thus, nations are less motivated than individuals and are on top of that unequally motivated to enter a social contract by establishing supranational institutions of authority. Instead, according to realist expectations, they will forever remain in a natural condition of anarchy: the international state of nature.[131]

Interestingly, it is precisely because the analogy between the state of nature and the state of nations is only partial that Hobbes's political philosophy does, indeed, have profound implications for international political theory. Hobbes does not develop a theory of international politics. Instead, he develops, like Machiavelli and with virtually identical political aims, a theory of the impact of human nature on politics, in general. His judgment of human psychology allows Hobbes to predict how human beings will behave under certain conditions, such as anarchy or civil society.[132] In relations among nations, anarchy persists. At this level of political interaction, there exists no realistic institutional solution to the problem of human conflict. The solutions that remain are psychological. First, like Machiavelli, Hobbes understands that domestic stability will make a nation more powerful and thus a less likely target for attacks from abroad. A strong government at home will deter aggression at the international level. Second, insight into the irrationality of pride and ideology and the importance of rational fear will lead nations to be less aggressive themselves. Thus, Hobbes counsels an outlook on politics that emphasizes rationality and caution, while recognizing the centrality of power in relations among individuals as well as among states.

It is worth quoting Johnson at length:

> The school of realism is essentially Hobbesian in that it (1) counts on the predictability of actors' motivations and behavior; (2) equates anarchy with constant fear, struggle, and danger; (3) claims that the national interest, defined as self preservation and advancement against others is a dictate of nature—either a state obeys it or is destroyed; (4) takes all other motivations besides the national interest as irrational and dangerous and therefore to be counseled against, so that such motivations as national pride and ideological or religious fervor cannot be accounted for except as fatal anomalies or covers for power interests; (5) disregards the character of individual leaders as irrelevant, considering the overriding dictates of the international power structure; (6) disregards political rhetoric because it is seen as epiphenomenal; and (7) counsels prudent adherence to the realist view of the world put forth by the scientists of the realist paradigm that science is a better source of wisdom than the cultivation of excellence in leaders and their followers.[133]

While recognizing how Hobbes has been interpreted within the realist school of thought, it is important to keep in mind that not all critics of realism are equally critical of Hobbes. As Navari points out, "Hobbes's rights, laws and states of nature are not primarily descriptions of states of affairs, and it is more a mark of ignorance of Hobbes's thought than philosophical proximity to suppose that they are intended as such. They are logical constructs."[134] The fact that, nonetheless, "Hobbes's prescription has often been mistaken for his diagnosis"[135] stems from the difficulty of recognizing the distinctness and complexity of his scientific goals, on the one hand, and his political or ideological ones, on the other.[136]

Hobbes's impact on realist international relations scholarship has everything to do with the motivational assumptions underlying his theory. His portrayal of human nature in the *Leviathan* has provided realists with the rational egoist who populates their theories. However, while for Hobbes this person was a much wished for but quite unrealistic alternative to the emotional fools human beings actually are, contemporary realists consider it the norm. Realist followers of Hobbesian logic quite frequently mistake his ideological strategy of justifying the absolutist state through an eloquent but entirely hypothetical portrayal of the consequences of its absence for a descriptive model of political reality. They overlook that Hobbes's theory is actually designed to "create" a new reality. By doing so, they not only fall prey to the rhetoric of one particularly clever man but also elevate him to the status of a prophet. Ironically, it is Hobbes himself who warns (or tempts) posterity with the remark that "prophesy . . . [is] many times the principal cause of the event foretold."[137]

Summary and Conclusions

While I have characterized both Hobbes and Machiavelli as political realists, their views are complex, and it is extremely difficult to compare their political philosophies in their entirety. Each of them deserves separate and detailed treatment. In fact, it is hardly possible to do justice to the thought of Machiavelli or Hobbes without identifying enough contradictory facets in either to defy categorization. Still, it is necessary to compare them to identify those commonalities that make us call them both "political realists." The question is, after all, not whether they deserve the label but what we mean to say when we apply it

On the brink of modernity, the Florentine statesman Niccolo Machiavelli helped set in motion a powerful reaction to Medieval political thought and practice. In opposition to the hypocrisy of political systems in rhetoric inspired by Christian values and in reality among the most corrupt known at the time, he elaborated a passionate defense of political realism, an attitude which elevated to the status of necessity the requirements of political success and rejected a legitimate role for moral arguments and idealist schemes in political discourse. His defense was inspired by those superior political agents he identified in history who were able to prove that leadership qualities, summarized in the concept of *virtu*, combined with a realistic judgment of the rules of the political game, could lead to lasting political success.

His primary purpose in his theoretical writings was to teach his view of political reality. At its foundation we find a view of man that is overwhelmingly pessimistic. According to Machiavelli, men are selfish, greedy, and cowardly opportunists, who will never willingly do anything that does not further their own interests. They are status hungry and power hungry, disposed to quarrel at the slightest opportunity, and do not empathize or identify with others. As a consequence, they are atomistic individuals who live in permanent latent (if not open) conflict with each other. All of man's ends must of necessity be selfish because human motivation is exclusively egoistic. Human reason is useful only insofar as it may be able to develop and recognize superior strategies to achieve man's selfish ends. Reason and science are always only instrumental to the achievement of human goals and cannot transcend the dictates of selfish motivation.

Machiavellian political theory is concerned with how, given this abysmal judgment of human nature, political order and stability can be achieved. Since men are fundamentally incapable of overcoming their basic nature, it is important that political leaders act on their knowledge of reality rather than on their normative aspirations. Machiavelli advises the prince on the facts of the political world. To persuade him to act on what is, after all, Machiavelli's judgment of the facts of the world and Machiavelli's judgment of their implications, he needs to persuade the prince, who is of course as selfish as anyone else, that it is in his own best interest to do so. The purpose of Machiavellian political science is, then, first, to observe and correctly interpret the relevant aspects of reality and, second, to communicate them to the relevant decision makers in such a way as to persuade them to follow the scientist's recommendations. Machiavelli's epistemology is positivistic, his method didactic.

The ultimate purpose of Machiavelli's theorizing is to find the right ways to ensure the survival of the state. The goal of *mantenere lo stato* is conceptualized as an absolute necessity, which means that it justifies any actions taken to ensure its achievement. This idea is captured in the concept of *ragione di stato*. To survive, a state requires capable government and the power to defend itself against foreign as well as domestic threats. Machiavelli attempts to define capable government and to identify the ways by which the power of government can be maximized. A knowledge of psychology is particularly useful to achieve and maintain such power and capability because once we know how human beings are motivated we can better control their behavior. Machiavelli counsels the prince to make use of the motive of fear by using intimidation tactics and terror against his opponents if necessary. He also counsels him to use, cautiously, the motives of greed and pride to rally his subjects behind his causes. He needs to do so, because human beings would not sacrifice their selfish pursuits solely out of a sense of duty, loyalty, or patriotism. Instead, they need to be made to believe that they are helping themselves when they are in fact doing as the prince wishes them to. The prince needs to be careful and clever when trying to exploit the motives of greed or ambition because such motives, attaching themselves to whatever objects promise the best chances for achievement, operate within human beings in an unstable manner. He needs to be able to manipulate appearances, lie, and trick human beings into working for his designs. Since this is not always possible it is important for him to possess enough raw power to fall back on the reign of fear, if he has to.

Machiavelli's view of human nature and, consequently, of politics, international as well as domestic, is profoundly amoral. Moral values not only do not apply, the illusion that they do is destructive of the only legitimate end of government—its success, defined, minimally, as survival and, beyond that, as the expansion of its power. This is so because the assumption that morality has a place in politics leads us to misjudge the motivation and intentions of others, to develop naive expectations, and to proceed with insufficient caution and insufficient mistrust. Those who are more "realistic" will take advantage of our blindness, and we will be destroyed. The only defense against the imperial designs of others is to be better at the "game" than they are, to be more "realistic" and more determined to break all rules of morality if we are required to do so by "reason of state." Even today, the suggestion that threats must be met with counterthreats has the status of common sense, in politics as well as in many other areas of life. It has received its rationale from ideological realism, which finds its purest expression in the writings of Machiavelli.

Thomas Hobbes shares Machiavelli's judgment of human nature. However, he embarks on a more systematic treatment of the role of human motivation in politics, which he then employs as the axiomatic foundation for a complex deductive theory of politics. He perceives human beings, in explicit agreement with the Athenian thesis, as self-interested and motivated primarily by fear, pride, and a desire for material comfort. All three of these motives will lead them to seek to expand their power, which brings them into constant conflict with each other. Hobbes's mechanistic view of the workings of human motivation, combined with his deterministic judgment concerning the persistence and effects of anarchy in the absence of absolute government, lead him, more so than Machiavelli (whose psychology is somewhat less deterministic) to seek the remedies for the inadequacies of human behavior among their causes. He identifies fear as the main driving force for human behavior and sets out to show how, from an assumption of the primacy of fear, strategies may be developed which can help to suppress some passions and allow more reign for others and which can thus, through a manipulation of human motivation, further his goal of domestic stability. Hobbes's condemnation of the destructive impact of norms, ideologies, and "moral passions" in political life is both scientific and normative. He attempts to defend both the rule of the *Leviathan* and the laws of nature scientifically, by showing that they must logically follow from the minimal assumption that all human beings above all wish to survive. However, in so doing he shows a clear normative preference for those psychological characteristics, such as caution, prudence, acquisitiveness, and intellectual ambition, that are compatible with his hopes for scientific advancement and the doctrine of rationality, and against others, such as religious beliefs or reformist political ideologies, that he perceives as irrational and dangerous.

Hobbes is a skeptical positivist and empiricist. He is pessimistic of man's ability to see reality as it is as well as of his ability to communicate his observations without distortion. This causes a strange tension in his overall political theory between his hopes for positivist science and rationality to teach man to see the world as it should be seen and to lead him toward less disruptive behavior patterns, on the one hand, and his understanding and use of rhetoric to persuade his readers to see the world as he does, on the other hand. Both Hobbes and Machiavelli believe that a reliance on instrumental rationality and positivistic science, which is designed to see the world as it really is, can, in principle, help human beings adapt more successfully to the conditions of the (political) world. However, their instrumental view of science leads them to include didactic and prescriptive elements in their theories, which in turn require them to rely on rhetorics to persuade their readers that they should "buy into" the view of reality presented, as well as the recommendations that go along with it. The theories of both Machiavelli and Hobbes are normative insofar as they are, first, guided by the specific goal of ensuring the stability of the state and, second, designed to further this goal by educating political actors in the appropriate ways. Their obvious reliance on rhetorics, in the case of Hobbes even on rationalist argument, contrasts, as it does in the Athenian thesis, with the realist positivist–scientific aspiration to overcome the influence of rhetorics in scientific communication through the employment of a technical language that could approximate the objectivity assumed to be characteristic of the worldview presented.

The thought of both Machiavelli and Hobbes contains a structural along with a psychological dimension. In Hobbes, the second is as deterministic as the first. In Machiavelli's thought there exists no clear boundary between the two. Agency is presented to be able to overcome structure to some extent, depending on the character and capabilities of the actor. Like Hobbes, Machiavelli relies on the assumption that human nature is basically uniform, but he incorporates into his theory an elitist admiration for able leadership that counteracts his psychological determinism at least with respect to the psychology of "princes." As a consequence, he gives advice on how superior leadership can overcome presumed structural constraints. In comparison, Hobbes's views are more egalitarian, and he seems profoundly pessimistic concerning the possibility of extending the realm of agency. Instead, he counsels a reliance on prudence, caution, and rational procedure in the pursuit of self-interest, as well as an acceptance of and adaptation to constraints.

Both Machiavelli and Hobbes view human nature as stable and uniform. Both characterize human beings as independent, atomistic, selfish, untrusting, and untrustworthy. Both believe that human beings are inherently self-interested and that their basic motives lead them to pursue power, which, in turn, causes constant conflict among them. Both accede a central role in their psychology to the motive of fear, which both believe can and should be exploited by the powerful to exert a stabilizing influence on political order. Both believe with the sophists that moral values are inherently subjective and, since they possess no objective reality that science could examine, are a constant source of unsolvable disagreements. As a consequence, both are moral skeptics.

However, while Machiavellian realism remains "ideological," Hobbesian realism is realism turned "paradigmatic." Machiavelli shocks the world with his unabashed presentation of the full implications of realist arguments and even more so with his unabashed defense of those implications. Hobbes's approach, by comparison, is more subtle. It involves the use of realist motivational assumptions as axioms in a powerful deductive theory.[138] The practical recommendations that emerge from his arguments are, however, no less radically "realistic." In addition, they are likely more influential, since Hobbes ostensibly takes such care to proceed according to the conventions of positivist science. While Machiavelli represents realism as an ideology, it is Hobbes who emerges as the "father" of realism as a paradigm.

4

Realism Today

This chapter examines the work of representative realist scholars of the twentieth century and brings the historical analysis of the development of the realist view of human nature and motivation up to date. It includes treatments of both the "classical" and the structural, or neorealist, schools of international relations theory as well as of important contemporary developments in realist scholarship. The third section briefly analyzes the impact of rational choice and game theory on the development of the realist psychology.

Introduction

Realist arguments, as formulated by Thucydides' Athenians, by Niccolo Machiavelli, and by Thomas Hobbes, among others, continued to gain currency after the seventeenth century. During the eighteenth and nineteenth centuries, a number of important figures developed various elements of realist thought. One of them was Jean-Jacques Rousseau. Jim George states that, "a social contract theorist with explicit concerns about justice and morality among citizens of the modern state . . . , Rousseau, nevertheless, is granted Realist status because of his perspectives on the inter-state system where, he argued, a paradox exists which makes structural anarchy inevitable."[1] This paradox is that the formation of sovereign states, designed to protect domestic peace and the property rights of individuals, has the effect of transposing the problems solved by the social contract onto the next higher level, that of relations among the sovereign states. Rousseau notes that while "the hands of nature set bounds to the inequality among men, . . . the inequality among societies can grow endlessly, until one absorbs all the others."[2] The lack of natural equality among nation-states has the effect that a contractarian solution to the problem of social organization is not feasible at the level of the international system, where, instead, anarchy persists. Rousseau also makes the additional realist argument that, under such conditions, social relations are likely to be characterized by competition rather than cooperation. He employs the famous metaphor of the stag hunt to show "how common purposes and common interests are not enough—absent constraining rules and institutions—to procure collaboration in pursuit of some collective good."[3]

The 1830s saw the publication of Carl von Clausewitz's *On War*, which resurrected the Machiavellian defense of expediency as the proper guiding principle in political decision making.[4] As Gregory Crane has pointed out, the Machiavellian identification of the political realm as one where action is judged by the criterion of expediency rather than by moral standards continued to inform such politically influential concepts as "the *raison d'etat* of Richelieu, the *Realpolitik* of Bismarck, the 'big stick' of Theodore Roosevelt, and the cold war balance of power for which George Marshall was a primary architect."[5] The term *Realpolitik* was coined in 1853 by the German liberal nationalist August Ludwig von Rochau as a rhetorical weapon in his fight for the consolidation of the nation-state of Prussia and the assertion of its interests against Austria. The introduction of the term coincides with a shift in mainstream continental political thought away from the influence of idealist approaches inspired by Enlightenment philosophy toward the realist strategic rationale of the European concert of powers.[6]

Meanwhile, the ascension of positivist epistemology to its paradigmatic status in virtually all scientific departments served to support the belief that a realistic psychology should be the basis for political theorizing. Albert Hirschman writes: "That man 'as he really is' is the proper subject of what is today called political science continued to be asserted—sometimes almost routinely—in the eighteenth century."[7] As we have seen, realists claim that their theories are based on such a view of man, "as he really is," and are therefore realistic. By comparison, they characterize idealist approaches as "unscientific" for being based on an unrealistic vision of man and criticize the exaggerated rationalism and utopian progressivism, which they perceive to be the consequences of this vision.[8]

The liberal and other progressive approaches to international politics that had been inspired by Enlightenment rationalism were not to regain status until the period between the two world wars.[9] After this period, as a result of their perceived destructive consequences, they were once again discredited in large sectors of mainstream academic discourse and policy making. As George has put it, "[T]he time was right for the emergence of contemporary power politics Realism, and subsequently, for a Cold War 'catechism' opposed to all 'utopian' notions of a universal moral order."[10]

Realists such as E. H. Carr and Hans Morgenthau played an important role in establishing international relations as an academic discipline, especially in Great Britain and the United States.[11] The development of this discipline brought with it the systematic formulation of various tenets of realist political thought in the form of a paradigm of international relations theory. Francis Beer and Robert Hariman observe that "as it was linked to the modern valorization of the scientific method, the doctrine of political realism became the dominant theory within the contemporary discipline of international relations."[12]

The basic and stable elements of the realist paradigm of international relations are as follows:[13] The international system is comprised of nation-states, which are the primary actors in international politics.[14] These states exist in an anarchic, self-help environment. In other words, there exists no authority above the level of the states that is capable of coercing them to carry out its decisions, and international organizations cannot properly provide for states' needs. The condition of international anarchy is viewed as a powerful structural constraint that limits the rational policy options of states to such an extent that they are expected to behave in virtually identical ways when confronted with similar situations.[15] Most important, to provide for its own security, every state has to attempt to maximize its power relative to the others. While, for any state, power may or may not be an end in itself, it is always a necessary means to achieve security. Since realism is primarily concerned with military conflict, which is considered to pose the most immediate threat to a nation's security, it traditionally considers military capabilities the most important type of power resource. Thus it expects states to try to maximize primarily, though not exclusively, their military power.

It is important to note that the deduction of this expectation from the premise of international anarchy rests on the motivational assumptions of realism, which define what states want—the so-called national interest—and provide some insight into why states respond to structural constraints the way they do. They include at a minimum the assumptions that states are self-interested and rational, that they seek physical security, that they consider their security to be threatened by other actors, and that, to reduce the threats they perceive, they will want to increase their power vis-à-vis those others.[16]

Relying on deterrence as the only reliable means to prevent aggression, realism accepts the advice of the fourth-century Roman military theorist Vegetius: If you want peace, prepare for war. Realists frankly acknowledge the principal danger contained in this logic: One state's attempts to make itself secure may easily be interpreted as threatening by others. These others will react by stepping up their own military preparations in turn. Arms races may result, and defensive posturing may easily end up provoking aggression rather than deterring it.[17] Realism sees no way out of this "security dilemma" because states cannot trust one another enough to forsake their own protection. Given the lack of predictability of the behavior of others, which is created by the condition of international anarchy, political prudence forbids such trust.[18] Robert Jervis and others have pointed out that "deterrence is [thus] fundamentally a psychological theory. It is based on a series of 'hidden' assumptions about the relationship between power and aggression, threat and response, and the ability of leaders to influence the calculations and behavior of their would-be adversaries."[19]

Realists argue that collaboration among states is highly unlikely, even where common interests would seem to demand it.[20] This is the case in spite of the assumption that states are self-interested and act rationally. The problem is that, in the words of Michael Loriaux, their "rationality is unable to attain some of the more enlightened conceptualizations of self-interest because of the structural obstacles that international anarchy places in its path."[21] In other words, realism posits that due to environmental constraints and the "laws" of international political life states can never feel safe enough to make it rational for them to divest the pursuit of power of its top priority. On this basis, realism rejects idealistic along with utilitarian hopes that human reason could actually transform the realities of the international competition for power for the benefit of all.

Since the security dilemma cannot be avoided, the best that can be done to work for peace is to create conditions under which it is less likely to lead to open conflict. This is the raison d'être of balance-of-power politics, the principal international policy strategy advocated by realists. Security relations among states may be stabilized through the balancing of power among states and alliances, which in effect works by reducing aggressors' chances of success.[22] The conduct of successful balance-of-power politics, in turn, is seen to require foreign policies that are informed by a view of international political reality as well as by strategic recommendations developed in accordance with the realist rationale. The policies that result from this rationale are not guided by idealist hopes or dominated by ethical considerations. Instead, they are Realpolitik. After all, in the words of Loriaux,

> realism is, first, an expression of doubt regarding the prospects of achieving "perpetual peace" in international relations. It is, second, the advocacy of a politics of prudence informed by that foundational skepticism. It is, third, the recognition that the statesman must be willing to commit morally unpalatable acts—to kill, to deceive, to break promises—if such acts are required by the prudent defense of the national interest.[23]

It is a widely known fact whose implications are rarely fully appreciated that during the early years of the Cold War the foreign policy establishments in the United States as well as other nations entered into a symbiosis with realist scholarship that, in many cases, was to last until the present day.[24] Immediately after the Second World War, realist interpretations of the events of political history were widely viewed as invaluable to an appropriate understanding of the contemporary state of the international system.[25] In addition to developing realist interpretations of historical (including the most recent) political events, realist political theorists during the Cold War, relying on such interpretations and rejuvenating the arguments of illustrious forebears such as St. Augustine, Machiavelli, and Hobbes, reformulated realist theory in part to fit the requirements of their foreign policy-making establishments. Thus, for example, realist scholarship had a profound impact on U.S. diplomacy, as reflected in the work of George Marshall, George Kennan, and Henry Kissinger.[26] Mary Maxwell points out that "this was a most dramatic instance of academic theory persuading the practitioners,"[27] during which, as John Garnett has observed, American policy makers "swallowed Realism, hook, line, and sinker."[28]

Michael Mastanduno has found that after the Cold War "U.S. foreign policy is still consistent with realist principles, insofar as its actions are still designed to preserve U.S. predominance and to shape a postwar order that advances American interests."[29] Frank Wayman and Paul Diehl suggest that, at this point in time, "realism's tenets are widely adopted, if not worshipped, in many policy-making circles around the globe."[30] This observation, of course, legitimizes realist scholarship, which, in turn, serves to legitimize realist policies, in the United States and elsewhere.[31] All states, so argue the realist scholars, "continue to pay close attention to the balance of power and to worry about the possibility of major conflict."[32] This "enduring preoccupation with power and security" shows that "the end of the Cold War did not bring the end of power politics, and realism is likely to remain the single most useful instrument in our intellectual toolbox."[33]

"Classical" Realism in the Twentieth Century

The generation of political realists writing around the time of the Second World War and especially during the early years of the Cold War are commonly referred to today as "classical" realists. The most influential twentieth-century classical realists include Hans Joachim Morgenthau, Reinhold Niebuhr, E. H. Carr, Martin Wight, Raymond Aron, and John Herz.[34] While all of these and many other thinkers have had an impact on the further development of the realist paradigm of international relations, their theories are by no means identical. A comparison of the arguments of the major classical realists uncovers a wealth of interesting disagreements.[35] However, to identify the central unifying elements of classical realist thought, I will simplify the arguments of the classical realist scholars and eschew a treatment of the complexities and idiosyncrasies of their individual works.[36]

The classical realists wrote in reaction to the spread of totalitarianism and aggressive nationalism in the early decades of the twentieth century, as well as the devastation of the world wars, intending, in the words of Carr, "to analyse the underlying and significant . . . causes of the disaster" they had experienced.[37] They attributed a large portion of the blame to the failures of interwar diplomacy, which, according to classical realism, were due largely to a deluded idealism à la Woodrow Wilson and to the policy of appeasement that resulted partly from this idealism. The preeminent classical realists themselves tended to be disappointed idealists.[38] Classical twentieth-century realism thus received its raison d'être to a large extent from the blows that had been dealt idealist approaches (and idealists) by the brutal historical realities of the first half of the twentieth century. It continued to receive ideological justification by the systemic polarization, confrontational rhetorics, and power struggles by proxy that became part of everyday life during the Cold War. Just like Machiavelli's exposé of political corruption and the Hobbesian response to the English Civil War, classical twentieth-century realism must thus be understood as an attempt to learn from the realities of political conflict as it had been and was experienced at the time.

Whereas Hobbes was concerned with conflicts between groups within the state, twentieth-century realism, as a theory of international politics, is primarily interested in conflicts between states. Classical realists attempt to explain the behavior of states largely by analogical reasoning through reference to the traditional realist view of human psychology. This strategy is most obvious in the work of Morgenthau, who establishes as the first principle of political realism that "politics . . . is governed by objective laws that have their roots in human nature."[39] In their characterization of human nature, the classical realists place a strong emphasis on egoistic passions and evil in man. In addition, they believe the negative traits of human psychology to be inevitable and permanent. In the words of Morgenthau, "the sinfulness of man is . . . not . . . an accidental disturbance of the world sure to be overcome by a gradual development toward the good but . . . an inescapable necessity which gives meaning to the existence of man."[40]

Morgenthau explains the observation that nations seem constantly embroiled in conflict with reference to what he calls "elemental biopsychological drives" characteristic of human beings.[41] Two of these drives are particularly important: The first is "an elementary egoism which arises from the competition for those scarce material and ideational goods that enable human beings to survive."[42] The second is the human will to power, or, as Morgenthau puts it, "the desire to maintain the range of one's own person with regard to others, to increase it, or to demonstrate it."[43] While "there is in selfishness an element of rationality presented by the natural limitation of the end," since any human being or state only needs a finite amount of resources to survive, the will to power is, according to Morgenthau, both infinite and irrational.[44]

In the thought of Morgenthau, the "tendency to dominate" that is apparent in "all human associations, from the family . . . to the state," that omnipresent human "aspiration for power over man," is "the essence of politics."[45] Inhabited by selfish and self-aggrandizing beings, the realm of international politics becomes a realm of evil, characterized by constant struggles between selfish and self-aggrandizing states, seeking power both as an end in itself as well as a means to all their other ends. This is how the classical realists assimilate, for purposes of creating a realist theory of international relations, "the core argument offered by previous realists, namely that the egoistic nature of man is the cause of all political strife."[46]

Niebuhr, whose lectures at Harvard Morgenthau attended, complements the realist view of human nature with a theory on the psychological egoism of groups.[47] He is known as a theologian for taking the position of "Christian realism," which aims to identify and openly confront the roots of evil in human nature. He begins by noting that man's quintessential experience as a mortal being is a pervasive sense of insecurity. From this insecurity results over-defensiveness. Both man's never-ending quest for power and the cardinal sin of pride, which is nothing less than an attempt to transcend mortality, are expressions of this over-defensiveness. These dangerous traits of human nature are magnified in relations among groups because, for a variety of reasons, group relations will always be even less affected by ethical considerations than individual relations. Thus, the behavior of nations (as well as classes) is motivated almost exclusively by the quest for power and status.[48]

Niebuhr's arguments are reminiscent of Hobbes's. Like Hobbes, he identifies the lack of physical security that is naturally experienced by human beings as the cause of over-defensiveness, or irrational fear. Such irrational fear, in turn, is seen to be the root of those passions which lead human beings into conflict. Like Hobbes, Niebuhr is particularly critical of the passion of pride. As a motive that combines a strong sense of competition with the perceived need to use one's power over others to influence their perceptions, pride has the unfortunate tendency to corrupt idealistic endeavors. As a consequence of his own experiences as a political activist as well as of his observations concerning the fate of ideologically motivated reforms in the Soviet Union and elsewhere, Niebuhr became known for his powerful polemics against liberal progressivism and utopian radicalism.

Niebuhr's thought is strongly influenced by St. Augustine, to whom he refers as "the first great 'realist' in western history."[49] According to Loriaux, who has called Niebuhr "the bridge that spans the centuries separating Augustine from the modern realist," "Niebuhr looked to Augustine to reconcile a growing disillusionment with progressive politics and a steadfast refusal to retreat into a cynical conservatism."[50] His solution resembles that of Wight, who, as Fred Halliday has pointed out, was "in 'public' . . . a power politics Realist, . . . [and] in 'private' a Christian pacifist."[51] Wight's conclusion that "hope is not a political virtue: it is a theological virtue"[52] has been termed by George to be "perhaps the most explicit representation of an ancient pessimism on the human condition to be found in Realist literature."[53] This "neo-Augustinian" influence profoundly affected the subsequent development of realist political philosophy by reaffirming and legitimizing its "foundational skepticism"[54] concerning human nature and the possibility of worldly progress.[55]

As we have seen, classical twentieth-century realists are generally highly skeptical of progressive, or idealist, approaches.[56] In this context, Carr's admonitions against the assumption of a "natural harmony of interests" are particularly impassioned. He writes in *The Twenty Years' Crisis*, that "the exposure by realist criticism of the hollowness of the utopian edifice is the first task of the political thinker."[57] The classical realist critique of political idealism rests on three empirical claims: First, realists hold that idealistic policy schemes have a high probability of being mere cover-ups for underlying power–political interests. In other words, they tend to be ideological in nature. Second, ideologically motivated policies threaten international peace and thereby national security. Third, genuinely idealistically motivated policies by one's own government directly undermine one's own national security. Depending on whether the first or the third of these claims plays a larger role in their arguments, realists may suggest either that true idealism *does* not exist or that it *should* not.[58]

According to Loriaux, Carr expresses skepticism concerning idealist schemes on the basis that "moral values cannot be disentangled from the political order that generates and enforces them."[59] Instead, he observes that "power goes far to create the morality convenient to itself."[60] As, for Carr, moral codes tend to reflect "the interests of the classes and nations that create and defend political order,"[61] he does not "share the Wilsonians' faith in the capacity of human reason to recognize in liberal philosophy the most abstract and universal expression of the real interests of humanity as a species."[62] Morgenthau confirms that "political realism refuses to identify the moral aspirations of a particular nation with the moral laws that govern the universe," because "all nations are tempted—and few have been able to resist the temptation for long—to clothe their own particular aspirations and actions in the moral purposes of the universe."[63]

This skepticism concerning idealist arguments is motivated by the observation that ideologies wreak havoc in the international system. As Laurie Johnson Bagby has pointed out, for the classical realists as well as for Hobbes, "it is ideological zealotry which can lead to the most dangerous doctrinal warfare, warfare not over security (which in the realist's view is the only legitimate reason for war) but over ideas."[64] If ideologies are so dangerous, it makes sense to be on the lookout for them. Since they usually hide behind idealist "cover-ups," it makes sense to be generally skeptical of idealist arguments. However, when it comes to counseling governments on appropriate foreign policy strategy, realists adopt a different emphasis. Rather than claiming that true idealism does not exist, they argue that it is dangerous for any one government to take an idealist position. The reason is, simply, that it is unlikely that any other government will do the same.

The classical realists follow Machiavelli (and the Athenians) in stressing the amoral nature of interstate relations.[65] While they may or may not regard domestic politics differently, realists view international politics as an arena in which nations compete for power and, in defense of the national interest, ruthlessly exploit any advantage they may acquire. In the words of Morgenthau, "the main signpost that helps political realism to find its way through the landscape of international politics is the concept of interest defined in terms of power."[66] Defending the concept of the national interest as both the appropriate interpretive tool to understand the behavior of nations in general as well as the proper objective of foreign policy, he refers to it as "the one guiding star, one standard of thought, one rule of action" in the international sphere.[67]

The concept of the national interest is not by definition opposed to moral principles. However, it needs to be divorced from such principles if the statesman is to avoid unrealistic judgments and expectations.[68] According to classical realism, political prudence, or the requirements of Realpolitik, demand that policy makers realize that the true nature of international relations is more akin to Hobbes's state of nature than to civil society. This is not to say that statesmen always actually behave as if in a state of nature. As Johnson Bagby points out, Morgenthau, for example, realizes that "ethics, mores and laws do limit and regulate somewhat the struggle for power" even in the international realm.[69] He does not claim that politics is amoral by nature or that political action has no ethical implications.[70] Still, it is too dangerous to attempt to conduct foreign policy according to idealistic aspirations or moralistic hopes. Morgenthau writes, "We have no choice between power and the common good. To act successfully, that is, according to the rules of the political arts, is political wisdom. To know with despair that the political act is inevitably evil, and to act nevertheless, is moral courage. To choose among several expedient actions the least evil one is moral judgment."[71]

Morgenthau reformulates in terms more palatable than those of Machiavelli the necessity of separating the realm of international politics from the realm of morality.[72] Michael Doyle points out that, like Machiavelli, "Morgenthau finds moral considerations unfit for the necessities that characterize politics, particularly international politics. Traditional moral considerations are real, but they should (can) restrain otherwise expedient policy only where necessity does not override them."[73] However, Morgenthau's position is more ambiguous than Machiavelli's because he is not as easily characterized as a general moral skeptic.[74] Rather, he appears caught between two contradictory impulses. On the one hand, he bases his hopes for policy improvement on a realist science of politics, which requires that the realm of international politics be clearly separated from the realm of ethics. He dismisses alternative approaches for involving "a fundamental misunderstanding of the real world which seeks in utopian/idealist/ideological fashion" to deny the inescapable conditions of human existence.[75] On the other hand, he does not deny the relevance of ethical constraints in international politics and even ventures to evaluate the role they do and should play. Morgenthau is akin to Thucydides in his acknowledgment of the tension between moral and political imperatives.[76] It is his commitment to a practical art of politics that appears to lead Morgenthau to embrace realism as opposed to any openly normative approach. In his advice to policy makers, he assigns merely a minimal role to morality in foreign policy by advising that the standard of "prudence" be used in addition to the standard of success.[77] Beyond his role as a political theorist, as a moral thinker and a private citizen, Morgenthau may, however, easily be characterized as a moralist. In this respect, he resembles the neo-Augustinian realists Niebuhr and Wight.[78]

In *Scientific Man vs. Power Politics*, Morgenthau accuses rationalist idealism of "scientism," claiming, in essence, that such idealism attempts to establish a managerial science of politics based on a vastly exaggerated judgment of the human capacity to understand and predict political phenomena.[79] By comparison, classical realism is characterized by a fairly deterministic pessimism. Carr, for example, stresses the operation of "historical forces" beyond man's control, and Morgenthau himself warns that, the "laws [by which society lives] being impervious to our preferences, men will challenge them only at the risk of failure."[80] The classical realist logic depends on deterministic elements because, in the words of Steven Forde, "what gives the realist argument its scientific character is its grounding in necessity."[81] After all, it is the "laws by which society lives" into which realism purports to provide a particular insight.[82] As we have seen, the realist search for a science of international relations, firmly based on a realistic understanding of the world, which can avoid the pitfalls of ideology and provide us with the means to properly understand and control the realities of political life, has always been motivated by the hope that a better understanding of political reality can help policy makers make more informed decisions with more promise of success.[83] Robert Gilpin has written that "political realism is, of course, the very embodiment of this faith in reason and science. . . . Realism holds that through calculations of power and the national interest statesmen create order out of anarchy and thereby moderate the inevitable conflicts of autonomous, self-centered, and competitive states."[84]

The primary practical purpose of the science of international politics as envisioned by Morgenthau is to guide policy makers in the conduct of foreign policy. Based on his six principles of realism, he suggests, in *Politics among Nations*, four fundamental rules of realist diplomacy.[85] Diplomacy, according to Morgenthau as well as realist diplomats such as George Kennan, is the only policy tool beyond deterrence that is useful for averting war, since nation–states will always resist "limitation," in the form of disarmament, international law, or collective security arrangements, just like the international system will always resist "transformation" from an anarchic realm inhabited by individual nation–states into a global community. To conduct the kind of "rational" diplomacy that will help avoid violent conflict, policy makers first need to gain a realistic insight into the constraints and incentives operating in international politics.[86] In the words of Morgenthau, "[T]o improve society it is first necessary to understand the laws by which society lives."[87] Realism attempts to provide this insight by "speaking truth to power" and to teach decision makers how to properly respond to the constraints and incentives they face.[88]

Forde has pointed out that, as compared to neorealists, classical realists do not rely with equal ease on restrictive psychological assumptions in stipulating the "laws" of politics; instead, following the example of Thucydides, they "embed the scientific elements of their theories in rich and comprehensive analyses of human nature and domestic as well as international political practice."[89] It is indeed true that the continued development of the realist paradigm would lead still further away from a concern with the impact of psychological and domestic political factors on international politics and toward a concentration on structural factors operating at the level of the international system. However, the seeds of this strategy are clearly sown in classical realist thought.

According to Morgenthau, realist political theory guards against "two popular fallacies: the concern with motives and the concern with ideological preferences."[90] He holds that "to search for the clue to foreign policy exclusively in the motives of statesmen is both futile and deceptive. It is futile because motives are the most illusive of psychological data, distorted as they are, frequently beyond recognition, by the interests and emotions of actor and observer alike."[91] Not only are the motives and convictions of statesmen difficult to know. Even if we could know them, Morgenthau claims, "that knowledge would help us little in understanding foreign policies, and might well lead us astray."[92] This judgment implies that statesmen are constrained from acting in ways of their own choosing. Classical realists are skeptical of psychological approaches to foreign policy analysis because they perceive political actors to be powerless to change the essential conditions imposed by both human nature and the realities of international political life. Rather than examining the motives relevant for state behavior, they rely on an axiomatic minimal consensus concerning state motivation, which they use to explain the strategies states adopt in response to varying external circumstances. By adopting this perspective, they lay the groundwork for their structural realist successors.

As we have seen, realist political theory has always contained structuralist elements.[93] However, what distinguishes earlier structural realist arguments is that they typically include explanations of how structural causes effectively translate into the behavior of states.[94] While the classical realists tend to follow Machiavelli and Hobbes in making reference to human nature to explain why states react in the specified ways to the stipulated constraints, neorealists such as Kenneth Waltz or Robert Gilpin aim to bypass a concern with human nature and focus exclusively on system-level variables to explain variation in the behavior of states. In an attempt to develop highly parsimonious explanations for international political events, they seek to circumvent a concern with the obscure mechanisms of the human mind or the unpredictable processes of foreign policy making by modeling direct connections between "objective" phenomena at the systemic level and the observed reactions of states. Thus the main difference between the so-called classical realists of the mid-twentieth century and their neorealist successors is their choice of primary level of analysis.[95]

Neorealism and Beyond

The "father" of neorealism as a general theory of international relations is Waltz. Drawing on earlier arguments, which can, for the most part, be found in his 1959 publication *Man, the State, and War*, he formulates the mature version of his approach in his *Theory of International Politics*, which was published in 1979. Just like classical realism, neorealist theory makes assumptions about the motives of states based on a particular understanding of human nature. Waltz himself sounds like St. Augustine when he writes that "our miseries are ineluctably the product of our natures. The root of all evil is man, and thus he is himself the root of the specific evil, war."[96] However, he rejects as useless for purposes of international political theorizing the argument that "struggles of power arise because men are born seekers of power."[97] Instead, he suggests that human nature is ultimately too indeterminate to be considered the primary cause of war and that we should instead focus on the structural constraints that compel men, regardless of their nature, to vie for power.[98] His theory is based on the rationale that "struggles for preference arise in competitive situations and force is introduced in the absence of an authority that can limit the means used by the competitors."[99]

According to Robert Keohane, the main significance of Waltz's theory lies in his "attempt to systematize political realism into a rigorous, deductive systemic theory of international politics."[100] The novelty of this approach consists in his claim that it is possible to develop explanations and predictions of state behavior without paying attention to first-image (psychological) or second-image (state-level) variables. Instead, Waltz attempts to explain the behavior of nation–states and its effects on the international system exclusively with reference to third-image variables, structural causes that operate at the same systemic level. Thus, neorealist theory is structuralist and systemic. As Waltz himself points out, it cannot serve as a theory of foreign policy, since it is not designed to explain the process or the outcomes of foreign policy decisions, only their systemic effects.[101]

By Waltz's own admission, neorealist theory thus can never fully explain individual political decisions.[102] Bruce Porter observes that "neorealist theory has always admitted that a full understanding of a *specific* event requires that unit-level features be taken into account."[103] However, Waltz argues that a concentration on the impact of structural constraints can help identify important factors that generally influence state behavior. According to Keohane, Waltz believes "that a good theory of international politics must be systemic, since how the relationships among states are organized strongly affects governments' behavior toward one another."[104] In addition, Waltz argues that the "construction of a *general* theory of international relations . . . requires that . . . [unit-level features] be disregarded."[105] He regards approaches that explain state behavior with reference to psychology as "reductionist"[106] and disputes their status as proper theories of international relations. In his own judgment, his "structuralist-realist theory . . . is the only pertinent theory" extant in international political analysis because it combines explanatory power with general scope and parsimony.[107]

Waltz agrees with the classical realists that the international system consists of nation–states as primary actors. His theory posits that the structure of the international system, which "defines the arrangement, or the ordering, of the parts,"[108] has three dimensions: its ordering principle, the specific functions of its parts, and the relative capabilities of its parts. Following realist orthodoxy, Waltz treats the ordering principle of the international system as a given: International relations is an anarchic realm, a self-help environment, akin to the Hobbesian state of nature. His second crucial assumption is that the units of the system, that is, the individual states, perform similar functions within the system. This second-image assumption allows him to treat states as if they were alike.[109] With two dimensions "held equal," then, the structure of the international system varies only along the third dimension, that of the distribution of capabilities, or power. According to Waltz, the international system changes whenever the distribution of power among its units changes enough to cause a shift in the overall balance of power. Neorealist theory, in general, explains major international events with reference to such shifts.[110]

Waltz's third major assumption concerns the first image, or the level of analysis of the political decision maker. It establishes expectations about how states will react to structural constraints and thus plays a crucial role in implicitly supporting Waltz's second-image assumption. States are seen as rational "unitary actors who, at a minimum, seek their own preservation and, at a maximum, drive for universal domination."[111] The fact that all states function as rational security-maximizing units within an anarchic realm explains, in Waltz's theory, the continual tendency toward the establishment of a balance of power exhibited by the international system.[112] Waltz clarifies that he conceptualizes power balancing as a systemic effect, not a foreign policy choice. In other words, it can be explained without reference to the intentions of states.

A highly ambitious approach, Waltz's neorealist theory has, not surprisingly, been subject to various kinds of criticism. Most critics are concerned that the broad scope and parsimony of Waltz's theory require an exaggerated degree of abstraction, leading to a lack of explanatory and predictive power.[113] Neorealist theory has been accused of being particularly weak when it comes to explaining change in world politics.[114] By Waltz's own admission, while it claims structural causes to be paramount in producing systemic stability and defines changes in the structure of the system as change from one system to another, systemic theory is unqualified to account for changes *within* systems.[115] His theory has met with increased skepticism since the end of the Cold War, as a large number of studies have accumulated to suggest that the transition to the post–Cold War world cannot be explained without reference to the changes within the Cold War system that preceded it.[116]

Another criticism levied against structural realism, in general, and Waltz's theory, in particular, is that it contains normative elements that are not acknowledged.[117] As interpreted by Ian Clark, for example, Waltz's

> central theoretical position is the significance of the structure of the international system which requires realist policies by states. . . . Neorealism . . . may be said to require for its objective explanatory power a subjective understanding by the actors of the requirements of the system and, to this extent, to be influenced by the role of ideas and values. Thus it has been said that Waltz's work should be read "as exhortations to policy makers and fellow citizens about how they *ought* to respond to the structure of power."[118]

A problem that has not received enough attention in the literature is the degree to which neorealist theory relies on strong assumptions concerning the characteristics of the "units" that comprise the international system.[119] As Waltz himself explains,

> balance-of-power theory is a theory about the results produced by the uncoordinated actions of states. The theory makes assumptions about the interests and motives of states, rather than explaining them. What it does explain are the constraints that confine all states. The clear perception of constraints provides many clues to the expected reactions of states, but by itself the theory cannot explain those reactions. They depend not only on international constraints but also on the characteristics of states.[120]

The problem is that neorealism, even while admitting these limitations, does purport to explain and predict the reactions of states to the stipulated structural constraints and develops policy advice based on the expectations created by the theory. The only way it can do so is by making assumptions about the characteristics of states, most importantly by making assumptions about the motives for state action.

We do not even know that the structural constraints stipulated in neorealist theory are "real."[121] In fact, the realist characterization of the international system as an essentially governance-free self-help environment comprised of largely independent states is rejected by entire schools of international relations theory as outdated at the very least.[122] The fact that neorealism also relies on strong unit-level assumptions, which it generally does not even defend, is even more problematic, since these assumptions largely determine the expectations developed by neorealist theory. It is likely that, as Alexander Wendt has argued, neorealist theory becomes unduly static and pessimistic by treating "self-interested actors as constant and exogenously given and focus[ing] on the selective incentives that might induce them to cooperate."[123] As Richard Ashley claims, neorealist views concerning human nature may even function in defense of an approach to international politics that "combines the superficiality of positivistic atomism and structuralism's inability to account for change with an ideological aversion to critical thinking about values."[124]

While neorealism is approaching the status of the next "classic" theory of international politics, a more recent development in the history of realism is the introduction of offensive–defensive theory by such scholars as Robert Jervis, George Quester, and Stephen van Evera.[125] According to offensive–defensive theory, the magnitude of the security dilemma in which states find themselves is not fixed, it varies depending on what Jervis has termed the "offensive–defensive balance" and "offensive–defensive differentiation."[126] The first refers to the relative degree of "difficulty" that nations associate with pursuing a policy of aggression versus the difficulty they associate with defending themselves. The central hypothesis here is that to the extent that defense is "easier" than offense, nations become less motivated to attack. The second crucial variable is the degree to which offensive weapons can be distinguished from defensive weapons. The hypothesis is that the easier weapons can be differentiated, the easier it becomes for nations to build up their defenses without appearing threatening to others.

The introduction of offensive–defensive theory has led to a split of realist scholarship into two camps.[127] So-called defensive realists, such as van Evera and Jack Snyder, argue that states are not intrinsically motivated to expand and conquer others and that they must not necessarily try to maximize their relative power to pursue security.[128] Instead, they will not attack others if their chances of failure are not outweighed by the potential benefits and thus may find it more rational to preserve the status quo. Defensive realists argue that offense is becoming increasingly irrational, at least among Western industrial nations, because "the costs of expansion generally outweigh the benefits."[129] In their opinion, great power wars even in the past usually resulted from "militarism, hypernationalism, or some other distorting domestic factor."[130] They "occurred largely because domestic groups fostered exaggerated perceptions of threat and an excessive faith in the efficacy of military force."[131] When defense is realistically judged to be easier than offense, states experience a higher level of security and less incentives to expand, under which conditions peaceful coexistence or even cooperation among them become more viable. Defensive realism is fairly optimistic concerning the possibility of such cooperation because better defense capabilities and the ability to distinguish between offensive and defensive weaponry, in principle, can enable states to achieve an acceptable level of security without threatening others. This, in effect, means that they can overcome the "security dilemma" and thus break the automatic tendency of international anarchy to lead states into violent confrontation.[132]

Defensive realism is criticized primarily for its two major claims: that states must not try to maximize their power in the pursuit of security and that conquest is, at least today, generally not cost-effective. The first claim is questioned, for example, by Randall Schweller, who argues that it underestimates the threat posed by predatory revisionist states, much like interwar idealism did.[133] "Offensive" realists, such as John Mearsheimer, Eric Labs, and Fareed Zakaria, argue that precisely because no state can be sure when a predatory revisionist power may emerge, all states are motivated to maximize their relative power.[134] According to offensive realists, the assumption that states seek security is by itself too weak. Instead, a realistic judgment of international politics requires the assumption that all states seek to expand their power and that they "will take advantage of opportunities to expand their power, regardless of the status quo or whether they confront a specific threat."[135]

In addition, the second major claim of defensive realism is contradicted, for example, by Peter Liberman in his book *Does Conquest Pay?*[136] Offensive realists point out that situations in which it may be rational to initiate war are far more common than defensive realists claim, that "anarchy forces great powers to compete irrespective of their internal characteristics,"[137] and that security competition is the natural state of the international system even where economic interdependence is strong. They draw support from a recent current of realist scholarship that stresses the distinction between absolute and relative gains and its consequences for rational foreign policy making. Scholars writing in this context react primarily to neoliberal institutionalist claims that international institutions can play an important role in world affairs because states realize that their cooperation in such institutions will provide them with long-term gains. For the sake of such gains, liberal theorists argue, states can and will rationally make short-term sacrifices with respect to independent authority and power resources. In response, realists such as Joseph Grieco and Stephen Krasner point out that states have to be concerned not only with their absolute gains from cooperation but with their relative gains, meaning with how much they stand to gain in comparison with the other participants.[138] States are not expected to cooperate if such cooperation in the long run will serve to decrease their power relative to other states. Such a view assigns a markedly less significant role to international institutions and drastically reduces the expected potential for international cooperation.[139]

The distinction between offensive and defensive realism is useful today because it helps explain why realist scholars quite frequently arrive at contradictory judgments with respect to crucial questions, such as, for example, the relationship between structural characteristics of the international system, such as polarity or the distribution of capabilities, and the likelihood of war.[140] The fundamental difference between the two contemporary currents of realist scholarship is that they employ slightly different motivational assumptions. While both assume states to be rational, self-interested, and motivated to maximize their security, defensive realism does not assume that states always seek to maximize their relative power nor does it assume that they prioritize military power. Instead, they may perceive themselves in a position secure enough to grant high priority to other goals.[141] Offensive realism assumes that this is not, and believes that it should not be, the case. It assumes instead that states always attempt to maximize their relative power, and that military power is their highest priority. Representative here is John Mearsheimer, whose views on state motivation are summed up as follows: "The most basic motive driving states is survival. . . . States in the international system fear each other. . . . Fear is [thus] an important force in world politics. . . . States in the international system aim to maximize their relative power positions over other states."[142]

This distinction is certainly not the only plausible way to categorize contemporary realist scholarship. Stephen Brooks, for example, distinguishes between neorealist theory, as represented by Waltz, and "postclassical realism." He argues that these two currents of realist scholarship are distinguished by three crucial assumptions concerning state behavior. Most significant, while neorealism holds that "states are conditioned by the mere possibility of conflict," which leads them to always adopt a "worst-case perspective," postclassical realism holds that states "make decisions based on the probability of aggression."[143] The other two points of disagreement between the two currents of scholarship depend on this distinction. The first concerns the so-called discount rate. Neorealists assume that states heavily discount future security for the sake of short-term military preparedness, while postclassical realism does not. The second concerns state preferences. Neorealism assumes that military power is always more important to the state than economic power, while postclassical realism holds that "rational policy makers may trade off a degree of military preparedness if the potential net gains in economic capacity are substantial relative to the probability of security losses."[144]

Brooks's distinction is broadly analogous to the distinction between offensive and defensive realism. The important lesson to draw from such attempts at categorization is that, apparently, unit-level assumptions play a crucial role in the development of realist explanations and predictions of international politics. In fact, since the end of the Cold War, it has become especially apparent that the different motivational assumptions employed by different "types" of realists lead scholars to develop radically different expectations and, consequently, policy recommendations. For example, defensive realist van Evera judges post–Cold War Europe to be "primed for peace" since he believes that relevant decision makers agree that the benefits of present and potential peaceful cooperation vastly outweigh the potential net benefits of imperialism.[145] In contrast, offensive realist Mearsheimer believes that a withdrawal of U.S. hegemonic dominance from Western Europe is bound to revive security competition between European nations. He agrees with Waltz that the demise of the bipolar order of the Cold War, stabilized as it was by the nuclear stalemate between the eastern and western alliance, and the emergence of a multipolar structure will create a high risk of armed conflict, in Europe and elsewhere.[146]

Rational Choice and Game Theory

In tracing the flaws in *The Logic of Leviathan*, David Gauthier has touched on an important element of realism, both classical and structural: its reliance on the assumption of rationality.[147] According to Keohane, "[E]ven as long ago as the time of Thucydides, political realism . . . contained three key assumptions: (1) states . . . are the key units of action; (2) they seek power, either as an end in itself or as a means to other ends; and (3) they behave in ways that are, by and large, rational, and therefore comprehensible to outsiders in rational terms."[148] Rational choice theory, which is a relatively new and fast developing methodological approach rather than a substantive theory in itself, has had the effect of strengthening the overall reliance of realist theory on the rationality assumption and has been enthusiastically employed by many realist scholars.[149]

While rational choice theory is neither coterminous with nor dependent on the framework of realist theory, it does share important, if often implicit, assumptions with the thought of Hobbes and other realists. These assumptions concern both human psychology and expectations about "the way the world does and should work."[150] Our interest in the relationship between realist and rational choice theory warrants an aside on the origins shared by these two schools of thought. The historical roots of rational choice or rational actor theory are commonly sought in the classical liberal microeconomics of Adam Smith, who attempted to solve a problem that, according to Kristen Renwick Monroe, "had troubled philosophers since Hobbes made his famous argument that there was one basic human nature and that this nature was self-centered."[151] This problem is, "How can a society of selfish citizens produce collective welfare without authoritarian government?"[152]

We have earlier heard from Hirschman that both political realism and economic liberalism emerged from the seventeenth-century strategy of "opposing the interests of men to their passions and of contrasting the favorable effects that follow when men are guided by their interests to the calamitous state of affairs that prevails when men give free reign to their passions."[153] We know that the concept of interest originally did not have primarily material connotations. Instead, "it comprised the totality of human aspirations, but denoted an element of reflection and calculation with respect to the manner in which these aspirations were to be pursued."[154] In other words, it represented the idea of man seeking his own good in a way that we would today call "rational." The rational pursuit of self-interest was deemed essential to the prevention of conflicts brought about by the rash and ignitable nature of human passions. Thus, early arguments revolving around the principle of countervailing interests fed into the realist political arguments that were brought forward by Hobbes.[155] They also fed into the development of economic liberalism, in which "the term 'interests' actually carried—and therefore bestowed on money-making—a positive and curative connotation deriving from its recent close association with the idea of a more enlightened way of conducting human affairs, private as well as public."[156]

Liberal economics asserts that, at least in the economic realm, the problem of making the selfish passions of man contribute to a common good can be solved through the operation of the "market," which transmits the relevant information and creates the proper incentives to lead individual decision makers to collectively acceptable decisions. Liberal economic theory implicitly relies on the assumption of the rationality of individual decision makers, without which it would be incomparably more difficult to predict how these decision makers might respond to the incentives created by the market.[157] Rational choice theory is the methodology that has emerged from this and supplemental assumptions implicit in liberal economics. Rational choice theorists attempt to apply such assumptions to other contexts of human behavior, most notably to politics, and today political scientists both of liberal and of realist persuasion frequently make use of rational choice methodology.

Donald Green and Ian Shapiro identify the following assumptions as generally shared by rational choice theorists today.[158] First, rational behavior involves the maximization of an actor's utility, that is, actors are assumed to choose the course of action they believe will lead to the outcome most desirable to them. Behavior is rational, in the words of Mancur Olson, if objectives are "pursued by means that [seem] . . . efficient and effective for achieving these objectives," given the actor's information and beliefs.[159] Second, rationality requires that actors pursue their objectives consistently. At a minimum, two conditions must be met to ensure consistency. First, rational choice theory assumes the "connectedness" of actors' preferences, that is, it views actors as, in principle, able to rank-order their various options. When comparing options, an actor must either be able to prefer one over the other or decide to value them equally. In addition, rational choice theory assumes that actors' preference orderings are transitive. This means that if an actor prefers option A to option B and option B to option C, then he must also prefer option A to option C. A third assumption is that, since decision making usually takes place under conditions of uncertainty, actors maximize their *expected* as opposed to their *actual* utility. Usually, actors are modeled to attach probabilities to all specified possible outcomes and to consider these probabilities when choosing a course of action. Sometimes, such a model will allow for varying predispositions with respect to risk, so that a risk-averse actor might attempt to pursue a smaller payoff with a higher probability of success, while a risk-acceptant actor might "gamble" for a higher gain. The fourth important assumption of rational choice theory identifies individuals as the relevant agents. Rational choice theorists generally "explain collective outcomes with reference to the maximizing actions of individuals."[160] The behavior of collectivities, such as nation–states, is commonly examined by treating such collectivities as if they were rational individuals. In sum, "rational choice theorists generally agree on an instrumental conception of individual rationality, by reference to which people are thought to maximize their expected utilities in formally predictable ways."[161]

Above and beyond this minimal consensus, different conceptions and applications of rational choice theory introduce additional, more or less far-reaching assumptions. There exist two main areas of disagreement among rational choice theorists with respect to their general theoretical assumptions. The first concerns the question of how much information actors can be assumed to possess and to be able to use when making their decisions. Critics of rational choice theory frequently target what they perceive to be unrealistic assumptions with respect to actors' information acquisition, retention, and processing capabilities as well as their abilities to estimate the values and probabilities of potential payoffs. For example, Monroe spells out the assumptions underlying rational actor theory as follows:

> (1) Actors pursue goals. (2) These goals reflect the actor's perceived self interest. (3) Behavior results from a process that involves, or functions as if it entails, conscious

> choice. (4) The individual is the basic agent in society. (5) Actors have preferences that are consistent and stable. (6) If given options, actors will choose the alternative with the highest expected utility. (7) Actors possess extensive information on both the available alternatives and the likely consequences of their choices.[162]

In fact, few rational choice theorists today would subscribe to the seventh of these assumptions. Generally, rather than assuming that actors possess all information that would be relevant for assessing their options, they require that actors make consistent use of the information they do possess and, sometimes, that they are able to "learn" by properly assimilating new information. However, for the actual prediction of behavior the actual amount and quality of information that actors are assumed or known to possess is, of course, crucial, and individual models differ greatly with respect to their auxiliary, often implicit, assumptions about such information.

Even if no additional assumptions are made, it is clear that the consensual view of rational choice as "value-maximizing adaptation within the context of a given payoff function, fixed alternatives, and consequences that are known (in one of the three senses corresponding to certainty, risk, and uncertainty)"[163] is rather demanding in and of itself. The concept of rationality that is commonly employed today is patterned after what Herbert Simon refers to as "bounded" rationality and admits for the possibility of insufficient capabilities for the processing of information. Such limitations cause actors to adopt rules of thumb, which can only approximate full rationality and which will, strictly speaking, lead them to "satisfice" rather than "maximize" their expected utilities.[164] The idea of bounded rationality, however, while it is inarguably more realistic, brings with it the serious problem of how to define the "bounds" of rationality in any given context.

This problem brings us to the second area of disagreement within rational choice theory, which concerns the question whether the assumption of rationality includes or should include expectations about actors' goals. It is common to distinguish between "thin-rational" accounts, in which agents are only assumed to "efficiently employ the means available to pursue their ends," and "thick-rational" accounts, in which "the analyst posits not only rationality but some additional description of agent preferences and beliefs."[165] Individual rational choice theories must generally introduce information about actors' preferences to develop predictions. Their propositions may be tested, and, thus, their views on actors' preferences, are, in principle, vulnerable to empirical evaluation. However, assumptions about actors' preferences, while crucial for establishing empirical expectations, may also remain implicit.[166] In such cases, the problem is not only that these assumptions will escape tests but also that the implications of any tests that are conducted on the theory from which the propositions are derived are impossible to adequately determine.

As James DeNardo has warned, the use of the concept of "bounded rationality" actually "generates" policy preferences, in the sense that the identification by the analyst of the options that can rationally be considered as well as of their utilities, in effect, creates expectations concerning actors' preferences.[167] He argues that, while, theoretically, preferences are exogenous and logically prior to rational choice models, in practice, applied rational choice theory frequently introduces preferences based on the "structure of the problem" or the "logic of the situation." This strategy presupposes fundamental assumptions about what actors want and how they view their choices, in spite of the fact that there is usually little or no evidence that the preference structures assumed in theory actually describe actors' real understanding of their situations. Simon has written that "it is far easier to calculate the rational response to a fully specified situation than it is to arrive at a reasonable specification of the situation. And there is no way, without empirical study, to predict which of the innumerable reasonable specifications the actors will adopt."[168]

The reason why, in spite of such serious problems, it is still very tempting to assume rationality in the analysis of human behavior is made clear by John Harsanyi: "From the point of view of a social scientist trying to explain and predict human behavior, the concept of rationality is important mainly because, if a person acts rationally, his behavior can be fully explained in terms of the goals he is trying to achieve."[169] The general logic of rational choice theory has been formulated most stringently in contemporary microeconomics, decision theory, and game theory. According to Graham Allison,

> in economics, to choose rationally is to select the most efficient alternative, that is, the alternative that maximizes output for a given input or minimizes input for a given output. In modern statistical decision theory and game theory, the rational decision problem is reduced to a simple matter of selecting among a set of given alternatives, each of which has a given set of consequences: the agent selects the alternative whose consequences are preferred in terms of the agent's utility function which ranks each set of consequences in order of preferences.[170]

Rational choice methodology can be no less useful as a tool in foreign policy analysis. In his seminal work *Essence of Decision*, Allison identifies the rational actor model as the most commonly employed theoretical framework used to explain foreign policy decisions. Indeed, he claims that, by the early 1970s, it had already achieved the status of the "classical" model of foreign policy making.

Rational choice theory perceives foreign policy decisions as the purposive acts of unitary actors. To explain such acts, it asks "how the nation or government could have chosen to act as it did, given the strategic problems it faced."[171] To predict foreign policy behavior, it asks for "the rational thing to do in a certain situation, given specified objectives."[172] Rationality in this context means "consistent, value-maximizing choice within specified constraints," a notion that Allison calls "essentially Hobbesian."[173] Morgenthau explains:

> We put ourselves in the position of a statesman who must meet a certain problem of foreign policy under certain circumstances, and we ask ourselves what the rational alternatives are from which a statesman may choose who must meet this problem under these circumstances (presuming always that he acts in a rational manner), and which of these rational alternatives this particular statesman, acting under these circumstances, is likely to choose.[174]

By assuming the reality of the "rational statesman," it becomes possible for the analyst to develop parsimonious explanations and predictions of political decisions.[175]

The difficulties political analysts have encountered in their attempts to apply rational choice theory in their study of political behavior have helped to inspire important theoretical and methodological developments. Efforts to explain instances of cooperative interaction among self-interested rational actors have helped motivate the sophistication and increasingly frequent application of strategic, or game, theory.[176] Game theory incorporates the assumptions of rational choice theory. Thomas Schelling, whose work in the area of deterrence theory represents particularly influential applications of game theory in political analysis, recognizes as the foundation of strategic theory "the assumption of rational behavior—not just of intelligent behavior, but of behavior motivated by a conscious calculation of advantages, a calculation that in turn is based on an explicit and internally consistent value system."[177] What is different in game theory is that it models the behavior of two (or more) actors involved in some type of interaction. In an interactive context, decisions are interdependent, that is, any decision made by actor A depends at least on decisions previously made by the other actors and may also depend on the decisions actor A expects other actors to make in response to his own.[178] In the words of Allison, game theory as applied to the analysis of international political behavior

> analyzes and explains the maze of national actions and reactions as more or less advantageous moves in a game of interdependent conflict. Nations act in situations of tempered antagonism and precarious partnership, each nation's best choice depending on what it expects the other to do. Strategic behavior influences an actor's choice by working on his expectations of how his behavior is related to his adversary's.[179]

While, at a minimum, game theory only needs to assume rational "goal-seeking behavior in the absence of coercive authority,"[180] game theoretical approaches to international politics are particularly compatible with realist theory because they usually perceive of rational power-maximizing nation–states as the principal actors. Game theory can be particularly useful to realists because it models the behavior of Hobbesian egoists in the absence of central coercive authority. Consistent with realist expectations, game theoretical analyses frequently model such actors to be trapped in the famous "prisoner's dilemma," in which "a cool aversion to being suckered wrecks havoc on social cooperation."[181] On the other hand, game theorists are able to show how, under some circumstances, cooperative strategies can emerge over time through repeated interaction. The rationale here is that observing cooperative behavior by the other players helps create expectations that such behavior will continue. In other words, it helps develop trust. Such expectations will make it more rational for an actor to be cooperative as well, creating a pattern of cooperation, which is precarious but can, in principle, last until one player defects.[182] This is why Duncan Snidal can claim that "the ultimate promise of game theory lies in expanding the realm of rational-actor models beyond the restrictive confines of the traditional Realist perspective to a more complex world where concern is less exclusively with problems of conflict and as much with problems of cooperation."[183]

Taking a different approach to the same problem of modeling political reality more completely, so-called institutional rational choice theory examines how political institutions, variously defined, interact with actors' motivation to more fully determine political behavior.[184] As James Morrow explains, rational choice theorists generally "deduce actors' goals from observing their prior behavior or by experimentation. . . . [They] then assume that actors will continue to pursue the goals . . . [they] have . . . pursued in the past. . . . [They] fix actors' preferences and allow the information they have and the situation they face to change, creating variation in their actions."[185] Institutional rational choice theorists hold that, while "preferences provide the motivation of individual action, institutions provide the context, allowing causal explanation."[186] They are, first, interested in the ways in which "institutions both constrain what is possible and 'structurally suggest' individual interests."[187] Second, they study the role of institutions in the solution of collective action problems.[188] According to Michael Laver, for some of the authors concerned, "the state fulfills . . . a role rather like that of the Hobbesian sovereign, bringing about peace and productivity rather than a destructive war of all against all."[189] Once again, it is apparent why rational choice approaches are particularly compatible with realist theory when it comes to explaining the behavior of nation–states in the international system. Realism and rational choice theory share similar views on actors' basic motives, the way they go about achieving their goals, as well as on the ways in which their behavior may be "regulated" by affecting their preference orderings or probability calculations.

Beyond its use as a tool to simplify the explanation and prediction of foreign policy decisions, the rationality assumption, as we have seen, serves as a crucial axiomatic building block in both classical and neorealist theories of international politics.[190] Mark Petracca has pointed out that "the assumption of rationality is essentially an assumption about human nature."[191] Employed in a deductive theory, it allows the analyst "to predict that certain actions and consequences will follow from basic assumptions about the motivational force of human nature."[192] Rational choice theorists commonly claim that they do not make assumptions about the motives or goals, or, in the language of the theory, the preferences, of actors. However, as Simon has pointed out, rational choice models must rely on auxiliary assumptions to be able to predict human behavior,[193] and such auxiliary assumptions do concern the motives and goals of human beings.

Keith Dowding and Desmond King have found that rational choice theory of necessity relies on an "egotistical viewpoint": "The rational actor is self-centered, which means that the world is viewed from the perspective of the individual decision maker rather than from an essentially social viewpoint."[194] In the words of Petracca, "the picture of human nature that emerges [from such a viewpoint] is one of egoistic individuals seeking to maximize their own good or well-being."[195] In addition, rational choice models exhibit a strong tendency to "equate 'rational' with narrowly self-interested behavior."[196] Using the game-theoretical model of the Prisoner's Dilemma as an illustration, Jane Mansbridge has examined the gains and losses involved in simplifying motivation in this manner.[197] She finds that, in the trade-off between theoretical parsimony and descriptive accuracy, the theoretical "enterprise loses when, as is usually the case, the simplified view of motivation that helps us work out the long-term logic of interaction leads us to ignore or discount motives other than narrowly defined self-interest that also affect moral and political choices."[198]

It is true that

> formal modelers and rational choice theorists usually make . . . assumption[s] only for heuristic purposes, to clarify our understanding of one subset of interactive relations. They do not usually claim that this subset exhausts human behavior, but rather that tracing the interactive dynamics that would follow from pure narrow self-interest illuminates important, or in some cases the most important facets of real world interaction.[199]

It is commonly granted that rational choice theory takes what might be called an a priori as opposed to an empirical approach to modeling, which attempts first and foremost "to construct a logically coherent potential explanation of the phenomenon under investigation."[200] Such models can be employed to generate hypotheses that may then be subjected to empirical testing. If the logic of the model is flawless, such tests are in fact tests of the model's underlying assumptions.[201] However, problems arise when theorists "in the same account of politics, . . . alternate *a priori* and empirical methodologies."[202] According to Laver,

> a number of rational choice theorists have fallen into this trap, starting with a set of a priori motivational assumptions, arriving at a point where their deductions seriously diverge from observed reality, and solving their problems at a stroke by switching into the empirical mode of analysis. They use their empirical findings to modify their a prioris in such a way as to allow them to deduce observed reality, and then proceed blithely on their way as if nothing at all had happened.[203]

Part of the temptation to adjust assumptions in this way stems from the insight that, in spite of all the potential benefits of mind games, "it is obviously useful to construct at least some of our models on the basis of plausible, rather than implausible assumptions."[204] Thus, rational choice theorist Gordon Tullock defends his thick-rational account by concluding, "as a result of empirical research," that "the average human being is about 95 percent selfish in the narrow meaning of the term."[205] While the reasons are by no means clear, it appears as if, aside from the heuristic uses of assumptions of egotism and selfishness, "many [rational choice theorists] also show a disturbing tendency to assume that most important behavior . . . is in fact so motivated."[206] Interestingly, the resulting obscurity in the rational choice literature that surrounds the distinction between model depictions of a partial reality, which, for methodological reasons, concentrate on some facets of reality at the expense of others, and the actual subject matter of the theory is also characteristic of realist theory. It is at the root of the realist misreading of Hobbes's model theory of social organization as an empirical theory. It pervades classical realist thought with its ever-present tension between descriptive and prescriptive arguments. Finally, it has only been exacerbated by realists' use of rational choice and game theory and their attempts to develop highly parsimonious theories of international relations, which rely strongly on implicit empirical assumptions. The complementarity of rational choice methodology with realist international relations theory is both more firmly established historically and more far-reaching philosophically than is often acknowledged. The consequences of this theoretical affinity for the axiomatic psychological bases of realist thought clearly deserve our critical attention.

Summary and Conclusions

Common to twentieth-century realist approaches to international relations, be they classical or structuralist in orientation, are the following motivational assumptions: States are self-interested. This means that they will attempt to achieve their own goals and interact with others only for their own benefit. By and large, they will act rationally in pursuit of their national interest, which means that they will choose the most efficient means to achieve their goals, in order to maximize their benefits and minimize the necessary sacrifices. The national interest is defined primarily as physical security. In other words, states are primarily motivated by the fear of disappearing from the world map. As a consequence of this fear and the condition of international anarchy, they are motivated to maximize their power relative to other states. Thus the national interest also includes the maximization of power, which is defined primarily in material, and especially in military, terms.[207] The goals of security and power may well require contradictory strategies. In fact, this problem is the core of the "security dilemma," in which states are likely to end up less secure by trying to become more powerful. Realist approaches differ with respect to which of the two possibly contradictory goals they emphasize, which leads them to develop different expectations about how states will react to various constraints. Such different expectations illustrate the crucial role played by motivational assumptions in international relations theory.

Perhaps the most important developments in twentieth-century realist psychology are the ever-increasing tendencies to accept without question strong motivational assumptions concerning the selfishness, sense of insecurity, and lust for power of human beings (and, by extension, states) and to assert the empirical validity of rationality. As we have seen, realist arguments have always been based on a view of human nature as essentially selfish, and realist attempts to explain and predict political behavior have always relied on an assumption of the rationality of human behavior. However, Machiavelli and Hobbes still felt that their characterization of human nature as essentially wicked required some persuasive argument and empirical support. They went to great lengths to explain how they arrived at such ideas. By comparison, twentieth-century realism exhibits a progressively stronger tendency to take the realist view of human nature for granted. While classical realists commonly at least present their views on human nature and the motivation of states, neorealists tend to pretend that their theories do not depend on such views, an argumentative strategy that is blatantly misleading.

In addition, while Machiavelli and Hobbes were primarily interested in advocating self-interested rationality as a promising solution to the problem of passions in politics and civic life, contemporary realism increasingly relies on rationality as an empirical assumption. Realist theories now commonly assume human beings and states to be not only selfish, power-hungry, and chronically afraid but also capable of pursuing their self-interest rationally. Based on these motivational assumptions as well as other assumptions concerning the constraints under which states operate, they develop strategic suggestions or concrete policy advice. By adhering to the principles of empirical science and formulating their theories in such a way that they could, theoretically, be subjected to empirical testing, they dodge most normative critiques with the exception of the accusation that they serve to perpetuate the status quo.

The increasingly unquestioned reliance of realist theory on a particular view of human nature and the assumption of rationality may be explained by the demands placed on international political theorizing. Mainstream political science, as well as its subdiscipline of international relations, have tried hard to gain the status of a science, whatever methodological efforts this label was thought to require at any point in time. During the first half of the twentieth century, a consensus emerged in Western academia that scientific theories should be empirical–analytical in nature. It may be considered an irony of fate that the task of building an empirical–analytical theoretical footing for international political realism fell to thinkers with such profound and persuasive moral convictions and rich historical knowledge as Morgenthau, Carr, or Niebuhr. Unsurprisingly, the classical realists never ventured far from their moral concerns or preference for inductive theorizing. However, the paradigm continued to evolve. As a result primarily of the behavioral revolution of the 1950s and 1960s, it became acceptable in the social sciences to employ highly simplified accounts of the causes and patterns of human behavior for the sake of developing instrumentalist theories designed to improve human control of the social world. Finally, the particular problems of the fragmented discipline of international relations, in which there exists no substantial scholarly consensus on even the most basic issues, has motivated some of the most ambitious of its members to search for integrative frameworks, similar to those Marx, Weber, or Durkheim provided to the discipline of sociology, or similar to the theory of the market that has done so much for liberal economics. Such a framework, of course, needs to be broad and comprehensive. If it is also to be, in principle, testable, which is a crucial requirement of empirical science, it needs to be general and parsimonious as well. It is clear that the more parsimonious a theory, the stronger it must necessarily rely on foundational assumptions. In particular, structural theory must rely on assumptions concerning agency. Systemic theory must rely on assumptions concerning the "units" comprising the system. A structural systemic social scientific theory, such as neorealism, is by definition forced to make assumptions about human nature. It is important to note that, while such assumptions might be "exogenous" to the theory, this does not mean that human nature is not an explanatory factor within it.

Aside from its psychological determinism, political realism has always contained structural deterministic elements. Aside from seeking the causes for political behavior in inescapable facts of human nature, it has always examined the impact of various structural constraints on such behavior and attempted to establish "laws" of political behavior based on the observed regularities. As a theory of international politics, realism grounds the logic of its arguments firmly in the assumption of international anarchy. While rational choice theory has served to exacerbate its psychological determinism, neorealist theory has exacerbated the structural deterministic tendencies of realist thought. Within Waltz's theory there is no room for diplomacy or statesmanship. Structural constraints determine state behavior, as the fact of anarchy and the need to preserve relative power absolve decision makers of political choice. Whether it be full-blown moralism or fellow-realist Morgenthau's prudent restraint, human attitudes toward political reality are irrelevant.

We find that neorealism and rational choice theory are fundamentally complementary. While rational choice theory helps establish expectations about how states as rational unitary actors will react to various incentives and disincentives, neorealism examines the insurmountable systemic constraints that such states are assumed to face when making their choices. In addition, the two schools of thought can provide support for one another. For example, Sidney Verba suggests that it may be appropriate to assume self-interested rationality in foreign policy making because the structural constraints operating in the international system are so strong that they leave states little room to indulge in irrationality.[208] In so arguing, Verba defends the assumptions of rational choice theory as empirically appropriate within the international political realm. In turn, by adopting its fundamental assumptions, structural realists can employ the logic of rational choice theory to predict how actors should respond to the assumed structural constraints.

Traditionally, realism has been beset with a serious problem encountered by Hobbes, the problem that the sensibility of its normative advice depends on the idea that human beings can in fact be rationally self-interested, while its diagnosis of the ills of the world includes the observation that they commonly cannot. The resulting tension between prescription and description in realist theory is handled differently by different theorists and schools of thought. In the works of the classical realists, normative arguments are typically quite important, since their aims, at least in part, tend to be critical–rhetorical. For example, Morgenthau, in his later years, suggested that perhaps *Politics among Nations* should be read as a polemic, similar to Hobbes's *Leviathan*, and not as an empirical theory of international relations.[209] The problem is that, just as Hobbes's *Leviathan*, it did tend to be read as the latter, especially by fellow-realists to whom it was invaluable as a guide in their own theorizing. Recent developments in realist international relations theory only tend to lead further away from the normative basis of realist thought and toward uncritical empiricism. Both Carr and Niebuhr characterized realism as a negative theory, primarily useful for exposing the problems of other approaches. They rejected it as a positive theory for delivering an incomplete, perhaps even distorted, image of reality.[210] Contemporary realists, with some exceptions, tend to be far less modest.[211]

It may be said that, during the course of its history, realist theory has focused on description where it has sought support through empirical observation and where it has defended its approach to political affairs as particularly scientific. It has been able to emphasize prescription wherever the above could be assumed to be sufficiently established. In light of this tendency, which is an all but universal strategy of persuasion, it seems that realism today is on the defensive. More important, the tension between descriptive and prescriptive elements in realist theory should draw our attention to a set of crucial questions. When realist theory describes reality, that is when Machiavelli recounts Roman history, when Hobbes describes the events of the English Civil War, or when Waltz traces superpower balancing policies, what impact do their theoretical and normative aspirations have on such descriptions? Realists, understandably, claim that their influence is minimal. However, if this is true, why are these descriptions so commonly accepted as accurate depictions of reality, even though hardly anybody is willing to defend the realist view of human nature as actually "realistic"? It seems unlikely that they would be, were it not for the fact that the relevance of psychological assumptions for the logic of realist arguments has received such little attention. At best, twentieth-century realists, such as Morgenthau or Waltz, have claimed that their psychological and other assumptions are realistic enough, in the sense that they do not negatively affect the explanatory and predictive power of their theories.[212] However, this argumentative strategy may be just what is putting realism on the defensive: Every counterexample needs to be explained, and the temptation to revise individual theories ex post facto is great indeed.[213]

In turn, when realists theorize and advise policy makers about reality, we may want to inquire about the impact of their descriptions of reality on their interpretations and judgments. It is commonsensical that our assumptions about and perceptions of reality affect our interpretations and, thus, our strategies. In addition, realism defines itself as a scientific paradigm to a large extent by its supposed empirical basis. From accurate description, it is argued, realist theory develops the appropriate conclusions. This is in fact a very strong claim, which warrants our critical attention. If realist description is not accurate, what consequences does this have for realist theorizing and policy making? What is more problematic still, if assumptions take the place of description, the empirical basis for realist theorizing becomes more difficult to assess. If such assumptions are not even made explicit, the merits of realist theory become unduly difficult to evaluate.

5

Realist Man through the Ages: A Synopsis

This chapter draws conclusions from the historical analysis that comprises the previous three chapters. Specifically, it answers the following three questions: First, what are the motivational assumptions of realism? What is their nature? Second, what role do they play in realist theory? How are they used? What is their function? Third, what are the effects of using these assumptions in the ways described? Of interest here are both effects on realist scholarship and its findings and predictions, as well as the effects such findings and predictions may have on the policy-making process. Based on the answers found to these questions, the next chapter will provide a critique of the nature, function, and effects of realist motivational assumptions.

The Realist Image of Man

It is clear that, for purposes of specific applications of realist theory, different scholars may emphasize different aspects of human psychology. In addition, while the axiomatic "core" of the realist paradigm is relatively easy to define, the realist consensus concerning appropriate motivational and other assumptions, naturally, falls apart at its borders. "Defensive realism," for example, which was discussed in chapter 4, does not fully share in the consensus I will describe. It may thus be viewed not as realism proper, as I define it, but rather as a distinct approach in opposition to the realist mainstream. In spite of the usual difficulties of generalization, however, studying the similarities among different realist theories makes it possible to identify a consensual view of human nature and motivation, which is shared by the paramount writers of the realist tradition. In fact, when we study the arguments made by political realists throughout the centuries, we find that this consensus is not only relatively obvious but also astonishingly stable. It is necessary to identify this consensus in order to observe the crucial role motivational assumptions play in realist theory.

The realist view of human nature is distinguished by three basic characteristics. To begin with, realists view human nature and motivation as both universal and stable. The realist view of human nature is egalitarian in the sense that realism does not distinguish, for example, between more or less selfish or evil human beings. Instead, it holds that all human beings are identically motivated and thus cannot be judged by their basic motives. The realist view of human nature is also nonevolutionary, or static. Realism expects that the basic elements of human nature and motivation will not change with time. The third characteristic of the realist psychology is its profound pessimism. Realism perceives human motivation to be essentially conflictual and thereby destructive of idealist hopes for peace and justice. Realists believe that human motivation is at the root of conflict among human beings, and that, since such motivation is always and everywhere the same, conflict is an indelible feature of social life.

When we speak of the motivational assumptions of realism, we speak of assumptions concerning the basic driving forces underlying human behavior. The specific motives emphasized in realist psychology are understood to be self-referential, exclusive, and competitive. Realism views human beings as atomistic individuals, who are profoundly independent of each other. While actors are perceived to be identically motivated and thus to attempt to achieve the same basic goals, these goals themselves are not "shared" by actors; instead, they are pursued by individuals independently of social context. Not only do individuals define their own goals for themselves, but they pursue these goals selfishly, without regard for others, accepting and even inviting competition and conflict. Rather than identifying with one or various collectivities, individuals remain egoists, pursuing only their own narrow self-interest. Besides being self-referential and exclusive, the motives that determine human behavior are also understood to be competitive in the sense that they lead actors to pursue ends which will likely conflict with those of others.

The most basic of these motives, according to realism, are fear and self-interest. The motive of fear is associated with the goal of survival. Realism assumes that human beings want, above all, to survive. This goal, often considered an instinct, aside from inspiring ingenious strategies to deny their mortality, leads them to try to find ways to protect themselves from natural dangers. Human beings know that they are always vulnerable to other human beings. As Thomas Hobbes observes, even the weakest of men can find ways to kill even the strongest.[1] Therefore, as human beings can never truly feel safe from one another, they remain distrustful of each other. At the same time, they are also profoundly untrustworthy because, being egoistic and distrustful, they would naturally take advantage of any opportunity to secure themselves at the expense of others. A person who knows that he himself is in this sense untrustworthy is likely to assume that others are untrustworthy as well, and act accordingly. Distrust among human beings is thus perpetuated by interaction.

The motive of fear and the distrust that accompanies it lead human beings to seek security. The goal of security, in turn, will lead them to seek power. The most important type of power for purposes of sheer survival is "physical" power. Not to be understood in a narrow sense, physical power resources could include anything from bodily strength to a burglar alarm or even a pair of glasses. It is the kind of power that affords protection from any type of physical harm which could be afflicted by other human beings. Physical power is considered valuable because, given the realist view of motivation, only being more physically powerful than others will deter them from attack. If they should attack anyway, because they are unaware of the danger or because they do not act rationally, only superior physical power guarantees that they can be overcome.

The motive of fear, while its intention is defensive, leads to conflict because it makes human beings compete for physical power and because it leads them to threaten each other in order to deter attack. The problem is that one human being's attempts to make himself more secure will likely be understood as threatening by others. For example, if a person carries a handgun to defend himself in case of attack, he becomes more of a threat to everyone around him, whether they intend to attack him or not. In response, others may step up their security precautions as well, and a kind of "security competition" may result. Such competition can escalate and thereby increase the risk of violent clashes or at least the level of destruction that may be caused by such clashes. Persons with guns, for example, can do more damage to each other than persons without guns. What is more, being threatened, rather than deterring, can lead others to attempt to remove the threat. Deterrence, by inspiring preemptive aggression, may thus have the opposite of the desired effect. Realism sees no way out of this dilemma, for it reasons that, while human beings feel that their survival is threatened by others, they have no choice but to seek to increase their physical power relative to those others. In other words, it holds that because the motive of fear is an indelible and paramount feature of human life, so is the risk of violent conflict.

The second basic motive underlying human behavior in realism is the motive of self-interest. The goal it is associated with is a comfortable life. Beyond merely wanting to survive, human beings also want to live well. Only through acquiring more than the essentials needed for survival can human beings experience leisure, or temporary freedom from worry. Such freedom from worrying about how to survive the next day may well be the prerequisite for what is called "happiness." The goal of a comfortable life leads human beings to pursue primarily two "goods": social status and material wealth, or, as the Athenians put it, "honor" and "profit."[2] Both status and material wealth are also types of power resources. We are familiar with the claim that "money is power," and status is frequently considered to be nothing more or less than power over other human beings. Being power resources, both material wealth and status can enhance one's physical security as well. For example, money can buy guns, and having leadership status helps rally one's gang in a streetfight.

The quest for power is the third important driving force of human behavior, according to the realist view of human motivation. It may be considered a secondary motive, since, unlike survival and a comfortable life, power is not commonly sought for its own sake, but rather as a means to achieve those two primary goals. Still, since, according to realism, the goals of survival and a comfortable life inevitably demand the pursuit of relative power, it, too, is a permanent and pervasive feature of human life. In fact, as we have seen, it is the pursuit of relative power, as a consequence of the primary motives of fear and self-interest, which makes human relations so conflictual. I have also shown how the pursuit of physical power for the sake of security can perpetuate or even exacerbate conflict. The pursuit of material gain as well leads to conflict because the material resources human beings crave are limited. The pursuit of status also leads to conflict, since status, just like physical power, is a relative good. The desire for status is, after all, nothing but the desire to be distinguished from others as in some way superior. It may even be, as Hobbes suggests, a particularly destructive motive because it attaches itself in an unpredictable way to different objects. It is difficult to know how others estimate their self-worth, whether it be, for example, through material possessions, religious conviction, or a particular ability. While it is comparatively easy not to directly threaten another human being's life or livelihood, it is thus considerably more difficult not to offend his pride.

We remember that Hobbes, when discussing the more or less destructive effects of various human motives, also distinguishes between what we might call irrational, or paranoid, fear and rational fear. Rather than motivating human beings to take appropriate precautions for their security, irrational fear, like pride, attaches itself to various objects in unpredictable ways, leading people to panic and overreact, jump out of a tenth-floor window at the sight of a mouse, or spike their suburban lawns with land mines. Rational fear, on the other hand, is caution. It leads to what common sense would consider sufficient yet not excessive levels of distrust and defensive preparation aimed at the appropriate, that is, actually dangerous, objects or persons.[3]

Realism perceives of human beings as, by and large, rational. Excessive pride and paranoid fear are exhibited quite frequently, but, at least in the context of statecraft, they are regarded as deviations from "normal" human behavior. Rationality, then, is the next important ingredient in the realist view of human motivation. To be sure, rationality itself is not a motive. The assumption of rationality may be called a "cognitive," rather than a "motivational," assumption because it does not specify what human beings want, what they are after. Instead, it specifies how people go about acquiring what they want. However, as we have seen, the rationality assumption does play a central role for the realist image of human nature. In fact, a complete understanding of the nature, function, and effects of realist motivational assumptions requires that we pay close attention to realist views on rationality.

The assumption of human rationality has two elements: First, it holds that human beings will attempt to achieve their goals and, second, that they will try to use the most efficient means to do so. The rationality assumption thus suggests that human beings can define their goals and rank them, that is, that they can ascertain their own interests in any situation requiring a decision. It also suggests that human beings will pursue the interests they have identified as their own. It does not tell us what human beings will want, but it does tell us that they are self-interested goal seekers. If we are willing to grant that this is the case, as realism does, it becomes commonsensical that efficiency should be another element of rationality. Ceteris paribus, if a person wants to buy an apple, it would clearly be irrational to buy one for one hundred dollars if he can get one for fifty cents.

The motives that realist international relations theory ascribes to nation–states are identical to those which define the realist view of human nature. The logic that connects them is analogous. This is true for traditional as well as neorealism. In the words of Laurie Johnson, "[B]oth assume, first of all, a uniformity of nature. . . . It is this theory of human nature that is projected on the state by realists. Human beings, as Morgenthau so aptly puts it, are driven by their passions—especially the passion of self-interest. States in anarchy, likewise, must be expected to pursue their interests, which can be summed up in security and in the pursuit of power."[4] Nation–states primarily seek to survive, that is, they are primarily motivated by a desire for physical security. This motive requires them to maximize their power relative to other states. For nation–states, military power is the most important type of power resource. Beyond security, states seek material wealth and status. Both are also power resources, which may be used to increase the state's physical security. Imperialism can be explained, as it is by the Athenians, through the operation of all three basic motives: fear, the desire for profit, and the desire for status. As with human beings, the motivation of states is stable and universal. It also leads them into conflict, for the same reasons as it does individuals.

States compete for material wealth, status, and military power. In particular their competition for military power leads them into a security dilemma in which their attempts to increase their security can lead to arms races and increase levels of hostility and threat perception on all sides. Given the high defense expenditures, psychological strain, and actual danger which may result, how can realists still believe that states act rationally? The answer is simple: because they assume that security is the most important end of all state action and fear its most important driving force. Given that they perceive them as threatening, all states are therefore forced to try to maximize their power relative to the others. (See Table 5.1.)

Table 5.1
The Realist Image of Human Nature in Context

Level of Analysis	Main Assumptions	Theoretical Approaches Most Directly Contradicted
Individual Psychology	Human beings above all want to survive; they are motivated primarily by fear of relative weakness and potential violation and death; therefore they compete for power; they are selfish schemers, usually wickedly rational, at times dangerously irrational; they are asocial, untrusting, as well as untrustworthy.	Idealist approaches; much of psychological theory and liberalism
Interaction between Individuals	Human beings are threats to one another; they compete relentlessly; they are by nature independent, not social beings; all voluntary interaction is selfishly motivated; human beings do not redefine their basic motives in response to social membership or moral obligation.	Social psychology; much of sociology and political philosophy
Human Collectivities	All cooperation and affiliation is needs-based and likely temporary; as long as they last, conflicts within the group are suppressed and emerge instead in relations with other collectivities; collectivities act and interact just as individuals would in asocial space.	Globalist approaches; much of liberalism
Interaction between Human Collectivities	Human collectivities are threats to one another; they compete relentlessly; they are independent entities not inclined to merge with others; all voluntary interaction with other collectivities is selfishly motivated; collectivities such as nations do not redefine their basic motives in response to social membership or moral obligation.	Constructivism and sociological institutionalism
Environment of International Politics	The world of international politics is an anarchic self-help environment in which one cannot rely on the goodwill or promises of others and which poses constant dangers, especially for the less powerful.	Idealist approaches; much of liberalism

The Role of Motivational Assumptions in Realist Theory

Motivational assumptions are used in realist political theory in three distinct yet related ways. They are established inductively in scientific realism, where they serve to explain political phenomena. They are employed in paradigmatic realism as the axiomatic psychological foundation for deductive political theories. Finally, they are employed rhetorically to justify the prescriptions of ideological realism. Realist applications of motivational assumptions in individual theories may involve more than one of these functions. Hobbesian realism, for example, involves all three.

Whether the method of inquiry is inductive or deductive, the purpose descriptive–explanatory or prescriptive, motivational assumptions always fulfill an important function as the psychological dimension of realist political theory. This is true no matter where individual theories locate their primary explanation(s) for the phenomena they seek to elucidate. Sometimes motivation itself is identified as a crucial explanatory factor. For example, the Athenians at Sparta offer a psychological explanation for their imperialist policies: They had to expand the power of Athens because they were motivated by fear, honor, and profit. In contrast, neorealists such as Kenneth Waltz do not make reference to motivation but, instead, explain international systemic outcomes primarily with reference to environmental constraints, such as the distribution of power in the international system.[5] However, we have seen that to be able to do so they must rely on motivational assumptions, which provide at least a first-image foundation for their theories.

Wherever realist theory expects states to react in identical ways to the same conditions, as is the case in structural realism, motivational assumptions provide not only the first-image foundation but, in effect, the second-image foundation for the theory as well.[6] In this case, they are used, often implicitly, to establish expectations about how states will react to the specified structural constraints. Johnson has observed that "the emphasis that realists place upon the environment or circumstances in which actors are placed is a direct result of the uniformity that they posit in human nature. . . . Realists' assumptions about human nature and therefore the nature of states produce the conditions for structuralism."[7]

The role played by motivational assumptions in this type of realist theory is obscured because, by definition, structuralist social scientific theory seeks explanations for human behavior not by asking what human beings want but by asking what it is possible for them to have. In addition, the higher the level of analysis at which explanation is sought, the smaller the perceived role of agency, as opposed to structure, in realist arguments. Motivation is by nature an attribute of individuals. By suggesting that a knowledge of structural constraints may be sufficient to predict what choices political actors will make, neorealism suggests that such actors do not have much choice in making their decisions. If individual actors have no choice, one may argue, why would it matter what they want? To use an example: A prisoner in a cell has only apples to eat. We want to predict what he will do when he gets hungry. In this case, it does not matter whether the prisoner likes pears better than apples or not: We may safely predict that it is apples he will eat.

Given that constraints can be understood to be able, in principle, to fully determine behavior, does motivation still have to play a role in structural realism at all? Or may we safely ignore it, as we may in the above example? The answer is: We may not, as long as we cannot be completely sure which constraints actually operate. Within the complex realm of international relations, no matter how narrow and well-specified our theory, we can only predict responses to the constraints we perceive if we make assumptions about how the relevant actors will perceive the same constraints. Take, for example, the simple expectation that states will react to the emergence of a hegemon by counterbalancing, if need be by forming a military alliance. The main constraint states are perceived to face in this scenario, according to realism, is structural anarchy. It is impossible to predict that the rise of a hegemon will lead to the formation of a counter-alliance simply by knowing that there exists no governing authority above the individual national governments. The logic that connects the assumed constraint to the expected effect is incomplete. Instead, to arrive at our expectation, we have to follow a chain of argument roughly as follows: The emergence of a hegemon constitutes a threat to the national interests of the other states. This is because all states are motivated to maximize their relative power vis-à-vis others. This is because they primarily seek physical security and perceive others as threatening their security. States are rational. Thus, they will not challenge the new hegemon by themselves, risking destruction. Instead, they choose the next best option: They pool their military power to be able to deter the hegemon from conquest. They feel so threatened by the hegemon that they are willing to curb, though never relinquish, their natural distrust with respect to their new allies.

Even if we are willing to follow this entire line of argument, we still cannot be sure that what we predict will actually occur. Our expectation is still underdetermined. The important point is that without making assumptions about what states are after, we could get nowhere close to explaining or predicting their reactions to the constraints we perceive to operate. In fact, it is generally the case that the higher the level of analysis—that is, the more realist theory abstracts from individual psychological explanations for political decisions—the more crucial the role played by motivational assumptions is. Waltz's neorealism, for example, is a highly parsimonious theory. This means that it is "scientifically efficient," in the sense that it maximizes the amount of information won while minimizing the amount of information spent. A parsimonious theory, in other words, purports to explain a comparatively large range of outcomes with recourse to comparatively few explanatory factors. Parsimonious theorizing is easy as long as there are only relatively few important explanatory variables. If there are more, parsimony can be achieved by "holding constant" those variables in which the theorist is not particularly interested. This is exactly what neorealism does by rejecting the, as Waltz has put it, "profoundly unscientific view that everything that varies is a variable."[8] It "holds constant" the motivation of states in order to examine the impact of systemic variables on the outcomes of state behavior that are observable at the systems level. This strategy receives legitimation from the static and universalist realist view of human motivation that has been propagated through the centuries.

Where realist theories rely on human motivation for the explanation of political phenomena, they explain unchanging aspects of reality. After all, human motivation is perceived to be stable. Thus, according to the Athenians, city–states will always be tempted to conquer others and, according to the neorealists, one or the other balance-of-power configuration always results from states' attempts not to end up at a disadvantage. Human motivation, or human nature in general, is not used as an explanatory variable in realist theory. It is a constant. It may be used to explain phenomena, as the Athenians use it to explain imperialism. Alternatively, it may be used more like a "control," as it is in neorealism. When it is used as a control, realists are interested in examining the impact or causes of other, higher-level variables. They then may go on to test hypotheses that take one of the following forms: Given that states try to maximize power, we can expect our variable of interest, x, to have effect y, or, given that states maximize security, the effect we are interested in, w, can be explained with reference to explanatory variable z. The fact that realist theory perceives human nature as a given allows it to employ motivation as a control in order to examine the impact of other explanatory factors. It also allows it to rule out alternative explanations that would be incompatible with its motivational assumptions. This is how realism uses its view of human motivation in combination with information on various other factors that might explain political behavior in the search for "laws" of such behavior, which could explain the mysteries of international politics.

Political realism generally addresses two basic questions, Why does conflict occur? And what can be done about it? While the first question asks for an explanation, the second asks for a prescription. Inasmuch as political realism is concerned with both of these questions, it thus contains both descriptive and prescriptive, or empirical and normative, elements. Descriptive realism makes use of assumptions concerning the motives for state action in combination with the assumption of rationality to explain and predict state behavior. According to descriptive realism, human motivation helps explain why conflict occurs: In the absence of law and order, their egoism and sense of insecurity lead human beings to fight. However, according to prescriptive realism, human motivation could as well provide solutions to the problem of conflict: Their egoism and sense of insecurity could lead human beings to avoid fights, if they could just know how.

How does realism get from the problem to the solution? Prescriptive realism hopes that rationality may be employed to curb the worst effects of human motivation. It suggests that the impact of motivation on human behavior may be modified through adjustments in human beings' incentive structures plus the removal of constraints that inhibit the rational pursuit of self-interest. First, it is necessary to teach human beings how it is in their own best interest to act in ways that would minimize conflict for the benefit of all. When employing this strategy realism of course relies on the hope that human beings are not only selfish but also rational. Knowledge of the motivation of actors makes it possible to rely on their rationality to manipulate their behavior. An example: In a civil war, warring factions are fighting for control of the nation's capital. The mediator knows that both sides want to use the capital to set up their government there, once the war is won. The mediator could now try to persuade the warring parties that it is in neither side's best interest to continue to battle over the city, destroying it in the process. After all, what would either side want with a pile of rubble, once it would have won the war?

The creation of incentives for individually rational and collectively acceptable behavior, however, is usually not enough. We also need to remove the constraints that make it impossible or irrational for human beings to act in the ways we recommend. Hobbes believes that this requires the establishment of authoritarian government. The absolute rule of the *Leviathan* strongly discourages others from acting lawlessly and thereby creates the conditions under which peaceful exchange and accommodative social behavior become options for the rationally self-interested, cautious, and distrustful individual. In the case of the above example, the warring parties might be persuaded to strike an agreement to discontinue the battle for the city. The crux is that both parties would have to be ensured that this agreement would be enforced by an impartial authority.

The particular problem which, according to realism, afflicts the international realm is that the primary constraint inhibiting collectively beneficial behavior by nation–states can never really be removed. That constraint is anarchy. The condition of anarchy in the international realm allows states to pursue their goals without fear of punishment by any authority. For example, nothing could really stop either of the warring parties in our civil war example from breaking the agreement to save the capital, if there were no one to enforce this agreement. What is more, in the absence of hopes for proper enforcement, they probably would not even consider an agreement in the first place, because they are by nature distrustful. Paradoxically, then, the primary constraint faced by states in their rational pursuit of self-interest is that they do not face constraints; instead, they are aware that nothing but the risk of defeat exists to stop their competitors from attempting to overrun them. Under such conditions, fear will always remain the most important driving force underlying state behavior. Since fear leads states to pursue relative power, there seems to be no way out of the security dilemma. Prescriptive realism operates within these limitations, which are upheld by its combination of motivational with structural assumptions.

The rationality assumption plays a crucial role in realist theory as the logical connection between empirical statements about motivation and statements that judge or commend behavior. In other words, it is the connection between the descriptive and the prescriptive dimension of realist thought. An illustration: Hobbes holds that human beings above all want to survive. He condemns behavior that is motivated by paranoid fear and vainglory. His argument is: If human beings were really rational, seeing that paranoid fear and vainglory lead them into violent conflict, which threatens their survival, would make it obvious to them that they should behave differently. If there is no hope that human beings can be rational, Hobbes's prescription is hopeless as well.

It is important to understand that whenever we call behavior rational, we purport to know what it is the person we are observing wants. To identify what constitutes rational behavior, realist theory requires information on the goals human beings pursue. After all, if Hobbes were wrong about the fact that human beings above all want to survive, the motives of paranoid fear and vainglory might well be wellsprings of rational behavior. For example, for a person who values escaping from a mouse more highly than survival, jumping out of a tenth-floor window might not constitute an irrational action. Realist motivational assumptions provide the information on human goals that is needed to judge the compliance of human behavior with the standard of rationality. In fact, realism can make use of its motivational assumptions to defend the empirical accuracy of the rationality assumption. For example, it can explain that it is rational for nations to risk bankruptcy to stockpile nuclear weapons, because security is so important to them. In turn, realism can rely on the assumption of rationality to predict state behavior. A knowledge of the motives and options of states is by itself not enough to do so.

When prescriptive realism recommends a particular kind of behavior as rational, it does in effect advocate particular goals. When Hobbes recommends rational behavior to solve the problem of civil strife, he, in effect, recommends that human beings should value some ends over others, that they should follow some motivational inclinations, rather than others. As we have seen, Hobbesian realism as a prescriptive theory relies on the primacy of rational fear. If rational fear could be made the most important driving force for human behavior, so Hobbes, human beings would not continue to quarrel for what he considers to be unimportant reasons. Overall, so Hobbes hopes, they would quarrel less. The hope that the rational and cautious pursuit of their self-interest could motivate human beings to quarrel less is the defining characteristic of prescriptive realism. Realism thus uses motivational assumptions in conjunction with the assumption of rationality, both to explain and predict political behavior and to recommend proper responses.

The Effects of the Realist Use of Motivational Assumptions

While realist arguments have always rested on the claim that realist theory sees the world as it really is, realism has evolved from a primarily prescriptive to a primarily descriptive–explanatory theory, or, in other words, from a normative to an empirical theory. Where realism operates as a primarily prescriptive theory, it does contain as its main descriptive element a particular view of human nature. This is the view of man as it was expounded in the works of Niccolo Machiavelli and Thomas Hobbes.[9] It is employed as the axiomatic foundation of deductive realist theory. As such, it may be used explicitly as an important explanatory factor, as it is by Hobbes, or implicitly as a control, as it is in neorealism. In the latter type of realist theory, it is both less well explained and more restrictive. It is less well explained because it is largely taken for granted or presumed to be relatively unimportant. It is more restrictive because of the different aspirations of contemporary social scientific theory. While the view of human nature underlying realist arguments has essentially stayed the same over the centuries, Hobbes and Machiavelli spent much time explaining and defending their views on human nature, developing a rich, if profoundly pessimistic, portrait of human motivation. Empirical realism, in its search for parsimony, has had to simplify this portrait, which appears merely as a sketch in most contemporary realist works, if it appears at all. The evolution of the realist use of motivational assumptions has thus led to a progressively more simplified and, arguably, less realistic view of human nature and motivation.

As we have seen, the traditional realist view of human motivation is both static and universalistic as well as profoundly pessimistic. It provides realism with what may be called its "foundational pessimism," which extends into all elements of realist thought. In addition, the motivational assumptions of realism contribute to its determinism. They do so in the following way: Realism perceives of human motivation as stable and universal. Motivation determines how human beings react to varying constraints. At the same time, constraints inherent in their situations limit the options human beings have to choose from when making their decisions. Exterior constraints can thus further restrict the range of operative human motives. In addition, the decisions human beings make affect the reactions of others by limiting their options for rational responses. Interaction can thus reduce the range of operative human motives even further.

At least partly as a consequence of its restrictive motivational assumptions, realism generally minimizes the role of human agency in politics. Human beings are portrayed as having little choice but to act in the ways predicted by realist arguments, because their options are limited not only by external constraints but also by the fact that their objectives are fixed. Partly as a consequence of the determinism thus introduced, the role realism prescribes for morality in politics is minimal as well. If nations really have as little choice in reacting to the realities of international politics as realism suggests, it makes little sense to judge their actions by the demanding standards of any type of morality.

Realism is profoundly distrustful and skeptical of attempts to advocate a role for morality in politics. We remember that its view of human nature does not include a genuine moral component. Instead, the pursuit of moral ideals is portrayed by Machiavelli as scheming hypocrisy and by Hobbes as the result of irrational and destructive passions. In general, realism tends to believe that assurances of goodwill in politics are motivated either by an intention to deceive, by a need to assuage, or by a delusional idealism dangerously akin to madness. Any type of reformism, whether it be only mildly or more profoundly idealistic in appearance, is met by realism with this kind of skepticism.

Its pessimistic view of human motivation leads realism to counsel against political idealism. In fact, idealism is directly contradicted by realist skepticism concerning claims to idealist motivation as well as its pessimism concerning progress. Both result in the risk-averse conservatism that characterizes prescriptive realism. Both are explained by the realist image of man. Idealistically motivated foreign policies are considered suicidal, because human beings are considered to be selfish and untrustworthy. Idealism as a political worldview is considered utopian, because human beings are not expected to change for the better.[10]

The motivational assumptions of realism also have an impact on its views concerning the proper conduct and the role of science, in general, and of realist international relations theory, in particular. We remember that realism as a worldview emerged concurrently with positivist epistemology, in the context of a secular and anthropocentric ontology. We remember that the elements of positivist epistemology are the beliefs that objective facts exist, that it is possible for human beings to gain direct access to these facts, to "know" them, and that the phenomena we observe can, in principle, be explained with reference to other observable facts.

As a scientific paradigm, realism is inexorably positivistic. It purports to describe and explain the world as it really is. To do so, it adopts the stance of the "detached" and neutral observer. To speak about the world "as it really is," it seeks to employ an "objective," technical language, which can minimize the impact of the speaker's personal interpretation of the phenomena observed, as well as of his values. Positivist science seeks to be noninterpretive and value-neutral. It is anti-normative and anti-rhetorical insofar as it believes that normative aspirations should not find their way into scientific theories, and that the value of scientific theories should not be judged by the persuasiveness of the theorist's argument but only by the accuracy of the theory's predictions.[11] Both positivism and realism adopt the view, originally propagated by the sophists, that normative ideas are inherently subjective, that they cannot be true or false. Other human beings can always only either be forced to do as one wishes them to or manipulated through rhetorical persuasion to share one's normative views. Realist views on the role and relevance of morality in politics as well as political theory can be properly understood only with reference to its epistemological heritage. After all, both Thucydides and Machiavelli "see realism as inherently amoral precisely because of its grounding in necessity and compulsion, that is[,] because of its scientific character."[12]

Because it is anti-normative, positivist science must of necessity be purely instrumental science. Rather than advocating one or the other ideal, positivist science merely provides the tools with which reality might be manipulated, leaving it to practitioners to decide what to do with the knowledge thus won. The pessimistic determinism that characterizes realism as a consequence of its judgment of human nature leads it to minimize its own usefulness as a practical science of international affairs. If nations had really no choice at all in how to react to the realities of international politics, there would be no need for a science of international relations. Since their range of options is so minimal, so is the role of the science of international relations, as propagated by realism: It is primarily adaptive and, beyond that, minimally instrumental. Realist political science is therefore never reformist in orientation.

This conservatism should not excuse realists from having to defend their positions. After all, Steven Forde is correct to point out that any "social science that discovers 'laws' of behavior is not just a form of the search for truth, but also a potent political weapon."[13] The realist reliance on positivist epistemology may well serve to obscure its ideological dimension. Specifically, it disallows the open advocacy of political goals as well as the use of rhetorical argument. Realism adopts positivist criteria for the proper conduct of science. However, as any social scientific paradigm, it has to have recourse to rhetoric to persuade potential critics that its models of reality adequately capture what is in fact real and that the advice realism has to give is therefore justified. Truly prescriptive realism in the Hobbesian mode faces an obvious dilemma. While aspiring to be scientific in the positivist sense, it really cannot be, for the simple reason that it attempts to be prescriptive. Hobbes is quite obviously concerned with maintaining order within the state, and his theory is specifically designed to contribute to that end. Hobbes thus grudgingly recognizes that prescriptive realism must rely on rhetorics to persuade. Ever since, realist theory, by teaching reality, combines positivist epistemology with a didactic rhetorical method.

So what is the nature of realist rhetorics? Realist arguments are usually noncognitivist and antirationalist. This means that they deny that ideas and norms may possess universal value and that, even if they did, their value could be understood by human beings. For example, Hans Morgenthau defines his approach to the role of ethics in politics in explicit opposition to the view that human beings can employ reason to understand what is right and what is wrong.[14] Instead, human reason is understood to be instrumental to human ends. It is, in essence, no more than what we understand by rationality. What, then, is the specific role realist political theory advocates for itself? Since it cannot teach us about right and wrong, it can teach us only to achieve our goals more easily. It can help us both to adapt more successfully to what is given and to manipulate more effectively what is not. Knowledge of the motives of human beings, for example, can be used to control and manipulate their behavior and thus to secure one's power position, as Machiavelli demonstrates to *The Prince*. Realist political science usually presents itself as instrumental, but to what ends?

Inherent in realist arguments are normative preferences concerning the behavior of individuals, the proper goals of foreign policy, as well as the ends of politics, and specifically international relations. With respect to individual motivation, realism, both Hobbesian and classical, suggests that the operation of "interests" as opposed to "passions" can provide for more collective well-being. Traditionally, the rational pursuit of self-interest provides the only hope for political realism (as well as economic liberalism) that the selfishness of man can be harnessed for the sake of the common good. The specific traits that are encouraged most strongly are caution and prudence, or foresight. With respect to the proper ends of foreign policy, realism obviously defends the goal of physical survival and independence as the core of the national interest, and the pursuit of relative power as the proper means to achieve it. It searches for the proper strategies and policies to achieve both power and security by emphasizing the requirements for rational decision making, such as sufficient information and level-headed leadership. With respect to the ends of politics in general, and international politics in particular, realism emphasizes the goals of stability and order. Political realism is radically risk-averse and, thus, conservative. Realists such as Morgenthau counsel against idealism in foreign policy because they perceive it to be too risky an outlook on international reality. Instead, they are usually prepared to defend the status quo, however unsatisfactory, for being preferable to an uncertain future. Realist political science seeks to achieve a higher degree of predictability with respect to the behavior of political actors. Such predictability can be useful in two related ways: It makes it easier for actors to make rational decisions, and it makes it easier for scientists to predict such decisions.

Prescriptive realist international relations theory relies on the hope that states are indeed rational. As is the case with Hobbes's prescriptions against civil strife, realist hopes for an improvement of international affairs rest on the hope that states can be helped to "be better at" being rational. Despite assurances to the contrary, prescriptive realism is in fact both cognitivist and rationalist insofar as it believes that the standard of rationality is defensible as well as accessible to human beings. However, realist foreign policy advice can never really counsel against power politics, since it does not acknowledge a goal higher than the preservation of the state and believes that the preservation of the state requires the rational pursuit of relative power. This is why Machiavelli, the "rebel realist," stresses that the goal of *mantenere lo stato* requires that expediency be the sole standard used in political decision making. This is why the concept of "raison d'état" conceptually unites that goal with the strategy realism suggests can achieve it: To do whatever is necessary and best suited to the end of maintaining the state, that is "rationality of state." Even Morgenthau, whose suggestion that the policy that is "best suited" in any case must be prudent, in addition to merely being successful, is obviously ethically motivated, cannot overcome the profound pessimism that afflicts realist theory by virtue of its restrictive judgment of motivation and resulting deterministic view of the requirements of Realpolitik.

Is there nothing, then, that can be done to make it easier for states to act in ways that are rationally self-interested yet not collectively destructive? Realism holds that what can be done is indeed fairly minimal. Realist foreign policy attempts to work within the constraints posed by international anarchy, rather than attempting to overcome them. At the same time it accepts as given constraints that are assumed to operate in human nature. With Hobbes, it thus has to seek the remedies to the problem of conflict among its causes. As a consequence, it works primarily by attempting to affect the rational calculations of other actors. It does so either by creating incentives to comply with the ends sought or by creating disincentives to noncompliance. Whether these incentives or disincentives are "real" is not even important, since what counts is only that other actors believe they are. Deterrence, for example, is considered the best way to discourage imperialism. Under conditions of mutually assured destruction, policy makers would indeed have to be mad to initiate a violent confrontation. Beyond advocating the pursuit of military power, political realism may suggest that balance-of-power politics can enhance stability in the international system. Stability means that the behavior of other actors becomes more predictable, and the predictability of the effects of one's decisions is an essential prerequisite for the calculations necessary for rational decision making.

Balance-of-power politics may have another remedial effect as well. According to Thomas Hobbes and Jean-Jacques Rousseau, the main reason why states are unlikely to subject themselves to a higher authority, which could afford them protection from one another, is that they, unlike individual human beings, are not by nature equal.[15] Stronger nations have no interest in transferring power, because they can feel quite safe as long as they remain stronger. They have nothing to gain and much to lose by subjecting themselves to a higher governing authority. Since only such strong nations would have the power to establish such a higher authority, none is ever established. However, if capabilities were distributed relatively equally among the world's strongest powers, they might indeed find it in their own interest to enter into contractual agreements. This process could also occur on a regional basis, or, perhaps, begin on a regional basis, and continue to spread.[16] The second part of the Hobbesian strategy, the removal of obstacles to behavior which is both individually rational and socially beneficial, may indeed be applied to the realm of international relations, and, if we consider, for example, arms control agreements, in limited ways it already has. Even the emergence of strong supranational authority is not in principle incompatible with realist logic. However, realism does not venture to predict the emergence of more cooperative arrangements among nation–states, because its hopes for a more rationally enlightened pursuit of national self-interest are severely limited.

This pessimism can only be understood if one remembers that the assumption of rationality is a very daring empirical assumption. Complete rationality requires complete information and superhuman cognitive abilities. It can always only be approximated. Descriptive realism always remembers with Hobbes that human beings are fools and finds that states behave in foolish ways. What is more, human beings are not harmless fools, who may very well live in complete harmony even under anarchical conditions; instead, they are offensive egoists, whose basic motivation prohibits them from getting along in the absence of compulsion.

Part II

Sunglasses at Night: A Critique of the Realist Psychology

6

What Is Wrong with the Realist Psychology?

This chapter will argue that the understanding of human motivation which is the foundation of realist theory is, first, incomplete and, second, biased in favor of divisive, competitive, and destructive aspects of human psychology. It will also address the most common defenses that are brought forward by realists on behalf of their motivational assumptions, explaining why such defenses do not constitute a sufficient justification for the bias that may be introduced by such assumptions into both realist theory and the praxis of foreign policy.

The Incompleteness of Realist Motivational Assumptions

There is ample evidence in the psychological as well as political–psychological literature to the effect that realist motivational assumptions are in fact incomplete, that is, that the actual motives underlying human behavior are more varied than those acknowledged in realist theory. The works of psychologists Henry Murray and David McClelland have been paramount in establishing the practice, now common in all social sciences, of classifying human motivation according to the primary need pursued. Both identify three basic needs: power, achievement, and affiliation.[1] These three motives have since been the most studied, and the practice of classifying motivation in this particular way has become very common across disciplines and issue areas.[2] For example, Abraham Maslow employs these three themes in his hierarchy of needs, where he places security and survival (power) at the bottom; love, affection, and affiliation (affiliation) in the middle; and self-actualization (achievement) at the top.[3] In the field of foreign policy analysis, Arnold Wolfers identifies three basic kinds of foreign policy goals: security (power), milieu (affiliation), and possessional (achievement).[4] Richard Cottam identifies as many as fifteen different foreign policy motives, but he classifies them as governmental (power), communal (affiliation), and economic (achievement).[5] More recently, Graham Allison and Gregory Treverton have claimed that American foreign policy makers must answer three basic questions to be able to develop foreign policy strategies: What are American national interests? How are those interests threatened by other nations and international actors? What opportunities are there to advance those interests?[6] These questions as well may be interpreted to address the needs of affiliation, power, and achievement, respectively.

Of the three basic motivational categories employed in the social sciences, realism concentrates on only one: the motive of power. By doing so, it may develop incomplete explanations and misleading predictions. What evidence is there that a broader view of motivation is more helpful in the study of international politics? Some support for this notion may be derived from studies that attempt to identify the types of basic values, beliefs, and attitudes which play consistent roles in the formation of public or elite opinions on foreign policy issues. For example, a study by William Chittick, Keith Billingsley, and Rick Travis finds that information on all three motives is needed to predict individuals' foreign policy opinions.[7] Using both elite and mass opinion data, Chittick and myself have shown that taking into account variation on three motivational dimensions, each based on one of the three motivational complexes identified in the psychological literature, improves our ability to account for and predict foreign policy opinions, in general, and public opinion concerning the use of force, in particular.[8]

If it can be shown that all three motives contribute to actors' behavioral intentions, it seems highly plausible that all three motives might also be relevant for the explanation of their actual behavior. Additional, substantial support for a broader view of motivation than the one that forms the psychological basis of realist theory can be found in studies of the relationship between motivation and conflict.

In 1975 McClelland first identified the power and affiliation motives as, respectively, the basic psychological causes of war and peace.[9] He specifically argues that an increase in the power motive combined with a decrease in the affiliation motive increases the risk of a nation becoming embroiled in war. Empirical studies by David Winter and others employ McClelland's motivational categories in attempts to link motivation to specific types of foreign policy decisions. Winter finds that war entry is indeed associated with the power motive, while the motive of achievement appears to be unrelated to the likelihood of violent conflict.[10] More recently, he concludes, as the result of repeated empirical tests, that the outbreak of war is made more likely by high power motivation and low affiliation motivation.[11] He also finds that, for wars to end, it is necessary for power motivation to decrease. Bill Peterson, David Winter, and Richard Doty have analyzed the results of three tests which suggest that international conflicts tend to escalate to violence when power motivation is high, the perception of the strength of power motivation in the opponent is exaggerated, and the actor reacts by becoming even more strongly motivated by its need to compete.[12] The cited and similar studies show that to actually explain and predict foreign policy decisions of various kinds a broader range of motives than those acknowledged by realism has to be taken into account. What is more, since they all find the strength of the motive of power to be positively related to the likelihood of violent conflict, they strongly suggest that the realist concentration on the motive of power at the expense of other motives can be expected to lead to an exaggerated estimate of the likelihood of such conflict.

That the assumption of self-interested rationality does not fully characterize human beings is, as we have seen, a fact that traditional realism typically acknowledges. Both the idea that human beings are self-interested and the idea that they can pursue their self-interest rationally deserve qualification. As Peter Ahrensdorf has pointed out, its supposed "founding father" Thucydides clearly judges political realism to be "psychologically naive" in this respect.[13] Ahrensdorf holds that

> while the insight that human beings are compelled to care more about their self-interest than about justice is true, it is also true that most human beings cannot simply live with that insight because to do so would require them to abandon their moral illusions and pious hopes. However unreasonable moral and religious passions may be, human beings are far from being simply reasonable creatures and those passions and hopes have a real power in political life.[14]

Thomas Hobbes's treatment of the impact of factors such as norms and passions on human behavior contains important lessons concerning the limits of self-interested motivation. Specifically, as Stephen Holmes finds, it acknowledges that "motives that remain irreducible to self-interest are especially powerful in complex choice situations where considerations of advantage do not clearly privilege one decision over another."[15] Paranoid fear and vainglory are examples of such motives, which will produce puzzling results for an observer who assumes rationality, and "complex choice situations" may well be viewed to be the norm, rather than exceptions, in international politics. Laurie Johnson Bagby concludes that, as a result of its psychological views, realism as an empirical theory is "vulnerable to the charge of not being realistic enough, not taking into account the impact of so many 'irrationalities' within the system such as religion, ideology, national and ethnic identity, the role of international organizations and regimes, or the impact of international law and ethics."[16]

Inasmuch as realist theory relies on the assumption of rationality, it is vulnerable to the kinds of criticism of cognitive approaches to social behavior that are brought forward on occasion in all social scientific disciplines.[17] Such criticism is commonly based on the contention that a concentration on cognition, or intrapersonal processes of decision making, combined with a lack of attention to the role of social processes in the formation of opinions and the judgment of behavioral options, serves to obscure the fundamental importance of social processes for all forms of social behavior.

The limited empirical adequacy of the assumption of self-interested rationality becomes particularly obvious if we examine its application in foreign policy analysis. In his comprehensive study of the impact of nonrational factors in foreign policy decision making, Yaacov Vertzberger identifies among the sources of such factors the personality and cognitive structure of the decision maker, small-group and organizational effects and their different impacts on persons in varying situations, as well as societal–cultural influences and their interplay with all other factors.[18] The rational actor model constitutes such a radical simplification of the reality of political decision making that it is hardly useful for developing predictions. As a consequence, rational choice theory commonly introduces auxiliary assumptions and hypotheses. As Herbert Simon has pointed out, its "model predictions rest primarily on the auxiliary assumptions rather than deriving from the rationality principle, . . . [which] implies that the principle of rationality, unless accompanied by extensive empirical research to identify the correct auxiliary assumptions, has little power to make valid predictions about political phenomena."[19]

Graham Allison identifies three distinct types of rational choice theory, as applied to the analysis of foreign policy. The first is the ideal type, which treats all nations as identically motivated unitary rational actors. A second type of analysis "focuses not upon nations in general, but rather upon a nation or national government with a particular character. Characteristics of this actor limit the goals, options, and consequences of the basic paradigm."[20] Finally,

> a related, but nevertheless different, type of analysis, focuses explicitly on an individual leader or leadership clique as the actor whose preference function is maximized and whose personal (or group) characteristics are allowed to modify the basic concepts of the paradigm. This individual's weighting of goals and objectives, tendencies to perceive (and to exclude) particular ranges of alternatives, and principles employed in estimating the consequences that follow from each alternative serve as the basic framework within which the choice must be located.[21]

In the second and third type of analysis, the broad and sweeping assumptions introduced by the rational choice framework are mitigated by other factors, which introduce serious limitations on the generalizability of the explanations and predictions the theory serves to develop. In essence, such modifications trade breadth and parsimony for depth and a lesser degree of abstraction. In so doing, they render the theory considerably more realistic.

The Bias of Realist Motivational Assumptions

It is interesting to see that the three basic motivational categories identified by McClelland and others correspond to the three motives of the Athenian thesis. The needs for power, affiliation, and achievement at least roughly correspond to the motives of fear, the desire for honor, or pride, and the quest for profit, or material success. We have seen that, perhaps as a result of sampling error, realist theory adopts a view of all three of these motives as essentially divisive, competitive, and destructive. This strategy, which is exposed by Thucydides, leads realism down the slippery slope toward a restrictive and one-sided view of human motivation. By contrast, the views on the range of important motives that are more common in psychological and political decision-making approaches include the desire for affiliation, or community, as well as the operation of altruism.[22] Such motives, which introduce social and cooperative elements into the image of human nature, have traditionally been disregarded by realism, which, as a consequence, has adopted a dim view of human nature and a pessimistic outlook on possibilities for sustained international peace and cooperation. Realism ignores the relevance of the human needs for community as well as morality. As a consequence, its judgments of the possibilities for inter-human identification, empathy, sympathy, and cooperation, as well as for human learning and social progress, are extremely pessimistic.

This pessimism is so strong that it appears at times even incompatible with other elements of realist thought. For example, realists generally fail to take note of the fact that noncooperative behavior is often in the long run self-defeating and thus ill-compatible with the assumption of rationality.[23] This is because individuals and states are bound to interact with others not only once and never again but often on a continuing basis, which requires them to cultivate a reputation for being acceptable "players." Inasmuch as nation–states in today's world are interdependent, at least economically, the motive of achievement could actually be expected to encourage states to value their "reputations" more highly. Thus it does not have to operate in the dysfunctionally competitive ways predicted by realism.[24] Neither does the motive of pride, if we consider that it is an important emotional element in, and driving force to support, an individual's identification with others. Such identification, in turn, plays a crucial role in the establishment of community. The fact that individuals can develop various overlapping identities and an inclusive sense of community at least counteracts the competitive and hostile aspects of Hobbesian vainglory.

It should be noted that, by insisting on their view of human nature, realists choose to disregard a host of contradictory findings. Assuming the stability of human nature, for one, flies in the face of the entire discipline of psychology, and especially its subfield of psychiatry, whose very raison d'être is that "human nature" contains a significant range of dependent variables, and that socially destructive behavior, for example, can be "cured." The very notion of "character" implies that any individual personality is composed of various traits, some aggressive, some nonaggressive, and that the strength of any particular trait varies and can be affected by experience or treatment. Fixed traits are found by psychologists to be minimal and to extend not far beyond instincts. They certainly do not include a choice of particular goals or strategies to achieve them. In addition, most psychological studies of motivation accede that needs or instincts function as "natural" motives only as long as actors are not conscious of their impact.[25] In this view, consciousness almost by definition implies choice. This perspective contradicts the deterministic view of human motivation which is propagated by realism. It is also worth noting that many psychological approaches view man as an inherently social being.[26] They point out that the interests and goals of human beings are not simply attributes of individuals but are developed in social interaction and can, through complex processes of identification, create interpersonal and communal bonds, which, in turn, shape individual preferences and strategies. While such approaches also take note of the problems that affect social interaction, their judgment of its possibilities tends to be vastly more optimistic than that which characterizes realist theory.[27] In fact, their view, which emphasizes the possibilities of adaptation, learning, and social evolution, is considerably closer to the view of human nature that informs political idealist approaches.[28]

Realist Defenses

How may realists defend themselves against accusations that their assumptions concerning the motives of states are unrealistic? One possible strategy involves the argument that, because realism examines the behavior of states as opposed to individuals, it need not pay attention to what we know about the motives of human beings. For example, it is sometimes argued, that the "motivation" of states generally differs from the motivation of individuals, perhaps because nation–states are represented by elites rather than average persons or because their "goals" must of necessity be different from those of individuals, because they are different "creatures." A second possible counterargument might hold that, even if nation–states possessed basic motives identical to those of individuals, the different types of constraints operating at the level of international interaction may produce different types of behavior. As a consequence, actions that would appear irrational from a psychological point of view, which emphasizes choice, may be rational given the realist view of state decision making, which emphasizes constraints.

The first of these strategies of defense serves to expose a vulnerable aspect of the realist logic, which involves the issue of cross-level inference.[29] Realist theory, as may be expected from any grand theory of international relations, involves different levels of analysis. Wherever relations among them are underspecified, level-of-analysis problems arise.[30] Realist international relations theory is primarily concerned with the "behavior" of nation–states, and it is one of the defining characteristics of realism that it treats these nation–states as if they were unitary actors. It is obviously a strong empirical simplification to speak of states possessing interests or motives. However, it is believed that individuals do, and it is the prerogative of social scientists, within limits, to speak of aggregates of human beings as if they behaved like single individuals.

The analysis of the evolution of realist motivational assumptions that comprises the earlier chapters of this study clearly shows that realist expectations about the goals of states in the international realm have been shaped by the realist view of human psychology and the nature of social relations. As we have seen, realists make assumptions about the motives of states by means of analogical reasoning beginning from their views on human nature. States' goals are, as a consequence, assumed to be analogous to those of individuals. The problem with the realist logic is not that it treats states as if they were human beings;[31] rather, it is generally unclear about just when and how the psychological assumptions made about human nature actually inform realist interpretations of the behavior of states. It is obviously unacceptable for realists to base their expectations about the likely behavior of states on assumptions about individual motivation, only to deny having done so when confronted with empirical criticism of such assumptions. On this basis, we may question whether it is legitimate for realists to argue that the motives of states generally differ from those of individuals, even though this may well be the case.

The second argument, which suggests that the constraints faced by nation–states are systematically different from those faced by individuals, can ultimately be refuted (or confirmed) only through empirical evidence, which, given the nature of the problem, would be exceedingly difficult to come by. While Reinhold Niebuhr has argued, for example, that collectivities face greater constraints to ethical behavior than individuals, the reasons he suggests for why this should be the case, although numerous, still do not add up to persuade critics of the merits of his argument.[32] It cannot reasonably be disputed that states face constraints that are, prima facie, different from those faced by individuals. However, it is not at all clear whether those constraints are not nonetheless analogous to those faced by individuals (as states' motives are analogous to those of individuals), and even if they are not, whether they are systematically different, as opposed to simply not the same.[33] A large part of the problem is that, when we speak of constraints, we are of course not speaking of actual objects, but of mental constructs. Does it constrain foreign policy making to live with Soviet nuclear missiles aimed at New York City? Strictly speaking, only if the relevant decision makers think it does. The fact that common sense tells us that they would should not lead us to overlook the fact that the interpretation of the situations they face requires decision makers to make judgment calls. The quintessential realist assumption that states face the constraint of international anarchy is, ultimately, such a judgment call. Do decision makers act as if it were so? Apparently, sometimes they do, and sometimes they do not.

Another strategy that may be employed in defense of realist motivational assumptions, unrealistic or not, has to be met not with logical contradiction or empirical evidence but with a view to its full implications. It is common among academics to ask of potential critics what may amount to a "suspension of disbelief" with respect to the assumptions employed in their theories. The argument is that assumptions are scientifically justifiable only through the explanatory and/or predictive power of the theories they support. As long as a theory that employs particular assumptions delivers useful explanations, or the degree of compliance of the expectations it creates with empirical observations is statistically significant, so the argument goes, the assumptions it employs are useful within the context of the theory and thereby fully justified.

There are three obvious possible objections to this logic. The first problem is that it is by no means clear that we have anything to gain by suspending disbelief in assumptions that are difficult, if not impossible, to justify empirically. Even if they are employed in a theory that delivers impressive results, the relationship between the character of those assumptions and the success of that particular theory may well be spurious. Why waste our time, we may ask, assuming for the sake of neorealist theory that political culture has no impact on a nation's major foreign policy decisions, when everyone, including Kenneth Waltz, knows that this is blatantly untrue? In such a case, what is asked of us seems more like "suspension of better judgment" than mere "suspension of disbelief." Granted, we have to make assumptions to theorize even at the lowest level of abstraction. We need to assume to understand, and, to understand, we simplify. Our assumptions help reduce the complexity of mental impressions and processes by focusing our attention on those aspects of the phenomena of interest we believe to be essential. Our assumptions can never be mental reproductions of reality. Otherwise they would not be simplifications. Still, we may keep in mind that realism, rather than exploring "what-if" scenarios or engaging in political impressionism, purports to model the world as it really is. Models of reality by definition simplify based on what we believe to be "real" about reality, not based on what we know to be "unreal." For example, we may accept that a crudely carved piece of wood represents a locomotive, even if it does not have doors or wheels. However, we would be confused if it had wings, because we are quite sure that a real locomotive would not have wings. Instead, we may start to wonder whether we are not dealing with a model of a different aspect of reality, for example, that of an airplane. Alternatively, we may begin to question ours or the modeler's grasp of the relevant information needed to properly understand the object of interest.

The acceptance of empirically questionable assumptions may well pose problems much more serious than distortion introduced by artistic liberty or waste of scientific resources. The second major concern with the use of strong assumptions in social scientific theorizing involves their potential to affect the researcher's expectations in such a way that observations will be interpreted in line with those expectations. As a consequence of such interpretation, expectations as well as the assumptions on which they are based are considered empirically confirmed. This confirmation then leads the researcher to develop explanations, predictions, and policy suggestions that take for granted the assumptions underlying the theory. Scholarship can, in such a way, introduce interpretive patterns and policy strategies into the "real world," which, in time, may well transform reality in accordance with the theorist's expectations.

If it is possible to judge the empirical accuracy of the results of an analysis, it is also always possible to judge the empirical accuracy of its assumptions (as long as these assumptions are empirical in nature). We do not have to settle for assuming, for example, that nations always try to maximize their relative military power. We can, if we want to, take a look at history to see if this has really been the case. However, we can also choose not to test this judgment of ours. We might simply not be interested in doing so, because whether or not nations always try to maximize their relative military power is not our research question. In addition, we commonly believe that our assumptions are so sensible or so widely accepted that we may take them for granted, especially if our results do not surprise us. However, it is important to keep in mind that empirical assumptions are, in principle, always testable. In light of their potential for distortion, we should be prepared to evaluate their empirical accuracy whenever this is realistically possible.

Perhaps the only thing we may safely assume is that nothing is ever safe to assume.[34] When we make an assumption, what we actually do is to decide not to question a particular judgment we have made about reality. When we assume human beings to be rational, for example, we decide to think about human beings as if they truly were rational, even if we may not believe this to actually be the case. The fact that the rationality assumption is not commonly intended by the theorists who use it to be descriptive of reality does not change the fact that, for the theories in which it is employed, it fulfills the function of an empirical assumption: It models a particular aspect of reality so that this "piece of reality" may be taken for granted in subsequent information processing and in subsequent logic of argument. The more parsimonious our theories are, the more abstraction they require. The more abstraction they require, the stronger their reliance on assumptions. What this means in fact is that a highly parsimonious theory, such as, for example, structural realism, requires us to question less and take for granted more of the theorist's judgments about reality than a less parsimonious theory. If it is the obligation of the theorist to make his assumptions explicit, it is our obligation to examine them critically.[35]

7

The Effects of the Realist Bias

This chapter suggests that the bias contained in realist motivational assumptions can translate into a bias in realist interpretations of political events, and thereby into a bias in realist policy making. I begin by briefly introducing the general problems associated with choosing frames of reference to employ in scientific study. I continue by outlining the processes by which assumptions, via perception and cognition, can orient actors vis-à-vis their environment and thereby affect their behavior. I then examine in more detail some of the particular effects realist motivational assumptions can have on the foreign policy–making process.

How Biased Assumptions Produce Biased Interpretations

How is it that the bias in the assumptions underlying realist theory can translate into a bias in the findings which result from the application of that theory? When choosing to study a particular aspect of reality, we always also have to choose a particular approach to the subject of interest. Thomas Kuhn has pointed out that, if two persons are committed to different theoretical approaches, "we cannot say with any assurance that the two men even see the same thing, [that they] possess the same data."[1] While we may not be aware of the partiality which is introduced by our particular perspective, it nonetheless has a significant impact on how we will perceive our object of inquiry.

In his study of foreign policy decision making, Graham Allison has found that analysts "think about problems of foreign . . . policy in terms of largely implicit conceptual models that have significant consequences for the content of their thought."[2] His results suggest that the analyst's choice of the decision-making model to use in the study of political events has a profound impact on the findings of the subsequent analysis. Allison thus confirms that the analyst's choice of paradigm, which includes a choice of paradigmatic assumptions, does indeed help to determine how reality will be perceived. The analyst employs models of the relevant elements of reality and the relationships between them as heuristic devices in his quest for explanations and predictions of observable outcomes. Which kinds of explanations and predictions he derives, however, depends on which model, based on which assumptions, he uses to begin with. In short, conceptual models are based on foundational assumptions. Biased assumptions translate into particular explanations and expectations. These expectations then inform both scientific hypotheses and policy recommendations.

The type of bias introduced into science by theoretical assumptions is exceedingly difficult to eliminate. On the one hand, occurrence of the expected results is taken as proof of the correctness of the assumptions used. On the other hand, even results that contradict the researcher's expectations may well be explained away, rather than leading to a revision of those assumptions. This problem is commonly referred to as an "expectancy bias" in the theory of science.[3] It has been studied most thoroughly in the form of the experimental bias effect in experimental psychology, but, for methodological reasons, the kind of "fudging" that it typically encourages is even more common in nonexperimental social science.

The scientific standard of the intersubjectivity of conclusions cannot realistically be met if this problem exists. As a consequence of the biases introduced by different research strategies, scientific findings are too easily rejected by analysts who apply different models to the interpretation of the same events. Vice versa, they are not easily enough rejected by analysts working within the same approach. Perfecting the logic of the models only serves to exacerbate this problem to the point where anyone who shares the assumptions underlying the model must agree with the results of the analysis, and anyone who does not cannot logically agree with the analyst's explanation of those results. To escape this logic, which threatens to reduce the social sciences to rhetorical arts, it is necessary to examine the various assumptions that allow analysts who are ostensibly examining the same reality to develop their divergent conclusions.

According to Alan Lamborn, specialized theoretical approaches to the study of international relations have evolved from empirical disagreements concerning the relevant "types of issues, actors, political arenas, and strategic situations."[4] Lamborn claims that among the "effects that restrictive empirical assumptions in issue-oriented theories have on analysts' understanding of the political process," are "subtle forms of selection bias that . . . threaten both the validity and generalizability of much existing theory."[5] By accepting highly restrictive motivational assumptions, realism can capture but a small part of human reality. Since these assumptions are biased, the theory is empirically misleading. This causes a serious risk of inaccurate interpretations of political reality. In the words of Robert Jervis, "[I]t is both easy and dangerous to build models on the assumption that a general knowledge of what we take to be human nature, combined with our understanding of the situation, will tell us what incentives are operating."[6] It is easy because it absolves us from finding out what actors actually want. It is dangerous because, as Mark Petracca points out, the assumptions about what it is that they want, which underlie such models, whether they are correct or not, "shape research strategies, which in turn affect political cognition as well as political possibilities and actual behavior."[7]

How Biased Interpretations Affect Realist Scholarship

The danger posed by biased motivational assumptions in realist theory is exacerbated by the fact that realism contains both prescriptive and descriptive elements. Contemporary realism follows Thomas Hobbes in arguing that it is reasonable to seek the most efficient means to achieve the primary end of self-preservation, now understood to consist in a strategic pursuit of power. Actions that do not correspond to this view of the nature of international actors and political reality are discouraged and are at the same time treated as exceptions or errors. As Jervis points out, as a consequence of this dual strategy, failings to conform with the expectations of realist theory should be "not only those of individual states and statesmen but of the theory as well."[8] However, when states fail to behave in the ways predicted by realist theorizing, realists, rather than considering their hypotheses falsified, typically argue that the case in question constitutes one of those exceptions.

If any explanation is given for such an exceptional case, it typically involves the suggestion that the state in question, for whatever reason, failed to act rationally, as specified (or, worse, left unspecified) in the theory. Perhaps it lacked the prerequisite information. Perhaps it reasoned in a way that the theory cannot account for. Once again we see that the dual usage of the concept of rationality as both an empirical assumption and a normative behavioral standard plays a crucial role in the defense of realist expectations.

Whenever it ventures into the field of policy development, realism can be found to argue from "is" to "ought." This is particularly disconcerting if the "reality" that is explained deviates substantially from the one we actually experience. Realism in this case delivers prescriptions that are logically unfounded and beg justification. Michael Loriaux finds that

> the modern realist has tried to ground his skepticism regarding the progressive power of reason in assumptions of rational behavior. The effort is, to say the least, counterintuitive. It has weakened the realist's claims to be a skeptic by making him a believer in rational strategic interaction. Thus the realist is dismissive of projects that aim at global reform through international cooperation because they require unwarranted assumptions regarding the behavior of other nations. Yet the realist embraces the doctrine of mutual deterrence though it requires the same assumptions.[9]

The considerable influence, which realist prescriptions may have, makes it necessary to examine their possible effects on the reality of international policy making.

Realist international relations scholarship follows a few trends that may be considered worrisome. For one, it is frequently accused of failing to incorporate a concept or even betray an appropriate understanding of morality. While Charles Beitz claimed even before the end of the Cold War that the "shallow moral skepticism" propagated by realism had been successfully overcome, George Kennan still insisted at the time that "moral judgment has no place in foreign policy."[10] Jim George has since concluded that realist ethical "premises—its ontological process of framing the ethical subject and the political community—have hardly been challenged."[11]

Steven Forde finds that "the essence of realism" is indeed "the replacement of moral principle by compulsions or necessities, by 'laws' of behavior."[12] Realism is frequently understood to signify the liberation of selfish impulses from any moral restraints, leaving us with the impression that "realist doctrine is . . . locked into an inveterate conflict with moral aspirations, giving any realism that desires to combine the two an inescapable complexion of tragedy."[13] Forde suggests that both Thucydides and Niccolo Machiavelli understand realism to be "an inherently antimoral phenomenon and a much more virulent one than modern realists, especially neorealists, believe. . . . Its virulence stems partly from the fact that it is based upon certain aspects of human nature rather than simply structural consideration."[14]

Forde makes a crucial observation when he points out that "the true character of realism as a scientific approach is missed unless this essential fact is grasped: the same logic that explains the amorality of international behavior excuses it; and this logic, if unchecked by something outside it, pushes us to the conclusion that there is no reason even to deplore this state of affairs."[15] Noncognitivism, the belief that there exists no objective "truth" about matters involving value judgments, does not have to lead from moral skepticism to amoral relativism.[16] Other, nonamoral positions are logically compatible with noncognitivist premises. Such positions simply imbue moral assertions with a different kind of cognitive status than empirical statements. It is at least plausible that the rejection of such positions in realist theory may be politically motivated.

Concerning the normative judgment of foreign policy, Loriaux finds that "modern realist literature either assumes uncritically that the defense of the nation is the highest good that can be achieved in international politics" or, if it comes from within the United States, "it assumes that what is good for the United States is good for the world because it is stabilizing for the world."[17] He observes as well that such views can hardly be explained with reference to moral skepticism. Interestingly, it was E. H. Carr who suggested that, while realism presents itself as the soundest theoretical approach to the development of foreign policy, it can do little to provide motivation or inspiration to the makers of such policy.[18] This criticism is based on the idea that "political society requires a moral ideal to drive it, which simple self-interest cannot provide."[19] To be sure, the defense of the national interest, as long as it does not go to immoral extremes, is commonly understood as a legitimate aim of foreign policy. However, a problem to which we have been alerted by Thucydides is that the logic of realism may become self-destructive by undermining the bases for the national community to function. This is because the notion of a "common good" is inherently incompatible with the realist view of human nature and motivation.[20]

As Kurt Taylor Gaubatz has argued, neither the internal security communities advocated by Hobbes nor the external security communities that may be pursued by realist strategic policy are the empirical norm or the most successful types of security communities.[21] Rather, unifying institutions and shared norms on which they may be based are necessary for the creation and maintenance of legitimate and cohesive domestic as well as international communities that can provide a sense of security for their members. Such communities possess "interests" of their own, which are neither simply the aggregates of nor equivalent to the interests of their individual members. This raises the important question of "whether self-interest—the core of realism—is a viable basis of political and, indeed, human life."[22] As Forde has found, communities actually tend to "resist realism partly out of a need to protect their moral consensus."[23] The fact that there is need for such resistance is supported by James Boyd White, who observes that "the language of pure self-interest proves to be parasitic upon the culture it destroys."[24]

In the realm of international politics, the realist perspective leaves little possibility for mutually beneficial cooperation. As Forde observes, for both Thucydides and Machiavelli "the paradigmatic manifestation of realism is imperialism."[25] For Machiavelli, "the realist logic inevitably points in the direction of universal imperialism and the repudiation of all ethical restraints," because "the 'law' that power rules the relations of states . . . points to expansion as constrained only by the limits of one's own power, or by countervailing outside power. It certainly absolves such expansion of any moral taint."[26] This is why "Thucydides believes that international ethics can be furthered only by limiting and resisting realism, not by manipulating it in some way."[27] Forde observes that Thucydides as well as some of the classical realists raise the question how an "ethical good can be reconciled with the necessities of international politics and, indeed, whether it remains plausible in the face of a world characterized by immoral necessities."[28] He explains that "what the classical realists were acutely aware of, and what most if not all twentieth-century Anglo-American realism has lost sight of, is the fact that realism, at its core, poses the question not only of why ethics has such little effect on the behavior of states, but of why it should have any effect at all."[29]

A realism that justifies imperialism clearly leaves little room for the pursuit of an international common good, on which peaceful relations among states depend. Forde points out that "the notion that realism can be employed as a science of peace rests decisively on the possibility of identifying an international common good, something that is in the interests of all states to pursue, and persuading them to embrace it."[30] Supporting Forde's view are the attempts of Hans Morgenthau and other classical realists to encourage a rationally limited concept of the national interest, which avoids incorporating ideological and other irrational ambitions.[31] Such a concept could function as a common denominator in attempts to coordinate the foreign policies of nation–states. Hegemony and regime theory as well as game theoretical approaches may also be viewed as attempts to identify the bases for a possible coordination of state behavior. However, a point of criticism which is frequently made is that what would truly be needed for the institutionalization of cooperative arrangements and the development of international community is a shared understanding of the moral or normative bases for political action.

According to Robert Axelrod, it is particularly important to know how cooperation can develop in situations in which individuals or nations might be expected to act selfishly to further their own interests: "The answer each of us gives to this question has a fundamental effect on how we think and act in our social, political, and economic relations with others. And the answers that others give have a great effect on how ready they will be to cooperate with us."[32] The answers suggested by realist theory are, by all accounts, rather discouraging, since the realist view of human nature and motivation leads it to generally expect interests to clash and to downplay the role of shared norms. In addition, its views on the structural obstacles to mutually beneficial interaction lead it to be pessimistic of possibilities for cooperation even where shared interests may exist. While realists' use of game theoretical models has helped to explain when, why, and how cooperation may occur under such circumstances, it has not been able to affect the profound pessimism with which realists continue to regard attempts at international community building. As Forde has put it, "[T]he devices uncovered by game theory can help identify and build on a common good among states, but they cannot create a common good where one does not exist."[33] The motivational assumptions of realism thus continue to uphold a bias in realist theory against expectations of peaceful cooperation among self-interested nations. Such a bias may well be expected to affect political behavior in ways that actually reduce the likelihood that international cooperative arrangements will succeed.

Michael Argyle has examined the cooperative side of human nature with respect to its innate components as well as to the possibilities that exist for the reinforcement of cooperative traits.[34] He criticizes the Prisoners' Dilemma and similar game theoretical models of social interaction for being not only generally unrealistic in their conception but biased specifically against important factors that commonly correlate with cooperative behavior. Such factors may include familiarity with the other players, the possibility of communication, a history of joint activity, and a knowledge of applicable rules or norms. All of these factors may facilitate the operation of trust. Without a minimum of trust, however, cooperative strategies are unlikely to be initiated by any player.

Jervis argues that "considerations of morality, fairness, and obligation are almost surely large parts of the explanation for the fact that individuals in society cooperate much more than the Prisoners' Dilemma would lead us to expect. . . . Indeed, it is possible that morality provides the only way to reach many mutual cooperative outcomes."[35] He suggests that the tendency to be self-righteous, to attribute the actions of others to selfishness or hostility while refusing to question one's own, inhibits mutually beneficial cooperation while narrow self-interest reigns. He observes that, at a minimum, the introduction of a norm that commands the reciprocation of accommodating moves is necessary to sustain cooperation. While he suggests that, at least in international politics, it is likely that actors will continue to perceive their situations as involving interaction between independent and self-interested actors, in any case, "without the power of at least some shared values, without some identification with the other, without norms that carry moral force, cooperation may be difficult to sustain."[36]

In his analysis of the potential of game theory as used within a realist framework to explain and predict instances of cooperation, Jervis finds that some of the problems of realist theory may actually be exacerbated rather than alleviated by the use of such models. The simplifications of realist arguments that are required to formulate models can increase their empirical bias and lead to the neglect of important questions. The assumptions on which such models are based thus require strict scrutiny. Jervis concludes that

> game theory can accommodate both uncertainty and differences between the perceptions of the two sides, but we must know what these perceptions are; they may be more important and difficult to understand than the resulting interaction. Problems that are even more fundamental arise if narrow self-interest is not the driving force behind national behavior: although game-theory models could be built around different premises, many of the realist arguments about anarchy would be undermined.[37]

A rather more philosophical yet complementary critique of realist uses of theoretical models comes from Loriaux, who complains that,

> by trying to construct a realist social science of international relations on the basis of abstract and even simplistic psychological and structural assumptions, [realists] . . . have ceased to hear the "tragic narrative" of Thucydides, they have become oblivious to the fickleness of Fortuna to which we are alerted by Machiavelli, and they have become insensitive to the mad-dash strivings of peoples—as dissected by Augustine—to achieve a happiness that always eludes them. In the process they have lost the capacity to provide a meaningful answer to the question that lies at the end of all our research: "What do we do? How do we act?"[38]

Realism is characterized by a pessimistic determinism, from which it never really escapes. Realist prescription does not transcend its diagnosis, imbuing realism as a practical approach to policy making with a pessimistic, if not cynical, outlook on its own possibilities. This hopeless determinism is perpetuated by realist motivational assumptions.

Thucydides watched the Athenian view of man and the laws of politics contribute to the downfall of Athens. Hobbes believed that similar insights might just have been able to do the opposite for England. Based on a view of man as equally stupidly irrational and ingeniously selfish, Hobbes pleaded for rational selfishness to curb the worst effects of irrational passions. Thinking rational goal-seeking behavior "safer," realism obeys the dictates of Hobbesian distrust. Is there evidence that rational self-interest and distrust have ever been "safer" motives in the conduct of states? Are they in this day and time? These are crucial questions to which we need to find answers if we want to evaluate the true merits of the paradigm of political realism.

How Theoretical Biases Affect Reality

Realist scholarship can influence real-world politics in three different ways: through the academic education of policy makers; through the active involvement of realist scholars in political decision making; and through the impact of the views propagated by realism on political common sense. Realist scholarship may exert influence on policy makers by communicating assumptions, including motivational assumptions, by communicating its interpretations of political events, which are at least partly determined by such assumptions, and by communicating its expectations and suggestions, which are derived from its interpretations. In turn, policy makers can confirm realist assumptions, interpretations, and expectations by acting in the ways prescribed by realist scholarship.

In addition to observing the interaction between realist theory and praxis, it is important to keep in mind that foreign policy making itself is always an interactive endeavor. If we are concerned with the relationship between two nations, we are, if we assume them to be unitary actors, dealing with two sets of motivational assumptions. They obviously do not have to be the same. However, there exists a tendency for such assumptions to become assimilated through interaction. Policy makers, too, need to theorize in order to be able to interpret the events they observe. Based on their assumptions and interpretations they, too, develop expectations concerning the behavior of other actors. Motivational assumptions as employed by decision makers are of course always assumptions about the motives of others. While they do not need to make assumptions about their own, they are usually at a loss about the motives of those with whom they interact, which gives them all the more reason to act based on preconceived ideas.

In addition, decision makers will always be tempted to interpret the reactions of others in ways that are compatible with their own expectations. Other actors, observing their behavior, may in turn consider themselves confirmed in their own, and so expectations can become self-fulfilling. As Yaacov Vertzberger finds, acting in ways that produce self-fulfilling prophesies, and thereby making their theories self-confirmatory, is an important source of individuals' confidence in their own beliefs.[39] In light of powerful psychological tendencies to avoid cognitive adjustments, such patterns, as long as actors remain unaware of their operation, are usually disrupted only as a result of overwhelming disconfirming evidence in combination with generational shifts.

The role played by realist motivational assumptions in foreign policy making cannot be properly understood without reference to research conducted in the fields of psychology proper as well as political psychology. Such research has explored the impact of assumptions concerning the motives behind the actions of others on the reacting individual. The consensus that emerges is that the beliefs a policy maker holds about the likely motivations of other individuals can be expected to have a strong influence on his interpretation of their actions and therefore on his own reactions. For example, in his case study of British policy toward Egypt between 1876 and 1956, Richard Cottam has found that domestic conflicts over different policy options usually rested on differences in assumptions concerning the adversary's motives. He suggests that differences in motivational attribution function as the hidden bases of major foreign policy debates.[40]

There are two comprehensive bodies of research that are particularly relevant when it comes to explaining the possible effects which the bias introduced by realist motivational assumptions may have on the foreign policy–making process. The first is associated with the perceptual perspective in the study of foreign policy decision making, which is, in general, concerned with explaining how perception intervenes between an "objective reality" and behavior to help determine foreign policy choice. This perspective assumes that state behavior is at least partly determined by the goals of decision makers as well as their perceptions of the situations they face and of how these situations relate to their goals. Perception in this sense may be defined as "an integrative process, by which stimuli become interpreted by the individual, the process taking place via the integration of the stimulus events with the prior knowledge and beliefs of the individual."[41] James Voss and Ellen Dorsey observe that such a definition assumes, "one, that perception and interpretation are interwoven processes and essentially cannot be separated and, two, that individuals act to provide meaning to the environment."[42]

The foundations for the decision-making approach to the study of international relations were laid in the 1950s by Richard Snyder and his colleagues as well as Harold and Margaret Sprout.[43] These early studies began by drawing attention to the influence of perceptual factors on actors' definitions of their situations. Since then, the decision-making approach has been able to profit from related developments in decision theory and cognitive psychology. Behavioral decision making and game theoretical approaches have primarily explored the logic of decision-making under conditions of rationality. They have been employed in the study of dyadic international interaction primarily by realists, such as, for example, Bruce Bueno de Mesquita.[44] Foreign policy analysts, on the other hand, have profited more from cognitive approaches, which overwhelmingly focus on the limitations that exist to the operation of rationality in political decision making. Among the pioneers in this area are Joseph de Rivera and Lawrence Falkowski.[45] As we will see, by focusing on nonrational factors in decision making, cognitive approaches have been particularly useful in identifying sources of misperception, bias, and error.[46]

It may be argued that the consideration of so-called cognitive factors in decision making opens the proverbial can of worms. Two objections are voiced most frequently. The first suggests that in order to explain or predict behavior while allowing for the operation of nonrational factors, too much information is required. In addition, it is a type of information—that is, information about the needs, goals, and cognitive capabilities of decision makers—that is extremely hard to come by. This objection is somewhat unfair, for theories that assume rationality as well require information concerning actors' preferences and realistic specifications of the rationality concept to be able to explain and predict actual decisions with any degree of success. The second objection suggests that cognitive approaches work to undermine the capacity of science in the positivist mode to make any authoritative judgments about the behavior of states. After all, if we admit that actors react not to objective phenomena but to their individual perceptions, which are inherently subjective, what basis do we have to assess their reactions at all? Who is to say what constitutes a *mis*perception? And what right do we have to speak of biases, if everyone's perception is fully explained by cognitive and motivational factors? These questions are important because cognitive approaches do indeed face a serious risk of introducing psychological determinism into the study of international relations, even while they are generally eager to expel structural determinism. The threat of relativism, however, can be avoided by the establishment of criteria for judgment. Voss and Dorsey suggest that

> what determines whether one's interpretation is "better" depends upon how a particular interpretation fits with other information and whether its implications are acceptable. The point that our representations and beliefs about international events are formed through the implementation of complex cognitive and affective components makes these processes critical, and any fictional assumptions about the inherent rationality of humans rests [*sic*] upon little, if any, foundation.[47]

Cognitive approaches are relatively marginal in the discipline of international relations not only because they are still in the early stages of theory development but also because, in significant respects, they have no place within the realist paradigm. Voss and Dorsey observe that

> the cognitive position implies that because humans build perceptions or representations of the world, and because such perceptions are influenced by one's goals, knowledge, and factors such as bureaucratic position, the cognitive viewpoint places responsibility for international activity squarely upon the decision makers. Their judgments are the determiners of the actions of states, not the presumed, but generally undefined, laws involving an abstract international structure.[48]

Cognitive approaches thus by definition fall outside the bounds of at least structural realist theory. In addition, the cognitive–perceptual approach poses significant challenges to the theorist, because "one component of the cognitive system, such as perception, cannot be separated from the other components; how a person perceives is related to how a person learns, remembers, solves problems, and makes decisions. How a person perceives is also related to that person's beliefs, knowledge, affect, and goals."[49]

Cognitive approaches generally have been prepared to sacrifice theoretical parsimony for the sake of exploratory research into a large range of factors potentially relevant in political decision making. Different case studies have focused on different processes, and attempts at theoretical integration tend to be highly unparsimonious.[50] While not losing sight of this context, I will focus my discussion on those findings developed from within the decision-making approach which are particularly relevant to an understanding of the potential impact of the realist motivational bias on foreign policy making.

Cognitive approaches concede that real-life decision makers cannot comply with the expectation of full rationality. Instead, political decision makers adopt a number of strategies to deal with the limitations imposed on them by their cognitive capabilities. It is important to remember that such strategies are, to a certain extent, necessary and unavoidable. They facilitate information processing and enable actors to make decisions. However, they may also lead to misperception and error. A number of processes are particularly relevant. The study of problem solving has proven the need to pay attention to actors' definitions of the problem.[51] Studies of the limitations of memory have drawn attention to the problem of information overload in both problem solving and decision making. Most important, the development of the concepts of 'cognitive dissonance' versus 'cognitive consistency' by Leon Festinger and Fritz Heider in the 1950s and 1960s has served to emphasize the need for stability in beliefs and perceptions, while at the same time alerting us to the costs of such stability: "misperception and biased interpretation, with individuals using denial, bolstering, or other mechanisms to maintain their beliefs."[52] According to Robert Art and Robert Jervis, "[P]eople simplify their processing of complex information by permitting their established frameworks of beliefs to guide them. They can then assimilate incoming information to what they already believe."[53] Thus there exists "a tendency for people to assimilate incoming information into their pre-existing images."[54] This tendency is explained by psychological theory as part of a strategy to avoid cognitive dissonance. There is little to stop this tendency, because "information is usually ambiguous enough so that people can see it as consistent with the views that they already hold."[55]

Voss and Dorsey observe that "individuals build mental representations of the world and . . . such representations provide coherence and stability to their interpretations of the complexities of the environment."[56] So-called image theory studies the role played in the decision-making process by such interpretive "blueprints," which have been variously called "images," "schemata," "scripts," or "mental models."[57] The concept of "image," which is most commonly used in foreign policy analysis, captures the notion of a schema, which is more popular in cognitive psychology. In the 1950s, Kenneth Boulding defined the term *image* as "the total cognitive, affective, and evaluative structure of the behavioral unit, or its internal view of itself and its universe."[58] He argued that "the images which are important in international systems are those which a nation has of itself and of those other bodies in the system which constitute its international environment."[59]

Images can introduce misperception and error into the decision-making process, especially if they function as stereotypes. Stereotypes can be defined as "images that are assumed to have attributes that characterize all elements of a particular group."[60] The role of stereotypical images, such as the "enemy image," has been explored by authors such as Ole Holsti, Richard Cottam, or David Finlay and his colleagues.[61] Such studies find that stereotyping generally leads to "over-generalization, that is, erroneously attributing characteristics to a particular country that may not have one or more of the given characteristics. The countries are thus not sufficiently differentiated."[62] According to Holsti, "[T]he relationship of national images to international conflict is clear: decision-makers act upon their definition of the situation and their images of states—others as well as their own. These images are in turn dependent upon the decision-maker's belief system, and these may or may not be accurate representations of 'reality.'"[63]

The impact of stereotypical national images in policy making was particularly obvious during the Cold War, when Boulding referred to them as "the last great stronghold of unsophistication" in international politics, observing that "nations are divided into 'good' and 'bad'—the enemy is all bad, one's own nation is of spotless virtue."[64] The bipolar system was commonly characterized as a "closed" one, in which "perceptions of low hostility are self-liquidating and perceptions of high hostility are self-fulfilling."[65] This is because both sides continue to interpret new information in ways that help preserve the enemy image, even if such information is meant to constitute a conciliatory gesture. Closed systems suffer from the dangerous problem of distorted "mirror images." Urie Bronfenbrenner explains:

> Herein lies the terrible danger of the distorted mirror image, for it is characteristic of such images that they are self-confirming; that is, each party, often against its own wishes, is increasingly driven to behave in a manner which fulfills the expectations of the other. . . . [The mirror image] impels each nation to act in a manner which confirms and enhances the fear of the other to the point that even deliberate efforts to reverse the process are reinterpreted as evidence of confirmation.[66]

Both Richard Cottam and Philip Tetlock have argued that the avoidance of complexity in information processing is what supports distortive stereotyping and thus encourages error in foreign policy making.[67] Tetlock finds that decision makers who exhibit a high level of cognitive complexity are more likely to develop sophisticated interpretations and take compromise positions, which enable them to perceive common interests and a larger range of policy options, including the option of integrative bargaining. By contrast, those who exhibit low levels of cognitive complexity are more likely to develop simplistic interpretations and take competitive positions, which lead them to perceive less opportunities, in general, and less reasons for international cooperation, in particular. As Voss and Dorsey have put it,

> [W]ith respect to conflict resolution, the results support the notion that integratively complex decision makers will be predisposed to evaluate the problem areas from the perspective of the other actors and will incorporate their differing perspectives into the proposals that are advanced in the bargaining context. This approach stands in contradistinction to that of the integratively simple decision maker, who will pursue only an approach designed to extract concessions from the other actors while rejecting any coordinating proposals.[68]

This judgment seems to disqualify "hawks" from the ranks of reasonable decision makers. However, both of the previous studies also suggest that cognitive complexity in the decision-making process is strongly discouraged by the perception of high "stakes" or risk. To avoid the psychological determinism of which I warned above, it is necessary to keep in mind that such perceptions can, of course, be justified by the situations decision makers find themselves in. For example, crises have been found to strongly discourage the operation of cognitive complexity, and the research of Holsti, among others, has shown how crisis situations can lead to escalation and war by inhibiting rational decision making.[69]

Images include ideas concerning the opponent's motives, which are considered part of the decision maker's belief system. A belief may be defined as "the information that a person has about other people, objects and issues. The information may be factual or it may only be one person's opinion."[70] By comparison, an attitude is "a persisting positive or negative feeling about a person, event, or object, including a country."[71] According to Holsti, whose work on the impact of belief systems has been particularly influential, a belief system

> is composed of a number of "images" of the past, present, and future, [and] includes "all the accumulated, organized knowledge that the organism has about itself and the world." . . . It may be thought of as the set of lenses through which information concerning the physical and social environment is received. It orients the individual to his environment, defining it for him and identifying for him its salient characteristics.[72]

As Holsti points out, both belief system theory and image theory emphasize that "a decision-maker acts upon his 'image' of the situation rather than upon 'objective' reality, and it has been demonstrated that the belief system . . . plays an integral role in the cognitive process."[73]

Belief systems fulfill a double function for the individual. They contain an actor's value judgments, and thus serve to order preferences and establish goals. They also help organize perceptions in ways that allow him to react to incoming information. As such, they may become dysfunctional by leading the individual to "block out" information that is inconsistent with expectations.[74] For example, Anatol Rapoport has found that "controversial issues tend to be polarized not only because commitments have been made but also because certain perceptions are actively excluded if they do not fit the chosen world image."[75] The more rigid the image, the more likely an individual is to reinterpret incoming information to accommodate it.[76] In addition, the more "closed" the decision maker's belief system, and the more monolithic the social system in which he operates, the more likely he is to employ rigid images.[77]

A number of studies have examined the influence of beliefs or attitudes on the judgment of foreign policy events.[78] They have generally found that

> beliefs influence perception through their relation to expectations and interpretations. Beliefs set up expectations, and when an event occurs, we are likely to interpret the event in relation to our expectations. Expectations have three effects that may be noted. They permit rapid identification of the expected object or event; they admit a relatively wide range of objects or events as fulfilling the expectation, a characteristic that produces misidentification as well as identification of the target object; and they may lead to a failure to observe significant nonexpected objects or events.[79]

Beliefs can also influence perception through the use of analogical reasoning, "a categorization process in which information such as the occurrence of an event or situation is perceived to be related to some other event or situation that bears some similarity to the current event."[80] The use of analogies is, of course, as problematic as the use of images. Analogies may be misleading, as preconceived ideas may have a strong influence on the choice of analogy or dissimilarities between the supposedly analogous events may be disregarded for the sake of simplicity.

Another crucial factor influencing perception is motivation. In practice it is difficult to separate the effects of motivation on perception from those of beliefs.

However, significant progress toward this differentiation has been made in the study of misperceptions. In this area, it has become common to distinguish between "motivated" and "unmotivated" misperceptions. Some gains in clarity are made through this distinction, as motivation is perceived to influence perception through the impact of actors' needs and goals, whereas beliefs do so through processes that function to ensure cognitive efficiency. Both beliefs and motivation can produce misperception by producing selective (in)attention. Drawing on belief system theory and studies of "operational codes," the work of Jervis has been particularly influential in elucidating the role of misperception in decision making.[81] Jervis examines the impact of expectations and beliefs on decision makers' perceptions and interpretations of their own situations as well as of the actions of others. He shows how misperception can threaten international relations, particularly if it involves a misunderstanding of the intentions of potential adversaries.[82] Scholars writing in this area commonly hold that incorrect assumptions about the general motives of other actors can cause decision makers to make erroneous judgments about the reasons behind the particular decisions made by those actors. Such erroneous judgments may then lead to conflictual reactions that may have been avoided given fuller, more accurate information about other actors' motives.

Several common types of misperception can affect an actor's judgment of others' motives. For example, as Jervis observes, there exists a "tendency for actors to see others as more centralized and calculating than they are."[83] In addition, there exists a tendency for actors to "see others' actions as autonomous as opposed to being reactions to the actor's own behavior."[84] In his study of the effects of misperception on the likelihood of war, Jervis finds that misjudgments of another state's intentions are particularly influential in affecting the likelihood of violent conflict. In this context, underestimating an opponent's strength while overestimating his hostility is especially dangerous.[85]

The concept of a bias implies that patterns of misperception remain stable over time. Vertzberger has demonstrated and explained the harmful effects of motivational as well as unmotivational biases in foreign and international policy making.[86] Such biases can affect judgment, inference, and prediction. "Unmotivational biases are the products of the complexity of the environment, the inherent limitations on cognitive capabilities, and the strategies used to overcome them."[87] They are especially prone to lead to errors in decision makers' definitions of their situations. Such biases are impossible to avoid altogether, since they are a natural function of the limitations of the human mind. However, psychological research suggests that the propensity to rely on the types of cognitive "shortcuts" that can cause such biases varies among individuals and is at least partly a function of the situation in which they find themselves. In addition, "training in how to monitor the use of heuristics as well as specific knowledge-oriented training . . . can improve the trainee's control over heuristically-based information processing."[88] Motivational biases, on the other hand, "arise from emotions, personal motives, and needs and have ego-defensive functions."[89] They lead decision makers to abuse incoming information in the service of their personal needs.[90] Motivational biases can be avoided, if decision makers become aware of them. However, if an individual's ego-defensive needs are strong, he will be likely to avoid such an awareness. "Hence the remedy for motivational, self-serving biases, if there is any, requires treating motives."[91]

The bottom line of image and belief system theory is that "beliefs and images act at least as a proximate cause of the statesman's behavior."[92] Such beliefs and images are usually fairly stable, and they may have disastrous consequences for political decision making. Thus, as Jervis points out, "[I]f images of others, once established, are hard to dislodge, it is especially important to try to understand how they are formed."[93] Increasingly, research is being conducted to contribute to such knowledge and to develop image categories that can be tested empirically. An example would be a recent study by Richard Herrmann and his colleagues, which attempts to develop systematic linkages between perceptional patterns and the formation and character of specific images.[94] Another important recent development is research on so-called ill-structured problems, which confront decision makers with unstable and changing stimuli. Such situations allow a larger role for psychological factors in decision making, because it is unclear how they should be "objectively" perceived. For example Charles Hermann argues that the present fundamental changes in the international system pose such problems for decision makers, and that foreign policy analysis now urgently requires insight into how they may be handled.[95]

How the Realist Bias Affects International Politics

The second comprehensive body of research relevant for an examination of the possible real-world effects of realist motivational assumptions analyzes more directly the operation of some of the particular biases contained in realism. The most promising approach to the empirical study of realist policy making is the case study approach. Unfortunately, the wealth of findings that has been collected by such studies suffers from a lack of theoretical integration. However, a survey of the relevant research is still useful, for it draws attention to those regularities which suggest that plausible hypotheses might be developed that can link realist judgments to particular types of political behavior.

Of particular interest is Ralph White's psychological analysis of U.S.–Soviet relations during the Cold War, in which he finds that an emphasis on the motives of fear and power, which is typical of realism, at its worst supports "paranoid" tendencies in foreign policy decision making.[96] I will examine White's arguments in some detail, as they serve us well by synthesizing a number of relevant points. White begins with the observation that much of the danger associated with the nuclear arms race stems from the fact that "each side imagines that it faces an inherently, implacably aggressive enemy, when actually it faces an enemy as fearful as itself—an enemy driven mainly by fear to do the things that lead to war."[97] Keith Shimko has examined some of the classic hard-line images of the adversary that were associated with realist arms control policies during the Cold War.[98] He confirms that these include the belief that adversaries seek limitless expansion, that they will "back down" only when forced to do so, that they will violate agreements when they can, and that they are not afraid of the actor's capabilities. He finds that these assumptions, combined with the actor's fear of the capabilities of the adversary, led realist policy makers during the Cold War to accept only extremely tight and highly asymmetrical arms control agreements and propagated a general skepticism concerning the promise of such agreements.

Richard Ned Lebow as well as Lebow and Janice Gross Stein have examined the risks posed by motivational and unmotivational biases for deterrence and nuclear crisis management.[99] Their findings support those of Holsti, suggesting that the fact that the world was spared a direct superpower confrontation during the Cold War is hardly attributable to the ingenuity of deterrence strategies.[100] According to Lebow, the realist strategy of deterrence "fails to address what may be the most common cause of aggression: . . . the perceived need to pursue a confrontational foreign policy because of weakness at home or abroad."[101] White discusses as the three conventional elements of deterrence theory the "Good Guys—Bad Guys" schema, the doctrine of flexible response, and the principle of mutual assured destruction. He confirms that a basic limitation of all three of those components is that most who defend and rely on them "give little attention to the motives for aggression that their deterrence is designed to counteract."[102] This is surprising, considering the fact that in order to successfully deter an actor from a particular course of action, it seems necessary to know the reasons why that actor might or might not take such an action in the first place. In other words, it is necessary to know which motives a potential opponent might have to engage in conflict, and which motives he might have not to. According to White, "[O]n the negative, war-preventing side are the motives the deterrer hopes to create in his opponent: fear of war and fear of defeat in war. On the positive, war-promoting side . . . both historical evidence and psychological evidence suggest that two motives stand out as frequent driving forces toward aggression: an exaggerated, misconceived, 'paranoid' form of fear and a macho type of pride."[103]

White's argument at this point is highly reminiscent of Hobbes, who, as we have seen, also emphasizes the destructive potential of pride and the distinction between "realistic war-preventing fear and unrealistic war-promoting fear."[104] As White points out, this distinction also parallels the Freudian distinction between "objective" and "neurotic" anxiety.[105] In a completely different context and with entirely different strategies in mind, then, White proceeds to propose a solution that is nonetheless essentially Hobbesian: First, "to keep the peace we should encourage realistic fear on both sides and discourage exaggerated fear on both sides."[106] Second, we should also discourage what White calls "macho pride" and defines as "undue satisfaction from, or an undue craving for, an image of oneself or one's own group as powerful, prestigious, tough, and courageous, usually with a strong underlying assumption that those are masculine attributes."[107] In comparison with Hobbes, it is necessary to note that White distinguishes between macho pride and what might be called "healthy" kinds of pride, involving the cultivation of self-confidence or self-respect.

White's case study suggests that realism may support "paranoia" in international politics. Psychiatrists commonly define paranoia in terms of two types of delusions: "delusions of persecution, usually regarded as primary, and delusions of grandeur—which often occur together."[108] Delusions of persecution can be seen to be motivated by exaggerated fear, and delusions of grandeur by macho pride. As Ross Stagner, for example, has pointed out, paranoia is also characterized by so-called possibilistic behavior: the "jumping" from suspicion to certainty. Such behavior involves severe motivated misperception, which functions to confirm the actor's initial suspicions. It can lead the actor to make erroneous judgments to convince himself that his suspicions were correct. Stagner discusses as an example of paranoia realist U.S. policy makers' attitudes toward the likelihood of success of moratoria on nuclear tests. He suggests that by functioning as self-fulfilling prophesies, the images and motivated biases that were involved in such attitudes obtained an even stronger impact, further reducing decision-making rationality.[109]

Drawing on Jervis, White distinguishes between two types of errors of judgment. He defines motivated misperceptions as those that can "readily be attributed to subconscious emotional or motivational factors such as macho pride or ego defense."[110] Among those, the image an actor has of an actual or potential enemy is especially important, since it plays a great role in his perception of that enemy's character and actions. According to White, "at a minimum we need to recognize the great perception-determining importance of a long-term, deeply ingrained diabolical image of a national enemy" (137). Such an image "powerfully and directly influences the specific perceptions that directly mobilize the motives and cause the actions that cause war" (ibid.). The psychological reasons for holding such an image may include exaggerated fear, worst-case thinking, guilt projection, and defensively motivated aggression. However, White holds that those explanations "seem tenuous when compared with the anxiety we create for ourselves by picturing human opponents, who are probably as frightened of us as we are of them, as villains or monsters" (140). He finds that at least two more reasons need to be considered: the appeal of "macho melodrama" and the satisfaction achieved by "grim realism" (142).

The first motive consists in the human fascination with stories of the "Rambo" type, in which good fights evil and in which "macho pride, glorified by an intense sense of righteousness, [operates] on a semi-fantasy level" (141). The second motive suggested by White is particularly relevant for a critique of the realist paradigm. The problem here lies not with being "realistic" in the literal sense of the word, but rather with being "grim" about it: "There is nothing wrong or conducive to misperception in getting satisfaction from feeling realistic. That is an appropriate reward and reinforcement for being realistic. There is often something conducive to misperception though (and akin to macho pride) in feeling more grimly realistic than other people" (ibid.). White draws attention to the fact that "realism actually calls for nothing but great respect for evidence and for orderly, honest thinking on the basis of evidence" (ibid.). He observes that

> for some reason, though, many people apparently assume that there is something hard, virile, and automatically realistic about condemning an outgroup that their own group condemns and putting the worst possible interpretation on anything it does. . . .
>
> Perhaps the line of association is that seeing an outgroup as diabolical connotes readiness for violent conflict, and readiness for violent conflict connotes virility. It is a fighting stance. In any case an association between a diabolical enemy-image and a macho self-image does seem to exist, and to distort realistic judgment. (142)

The chief process through which such images actually produce misperceptions of reality is through selective inattention: "Subconscious motives such as anxiety and macho pride influence a person's 'reality world' chiefly by first influencing what he thinks about—that is, what he pays attention to—moment by moment" (154–155). The main corrective for all forms of war-promoting misperceptions, according to White, is "realistic empathy." Such empathy, while clearly distinguished from sympathy, "is more than the cold, calculating chess-player's type of empathy" required for successful strategic interaction (160). Instead, it implies

> understanding or at least genuinely trying to understand the feelings of other people. . . . It means *being* the other person, at least for a while, and postponing skeptical analysis until later. It means trying to understand the other from the inside looking out, not merely from the outside looking in. Most of all, it means trying to look at one's own group's behavior honestly, as it might appear when seen through the other's eyes. . . . An honest look at the other implies an honest look at oneself. (161)

Robert McCalla has analyzed five U.S.–Soviet crises. He finds that realist statesmen consistently exhibit tendencies to believe that their threats will be accurately perceived by the adversary and to interpret the actions of the adversary as hostile or evil, and that they are generally led astray by lack of information and the power of their preconceived images and beliefs.[111] White's call for "realistic empathy" is supported by McCalla's finding that crises tend to end when adversaries come to see their situation in a similar way. Realistic empathy counteracts exaggerated fear that is based on the diabolical enemy-image, "since it immediately humanizes the image of the enemy and makes it possible to recognize, for instance, the possible defensive motives behind his most aggressive behavior."[112] It also counteracts "the process of selective inattention, because absence of realistic empathy is probably the most inclusive, the most predictable, and the most war-promoting of all the forms of selective inattention. What is or may be in the mind of an opponent is one of the most important things to think about if we want peace, but also one of the easiest to push out of our minds."[113]

According to White, three kinds of lack of empathy have been "pervasive on both sides of the East–West conflict, and perhaps on both sides of every acute international conflict:"[114] "not seeing an opponent's longing for peace," "not seeing an opponent's fear of being attacked," and "not seeing an opponent's understandable anger."[115] Additional problems may be caused by the operation of the assumption of self-interested rationality. Psychologists have shown that selfish motivation is commonly regarded with some degree of hostility. For example, Steven Fein and James Hilton argue that "perceivers evaluate social actors more negatively when suspicion about ulterior motives is present, even when those perceivers do not have strong evidence that those ulterior motives in fact influenced their behavior."[116] Dale Miller and Rebecca Ratner have recently drawn together the findings of five separate empirical analyses which strongly suggest that human beings generally overestimate the influence of rational self-interest on both the attitudes and the behavior of others.[117] If this is the case, the realist emphasis on rational self-interest serves to make the judgment of foreign policy makers rather less than more realistic. In addition, there seems to be a certain amount of risk that an assumption of the essential selfishness of all human beings could lead to paranoia about other actors' intentions, especially under the added pressure of a political crisis.[118]

A second type of misperception are those of a "cognitive" nature, meaning simply that they cannot be as readily attributed to underlying emotional or motivational inclinations as the above. Prevalent among these are the effects of preexisting beliefs, such as images or stereotypes, on present perception. During a process of "assimilation of information to pre-existing beliefs,"[119] all evidence that is "dissonant"[120] or "out of balance"[121] with such images or stereotypes is disregarded. According to White, "the most conflict-promoting form" of such an image "is an established Good Guys–Bad Guys picture of the political world."[122] He eloquently describes the establishment of such an image:

> The origin of that world-picture (apart from the considerable elements of realism that it typically contains) is probably mainly subconsciously motivated. Over a period of many years it can be gradually built up—a little motivated exaggeration of the opponent's wickedness here, and a little motivated selective inattention to one's own wickedness there, but almost always in those same two directions. It can be likened to a great flywheel, too heavy to be set in rapid motion all at once by any ordinary amount of force but having much momentum once it is well started. It creates confident expectations that whatever the diabolical enemy does will have evil motives and harmful effects, while whatever the good self does will have good motives and good effects. Those expectations, in turn, influence the perception of any new situation, especially if that new situation is at all ambiguous—open to varying interpretations—as most new situations are. *That* process is mainly cognitive, since there is a vast amount of evidence, in everyday experience as well as experimental psychology, that expectations influence perception. Expecting evil, human minds tend to put the worst possible interpretation on whatever the enemy does; expecting good, they tend to put the best possible interpretation on whatever their own group does. It is even possible that the whole effect of subconscious motives on present perception is the result of this two-stage process. They affect expectations, and expectations, by a process that is perhaps purely cognitive, influence perceptions of a present situation and behavior in it.[123]

This process is driven by two related psychological mechanisms: the tendency of dichotomous thinking to blur distinctions within either of the two categories and the spread of attribution within these categories. Together, they have the following effect: "When the political world is divided between Good Guys and Bad Guys, perceived distinctions within the Bad Guys part of the world tend to be blurred, and the attribution of evil therefore tends to spread throughout that part of the world."[124] Edward Jones and Richard Nisbett made the valuable distinction between dispositional and situational attribution, according to which an actor "tends to attribute his actions to the situation he is in. He feels that anyone faced with that situation would have done something like what he did or is now doing. An Observer on the other hand, especially if his interests are hurt by what the actor does, tends to attribute it to a lasting inherent 'disposition' in the actor. . . . The actor is, in two words, a Bad Guy."[125] Attribution theory finds that once a person is assumed to be "bad," his actions tend to be automatically perceived as "bad," and vice versa. Motivational assumptions play a central role in this process as a "bridge" between judgments of an opponent's actions and judgments of an opponent's character.

Two processes that attribution theory has found to play a major role in this context are the "injured-innocence mechanism" and the human tendency to universalize one's own perceptions. The first has to do with the fact that the judgment of another's actions is strongly affected by the context in which that action occurs. For example, "[B]ecause each nation believes it is obviously innocent of any aggressive intention, it tends to infer that any strenuous arming by its opponents must have an aggressive purpose."[126] Such a way of thinking presupposes that the opponent knows of the actor's "innocence" or lack of aggressive intentions, which is obviously rarely the case. The second process may reinforce this error by leading an actor to assume that what is obvious to him is equally obvious to the opponent. According to White, "[E]mpathy with the perceptions of others, when their perceptions differ from one's own, is an acquired art, calling for some mental effort as well as sophistication."[127] He comes to the conclusion that "in the business of preventing war the most vital kind of learning is to see the world in a more and more differentiated way, with more and clearer distinctions between its various parts and aspects."[128]

As studies such as White's can show, realist motivational assumptions may introduce error into the foreign policy–making process by supporting both motivational and cognitive types of misperception. As Vertzberger points out, "[W]hen motivational biases affect decision makers' behavior, the observer cannot easily predict the state's behavior because such obvious causal factors as the situation, state interests, or past behavior are modified by psychological needs and personality traits, which are difficult to observe directly or infer indirectly and about which information is almost impossible to validate."[129] What this means, of course, is also that hypotheses linking motivational biases to behavior are extremely difficult to test.[130] The realist psychology and logic of argument and the evidence that does exist, however, suggest that the bias introduced into policy making as a result of the dominant status of the realist paradigm can be expected to be divisive and competitive and, thus, potentially harmful in its real-world effects.

Contemporary realism assumes the empirical validity of self-interested rationality and the primacy of the motive of power. By assuming the essential selfishness of all human beings, realism creates a reliance on distrust, which favors negative interpretations of others' intentions and restricts the range of rational reactions for realist policy makers in ways that favor competition and conflict. Realist policy makers consistently fail to acknowledge that opponents may be motivated by fear or that they may not be inherently aggressive, even though they understand their own competitive and aggressive moves to be motivated by the need for self-defense and by rational self-interest. They also fail to acknowledge that opponents may be motivated by collectivist forms of pride, since such "social" motives are supposed to be irrelevant in international politics. It may well be expected that this particular failure of "realistic empathy" could cause major problems for Western policy makers in their interactions with less individualistic societies, such as those of the Islamic world. If it is obvious that other actors are motivated by some kind of pride, that pride is interpreted after the Hobbesian fashion as inherently irrational and destructive. Realists deny that they themselves may be motivated by any kind of pride, or by irrational fear, yet, as studies such as White's show, this is far from true.

Perhaps the psychological appeal of "grim realism" operates hand in hand with the incentives created by the status of realist theory to reinforce the kinds of misperceptions discussed by White. Whereas prescriptive realism would of course suggest that policy makers should try to avoid such misperceptions, since they lead them to act less than rationally, based on an unrealistic assessment of their situations, such misperceptions might in fact be direct consequences of the assumptions about human nature that underlie the realist paradigm.

In addition to studying the possible psychological effects of realist motivational assumptions on foreign policy decision making, it is useful to observe the political effects of the operation of the realist paradigm. If the above suspicions are supportable, we should be able to identify particular patterns in international interaction that are associated with realist policies. According to Margaret Hermann and Joe Hagan, "[T]he view that the world is anarchic . . . leads to a focus on threats and security, a sense of distrust, and a perceived need for carefully managing the balance of power. Leaders with this view must always remain alert to challenges to their states' power and position in the international system."[131] John Vasquez has even argued that "the rise to power of militant hardliners who view the world in such realpolitik terms is a crucial prerequisite for war."[132]

The work of Jack Snyder is interesting in this context, as he has made some headway in the study of the role played by strategic concepts in the formation of national policy. Attempting to explain "the recurrent problem of self-defeating aggression among great powers," he finds it largely attributable to the "myth of security through expansion."[133] This myth, which is the core of realist strategic advice, is found to affect the domestic process of policy development through functioning effectively as a foreign policy ideology. Snyder cites as an example of overexpansion U.S. global containment strategy during the Cold War and shows how this strategy was encouraged through the use of the "domino theory" and other arguments related to the "security through expansion" myth.

Ernst-Otto Czempiel has discussed the effects of the dominance of realism in Europe, during and after the Cold War. He begins by observing that realist balance-of power politics has always failed to actually prevent war here. In fact, between 1815 and 1945, seventy-one wars were fought in Europe, among them the two world wars. Between 1945 and 1962, twelve actual wars were fought, while "the greater east–west conflict . . . continually threatened to lead to nuclear cataclysm."[134] Czempiel quips that "realism has after all been successful. Only it has produced war, not peace."[135] The familiar claim that realist strategic policies have prevented the outbreak of nuclear war is, of course, impossible to either prove or disprove. What is undoubtedly true is that the perception of the danger of war, both conventional and nuclear, remained extremely high in Europe throughout the Cold War decades. Czempiel's judgment is clear: "To believe that the security dilemma can be ameliorated by a strategy of strategic balancing is to fool oneself."[136]

Czempiel suggests that the conception of a security dilemma, if it ever was appropriate, is dangerously anachronistic in the world of modern industrialized nations.[137] This is a world characterized by a high degree of interdependence, in which states, along with a large variety of other important actors, pursue a variety of goals, among them many that require international coordination and cooperation. It is a world in which national foreign policies are only partly determined by military security requirements and largely depend on varying constellations of societal interests.

Czempiel echoes early-twentieth-century idealist writers, who already held that "industrial modernization rendered [political realism] . . . increasingly anachronistic and dangerous."[138] Andreas Osiander observes that, while twentieth-century realists typically charged idealists with a naiveté that they were sure history would invalidate, "from a post-1989 perspective the picture seems reversed. It would now appear that it was the early twentieth-century IR Idealists who had the correct long-term prognosis, while the adoption of the rival realist paradigm by academic IR since the late 1930s was based on a shortsighted interpretation of events at that time."[139] Osiander answers Hedley Bull's accusation that idealists are guilty of an "unlearning of old lessons"[140] with the suggestion that it may be that "the most serious shortcoming of Realism is . . . its refusal or inability to learn the lessons of modernity."[141]

Steven Forde, as well, finds that "classical realists take the worst moments of crisis and war as epitomes of the international climate, something non-realists regard as tendentious. Under normal conditions, they argue, the costs or risks involved in moral action are not nearly as great as the realists claim, and the benefits of moral consensus and cooperation greater."[142] Nonrealists generally argue that mutually beneficial cooperation among nations is more common than realists contend, and that the realm of international politics is not "sufficiently *lawless* to be fairly depicted as a latent 'state of war.'"[143]

> Overall, non-realists would contend that few states are as aggressive and dangerous as Machiavelli would have them be and few exhibit the paranoid reactions to anarchy that Hobbes and other realists describe. Under actual conditions it is misleading to say that states are "compelled" to abandon all restraints to protect themselves. It is usually appropriate at most to speak of certain *risks* states run in acting ethically, and the traditions of moral thought would hold that such risks are ordinarily small enough that states have a moral duty to take them.[144]

According to many of its critics, realism overlooks that the pervasive insecurity concerning the motives and considerations of other actors which characterizes the security dilemma does not truly exist among at least the developed nations of today's world. Its outlook is not only anachronistic but dangerous, because, by assuming such insecurity and preparing the appropriate defenses, realist policies can create a security dilemma that is the more dangerous because it has been established in this way. The reason is that a potential opponent who observes defensive postures that are evidently not necessary has all the more reason to interpret them to be offensive preparations. Thus, "realism, through its policies, creates a threatening situation, which confirms these policies ex post facto. If it chose a different strategy, the threat would never occur."[145]

Finding that NATO strategy, which is of course based on the realist rationale, has won out against alternative conceptions in the scramble for a post–Cold War order, Czempiel argues that Europe can expect to continue to face the structural conditions of an "architecture of security," based on the same axioms that reigned supreme in the preceding decades.[146] "This does not make renewed conflict inevitable, but it does not establish political order, does not strengthen cooperation, and opens possibilities for fresh confrontations."[147] Czempiel even suggests that NATO leaders might be tempted to resort to a "self-fulfilling policy" strategy in order to provoke reactions that could "prove," ex post facto, "the appropriateness of its politics and the importance of its existence."[148]

8

A Self-Fulfilling Prophesy?

This chapter will argue that realism functions as a self-fulfilling prophesy and that this is an important reason why the paradigm has maintained its status in spite of the bias it contains. It also summarizes the role played by motivational assumptions in the self-perpetuation of the realist paradigm.

The Problem of the Self-Fulfilling Prophesy

A number of scholars have examined the potential of scientific theories to function as self-fulfilling prophesies. Most evidence for the existence of this problem has been gathered by critics of rational choice theory. Representative here is Mark Petracca, who suspects that "public policy fashioned on the assumption of self-interested behavior may beget precisely such behavior when implemented."[1] More recently, psychologists Dale Miller and Rebecca Ratner have warned that, even though "homo economicus is a social construction, not a biological entity . . . myth or not, the image of humans as self-interested agents has powerful social and psychological consequences. Myths can create reality."[2] In another recent study, which has received auspiciously little attention in rational choice circles, Robert Frank, Thomas Gilovich, and Dennis Regan have investigated the effects of studying microeconomic theory on the behavioral strategies of students. They begin with the observation that, "from the perspective of many economists, motives other than self-interest are peripheral to the main thrust of the human endeavor, and we indulge them at our peril."[3] While earlier studies had examined the likelihood of economists to exhibit behavior that corresponds with this view, they had failed to establish a causal relationship between theoretical perspective and behavioral strategy.[4] Frank, Gilovich, and Regan, on the other hand, find plausible and statistically significant evidence that the mere exposure to the idea that individuals are rational utility-maximizing egoists increases the tendency of individuals to display the corresponding behavior, that is, to "defect" or "cheat" in Prisoner's Dilemma or bargaining games as well as to be less inclined toward charitable giving.[5] The authors suggest that the types of behavior predicted by rational choice theory, such as for example "free riding," are less "natural" than assumed, but are instead learned and encouraged by exposure to the theory. They conclude that, "first, . . . economics training encourages the view that people are motivated primarily by self-interest. Second, there is clear evidence that this view leads people to expect others to defect in social dilemmas. Third, there is also clear evidence that when people expect their partners to defect in social dilemmas, they are overwhelmingly likely to defect themselves."[6]

If scientific theory does indeed have the potential of functioning as a self-fulfilling prophesy, the role of the theorist becomes precarious. Moreover, as Petracca explains, "[E]ven if the assumptions of rational choice theory were true and mankind was accurately defined by self-interest and maximizing behavior, we must ask whether this is a permanent state and whether political science should be employed to justify it."[7] It is hard to imagine that any member of the scientific community would make it their research goal to encourage selfishness among human beings. What is more likely is that rational choice theorists, just like realists, generally assume human nature to be stable or at least highly unlikely to respond to reform efforts. This assumption, however, which makes them pessimistic of their own power to improve the reality they examine, is in spite of its enormous implications not commonly made explicit nor defended by either realist or rational choice theorists.

A few scholars have levied criticisms similar to the above at the realist paradigm of international relations theory. Thus, Ernst-Otto Czempiel holds that "realism as a strategy recommends a behavior, the implementation of which serves to confirm realism as a theory."[8] Laurie Johnson agrees that, by counseling prudent adherence to the realist worldview, realism becomes a "self fulfilling prophesy."[9] The problem of the self-fulfilling prophesy is a complex one. The way theories actually become self-fulfilling is by establishing so-called reflexive predictions. A reflexive prediction is one that "comes true because it comes to the attention of actors on the social scene whose actions will determine its truth-value."[10] Reflexive predictions function as necessary conditions for the events they predict. They do so by influencing the perceptions and expectations of decision makers whose actions can bring about those events.

The concept of a reflexive prediction helps to explain how realist theory can come to support its propositions with evidence that it has itself created.[11] However, the fact that scholarly expectations are confirmed by policy makers that heed scholarly advice is not the only relevant aspect to this problem. The self-fulfilling prophesy of realism functions as well both within the policy-making arena and within the context of realist scholarship. It does so in the policy-making arena by encouraging both motivated and unmotivated misperceptions. These misperceptions encourage behavior that, in turn, tends to elicit the expected responses from other actors. It does so within realist scholarship by affecting the development of theories and models in ways that allow researchers to cling to their assumptions. While the former process was discussed in the previous chapter, the following section will examine the latter.

The Prophetic Status of the Realist Paradigm

Why has the realist paradigm been so successful over the years? Realists attribute its success primarily to its "inherent descriptive, explanatory, and predictive strengths."[12] In addition, they make the point that the realist image of the world "most closely approximates the image held by practitioners of statecraft."[13] The question is whether realism is realistic because it adequately captures a reality that is independent of the theory, or whether it is realistic because it has such an impact on our interpretations of reality that it can, in effect, function as a self-fulfilling prophesy. Realist responses to the suggestion that realism may function as a self-fulfilling prophesy have ranged from the fatalistic to the cynical. According to Paul Viotti and Mark Kauppi, realists may hold either that they have no interest in being policy-relevant, or that "there is nothing inherently wrong with being policy-relevant."[14] The first attitude is apparently assumed to absolve theorists from all responsibility for the consequences of their activities; the second fails to take seriously the risks introduced by realist biases. Critics of realism are commonly accused of basing their attacks on a selective reading of realist works, and it is never quite clear which works one would have to read to be able to criticize realism at all. Finally, as a last resort, realists rely on their pessimism, making the argument that, even if the critics were right, it would still be too dangerous not to counsel adherence to the dictates of Realpolitik. That, of course, begs the question.

It is difficult to deny that the success of the realist paradigm has much to do with the rhetorical strategies it employs in its justification. It is, for example, commonly acknowledged that the appropriation of the label of *realism* has served the paradigm exceedingly well. Viotti and Kauppi explain:

> Realists could claim that they were dealing with the world as it actually functioned. The idealists, on the other hand, were supposedly more concerned with what *ought* to be. "Yes," a realist might say, "I, too, wish the world were a more harmonious place, but that unfortunately is not the case." Those persons who were placed in the idealist camp certainly did not choose this particular label for themselves. Who did? The realists. By so doing, the opposition was stripped of a certain amount of legitimacy. Idealism conjured up images of woolly-headed professors, unsophisticated peace advocates, and impractical, utopian schemes.[15]

Realism is also seductive by virtue of its increasing association with scientific methodology. Over the course of its evolution, realism has become "better grounded scientifically and placed within the context of the positivist view of how we comprehend reality. The positivist approach to knowledge reigns supreme in the natural and social sciences. As a result, any image of international politics that can be presented in the cloak of positivism is immediately granted a certain stature."[16]

A recent collection of essays edited by Francis Beer and Robert Hariman explores how realism functions as a persuasive discourse. They point out that, grounded as it is in the history of political philosophy as well as in the history of science, and historically linked to the emergence of the sovereign nation–state, realism functions simultaneously as an epistemology, an ontology, and a rhetoric. They stress that the persuasive power of the realist "narrative" should not be underestimated. As an ontology,

> it produces a coherent account of the international environment that coordinates all the key elements for representing human motivation: an actor (the nation–state) in a scene (the condition of anarchy, a state of nature) uses an agency (calculation) to act

> (the application of force) for a purpose (the national interest). In addition, by articulating this simple but powerful calculus as a universal, even tragic condition, the narrative suggests that it, and it alone, can equip one to survive and explain the natural conditions of state competition.[17]

As a rhetoric, realism adopts an antirhetorical strategy. As Hans Blumenberg explains, "[I]n the modern age anti-rhetoric has become one of the most important expedients of rhetorical art, by means of which to lay claim to the rigor of realism, which alone promises to be a match for the seriousness of man's position."[18] Beer and Hariman observe that, as realism's ontological, epistemological, and rhetorical claims "are articulated together in realist discourse, and particularly as they are counterposed against other discourses labeled utopian, idealistic, moralistic, legalistic, ideological, partisan, emotional, or rhetorical, the persuasive effect is comprehensive. Realism becomes not just an account of world politics, but the predominant context for explanation, evaluation, and action."[19]

While all the above points contribute to the success of realism, a full understanding of the reasons for the status of the paradigm also requires us to ask how it could *not* have been successful. In the following paragraphs, I will draw on the theories of Karl Popper, Thomas Kuhn, and Imre Lakatos, all of whom have made their own significant contributions to contemporary views on the growth of knowledge and the evolution of science. In short, my argument will be the following: Realism widely functions as the "normal science" of international relations and foreign policy theory.[20] Thus, as Kuhn has pointed out, its status could only be weakened by an acknowledged accumulation of discoveries that contradict its central claims. In addition, as Lakatos explains, individual realist theories will only be discarded if they can be replaced with theories that can be shown to possess greater explanatory power.[21] The problem here is the following: First, the existence of facts that contradict central hypotheses of realism is simply not acknowledged by staunch realists.[22] Instead, they are more likely to adopt ad hoc assumptions or reinterpret their own arguments in an ad hoc fashion to protect their theory from refutation.[23] They do so, in the words of Popper, "only at the price of destroying, or at least lowering, its scientific status" by rendering it irrefutable.[24] Second, as a further consequence, it becomes virtually impossible for rival theories to demonstrate superior explanatory power. After all, realism seems in principle able to explain practically everything.

Popper is considered the "father" of critical rationalism, a scientific epistemology formulated in self-conscious opposition to methodological positivism. According to Popper, it is vitally important that theories be refutable.[25] Part of the reason are the difficulties involved with confirming theories.[26] However, refutability, or falsifiability, is not only important because it is so difficult, if not technically impossible, to verify empirical claims, but rather because, even if they could be, the knowledge thus derived would be useless to science if it were not also, in principle, falsifiable.[27] Falsificationism is primarily an epistemological strategy that rests on, first, a critical attitude toward supposed truths and, second, the belief in the power of human reason, properly disciplined, to avoid the worst temptations to rely on motivated misrepresentations of reality. It does not dispute the foundational assumptions of positivism, but rather rejects its "attitude" toward the growth of scientific knowledge and the role of the scientist.

Popper rejects as "pseudoscience" and "dogmatic" any epistemological approach that cannot pass the "falsifiability criterion" and that relies on predetermined "laws" of human behavior. He cites as examples Marx's historicism and Freud's psychoanalysis, which "saw confirming evidence everywhere; the world was full of verifications of the theory. Whatever happened always confirmed it."[28] He proposes a set of methodological rules which, in essence, suggest that science advances by initially unjustified guesses followed by unrelenting criticism and testing.[29] The proper "criterion of the scientific status of a theory is its falsifiability, or refutability, or testability."[30] While, strictly speaking, only single empirical claims, such as hypotheses, are falsifiable, theories and paradigms are refutable if they consist of falsifiable claims and if it is clear which evidence would lead to their rejection. Popper insists that knowledge grows only through trial and error, or the correction of mistakes.[31] To be able to learn from our mistakes, it is important to decide in advance what evidence we would accept as refutation of our theories, that is, we must define what would constitute a mistake.[32]

At least since Kuhn rocked the ivory tower with his sociological explanation of scientific progress, it has become difficult to deny that the practice of science is characterized by powerful pressures for conformity.[33] He argues that scientific theory and praxis is conducted in the context of paradigms, conceptual worldviews that consist of foundational assumptions, accepted theories, as well as trusted experimental setups, models, and methods. He suggests that science evolves through four distinct stages: one during which a paradigm takes hold, one during which this paradigm achieves the status of "normal science," one in which the appearance of anomalies slowly leads to increased questioning of the paradigm, and the fourth stage, during which the old paradigm declines and alternative research, or "extraordinary science," coheres around what may become the core of the next paradigm. It is misleading to speak of scientific progress from one paradigm to the next, because the knowledge gathered within different paradigms is radically incommensurable. Kuhn uses the examples of the Copernican revolution in cosmology and the replacement of Newtonian by quantum physics to explain that a paradigm shift constitutes a true intellectual revolution, which is triggered by a profound epistemological crisis and reinvents basic interpretive strategies. According to Kuhn, the status of a reigning paradigm can only be weakened by an accumulation of anomalies that contradict its central hypotheses. However, such anomalies do not simply occur and speak for themselves. Instead, they need to be discovered, and their implications need to be expressed by rival theories.

Lakatos holds that scientific progress is characterized by the development of research programs, which consist of methodological rules: "[S]ome tell us what paths of research to avoid (*negative heuristic*), and others what paths to pursue (*positive heuristic*)."[34] He believes that a research program has a "hard core," which defines the program and is not subject to modification, and a "protective belt" of auxiliary hypotheses, which "has to bear the brunt of tests and get adjusted and re-adjusted, or even completely replaced, to defend the thus-hardened core" (133); and he calls "auxiliary theories" those which are devised "in the wake of facts" and lack predictive power (175–176).

Lakatos holds against Popper that "there is no falsification before the emergence of a better theory" (119), that, in other words, "falsification cannot precede the better theory" (122). Not to be misread, Lakatos is not saying that, as long as a theory is not considered falsified, that means that there exists no better theory, nor that the emergence of a better theory would automatically lead to the falsification of the previous one. This is obviously not the case. His point is, instead, that, to reject any theory on the basis of its lack of explanatory power, we must have a set of alternative hypotheses that can be shown to possess more. Lakatos perceives of Kuhnian paradigms as research programs that have achieved a monopolistic hold on science. In opposition to the idea of "normal science," he holds that, instead, competition among different research programs is vital for scientific progress.

In a recent article, John Vasquez sets out to evaluate the realist claim to scientific rigor. He acknowledges three criteria by which scientific theories and paradigms may be judged: empirical accuracy, falsifiability, and the criterion established by Lakatos that legitimate scientific theory must produce progressive research programs.[35] Observing that "a number of analysts . . . argue that, despite anomalies, the realist paradigm is dominant because it is more enlightening and fertile than its rivals," he holds that, instead, "what some see as a theoretical enrichment of the realist paradigm is actually a proliferation of emendations that prevent it from being falsified."[36]

Vasquez holds with Lakatos that "no single theory can ever be falsified because auxiliary propositions can be added to account for discrepant evidence" and that the appropriate task is, thus, "to evaluate a *series of theories* that are intellectually related."[37] He observes that realist and neorealist theories do constitute such a "family of theories," or paradigm. Vasquez notes that "a paradigm can only be appraised indirectly by examining the ability of the theories it generates to satisfy criteria of adequacy."[38] He focuses his examination on a core research program within the realist paradigm: the empirical research conducted to test Kenneth Waltz's balancing proposition. He then sets out to determine whether this research program is "degenerating" or "progressive" by Lakatosian standards.[39] A research program is degenerating "if its auxiliary propositions increasingly take on the characteristic of ad hoc explanations that do not produce any novel (theoretical) facts as well as empirical content."[40] To find out whether a research program is degenerating or not, we must examine whether its "problemshifts," that is, its theoretical emendations, are "progressive" or ad hoc. According to Lakatos, progressive problemshifts must be both theoretically and empirically progressive, that is, they must explain novel facts as well as be able to corroborate their claims, while also being able to account for the findings of their rivals. By comparison, "a degenerating problemshift or research program

. . . is characterized by the use of semantic devices that hide the actual content-decreasing nature of the research program through reinterpretation."[41]

Vasquez observes that,

> while some latitude may be permitted for the development of ad hoc explanations, the longer this goes on in the face of discrepant evidence, the greater is the likelihood that scientists are engaged in a research program that is constantly repairing one flawed theory after another without any incremental advancement in the empirical content of these theories. What changes is not what is known about the world, but semantic labels to describe discrepant evidence that the original theory(ies) did not anticipate.[42]

One effect of such a development is that

> collectively the paradigm begins to embody contradictory propositions, such as (1) war is likely when power is not balanced and one side is preponderant and (2) war is likely when power is relatively equal. The development of two or more contradictory propositions increases the probability that at least one of them will pass an empirical test. . . .
>
> Carried to an extreme, the paradigm could prevent any kind of falsification, because collectively its propositions in effect pose the bet: "heads, I win; tails, you lose." A research program can be considered blatantly degenerative if one or more of the behaviors predicted is only predicted after the fact.[43]

Vasquez finds that this realist research program is "degenerating" because of

> (1) a protean character in its theoretical development, which plays into (2) an unwillingness to specify what form(s) of the theory constitutes the true theory, which if falsified would lead to a rejection of the paradigm, as well as (3) a continual and persistent adoption of auxiliary propositions to explain away empirical and theoretical flaws that greatly exceed the ability of researchers to test the propositions and (4) a general dearth of strong empirical findings.[44]

He concludes that "there have been too many empirical failures and anomalies, and theoretical emendations have taken on an entirely too ad hoc nonfalsifying character for adherents to say that the paradigm cannot be displaced until there is a clearly better theory available. Such a position makes collective inertia work to the advantage of the dominant paradigm and makes the field less rather than more rigorous."[45]

The judgment of Vasquez is supported by Bahman Fozouni, whose analysis of its epistemological liabilities leads him to the conclusion that "political realism, properly understood, is empirically an untenable theory."[46] Fozouni examines various attempts to rescue realism from potential falsifying evidence, among them strategies of "qualifying realism's universal claim by means of additional auxiliary assumptions, incorporating additional explanatory variables and/or changing functional relationships among them, or diluting the theories' nomothetic-deterministic claim by using statistical generalization" (507). He finds that the epistemological liabilities of realism are primarily a function of such attempts by realists and neorealists to save the theory from refutation. He holds that "in many cases such efforts have had the unsalutory effect of impoverishing the paradigm" and that "they all detract in varying degrees from the theory's most desirable epistemic features—amenability to falsification (testability), parsimony, scope, and content" (ibid.). His judgment is that "none of these modifications produces any apparent compensating gains in either the explanatory power or predictive accuracy of the theory" (ibid.).

While the judgments of Vasquez and Fozouni are particularly harsh, other scholars as well have observed that realist theory frequently introduces auxiliary assumptions or hypotheses or adjusts crucial concepts to cope with anomalies.[47] One example of the kinds of ad hoc adjustments that are employed to bolster the explanatory and predictive power of individual realist theories can be found in the varying conceptualizations of the term *power*.[48] The concept of "national interest," which, according to realist theory, motivates the behavior of states, is, of course, rather vague and could encompass any number of different aims.[49] By defining the national interest in terms of power, realists simply shift the burden of explanation to the task of defining a different term. This is a problematic move primarily because it is common practice in the relevant empirical research to define the concept of power not as part of the theoretical, that is, explanatory endeavor, but rather at the stage of the operationalization of variables, that is as part of the "proof."[50] Frequently, such analyses get away with defining the concept of power in whichever ways are covered or supported by the data used or the results expected. The reason such methodologically flawed research is so commonly accepted is that the implicit assumptions it uses to bypass the logic of scientific inquiry are so widely considered indisputable. Ad hoc definitions of the concept of power, which is after all central in capturing the assumed motive behind all state action and is therefore commonly hypothesized to carry great explanatory value, serve to obscure the boldness of realist theory, which consists in ignoring all other possibly relevant motives for state action.

Another example of the ad hoc adjustments employed to preserve the status of the realist paradigm is found in what Jack Donnelly has referred to as "hedges."[51] We have previously observed the tension between ethical and political imperatives that is acknowledged by paramount classical realists. Donnelly describes various ways in which realists actually "hedge the amoral statesmanship that they describe or advocate."[52] He observes that

> such hedges certainly increase the practicality and plausibility of realism in particular cases. They do so, however, by diluting its distinctive character and at the risk of inconsistency. Furthermore, realists typically apply these hedges in an apparently ad hoc or, at best, intuitive way that has led critics to contend that in the end the theory provides little practical guidance or social scientific insight. There is nothing inherently problematic with hedges, but without an account of when the rule applies and when the exceptions do—something that most realists do not even attempt—the power and value of the theory are radically reduced.[53]

Lakatos argues that a research program does not have to be refuted to be discarded. Instead, if it is found to be "degenerating," it will just go out of fashion. However, it is obvious that there exist powerful impediments to paradigmatic research programs or theories simply going out of fashion. Only a strong reliance on the criterion of refutability could counteract these forces. However, as we have seen, realist theories dodge refutation. The fact that realism functions as a self-fulfilling prophesy in the real world contributes to the ease with which the paradigm avoids its scientific refutation: The more widely accepted realist arguments become, the less it appears necessary to question the ad hoc adjustments that are employed to save the theory (and its assumptions) from refutation. The less such adjustments are questioned, the more widely accepted the paradigm becomes. This is how, as Jim George has observed, realism's "self-affirming logic" came to exert its "abiding influence on everyday mainstream theory/practice throughout the Cold War and into the post–Cold War era."[54]

The motivational assumptions of realism play a crucial role in this situation for a number of reasons. It is the realist view of human nature, in general, and of motivation (and rationality), in particular, that supports the self-fulfilling tendency of the realist paradigm: It encourages distorted judgments of the motives of others and creates incentives to respond to their behavior in exactly the ways predicted by the paradigmatic worldview. Realist motivational assumptions are usually not made explicit, which allows for the possibility of their ad hoc modification and the increased flexibility of realist arguments. Realist motivational assumptions also contain a bias in favor of that particular view of human nature which is consistent with the realist worldview as a whole. As a consequence, they function to support realist arguments ex post facto by favoring such interpretations of political events that are consistent with the same bias. By informing reflexive predictions they help render realist expectations self-fulfilling. This circularity, in turn, serves to uphold the traditional choice and usage of realist motivational assumptions. In addition, the use of the concept of rationality both as a prescriptive norm and as a descriptive assumption contributes to turning the realist paradigm into a self-sufficient and self-affirming "project" by blurring the distinction between realism as empirical and realism as normative theory.

Popper's insistence on a critical attitude and the importance of falsifiability is not widely shared. Waltz, for example, cautiously defends the possibility of verification, emphasizing how a theory may gain plausibility by collecting confirming evidence and pointing out that "in the end, one sticks with the theory that reveals most, even if its validity is suspect."[55] However, the refutability of its claims is a crucial prerequisite for replacing an old paradigm with a new one. As a Kuhnian paradigm, realism could theoretically reign indeterminately, not in spite but rather because of the fact that its research programs degenerate. Popper rejects Kuhn's suggestion that critical rationalism overlooks the reality of "normal science." In his view, "the 'normal' scientist . . . has been taught badly. . . . [He] is a victim of indoctrination. He has learned a technique which can be applied without asking for the reasons why."[56] Popper also rejects the normative–relativistic implications of what he calls Kuhn's "myth of the framework." He agrees that "at any moment we are prisoners caught in the framework of our theories; our expectations; our past experiences; our language."[57] However, he holds that this only gives us all the more reason to be critical of such frameworks, and that the position of the critical observer allows us to overcome theoretical incommensurability to make the necessary judgments.

Realism becomes completely irrefutable to the extent that the paradigm truly functions as a self-fulfilling prophesy. Falsifiability depends on our ability to compare the expectations that have been created by a theory to a reality which is independent of that theory. If there is no such independent reality, the criterion of falsifiability is useless. To the extent that science is considered to depend on this criterion, its practice becomes impossible. Realism therefore may not be able to live up to its own scientific standards, as long as it does not actively counter its own tendency to function as a self-fulfilling prophesy.

Ashley Tellis, who has evaluated the scientific status of realist theory historically, using the criteria of critical rationalism, concludes that realism "will not have crossed the threshold of acceptability as a minimally adequate scientific research program until it sheds the last vestiges of naive empiricism in favor of a rationalist-deductive system built around the construction of situationally-determined exit models explicitly incorporating acting individuals as the theoretical primates."[58] His judgment implies that the requirements of critical rationalist social scientific methodology go hand in hand with a need for "reductionism" in the analysis of political behavior. Such reductionism would view the individual as both the unit and the appropriate level of analysis and examine the operation of constraints and incentives not as impersonal forces that possess an independent reality but as they are perceived and interpreted by individual actors. In so doing, it could potentially counteract the high degree of scientific as well as metaphysical determinism that is characteristic of realism. The battle against determinism is part of the critical rationalist project.[59] It is part of the quest for a critical attitude, which may well be our only hope for "scientific objectivity." Popper explains: "The so-called objectivity of science lies in the objectivity of the critical method. This means, above all, that no theory is beyond attack by criticism; and further, that the main instrument of logical criticism, the logical contradiction—is objective."[60] The battle against determinism also counters tendencies toward both scientific hubris and resignation. Popper observes that "there is an influential school of so-called political realists who declare that 'ideologies' as they call them have little influence upon political reality and that whatever influence they have must be pernicious."[61] He disagrees with this view. Moreover, critiquing Hans Morgenthau's *Scientific Man*, Popper explains Morgenthau's realism as the worldview of a disappointed historicist, who has adopted the "irrationalist" position that the social sciences are incapable of offering predictions. Such a position declares social science to be essentially useless and betrays a general despair of reason.[62]

Concluding Observations

The problem of the self-fulfilling prophesy is of course not unique to the realist paradigm of international relations. We have seen that similar criticisms have been raised against other scientific approaches, and that, in principle, any interpretive framework, if it is influential enough, can become self-confirming. However, an exposure of these tendencies as they are exhibited by political realism may be considered particularly important. It is important because of the effects realist policies can have on the lives of human beings. It is clear that realism is enormously influential as a political ideology. It is far from clear that, through lack of proper judgment, it does not serve to inhibit peaceful coexistence and cooperation and increase the risk of violent conflict among and within nation–states. As long as there is only a slight risk that it might, it is necessary that at least part of the discipline of international relations theory adopt a critical as opposed to a defensive attitude with respect to its major assumptions. It is equally necessary that the other part listen.

Steven Forde observes that "drawing on analyses of human nature, on arguments about the necessary structure of international relations, and on laws of political behavior derived from both these sources, realists have quite frequently posed as the clear-eyed apostles of objective reason, confronting the deluded idealism or self-righteous moralism of their fellow men."[63] Certainly, nobody, whether political scientist or policy maker, likes to be called "deluded" or "self-righteous." However, it also seems a likely dictate of "objective reason" that we should not threaten the normative bases for community together with all hope for social improvement for the sake of any convenient paradigm of scientific inquiry.

It is important to keep in mind that "'scientized realism' . . . presumes what actually needs explaining."[64] Paradigmatic realism was, after all, born from ideological realism and follows the Hobbesian strategy of self-justification. As David Johnston has emphasized, Hobbes's works are not designed merely to be academic exercises in political theorizing, but to help persuade those who carry on conflicts between parties and factions to instead seek accommodation and domestic peace.[65] As Robert Walker points out, to modern realists, "Hobbes is perhaps easier to read as a corroboration of the external necessities of realpolitik, but only if his explicitly normative aspirations are read naively, as the way things are."[66] In the service of ideological self-legitimation, Hobbesian realism constructs "a myth of origins in which individuals arise out of an imaginary moment of utilitarian calculation: a fabulous story which continues to mesmerize those economistic utilitarians seated obediently upon the patriarch's knee."[67] The reason such a myth can actually become dangerous is that, when it is used as a theoretical framework for the development of policy, the constraints that are considered given for the purposes of analysis are also taken on faith as being given in empirical settings.

We may not want to conclude with Robyn Dawes that the claims social science makes about understanding human nature are altogether unwarranted and it might be better to withhold all judgment about it.[68] However, we should clearly allow for the possibility that human nature might not be entirely static nor fully determined by the dictates of rational egoism, but that, instead, human beings can and do develop "social" interests along with cooperative patterns of interaction.

In addition, we should counter the realist bias in political decision making by fighting both motivated and cognitive misperception. To do so, in the words of

Robert Jervis, is to "increase explicit and self-conscious judgment and decrease the extent to which decision-makers perceive without being aware of the alternatives that are being rejected."[69] It is commonsensical to expect the motivating power of fear to vary with actors' perceptions of threat. It is equally commonsensical to expect the importance of relative power to vary with the degree of opposition an actor expects in the pursuit of its goals. As Richard Herrmann and his colleagues have put it, "[O]bviously, if cognitive perspectives develop only the enemy image, then they will need to assume that all relationships are perceived in threat-based terms. This may be consistent with the assumptions of neorealism, but fails to capture the variation in both motivation and behavior that characterizes foreign policies. . . . Clearly other images and relationships should be explored."[70]

9

Conclusion: Great Debates and Small Suggestions

This chapter moves beyond the analysis and critique of the preceding chapters to identify some of the broader implications of the arguments made. It attempts to locate these implications within the context of the major scholarly divisions in the field of international relations theory. First, it briefly discusses possible realist responses to the findings of this study and examines options for the future development of realist theory. Second, it explores how a transcendence of theoretical divisions might help to ameliorate the problem of biased motivational assumptions in the study and conduct of international affairs. A comparison of three major schools of international relations theory—realism, liberalism, and constructivism—reveals that each of these schools coheres around one of the three basic motivational complexes of power, achievement, and affiliation. It is suggested that new integrative frameworks to the study of international behavior should incorporate all three of these motives to avoid the type of bias that has been identified in realist theory. Finally, this chapter argues that the search for such new frameworks stands to gain from disregarding entrenched epistemological divisions, which serve to uphold theoretical biases. It concludes with a number of related theoretical and methodological suggestions for the future development of international relations theory.

Realism—Where Do We Go from Here?

All theoretically guided inquiry proceeds from assumptions. In the social sciences, the most basic of such assumptions concern human nature and provide the researcher with an idea of how human beings operate and why they react to external stimuli the way they do. While we cannot make do without such assumptions, it is important to keep in mind that they may not be taken for granted but need to be justified. If they are empirically untenable, they can lead to misleading theories that produce incomplete explanations and inaccurate predictions. They can also function as ideological assertions to support a paradigm in which all respectable scientific inquiry into the subject is expected to take place and in which policy recommendations are developed that are not helpful, simply because human nature does not correspond fully enough with the assumptions made.

I have argued that realist international relations theory suffers from overly pessimistic assumptions about human nature, which can be traced through the Athenian thesis, the political philosophies of Niccolo Machiavelli and Thomas Hobbes, and the arguments of twentieth-century classical as well as structural realism, to contemporary research conducted within the realist paradigm. I have also suggested some of the possible consequences of the use of realist motivational assumptions in the interpretation of international political events and in foreign policy decision making. This study suggests that the problems of realist international relations theory are twofold. First, the assumptions concerning human nature and motivation that underlie such theory are biased in ways which adversely affect the ability of realism to both explain and guide the conduct of international politics. Second, the dominant status of realism as a paradigm of inquiry is associated with methodological practices that protect such assumptions, along with the hypotheses and theories they support, from refutation, while allowing the realist paradigm to function as a self-fulfilling prophesy.

It is usually easier to criticize the arguments of others than to come up with defensible claims of one's own. The purpose of this study has been primarily critical and, thus, perhaps the easiest way to reject its merits is to demand that I come up with a new and improved grand theory of international relations before venturing to question the old. However, it is clear that to be able to improve on what we have we must first know where improvements are in order. If we could not first identify the weaknesses in established theory we would not even possess a motive to begin thinking about new ones. This chapter is devoted to providing some suggestions both on what might become of realist theory and on steps that might lead away from the problems which have been identified in the preceding chapters.

This study has attempted to evaluate realist motivational assumptions on their own merit, as opposed to judging them from a particular theoretical or political perspective. Perhaps my arguments suffer from their own bias, without which my critique would lose all plausibility. I have no choice but to let the reader be the judge of that. I will help by pointing out that my argument is vulnerable to attack at various stages. Critics could, for example, attempt to show that realist motivational assumptions are justifiable representations of empirical reality. Second, they could show that, inaccurate as they may be, the assumptions underlying realist theories do not translate into biased interpretations. Third, they could attempt to make the somewhat self-deprecating argument that realist analysis does not inform policy making. Fourth, they could attempt to show that realist policies are indeed generally more conducive toward defensible political ends than the alternatives, or that at least none of the alternatives are more useful. Finally, they could argue that realist theory is refutable and that the paradigm thus does not have an illegitimate monopolistic hold on scientific inquiry within the realm of international politics and foreign policy. It is perhaps easiest to make the last of these arguments.[1] It would be most important, but extremely challenging, to make the fourth. For the first three of these possible objections, it seems difficult to provide empirical support.

While it is to be wished for that realists as well as their critics take time to engage in reasoned debate and empirical testing of the above claims, the evolution of the realist paradigm continues. A number of proposals concerning the future development of realist theory deserve mention. One course of action that might be suggested is to restrict the range of application of realist theory to those instances where its assumptions fit reality best. However, there may well be no instances in which those assumptions generally fit well enough to be defensible. In addition, it is difficult to know whether they do, as long as the methodological problems we have discussed persist. What is more, within the issue areas in which realism claims to be particularly justified in employing its restrictive psychological assumptions—that is, in the areas of security relations and defense strategy—the effects of such assumptions can be particularly dangerous. In light of the possible harmful effects that have been suggested, it seems risky to continue applying the realist perspective to the study and conduct of any aspect of international affairs.

Another possibility is to reenvision realism as a primarily prescriptive, or normative, theory. In normative realism, motivational assumptions do not have to be realistic, but could be justified as axiomatic tools that are ideally suited to deliver the prescriptions which ideological realism seeks to communicate. It is highly unlikely that realism will develop in this way. As we have seen, realist arguments, since their known inception, have been tied to positivist strategies of legitimation. This is true even for primarily prescriptive realist approaches, such as that of Hobbes. In addition, given the moral implications of and the dangers posed by realist arguments, which we have discussed, it is highly unlikely that realism could ever maintain its dominant status as an openly normative theory.

Stephen Brooks has observed that "neorealism's worst-case focus and emphasis on capabilities to the exclusion of other variables leads its proponents to see little hope for progress in international relations." He therefore suggests that "postclassical realism" with its "probabilistic focus" should split off neorealist theory to form a separate approach.[2] As we have seen, Brooks's characterization of postclassical realism is similar to what is elsewhere called "defensive realism." Thus we may identify as another option open to realists the possibility of retaining their label while attempting to evade the pessimistic determinism that stems from the axiomatic foundations on which the tradition rests. However, this would require a modification of basic assumptions extensive enough to call into question the retention of the realist label. This is why Bahman Fozouni has suggested that "if there is anything in realism worth salvaging it must first be saved from realists and neorealists."[3]

At a bare minimum, scholars who choose to operate within the realist paradigm need to revisit the motivational assumptions underlying their work and to reevaluate those assumptions, using not only the standards of scientific usefulness and practicability but also those of empirical accuracy and logical consistency with the normative objectives of the research effort as well as of the policies consequent to it. Any practical defense of realism as a sound theoretical approach to the study of international politics must at the very least include a recognition of the motivational assumptions used in any given case, of the role they play in the theory, as well as of their consequences for the findings and recommendations that result from the study.[4]

As empirical theorists, realists would be justified in employing any motivational assumptions to the extent to which they are able to defend them as empirically accurate. However, we cannot know the empirical validity of such assumptions as long as realist theory dodges refutation and to the extent that it functions as a self-fulfilling prophesy. As long as such conditions persist, it is safer to modify the motivational assumptions employed in realism to make them more broadly representative of the actual panoply of operative human motives. Doing so would mean sacrificing parsimony, but it would also reduce the temptation experienced by realists to interpret events to fit their theory. The removal of the empirical bias contained within realist motivational assumptions would counter the bias of realist scholarly findings and policies, which is a logical result of the assumptions used in their development.

One important trend in this context is the recent rise of attempts to base realist arguments directly on sociobiological, rather than implicitly or explicitly psychological, foundations. In his study of the role of power in social evolution, Andrew Schmookler has attempted to show how intersocietal conflicts have necessarily developed as human societies evolved.[5] In a recent article, Bradley Thayer employs such evolutionary theory to explain egoism and domination, two human traits that he rightly considers critical components of any realist explanation.[6] The crucial caveat for such research is that social Darwinist determinism as well as the use of selective evidence to bolster it must be avoided at all cost if realists are not to dig themselves in any deeper. It seems highly unlikely at this point that greater realism will be achieved for the paradigm by employing sociobiological assumptions, even as combined with an evolutionary as opposed to a static view of human nature.

On the other side of the revisionist spectrum, a number of economists and philosophers have recently attempted to draw on the disciplines of both economics and moral philosophy in an effort to reintroduce a more comprehensive concept of reason into the study of social interaction.[7] This, it seems to me, is a step in the right direction, which might serve as an example for those contemporary international relations theories that rely on a dubious cognitive model of man which has been uncritically borrowed from the field of economics. It is important for political scientists operating within any paradigm to periodically reevaluate the psychological assumptions on which their theories are based. If these can be shown to be too restrictive, some degree of parsimony might have to be sacrificed to make the theory more useful. The motives underlying human behavior are complex and hardly allow for much stipulation. While it is certainly not impossible to predict action based on motivation, this complexity must be taken into account in any viable theory of international relations. A broadening of motivational as well as cognitive assumptions would both reflect current psychological knowledge and deliver more complete explanations of political behavior, while at the same time countering the unjustified and potentially harmful dominance of the realist paradigm in the theory and conduct of international relations and foreign policy.

Realist international relations theory takes a particular perspective on world politics that is by no means inclusive of all relevant aspects of the reality in question. This is a natural consequence of the fact that this perspective has been developed and refined in opposition to other frameworks of understanding. In fact, over the course of millennia, it has been specifically designed, for political and moral purposes, to counteract such other ways of looking at the world as, most notably, political idealism. This is why both E. H. Carr and Reinhold Niebuhr were prepared to admit that, while realism has potential as a negative and normative theory, it is not, and should not be, understood as a positive and empirical theory of international politics.[8] A positive theory needs to be not primarily designed to point out the weaknesses in other theories, or to counterbalance a view of the world that may be equally skewed in the opposite direction, but it needs to be designed with the purpose of developing the most useful explanations possible for the phenomena of concern. The usefulness of all strictly empirical theory ultimately depends on realistic assumptions and accurate observation. Deductive empirical theory, which is only implicitly built on observation, is, ultimately, only as useful as its assumptions; similarly, inductive empirical theory, which attempts to draw its conclusions directly from an examination of reality, is only as useful as its observations.

In view of the limitations caused by its assumptions about human nature, and of the dangers these assumptions pose for accurate observation, realism is empirically, scientifically, and normatively an untenable theory. It is empirically untenable because it is not realistic. Its assumptions concerning human nature do not merely constitute a "harmless" simplification, but they create and propagate a one-sided and thus biased view of man. Realism is scientifically untenable because, in Lakatosian terms, its research programs are degenerative. To restate, research conducted within the paradigm is too concerned with sustaining the paradigm and not concerned enough with providing new insight. It is possible that such is the fate of all paradigms, yet even if this were the case, such a judgment is no reason to let paradigmatic hegemony continue forever. If we were to come to such a conclusion, it would be far more commonsensical to attempt to foster theoretical and methodological pluralism. Finally, realism is normatively untenable, because it poses risks for the role and functioning of morality and community in human life. At the same time, there exists some evidence that it may influence the process of foreign policy making and, thus, the conduct of international politics, in ways that are difficult to accept as long as we believe that we have the option not to.

The rejection of realism as a legitimate approach to the study of international politics is a bold move indeed. Of course no sensible comprehensive approach to the field will simply go on to ignore realist arguments and conclusions. In this sense, all international relations theory today, no matter how critical of realism, reacts to realist theory and, ideally, improves on one or more of its shortcomings. In addition, it is quite possible that other presently available approaches may be equally incomplete and, perhaps, pose their own practical dangers as well. Frank Wayman and Paul Diehl, for example, conclude that, while realism may not be completely "accurate," it is still the most useful approach we have and that there exist no good alternatives.[9] However, it is a jump from paradigmatic conservatism to the suggestion that even just the search for alternative approaches "throws the realist baby out with its dirty bathwater."[10] Such a view implies that any alternative would not incorporate the useful elements of realist theory. This obviously does not have to be, and should not be, the case.[11] In addition, it is at least worthwhile pondering the merits of Ken Booth's suggestion that neither of the dominant approaches today should be trusted to make sense of the changing realities we are facing and that it is perhaps necessary to reinvent legitimate approaches out of the maze of puzzles and scholarly disagreements that exist today.[12]

It is unlikely that today's world is inherently more complex or confusing to us than yesterday's world was to the ones who came before. What is required is thus not undue conservatism, pessimism, or a panicked search for new certainties but, rather, an assessment of the needs of policy makers and political analysts today and the willingness to address these needs even if this leads away from our theoretical or methodological predilections. Constructive suggestions for the development of new hypotheses have come from a variety of sources. Their theoretical implications are serious enough to warrant further study. For example, Joseph Nye has proposed that the typical threats to national security faced after the end of the Cold War tend to be of a more "communal" rather than a traditional military nature and that this suggests an increased usefulness of liberal as opposed to realist approaches to the study of conflicts.[13] Robert Jervis argues that the post–Cold War world is characterized by increased structural and cognitive complexity, and that, as a consequence, this world requires more value trade-offs and calls for a greater tolerance for ambiguity. Jervis holds that political psychological approaches are useful in drawing attention to several psychological variables that are likely to play important roles in such a world. Among those are actors' beliefs about security and the causes of war, personal propensities toward the aversion of risk, as well as motivated and unmotivated perceptual biases.[14]

While the above and similar plausible suggestions concerning the implications of recent political changes suffer from a natural lack of historical evidence, a comparatively well-defined and growing area of research which is able to develop such data is the study of small state behavior.[15] Realist and especially neorealist theory have traditionally based their arguments primarily on the observation of the behavior of great powers, such as, notably, of U.S. and Soviet defense policies during the Cold War. True to the age-old realist belief that the strong do as they can while the weak do as they must, realist theory does not expect the interests and goals of small states to play a significant role in international politics. The foreign policy options of small states are perceived to be severely constrained by the operation of external necessities, prominent among them the leverage of hegemonic powers. In addition, as we have seen, neorealist theory in particular claims that domestic factors, such as the internal characteristics of states, small and large, may be disregarded in the study of systemic political outcomes. All of these claims have received criticism in studies of small state behavior.

Miriam Fendius Elman has demonstrated the impact of domestic factors on the foreign policies of small states, especially established liberal democracies.[16] Domestic factors, such as public opinion and institutional characteristics, are shown to remain relevant even under conditions of acute external threat. The importance of domestic factors in foreign policy making is also stressed in a recent collection of essays in small state security studies edited by Efraim Inbar and Gabriel Sheffer.[17] Examining the foreign and defense policies of primarily ethnic small states, these essays question the validity of neorealist claims about the compelling influence of structural factors as well as of the assumption of rationality in decision making. Instead, they show how ethnic and other interests determine decision makers' perceptions of challenges and threats. Such studies confirm that motivation plays a crucial role in foreign policy making, and that economic and ethnic interests, which are derived from the motives of "profit" and "honor," respectively, can be particularly crucial. While the role of security considerations cannot be denied, the importance of other factors, such as ethno-national aspirations, remains high even for well-established states facing seemingly clear threats and constraints. According to Sheffer, such findings

> cast additional doubt on the relative significance of structural global and domestic factors in the determination of foreign and defense policies. They also cast doubt on the rationality of the policies pursued by the leaders of the small ethnic states. It is hence questionable whether the neo-realist theory or the "strategic threat perceptions" thesis can serve as adequate basis for predicting the behavior of small ethnic groups in the regional and domestic political arena.[18]

What about the realist argument that small states still do not matter in international politics, since they cannot pursue their interests effectively without the consent of the great powers? John Scott Masker has argued that realist and neorealist theory consistently underestimate the power of small states and of small state regimes to influence international policies. He presents evidence for this claim in the form of case studies of small state security regime politics, which also support the suspicion, voiced in both liberal and constructivist circles, that established patterns of cooperation decrease the relevance of relative power positions.[19] As Richard Ned Lebow has pointed out, an expansion of international relations and security studies to include a genuine interest in the behavior of less powerful states could deliver significant theoretical payoffs by providing the data to inspire as well as to test propositions drawn from competing schools of international relations theory.[20] It may well be suspected that a greater concern with the behavior of less powerful along with hegemonic states would serve to weaken empirical support for realist theory, while strengthening liberal and constructivist claims. In any case, it could help identify the conditions under which external constraints, domestic factors, and particular types of foreign policy goals are more or less relevant, clarifying the limits of either of the major competing approaches.

Alternative theoretical approaches to the study of international relations and foreign policy should be developed based both on such newly developing insights and on defensible trusted findings and arguments. To reevaluate realist insights for their genuine merits we need alternative approaches, new theoretical frameworks of inquiry. Approaches that have been developed in opposition to realism naturally are not useful for this purpose. Instead, what is needed are new integrative approaches, which are developed neither in defense of nor in opposition to one or the other existing approach, but which are based on an updated understanding of relevant actors, goals, and processes. Such approaches could serve us better both in explaining and in testing the findings of existing theories as well as in the development of new insights.

Complementary Motivational Assumptions in International Relations Theory

Contemporary international relations theory is usually presented as divisible into three major theoretical approaches: realism, liberalism, and a third, which usually serves as a catchall category for theories which, broadly speaking, are idealist in orientation and which, for various reasons, do not fit well within the liberal or neoliberal camp.[21] It is not surprising that realist theory has much to learn from the alternative approaches that exist.[22] However, it is particularly inspirational to observe that such alternative approaches cohere around alternative views on human motivation. We have previously learned that the three motives of the Athenian thesis parallel the basic motives that, according to relevant psychological research, in some form underlie all human behavior. These are the motives of fear, profit, and honor, which express the human needs for power, achievement, and affiliation, respectively. While realism concentrates on the first of these motives and needs, the other two categories of international relations theory concentrate each on one of the other two. (See Table 9.1.)

The cluster of theories that may be classed under the "liberal" label includes traditional liberal, neoliberal, traditional institutionalist, and neo-institutionalist approaches.[23] These approaches share basic tenets and are distinguished only through varying main interests and emphases. For purposes of this discussion they may be considered to form one theoretical perspective.[24] The liberal cluster of approaches to the study of international politics has its roots in the free-market liberalism of economic theorists such as Adam Smith, as well as in the thought of Jeremy Bentham and other utilitarians. In the last century, it was heavily influenced by functionalist accounts of international cooperation and gained empirical ground with the rapid development of communications and transport technology and the corresponding proliferation and rise in influence of nonstate international actors, such as nongovernmental or intergovernmental organizations or multinational corporations. The primary field of application of liberal theory widened along with its followership, as the number of liberal democracies across the globe increased throughout the twentieth century.[25]

Liberalism has traditionally been wed to free-market ideology and its insistence that competition without regulatory interference can ensure the harmonious pursuit of prosperity for each and all. The neoliberal approach, developed in the second half of the twentieth century, seeks to explain how, under some circumstances, the need for regulatory arrangements does arise. By stressing "the cultural–institutional context for state action,"[26] neoliberalism uses such explanations to account for coopera-

Table 9.1
The Complementarity of Motivational Assumptions in International Relations Theory

Theoretical Approach	Basic Motive Stressed	Motivational Complex Emphasized	Main Foreign Policy Goal Pursued
Realism	Fear	Power	Security
Liberalism	Profit/Self-Interest	Achievement	Prosperity/Rights
Constructivism/ Sociological Institutionalism	Honor/Recognition	Affiliation	Identity/Membership

tive arrangements, such as regimes.[27] In so doing, it emphasizes the role of economic and, to a lesser extent, other nonsecurity interests. It also acknowledges the effects of value commitments and shared norms on political behavior. As a consequence, it contributes to the identification of ways to overcome collective action problems.[28]

In contrast to realists, liberal theorists argue that the relative importance of nation–states as international actors has declined to the point where it is necessary to take into account the activities of various other political actors at supra-state and sub-state levels to provide meaningful and complete explanations of political outcomes.[29] In addition, liberals tend to question the realist treatment of nation–states as unitary actors, pointing instead to the complex bureaucratic and organizational processes within policy-making institutions that may contribute significantly to the character of the policies eventually adopted.[30]

Neoliberals argue that relations among at least modern industrialized nations are not anarchic but rather highly institutionalized, so that the behavior of these states depends to a considerable extent on rules.[31] The core claim of institutionalism is that "institutions are important determinants of state policy. They affect states' interests by creating both opportunities and constraints, and by legitimating collective norms and rules, which may then be taken for granted by governments."[32] John Ruggie has argued that the "anti-institutionalist posture" of realists such as John Mearsheimer has "failed to grasp the subtle yet integral role of institutionalist objectives" in all sectors of foreign policy making.[33] As a consequence, so Ruggie, realism is "not only wanting but potentially dangerous as a guide to the post–Cold War world."[34] Neoliberals also point out that states are becoming increasingly interdependent in the pursuit of their various goals.[35] Growing possibilities and incentives for communication and cooperation can be found to help redefine national interests and to lead states to adjust their strategies to achieve those interests. This may even lead to the creation of sustained patterns of cooperation, especially in relations among liberal democracies, where an expanded potential for cooperation can drastically reduce not only the significance of military threats and the role of force but also the general importance of relative power positions.

Both realism and liberalism view the world as an arena in which self-interested actors pursue their individual goals. However, realism emphasizes the conflicts that emerge between actors as a result of competition under conditions of vulnerability, whereas liberalism, owing to its traditional free-market optimism, draws attention to the possibilities for the identification of shared interests, the achievement of mutual gains, and the choice of cooperative strategies, which are options even in anarchical settings. The liberal world is one where actors are free to cooperate, even to the extent of entering contracts that will significantly constrain their own autonomy. It is the world of international trade, in which states may rationally sacrifice military strength for access to export markets. It is a world in which issues of military security are, for whatever reasons, less pressing. Absent the pervasive sense of insecurity that reigns in realist theory, the actors of liberal theory are free to pursue their other interests, which are defined largely in economic terms.

Given its philosophical roots as well as the fact that the liberal approach has proven particularly useful in explaining the development of cooperative strategies and institutions in the area of economic policy, it is little wonder that the primary motive assumed to explain foreign policy behavior in liberal theories is the desire for profit. In fact, the high degree of acceptance that the liberal philosophy has received in the Western world can help explain why the motive of profit is widely thought to be so important that it is at times even used synonymously with the idea of self-interest.[36] Generally speaking, liberals can contribute insights into the effects of the motivational cluster associated with the pursuit of happiness, which includes the desire for material comfort as well as the defense of certain personal rights, inasmuch as these rights are understood to be prerequisite to the pursuit of happiness. In psychological terminology, liberals thus contribute a concern with the motive of "achievement" to the realist concern with the motive of "power."

While both realist and most liberal approaches can be classified as materialist in that they perceive of foreign policy decisions as explicable in terms of the material interests of the actors involved, the approaches that form the third category of international relations theory could be classified as idealist, because they stress the impact of ideas and norms on the behavior of decision makers as well as on the ways in which these decision makers define their own needs.[37] Most of the work within this category is either sociological institutionalist or constructivist in orientation.[38]

Sociological institutionalists hold that, to properly understand the nature of international relations, we require knowledge about the motives of relevant decision makers and observe that, traditionally, "realists sidestepped or denied this issue by assuming a common motivation for all states."[39] This has made it difficult, if not impossible, for realists to account for variation and change in foreign policy. To be more useful in this respect, neo-idealist approaches generally draw on decision-making theory, which, as we have seen, naturally emphasizes the importance of decision makers' ideas for their subsequent behavior. Two bodies of research are particularly relevant. First, a range of studies has examined the role played by ideas in informing leadership decisions.[40] Richard Ned Lebow and Thomas Risse-Kappen observe that, "from such a perspective, the most critical feature of the international system is the distribution not of capabilities but of interests and aims."[41] Second, a theoretical approach that emphasizes possibilities for "governance" at the supranational level uses such insights to strengthen the case that "the object (and subject) of foreign policy is not the state but the individual, . . . not an anonymous entity, but human beings with their aspirations for well-being and democratic codetermination."[42]

Constructivist theories argue that "actors cannot decide what their interests are until they know what they are representing—'who they are.'"[43] They examine the processes by which international norms and cultures become part of a state's definition of its own interests.[44] Constructivists conclude that the realist argument that morality plays no legitimate role in international politics fails because it ignores, first, that states are embedded within systems of rules and, second, that interests and ideas are interrelated. They hold that even perceptions, definitions, and uses of power, on which realist theory concentrates, always occur "within a practice which is partly constituted by certain normative ideas."[45] According to constructivists such as Alexander Wendt, the fundamental structures of international politics are social, rather than merely material. These structures not only constrain the behavior of individuals, but they are directly involved in shaping individuals' identities and interests.[46]

Constructivist approaches include research into the development and operation of "epistemic communities," which is indebted to neofunctionalist and cognitive approaches.[47] Such research emphasizes that "between international structures and human volition lies interpretation. Before choices involving cooperation can be made, circumstances must be assessed and interests identified."[48] Recent work in the field of social cognitivism confirms such arguments by illuminating the mechanisms by which individuals develop goals and strategies through social interaction.[49] In addition, research conducted within the field of organization theory can be useful to cognitivists by pointing out ways in which insights concerning individual interest formation and decision-making strategies can be employed in the explanation and prediction of the behavior of social organizations, such as governments.[50]

Constructivist approaches explain progress and change in world politics with reference to changes in actors' perceptions and definitions of their own interests and options. They belong to the idealist "tradition of optimism" insofar as they believe that changes in attitudes can lead to changes in reality.[51] Such changes are usually expected to be the result of interaction. In the words of Wendt, "[C]ollective identity among states could emerge endogenously at the systemic level. Such a process would generate cooperation that neither neorealists nor neoliberals expect and help transform systemic anarchy into an 'international state'—a transnational structure of political authority that might undermine territorial democracy."[52] While the creation of a world state is by no means a necessary outcome of interaction at the systemic level, constructivist approaches are particularly valuable because they draw attention to the effects that such interaction has already had. Based on such insights, sociological institutionalism argues that "the allegedly inescapable consequences of anarchy have been largely overcome by a complex web of multilateral institutions that govern interstate relations and provide mechanisms for solving disputes."[53]

Sociological institutionalism, the idealist variant of liberal neo-institutionalism, relies on constructivist arguments and takes a modern approach to the traditional idealist purpose of elucidating the role of norms in international relations. It draws attention to the spread of a hegemonic culture with a distinctively Western flavor and claims that this culture includes "both a set of evaluative standards [norms] and a set of cognitive standards [rules] that define what social actors exist in a system, how they operate, and how they relate to one another."[54] Sociological institutionalists contend that such a global culture can "shape and define the preferences of actors in ways not related to internal conditions, characteristics, or functional needs."[55]

Together, social institutionalist and constructivist approaches claim that foreign policy actors can accept international norms as part of their own identities and use them to define for themselves what constitutes appropriate behavior. Identity is defined by constructivists to consist of "mutually constructed and evolving images of self and other."[56] Their examination of the role of identity in establishing interests has led constructivists to suggest that conflict in general erupts when actors do not identify with one another, while community and cooperation evolve from identification as expressed through rule-bound behavior.[57] If, for example, as an effect of globalization, foreign policy actors identify with a more inclusive type of international community, this will lead them to seek recognition by the other members of this social group. This recognition is awarded if they act in accordance with the norms and rules of that community and fulfill the expectations of its members.

Neo-idealist approaches in general, then, point to the importance of actors' self-definition or "identity" in policy choice, including an emphasis on the role of norms and the motivating power of community. They stress a third motive behind foreign policy decisions: the desire for "honor," or, in modern terms, the need to be recognized and accepted by one's community. In psychological terminology, constructivists contribute a concern with the motive of "affiliation" to the realist concern with the motive of "power." This motive can help explain foreign policy decisions that would seem irrational or unreasonable if we assumed the priority of fixed security or material preferences. It can also help explain how the roles of security or material preferences in decision making can change in response to changing patterns of international interaction.

Neither of the three approaches discussed above can make a persuasive claim that the other two do not also have a significant contribution to make to the explanation of international political phenomena. As soon as international relations and foreign policy theorists attempt to apply their general understanding of international politics to particular actors in the context of specific situations, they discover that they cannot account for behavior solely in terms of their preferred motive. Instead, it is commonly found that any exhaustive treatment of particular cases requires an examination of all three of the motives discussed.[58] In addition, as Alan Lamborn has argued, the different theoretical approaches basically share one view of how politics works, that is, they agree on the characteristics of the process of strategic interaction.[59] While we can identify such shared perceptual bases, it is difficult to argue that the different theories cannot be made to complement one another's choice of focus.

Some have called for a synthesis of realist and liberal approaches.[60] Such a synthesis would hardly be counterintuitive. The question is whether it would go far enough. While it is difficult to predict how the paradigm will develop in the near future, there are some indications that large parts of realism itself are evolving to approximate a liberal position. The term *mercantile realism* has been coined to characterize an emerging realist approach that recognizes the importance of economic stability and progress for the national interest and the importance of economic power for national security.[61] This approach suggests that realist estimations of the likelihood of conflict within an anarchic international realm still hold, but that, rather than expecting nations to drop bombs on one another, we can expect them to battle each other with tariffs and sanctions. Such analogical projections are, however, precarious, because the realm of economics differs in significant ways from that of foreign policy. For one, it is an area of political activity over which governmental institutions have always had and are, at least by some accounts, having progressively less control. "Mercantile realism" might well require a nonrealist view of the relevant political actors, which it would likely borrow from liberalism. As we have seen, "defensive" or "postclassical realism" as well is venturing far into liberal territory. Will we all end up being more or less pessimistic liberals, celebrating or despairing over the same "end of history"? There is indeed a possibility of the two giant paradigms merging, a grand coalition which, by all pluralist accounts, would require a dedicated extra-paradigmatic opposition. A catchall category of comparatively ill-funded neo-idealist approaches is unlikely to be able to do the job. Such an outlook can fail to worry only those who uncritically accept the traduced wisdom of either realist liberalism or liberal realism.

New integrative approaches should not only draw on realist and liberal theory, but they should also incorporate the basic insights developed in neo-idealist approaches. This is important primarily because both realist and liberal approaches traditionally treat actors' interests as given. Even though neoliberal and neo-institutionalist approaches today seem more inclined to examine how such interests are affected by institutional changes, they usually stop short of developing political strategies based on psychological insights. Neo-idealist approaches seem more promising in this respect. In fact, psychological analyses of foreign policy making foreshadowed the arguments of sociological institutionalism as early as in the 1960s.

When the psychiatrist Jerome Frank set out to examine the psychological aspects of war and peace, he began with the observation that it is reasonable to assume that "aspects of human nature are necessary, although not sufficient causes for war."[62] However, he also observed that "it is hard to discern what those aspects are because they manifest themselves only through sociopolitical institutions, and these change from one era to the next" (287–288). According to Frank, if impulses to power and violence are natural, it is crucial that institutions be developed that control their manifestation for the benefit of humanity. Interestingly, Frank develops a neo-idealist perspective that is supportive of global governance, based on psychological arguments.

He concludes that "the concept of unlimited national sovereignty and, its corollary, reliance on destructive capacity as the final resort in the settlement of international disputes must be replaced by an orderly rather than anarchic international system and by the development of faith in new non-destructive forms of power" (290).

Integrative approaches face a difficult battle against the dominance of the realist penchant for division. Hans Morgenthau could not have been any more clear in his insistence that realism must define the concept of the national interest in terms of power because the realm of politics must be separated from that of economics, in which interest is defined as wealth, as well as from that of ethics, where it may be defined in terms of moral integrity.[63] Integrative approaches must make the case that politics includes economics as well as ethics, and that this is why the interests of political actors must be defined more broadly. This is not a difficult case to make, but it has vast implications of which we need to be aware. A sacrifice in parsimony is probably the least offensive of these implications, while neo-idealist hopes for global governance, even though they are not a necessary component of the perspective, are likely to continue to cause significant political opposition to its integration into mainstream international relations theory.

The benefits of new integrative approaches should be practical as well as theoretical. Alexander George has argued that, besides factual knowledge as well as conceptual and practical guidelines for the employment of political strategies, foreign policy makers require behavioral models that are actor-specific.[64] While it is easy to observe that general theories of international relations are hardly designed to develop such specific models, it is equally clear that they must lay the theoretical groundwork for them. More complete and realistic general behavioral models would be helpful because they could more easily be modified for purposes of case-specific explanation and prediction.

To recapitulate, both the psychological and political psychological literature on the nature and effects of human motivation as well as the main rival theoretical approaches to the analysis of international relations and foreign policy have made important contributions to a more appropriate understanding of motivation that could serve as the foundation for such models and theories. The liberal and constructivist emphases on the motives of welfare and community, respectively, should be employed to complement realist motivational assumptions to provide a more complete account of human motivation. The purpose of this revised account would be to remove the realist bias from the study and practice of foreign policy and international relations and to inform more useful explanatory models. What is needed to accomplish this are integrative frameworks, which could enable analysts to examine the impact of all three motives on foreign policy decisions while avoiding unmanageable complexity.[65]

Transcending the Third Debate

In these final pages, I will suggest basic methodological guidelines that should inform new theoretical approaches to the study of international relations and foreign policy. Theoretical conflicts over the identification of relevant actors, goals, and processes take place in the context of larger methodological disagreements. As we have seen, the epistemology of realism is tied, perhaps inextricably, to the positivist approach to the development of scientific knowledge. If we reject political realism as the appropriate approach to the study of international relations, if we agree that its positivism gives realism not only a significant rhetorical advantage but also has served to support the tendency of the paradigm to function as a self-fulfilling prophesy, we have already assumed a perspective that is critical of positivist epistemology. The proponents of various methodological approaches are debating the values of alternative epistemologies. A cursory overview of major methodological fault lines can help us to identify useful directions for future theory development.

It is common to identify three "great debates" in the history of international relations theory in the United States and, to a lesser extent, in Europe.[66] The first is the debate between idealism and realism, which took its present shape in the late 1930s and early 1940s. The second is the debate between traditionalism and behavioralism, which began in earnest in the 1960s. The third debate has been taking place between positivism and postpositivism, or interpretivism. While there is a tendency for realist theory to be more strongly behavioralist and positivistic in orientation, and for idealist theory to be rather traditionalist or postpositivistic, it is important to keep in mind that the three dichotomies cannot be collapsed to become one without doing serious injustice to and creating harmful limitations for any of the approaches involved.

The third debate involves, first and foremost, the question whether we should attempt to locate explanatory variables in an outside reality or within actors' interpretations of their own "reality worlds." It also concerns the issue of "foundationalism," that is, the question where, if anywhere, to locate the epistemological foundation on which to ground scholarly authority. An early proponent of postpositivist arguments is Peter Winch, who claimed that the methodologies of the natural sciences cannot be usefully applied in the social sciences because the objects of analysis in the latter are self-interpreting actors and their understandings of social phenomena, which are not externally given but linguistically constructed.[67] Postpositivists accuse positivists of a dogmatic and static determinism that disempowers and degrades the human beings which are the objects of inquiry. They observe that positivist approaches tend to rely on empirical methods and behavioral data. As a consequence, they tend to be suspect of such methods and data. Postpositivists such as Mark Neufeld come to the conclusion that "emancipatory" social scientific theory requires both giving up the positivist logic of investigation and replacing it with a reliance on interpretive methods.[68] Interpretive methods generally involve attempts to enter the reality worlds of others, empathize with them, experience their unique worldviews, and then communicate these views to others.

Positivists react to postpositivist challenges by accusing the postpositivist approach of a relativism that threatens the raison d'être of all social science. They frequently reject the results of interpretive studies on the grounds that interpretive methods fail to uphold their own scientific standards of intersubjectivity and testability of propositions. In addition, they point to the strong tendency of postpositivist theory to be inherently normative, if not ideological or polemical in conception, arguing that the results that are developed from within such approaches necessarily fail to provide any generally valid insights.

It is not surprising that, on both sides, such accusations, primarily designed as they are to defend one's own perspective, fail to seriously address the points raised by the rival approach. While it is important to be aware of the conflicts they express, real progress can only be achieved by moving from an identification of areas of disagreement to an identification of better alternatives.

In an effort to transcend the division created by the third debate, Yale Ferguson and Richard Mansbach respond to Yosef Lapid's earlier call for a "third way" that could run between the extreme positions of "celebration" and "despair" to provide practical guidance in the face of prevailing theoretical as well as historical uncertainty.[69] They reject what they call "pseudorealism" and the "realist mythology," arguing that international relations theory instead needs to incorporate a concern with the role of values and the motive of affiliation as well as with the role of leadership and the causes and processes of political change.[70] Their third way involves the rejection of relativism and the defense of legitimate uses of empirical methods on the one hand, and a concern with problem solving and an openness toward interpretivist arguments on the other hand. It also supports interdisciplinary learning and the integration of knowledge created by different approaches. The authors suggest that opportunities for such learning and mutual enrichment could increase significantly if we could avoid getting "hung up" on epistemological debates.

John Vasquez, joining the search for a third way, observes that "post-positivism and postmodernism can have beneficial effects as long as they do not become the new orthodoxy."[71] Rather than the drawing of epistemological and methodological battle lines, what is needed is "more comparison of research findings using different methodologies and more rigorous appraisal of theories and paradigms."[72] Third-way approaches such as that of Michael Nicholson defend the applicability of empirical methods in the social sciences while attempting to instill greater sensitivity to the limitations of such methods and an awareness of the problems of positivist epistemology.[73]

New integrative approaches to the study of international relations and foreign policy should be informed by such attempts to overcome the artificial divisions created by all three debates and by the third debate in particular. In the following, I will identify some basic guidelines that could help to further define the third way for international relations theory. In short, the approach I advocate acknowledges the need for interdisciplinary perspectives and the role common sense can legitimately play in scientific inquiry. It transcends the division between idealist and realist political theory by avoiding grand schemes, on the one hand, as well as pessimistic determinism, on the other hand. In addition, it transcends the fruitless opposition between behavioralist and interpretive methods by stressing that we should employ the behavioralist–empirical capabilities that have been developed in the past decades. However, we should do so in awareness of their limitations and potential problems. It stresses that a concern with solving the problem at hand should lead researchers in their choice of methods, rather than the other way around, and that, within limits, any method of inquiry that can help us solve an important problem is a legitimate method.[74]

It is neither necessary nor desirable that the study of international relations and foreign policy proceed without the use of empirical theory or methods. While Winch's characterization of the objects of inquiry of the social sciences may well be correct, the very use of the term *object of analysis* indicates that even self-interpreting actors and their linguistically constructed understandings have to be "objectified" if we are to so much as speak about them. Karl Popper has defended the need for a conceptual detachment of scientific knowledge from the person of the scientist and for the criticism of such knowledge independent of its creator.[75] It is important to understand that the idea of the objectification of knowledge is legitimized not by its empirical content but by its usefulness as a guiding principle in the development and judgment of knowledge. It is problematic insofar as it may be abused to bolster the position of the scientist vis-à-vis his or her objects of inquiry, for political or other reasons. However, such abuse is not an integral part of the approach and thus may not be a sufficient reason to reject it. The strategy of basing the authority of the scientist on the hierarchy of observation does not have to and should not remain a prerogative of positivist science.

Finding the third way requires not only that criticism be regarded as a constructive endeavor rather than as an invitation to fortify one's own points of view at all cost, it demands that a critical attitude toward the data, methods, and findings that comprise our own analyses be considered an integral part of our own efforts. The divisions created by the three great debates can only be overcome by the identification of standards of judgment that both sides can accept as valid. Such standards cannot be "discovered." They have to be created and confirmed in praxis. Perhaps the norm of healthy skepticism toward the pronouncements of experts is as much common ground as is left to us. The only way to demonstrate that we share this common ground, if we do, is through a self-critical attitude. If we do not, the prospects for our mutual education are indeed bleak.

New approaches should be developed based on a concern with problem solving and the human relevance of our research efforts. Finding the third way requires the realization that "understanding" means more than pointing out relations between causes and effects. It means creating the preconditions for judgment. While this does not mean that observation and measurement should proceed simultaneously with judgment, or that we should officially allow personal preferences to affect the results of our analyses, it does mean that it is part of the analyst's responsibility to conduct such investigations that might be useful to human ends. The acceptance of the responsibility of science to contribute toward human ends must be motivated by a minimum of optimism. If we do not believe that human affairs can be improved, it is unclear what role science should play at all. To reject even minimal optimism out of hand as naiveté, as realist political theory frequently does, seems difficult to justify.

In our search for the proper assumptions that should underlie our theories we should, inasmuch as we do not test these assumptions, be guided more by common sense and less by ideology, no matter how benevolently motivated. To be sure, one man's common sense may well be the source of another's utter consternation. We do not have to forget that common sense is no objective category to be able to employ it as a standard. While it is not acceptable to reject a theory on the grounds that it does not correspond to the critic's idea of common sense, to reject common sense as a way of judging our own statements, just because our own idea of common sense may not be widely shared, is a particularly tragic case of throwing the baby out with the bathwater.

In addition to employing common sense in the choice of our assumptions, we need to cultivate a profound disrespect for disciplinary boundaries.[76] In particular, the disciplines of history and psychology are inseparable from that of political science, and, depending on the issue at hand, it may often be necessary to venture into other fields to develop sensible judgment in one's area of research. The discipline of political science rests on the discipline of history. It even makes sense to say that history—past, present, and future—is the very subject matter of our discipline. When developing inductive political theories based on the observation of historical events, it seems reasonable to consult the judgment of historians. While it may not in all cases be possible or even to be wished for, the compatibility of political–scientific interpretations with historical judgment, insofar as such judgment is discernible, can of rights be considered to increase their plausibility.

Moreover, as any social science, political science legitimately draws on the discipline of psychology to explain first-image phenomena, the preferences, perceptions, and decisions of human beings.[77] Once again, we do not have to become Freudian or Jungian political scientists and concentrate our political analyses on the inner workings of the human mind. However, to propagate views of the psyche which no psychologist could support, as assumptions or as explanations, seems a risky endeavor indeed. As Richard Herrmann insists, "the importance of motivation makes it imperative to base inferences about a country's foreign policy on its elite's perceptions of its goals, the nature of the environment in which it operates, and the foreign and domestic constraints it faces."[78] If we are to understand such perceptions, and properly evaluate the effect of motivation on political decisions, we require substantial knowledge of psychology.

We should be aware of the fact that psychological studies on motivation have been fighting to stand their ground against the cognitive revolution in their own discipline.[79] As Lawrence Wrightsman observes, "[T]he conceptions reflected in the humanistic-psychology movement and in personal-construct theory are in some ways shifts away from the predominant orientations (which heavily rely on determinism and an analysis of irreducible essences)."[80] Psychological approaches that employ such conceptions are fighting a difficult battle against those which employ more restrictive behavioralist assumptions. Not only can we learn from such parallel conflicts in other disciplines, but, by testing the findings of motivational studies in the nonexperimental analysis of social behavior, we can play a constructive role in them.

Another division that is not only arbitrary but a hindrance to the necessary integration of complementary research findings is the division between the areas of international relations and foreign policy as subfields of political science. This division has served to encourage the continued development of international relations theory toward a strong emphasis on structural systemic approaches, while it has upheld the focus on psychological approaches in the field of foreign policy analysis. The subfields are threatening to drift further and further apart, even though, as Valerie Hudson and Christopher Vore have observed, the subdiscipline of foreign policy analysis can provide the subdiscipline of international relations with a theory of human political choice, which is essential for the explanation of the behavior of collectivities.[81] What is truly needed is a rapprochement of the subfields to inspire integrative frameworks that take account of both psychological and structural factors to be able to actually explain and predict the behavior of international actors.[82]

Finally, perhaps one of the most important truths to keep in mind is that any war of labels is just that: a war of labels. Academic name-calling is no more productive than that of any other variety, and the intellectual amusement and career benefits that it provides are more than offset by its all too serious consequences. First, the abuse of labels creates divisions where none should exist. For example, we can find scholars fighting for hegemony in their niches of inquiry, rejecting the approaches of those who point out areas of agreement and possible fruitful cooperation. What less offensive and more effective way of defending one's turf than to call the other by a different name? Second, the abuse of labels obscures divisions where they do exist. The temptation is indeed great to seize on labels that promise rewards in recognition and a greater audience. As a consequence, labels change their meanings in ways that increase the temptation to appropriate them even more. Consider, for example, the difficulty of persuading someone that just because one says that one is not a "realist," one is not blind to the ways of the world. Such is the meaning the term has taken on, and it can only be dissociated from this meaning by a conscious effort. Stanley Hoffmann observed in 1981 that "we are all realists now, but there are not two realists who agree either in their analysis of what is, or on what ought to be, or on how to get from here to there."[83] Ambitious new or remodeled theoretical approaches to the study of international relations, no matter how idiosyncratic, frequently still seize the realist label.[84] The following remedy might be suggested: If what you mean is that you know the ways of the world, do not call yourself a "realist." Call yourself "smart." The careful use of labels is essential.

Above and beyond all rhetorical wars, it is important to keep in mind that the abuse of labels deprives them of their inestimable value as tools for communication. We spend years and years learning what a realist is, just so we can save ourselves and others some considerable time and energy later by employing the label correctly. If we find the label employed in the service of ideological justification or disparagement, its usefulness as a communication device is severely diminished, if not altogether lost. If we cannot talk to one another and understand one another, we cannot learn from one another; and if we cannot learn from one another, the concept of an academic community is a fiction. The alternative is depressing, for it is hardly worth our time to reinvent the wheel in the knowledge that our students and readers will have to do the same. One does not need to entertain a pre-Kuhnian faith in scientific progress to believe that there exists an attainable state of affairs somewhere in between that vision and one of unstoppable progress toward a set of final scientific truths.

Appendix: Biographical Notes on Authors of Classical Realism

Raymond Aron (1905–1983) was a French sociologist, historian, and political commentator known for his biting critiques of ideological orthodoxies. An expert on Carl von Clausewitz, he was particularly interested in issues of war and violence.

Edward H. Carr, who lived from 1892 to 1982, was a British political scientist and historian specializing in modern Russian history.

Carl von Clausewitz (1780–1831) was a Prussian general and an eminent strategist. He is famous for the statement that war is "a continuation of political activity by other means" (*On War*, 87).

Thomas Hobbes was an English political philosopher, who lived from 1588 to 1679. He attended university at Oxford and spent his life as a tutor and traveling companion to noblemen. His theory was most heavily influenced by his personal experience of the English civil war.

George Frost Kennan (b. 1904) has been a historian and a U.S. diplomat. He is best known for helping to formulate the Truman administration's policy of "containment" of the U.S.S.R.

Henry Alfred Kissinger (b. 1923) is a German-born political scientist, who served as national security adviser and Secretary of State during the Nixon and Ford administrations.

Niccolo Machiavelli (1469–1527) served as second chancellor to the city council and secretary in charge of military affairs to the Republic of Florence. As the city's emissary, he served as France's ambassador in several diplomatic negotiations, traveled to a number of European courts, and witnessed Cesare Borgia's loss of control of the Papacy in Rome in 1502. Back in Florence, he established and led a militia army to the conquest of Pisa in 1509. After the coup of 1512, in which the Medici family overthrew the Florentine republic, Machiavelli was imprisoned (and tortured) and later forced into premature retirement on his rural estate, where he put into writing the lessons of his own career in politics as well as his interpretation of primarily Roman history in *The Prince* and the *Discourses on Livy*. *The Prince*, addressed and delivered to Lorenzo II di Medici, is commonly interpreted as an attempt to regain the favor of the prince. In 1520, Machiavelli did regain some of his previous status when he was appointed the official historiographer of Florence.

George C. Marshall (1880–1959) was U.S. Army Chief of Staff during the Second World War, U.S. Secretary of State from 1947 to 1949, and U.S. Secretary of Defense from 1950 to 1951. In 1947 he proposed the European Recovery Program which became known as the Marshall Plan.

Hans J. Morgenthau (1904–1980), a German-born lawyer, political scientist, and historian, emigrated to the United States in 1937. He is identified by many to be the "preeminent modern Fundamentalist Realist" (Doyle, *Ways of War and Peace*, 106).

Reinhold Niebuhr (1892–1971) was a preeminent and politically active American theologian and philosopher, who, after the Second World War, enjoyed extraordinary influence in the U.S. State Department.

Thucydides, as a member of the Athenian board of generals, was both a politician and a military leader. He led and lost a strategic battle of the Peloponnesian War at Amphipolis in 422 B.C., after which he was exiled from Athens. Since his *History of the Peloponnesian War* breaks off abruptly several years before the final defeat of Athens in 404 B.C., it is assumed that Thucydides died in exile in the last years of the fifth century B.C.

Notes

Chapter 1. Introduction

1. It is common to distinguish between the fields of foreign policy, where the focus is on the decisions of individual actors, and that of international relations, where the focus is on the outcomes of interaction between them.

2. Kenneth R. Hoover, *The Elements of Social Scientific Thinking*, 5th ed. (New York: St. Martin's, 1992), 66.

3. May Brodbeck, "Models, Meaning, and Theories," in *Readings in the Philosophy of the Social Sciences*, ed. May Brodbeck (London: Macmillan, 1968), 583.

4. The term *theory* is employed in this book also in the more general sense that denotes the practice of theorizing. Thus, when I speak of "realist theory," I am referring to the theorizing that takes place within the realist paradigm. When I speak of individual theories, I am speaking of specific attempts at explanation.

5. As will become clear, there are "borderline" realist approaches, such as, notably, defensive realism, that lie beyond the image of the realist psychology which will be developed here. I make no claim to accommodating all those arguably realist theories located on the fringes of this difficult-to-define paradigm. For up-to-date treatments of the difficulty of defining realism, see Stefano Guzzini, *Realism in International Relations and International Political Economy: The Continuing Story of a Death Foretold* (London: Routledge, 1998); and Jack Donnelly, *Realism and International Relations* (Cambridge: Cambridge University Press, 2000). See also Robert B. J. Walker, "Realism, Change, and International Political Theory," *International Studies Quarterly* 31/1 (1987): 65–86; and Jeffrey W. Legro and Andrew Moravcsik, "Is Anybody Still a Realist?" *International Security* 24/2 (1999): 5–55.

6. Graham T. Allison, *Essence of Decision: Explaining the Cuban Missile Crisis* (Boston: Little, Brown, 1971), 38. In general, a "model" is a simplified representation of a particular aspect of reality. A "conceptual model" is a model of how we may think about and understand such an aspect of reality. However, the term *model* is also employed to denote a formalized theory whose elements are more thoroughly specified and whose propositions are thus, in principle, more easily tested than those of an ordinary theory. Compare Brodbeck, "Models" and Michael Nicholson, *Formal Theories in International Relations* (New York: Cambridge University Press, 1992).

7. Cornelia Navari, "Hobbes and the 'Hobbesian Tradition' in International Thought," *Millennium* 11/3 (1982): 207. As Navari points out, Machiavelli refers to these "real forces" as *necessita* or *fortuna*, E. H. Carr calls them "historical forces," and Hans Morgenthau refers to them as "the ingredients of national power."

8. See, for example, Stephen M. Walt, "International Relations: One World, Many Theories," *Foreign Policy* 110 (spring 1998): 29–46; or Paul R. Viotti and Mark V. Kauppi, eds., *International Relations Theory: Realism, Pluralism, Globalism* (New York: Macmillan, 1987).

9. Joseph S. Nye Jr., "Ethics and Foreign Policy," *An Occasional Paper* (Queenstown, Md.: Aspen Institute, 1985), vii.

10. Walt, "International Relations," 43.

11. See Thucydides, *Hobbes's Thucydides*, ed. Richard Schlatter (New Brunswick, N.J.: Rutgers University Press, 1975). The "Athenian thesis," a defense of realist political ideology by an Athenian diplomatic delegation to Sparta in 432 B.C., will be discussed in chapter 2.

12. Benjamin Frankel, "Introduction," *Security Studies* 5 (winter 1995/1996): ix.

13. John A. Vasquez, "The Realist Paradigm and Degenerative versus Progressive Research Programs: An Appraisal of Neotraditional Research on Waltz's Balancing Proposition," *American Political Science Review* 91/4 (1997): 899.

14. Steven Forde, "International Realism and the Science of Politics: Thucydides, Machiavelli, and Neorealism," *International Studies Quarterly* 39/2 (1995): 144.

15. Sidney Verba, "Assumptions of Rationality and Non-Rationality in Models of the International System," in *The International System: Theoretical Essays*, ed. Klaus Knorr and Sidney Verba (Princeton, N.J.: Princeton University Press, 1961), 95.

16. The emphasis on survival helps explain why realists have traditionally defined power primarily in terms of military capabilities.

17. Kenneth N. Waltz, *Theory of International Politics* (New York: McGraw-Hill, 1979), 118.

18. John J. Mearsheimer, "The False Promise of International Institutions," *International Security* 19/3 (1994/1995): 10.

19. Ibid., 11.

20. Waltz, *Theory of International Politics*, 118.

21. See, in particular, Hans J. Morgenthau, *Politics among Nations: The Struggle for Power and Peace*, 2d ed. (New York: Knopf, 1955).

22. See Thomas Hobbes, *Leviathan* (1651; reprint, Cambridge: Cambridge University Press, 1991). While it is common in political research to attribute interests and preferences to aggregates such as nation–states, it is uncommon to hear about states "feeling" fear. This seems inconsistent, given that there is no compelling reason why it should be possible to aggregate wishes and hopes, yet not emotions.

23. See Waltz, *Theory of International Politics*. The phrase *ontological foundations* refers to a set of basic assumptions about how the world operates. These assumptions are connected through argument to form a theory of reality.

24. This problem is further exacerbated in systemic realist theory, such as that of Waltz.

25. Realist arguments may be called "generally deterministic" because they maintain that, given that human nature is fixed and certain motives inevitably operate, decision makers can merely react in predictable ways to the threats and opportunities presented by their environments. A knowledge of environmental constraints can help predict behavior because options to react are limited not only by those constraints but also by the supposed psychological predispositions of the actors.

26. The term *cognition* refers to the processes by which human beings assimilate incoming information as well as the processes that determine their reactions to such information. Thus, cognition intercedes between characteristics of individual actors, such as their basic motivation, and the characteristics of the environment with which they are confronted.

27. K. B. Madsen, *Modern Theories of Motivation: A Comparative Metascientific Study* (New York: Wiley, 1974), 13. According to David McClelland, the complex of "personal causation" includes motivation along with cognition and personal skills. See his *Human Motivation* (Cambridge: Cambridge University Press, 1987). In the study of international relations it is common to conceptualize "skills" as an attribute of the international environment, since the most relevant skills are believed to involve relative capabilities. Compare James N. Rosenau,

Turbulence in World Politics (Princeton, N.J.: Princeton University Press, 1990) on the notion of a "skills revolution" in contemporary global politics.

28. For an overview see Madsen, *Modern Theories of Motivation.*

29. Russell G. Geen, *Human Motivation: A Social Psychological Approach* (Pacific Grove, Calif.: Brooks/Cole, 1995). See also Heinz Heckhausen, *Motivation and Action* (New York: Springer, 1991).

30. Some scholars question whether it makes sense to separate motives conceptually from incentives for action. However, if money is an example for an incentive and greed an example for a motive, it is clear that the concept of an incentive is both more narrow and more concrete. See, for example, David C. McClelland and Robert S. Steele, Introduction to *Human Motivation: A Book of Readings*, ed. David McClelland and Robert Steele (Morristown, N.J.: General Learning Press, 1973), vii–x.

31. A striking example is that realist theory at times relies strongly on the assumption of rationality and at others stresses the role of "irrational" motives, such as insatiable greed or lust for power.

32. Given the vast amount of material published that employs, defends, or criticizes realist theory, it is striking how few authors ever even address the psychological foundations of realism. I argue that this fact is not a reflection of the irrelevance of these psychological foundations but rather of a widespread lack of understanding of their nature, functions, and effects. Another shortcoming of the literature is that studies in international relations or foreign policy that do address realist motivational assumptions frequently neglect to incorporate important insights from the history of thought, while historically oriented analyses of realist works frequently fail to fully develop their theoretical implications. See the special section on the relationship between the disciplines of history and international relations in *International Security* 22/1 (1997).

33. While some academic trends, drawing on critical theory, tend to suspect all established paradigms to be essentially ideologies, I believe that not much can be gained from blurring the boundaries between politically motivated attempts to distort perception and the largely unmotivated influence of scientific theories and models on cognition. As will become clear, realism can, but does not have to, operate as an ideology.

34. Forde, "International Realism and the Science of Politics," 141.

35. I define a "bias" as a stable tendency to interpret information in ways consistent with expectations that are not justifiable on the basis of empirical evidence. A bias does not have to be ideologically or personally motivated.

36. As will become clear, realism has popular appeal partly because it does indeed generally fit the behavior of the most aggressive and thus the most dangerous leaders. Driven largely by paranoid fears and a matching denial of such fears expressed through aggressive machismo, such leaders personify the concerns addressed by realist theorizing and help to justify its propositions.

37. For example, John Vasquez has argued that it is one of the crucial prerequisites for war that political leaders view the world in the terms of *Realpolitik.* See his *The War Puzzle* (New York: Cambridge University Press, 1993).

38. Among the most illustrious examples are Henry Kissinger and Zbigniew Brzezinski, political scientists and senior foreign policy officials in the Nixon, Ford, and Carter administrations. See, for example, Kissinger's *Diplomacy* (New York: Simon and Schuster, 1994).

39. See, for example, Michael Mastanduno, "Preserving the Unipolar Moment: Realist Theories and U.S. Grand Strategy after the Cold War," *International Security* 21/4 (1997):

49–88. Mastanduno argued at the time that U.S. foreign policy was still generally consistent with realist principles. Foreign policy making under the current administration of George Bush Jr. has only made this more obvious.

40. Robert O. Keohane, "Realism, Neorealism, and the Study of World Politics," in *Neorealism and Its Critics*, ed. Robert O. Keohane (New York: Columbia University Press, 1986), 9.

41. Wherever realism operates as an ideology, its basic assumptions function as building blocks for an ideological strategy of self-justification.

42. This is a serious charge if we believe that "the criterion of the scientific status of a theory is its falsifiability, or refutability, or testability." See Karl R. Popper, *Conjectures and Refutations: The Growth of Scientific Knowledge* (New York: Basic Books, 1962), 37.

43. See Thomas S. Kuhn, *The Structure of Scientific Revolutions*, 3d ed. (Chicago: University of Chicago Press, 1996).

44. See Imre Lakatos, *The Methodology of Scientific Research Programmes* (Cambridge: Cambridge University Press, 1978).

45. See, for example, John J. Mearsheimer, "Back to the Future: Instability in Europe after the Cold War," *International Security* 15/1 (1990): 5–56. Mearsheimer's nightmarish predictions for the future of Europe rest on a denial of European integration and suggest that the political views and goals of relevant European nations have not changed since the Second World War.

46. See John A. Vasquez, "The Realist Paradigm" and *The Power of Power Politics: From Classical Realism to Neotraditionalism* (Cambridge: Cambridge University Press, 1998).

47. Popper, *Conjectures and Refutations*, 37.

48. An example for the kinds of ad hoc theoretical adjustments employed by realists to save their paradigm from empirical contradiction is found in Kenneth Waltz's reaction to the end of the Cold War. See his "The Validation of International-Political Theory" (paper presented at the annual meeting of the American Political Science Association, New York City, September 1994). Here Waltz switches back and forth between claiming that realist theory can explain the events that surrounded the end of the Cold War (while other approaches cannot) and safeguarding his defense by remarking that realism can make accurate predictions only where "the conditions that the theory contemplates obtain" (17). While he claims that international relations is the kind of system in which such conditions obtain, his explanations of actual historical events make reference to variables that are not properly part of the theory.

49. To quote Vasquez, "[U]ltimately, logic is only as good as the empirical accuracy of the premises used to establish the conclusion" (*The Power of Power Politics: From Classical Realism to Neotraditionalism*, 374).

50. For the purposes of this book, hermeneutics may simply be defined as an approach that, first, acknowledges that "the study of the social and historical world requires the use of methods which are different from those employed in the investigation of natural phenomena" and in which, second, "problems of understanding and interpretation are recognized as central." See John B. Thompson, "Hermeneutics," in *The Social Science Encyclopedia*, 2d ed., ed. Adam Kuper and Jessica Kuper (London: Routledge, 1996), 360, 361. It is a social science methodology closely related with philology, which employs textual criticism—exegesis—as its primary method, with the aim of understanding human thought as it is expressed through words and believed to guide subsequent behavior. My approach is historical in that it aims to analyze the development of realist thought over time.

51. The term *methodology* refers to a set of principles that determine under which conditions the information produced by scientists is considered "truthful" and/or useful. A "method," by comparison, is a particular strategy used in the production of such information.

52. See, for example, McClelland, *Human Motivation*. This book will partly rely on contemporary psychological scholarship on the operation of motives and suggest some ways in which international relations theory can profit from such scholarship. For an overview, see, for example, David McClelland and Robert Steele, eds.,*Human Motivation: A Book of Readings* (Morristown, N.J.: General Learning Press, 1973); Johnmarshall Reeve, *Understanding Motivation and Emotion* (San Diego, Calif.: Harcourt Brace Jovanovich, 1992); and Geen, *Human Motivation*. On the impact of motivation on specific types of policy decisions see, for example, David G. Winter, "Power, Affiliation, and War: Three Tests of a Motivational Model," *Journal of Personality and Social Psychology* 65/3 (1993): 535–545; and Bill E. Peterson, David Winter, and Richard Doty, "Laboratory Tests of a Motivational-Perceptual Model of Conflict Escalation," *Journal of Conflict Resolution* 38/4 (1994): 719–748.

53. The operation of the affiliation motive is explored to a small extent in the constructivist literature. See chapter 7. On the relevance of altruism in political decision making, see, for example, Kristen Renwick Monroe with Kristen Hill Maher, "Psychology and Rational Actor Theory," *Political Psychology* 16/1 (1995): 1–21.

54. The pessimistic outlook on humanity that is so typical of realism should be understood historically as a reaction to disasters which were attributed to idealist naivete.

55. See Yaacov Y. I. Vertzberger, *The World in Their Minds: Information Processing, Cognition, and Perception in Foreign Policy Decisionmaking* (Stanford, Calif.: Stanford University Press, 1990).

56. See Ralph K. White, *Fearful Warriors: A Psychological Profile of U.S.–Soviet Relations* (New York: Free Press, 1984). White's case study analyzes U.S.–Soviet relations during the Cold War.

57. Mark P. Petracca, "The Rational Actor Approach to Politics: Science, Self-Interest, and Normative Democratic Theory," in *The Economic Approach to Politics: A Critical Reassessment of the Theory of Rational Action*, ed. Kristen Renwick Monroe (New York: HarperCollins, 1991), 181. More recently, psychologists Dale T. Miller and Rebecca K. Ratner have warned that "homo economicus is a social construction, not a biological entity. But myth or not, the image of humans as self-interested agents has powerful social and psychological consequences. Myths can create reality" ("The Disparity between the Actual and Assumed Power of Self-Interest," *Journal of Personality and Social Psychology* 74/1 [1998]: 53–62).

58. Ernst-Otto Czempiel, "Governance and Democratization," in *Governance without Government: Order and Change in World Politics*, ed. James N. Rosenau and Ernst-Otto Czempiel (New York: Cambridge University Press, 1992), 270. This argument is also made by Laurie Johnson in *Thucydides, Hobbes, and the Interpretation of Realism* (Dekalb: Northern Illinois University Press, 1993).

59. See Karl R. Popper, *Conjectures and Refutations: The Logic of Scientific Discovery* (1934; reprint, New York: Basic Books, 1962); *Realism and the Aim of Science* (Totowa, N.J.: Rowman and Littlefield, 1983); and *The Open Universe: An Argument for Indeterminism* (Totowa, N.J.: Rowman and Littlefield, 1982). See also Kuhn, *The Structure of Scientific Revolutions;* and Lakatos, *The Methodology of Scientific Research Programmes.*

60. For a simple overview of the rival approaches see, for example, Walt, "International Relations." Generally speaking, liberals contribute insights on the motivational cluster associated with the pursuit of happiness, which includes the desire for material comfort as well as the defense of certain personal rights. Constructivists point to the importance of actors' self-definition or "identity" in policy choice, including an emphasis on the role of norms and the motivating power of community. In the terminology employed by McClelland in *Human*

Motivation, liberals and constructivists add a concern with the motives of "achievement" and "affiliation," respectively, to the realist concern with the motive of "power."

61. There exists a wide range of critiques coming from rival theories as well as from realist "revisionists." They are rarely directly and primarily concerned with realist motivational assumptions, but sometimes contain implicit criticisms of or have implications for an assessment of those assumptions. Examples range from the liberal critique of Robert O. Keohane and Joseph S. Nye Jr. (*Power and Interdependence*, 2d ed. [Glenview, Ill.: Scott, Foresman, 1989]) over the constructivist critique of Alexander Wendt (for example, "Constructing International Politics," *International Security* 20/1 [1995]: 71–81) to the radical critique of Richard Ashley ("The Poverty of Neo-Realism," *International Organization* 38/2 [1984]: 225–286).

62. See, for example, the concrete criticisms contained in Robert O. Keohane, ed., *Neorealism and Its Critics* (New York: Columbia University Press, 1986); or John Vasquez's broad methodological critique in "The Realist Paradigm."

63. Among the most passionate defenses are those of Kenneth Waltz and John Mearsheimer. See, for example, Waltz's "The Validation" and Mearsheimer's "Back to the Future." For a contemporary defense of classical realism, see Alan James, "The realism [*sic*] of Realism," *Review of International Studies* 15 (1989): 215–229.

Chapter 2. The Roots of Realism

1. It is worth remembering that the so-called ancient Greeks are not the geographical or cultural predecessors of the culture that now inhabits the state of Greece. When we speak about ancient Greek culture we refer to an intricate pattern of cultural traits shared by exchange through war, trade, and migration, which over hundreds of years took root in the area of the eastern Mediterranean. This amalgam of Dorian, Ionian, Persian, Egyptian, and many other cultural elements found its way into "Western" traditions through the writings of the "Greek philosophers," which entered Western intellectual discourse through Renaissance translations from the Arabic.

2. These two different options represent the contrast between idealist and realist expectations from science. Idealists accuse realists of impeding progress owing to a pessimistic view of the possibilities for improvement; realists accuse idealists of threatening our survival in the here and now by adopting a naive view of real constraints.

3. See, for example, historian David L. Silverman's "Generic Revolution," available at http://web.reed.edu/academic/departments/Humanities/Hum110/ThucLecture95.html. Like Herodotus, Thucydides breaks with epic tradition by presenting himself as the authority on the events he describes, rather than as a mouthpiece for the Muses. However, in the work of Herodotus, divine forces are cited as explanations for events, whereas Thucydides' explanations are entirely secular.

4. See Charles Norris Cochrane, *Thucydides and the Science of History* (New York: Russell and Russell, 1965).

5. Thuc. 1.21 (*Hobbes's Thucydides*, 40). The English translation of Thucydides used throughout this study is the one by Thomas Hobbes. Three other translations (see Bibliography) plus the etymological, morphological, and semantic commentaries on the original text which are accessible through Gregory R. Crane, ed., *The Perseus Project*, available at http://www.perseus.tufts.edu, were used to verify the interpretations provided here. For etymological commentaries, see also Arnold W. Gomme, *A Historical Commentary on Thucydides*

(Oxford: Clarendon Press, 1945); and Simon Hornblower, *A Commentary on Thucydides* (Oxford: Clarendon Press, 1991).

6. See, for example, Juergen Gommel, *Rhetorisches Argumentieren bei Thukydides* (Hildesheim, Ger.: Georg Olms Verlag, 1966).

7. In the preface "To the Readers" of his translation of the *History*, Thomas Hobbes calls Thucydides "the most politic historiographer that ever writ," explaining that "he filleth his narrations with that choice of matter, and ordereth them with that judgment," which makes the reader "draw out lessons to himself" (7). Eric Voeglin has described Thucydides as "the first craftsman, who tried to transform the empirical knowledge of politics into a science, using the science of medicine as his model." See his *Order and History*, vol. 2, *The World of the Polis* (Baton Rouge: Louisiana State University Press, 1957), 356–357. Steven Forde has found the *History* to resemble a theory-developing case study. See his *The Ambition to Rule: Alcibiades and the Politics of Imperialism in Thucydides* (Ithaca, N.Y.: Cornell University Press, 1989).

8. Thuc. 1.22 (*Hobbes's Thucydides*, 41).

9. Michael T. Clark, "Realism Ancient and Modern: Thucydides and International Relations," *PS: Political Science and Politics* 26/3 (1993): 491–494. A theory in this sense would consist of a number of logically connected statements clearly linking specific types of events to a limited number of suggested causes. It would have to introduce a degree of parsimony into our interpretation of events that, by focusing on some causal relationships at the expense of others, could increase the efficiency of our understanding.

10. Ashley J. Tellis explains that Thucydides prefers the "technique of conveying philosophical truths through a set of 'empirical facts'. . . over abstract theoretical specification (based on an explicit monocausal system of deduction), because 'history' and 'political science' are still identical for Thucydides and, hence, an 'insight into politics could be gained only by reliving history in [all] its concreteness.'" See his "Reconstructing Political Realism: The Long March to Scientific Theory," *Security Studies* 5/2 (1995/1996): 3–101; Tellis quotes Hajo Holborn, "Greek and Modern Concepts of History," *Journal of the History of Ideas* 10 (1949): 5.

11. The fact that Thucydides combines explanations at multiple levels of analysis has been stressed by, inter alia, Michael W. Doyle in *Ways of War and Peace: Realism, Liberalism, and Socialism* (New York: Norton, 1997); Tellis, "Reconstructing"; and Richard Ned Lebow in "Thucydides, Power Transition Theory, and the Causes of War," in *Hegemonic Rivalry: From Thucydides to the Nuclear Age*, ed. Richard Ned Lebow and Barry S. Strauss (Boulder, Colo.: Westview, 1991), 125–168.

12. See, for example, Kenneth Waltz, *Theory of International Politics* (New York: McGraw-Hill, 1979); Jacek Kugler and A. F. K. Organski, "The Power Transition: A Retrospective and Prospective Evaluation," in *Handbook of War Studies*, ed. Manus I. Midlarsky (Boston: Unwin Hyman, 1989); and Robert Gilpin, "The Theory of Hegemonic War," in *The Origin and Prevention of Major Wars*, ed. Robert I. Rotberg and Theodore K. Rabb (Cambridge: Cambridge University Press, 1989), 15–37. Gilpin claims to have based his theory directly on Thucydides. See his *War and Change in World Politics* (New York: Cambridge University Press, 1981). On attempts to draw lessons from analogy between the hegemonic rivalry described by Thucydides and the Cold War, see especially the essays in Richard Ned Lebow and Barry S. Strauss, eds., *Hegemonic Rivalry: From Thucydides to the Nuclear Age* (Boulder, Colo.: Westview, 1991).

13. See, for example, Mark V. Kauppi, "Thucydides: Character and Capabilities," *Security Studies* 5/2 (1995/1996): 142–168.

14. See, for example, Forde, *The Ambition to Rule.*

15. The importance of the speeches is stressed by virtually all Thucydides scholars. Prominent among them is Antonios Rengakos, who emphasizes that Athenian attitudes toward the pursuit and use of power in politics are clarified almost solely through this medium. See his *Form und Wandel des Machtdenkens der Athener bei Thukydides* (Stuttgart, Germany: F. Steiner Wiesbaden, 1984).

16. Luis E. Lord, *Thucydides and the World War* (New York: Russell and Russell, 1945), 196–197. Francis Macdonald Cornford concurs that the speeches are valuable primarily because of the emphasis they place on "the motives of individuals and the characters of cities." See his *Thucydides Mythistoricus* (London: Routledge and Kegan Paul, 1965), 64.

17. Lord, *Thucydides.*

18. Thuc. 1.22 (*Hobbes's Thucydides*, 41).

19. Thomas Hobbes, "Notes, Book 1, 19," in Thucydides, *Hobbes' Thucydides*, ed. Richard Slatter (New Brunswick, N.J.: Rutgers University Press, 1975).

20. Lord, *Thucydides*, 197. The accuracy of the speeches in Thucydides is also defended by most other commentators, prominently among them Gommel, *Rhetorisches Argumentieren*; David Grene, *Greek Political Theory: The Image of Man in Thucydides and Plato* (Chicago: University of Chicago Press, 1965); Marc Cogan, *The Human Thing: The Speeches and Principles of Thucydides' History* (Chicago: University of Chicago Press, 1981); and John Huston Finley, *Thucydides* (Ann Arbor: University of Michigan Press, 1963).

21. We are concerned here with realism as a political theory of international relations and foreign policy. As Gregory Crane has pointed out, it is possible to distinguish four kinds of "realisms." He identifies "'procedural' (getting the facts straight), 'scientific' (believing that there really are objective facts out there somewhere that can be gotten straight), 'ideological' (using your claim to privileged knowledge as a stick to beat your opponents), and 'paradigmatic' realism (seeing some phenomena more clearly and perhaps gaining a better view of the whole, but at the expense of simultaneously minimizing or ignoring other factors on which your predecessors had laid great emphasis)." See *The Ancient Simplicity: Thucydides and the Limits of Political Realism* (Berkeley and Los Angeles: University of California Press, 1998), quoted from http://www.perseus.tufts.edu/~gcrane/thuc.HC_ToC.html. In my interpretation, Thucydides emerges as a procedural and scientific realist. As we will see, the Athenian thesis combines scientific with ideological realism. Realism as a general political theory draws on all four elements.

22. See, for example, P. A. Brunt, Introduction to *The Peloponnesian Wars*, by Thucydides, trans. Benjamin Jowett (London: New English Library, 1966). Brunt, while seemingly accepting the conclusion that Thucydides' own views are reflected in the speeches of the Athenians, nevertheless points out some significant inconsistencies. See also Clark, "Realism Ancient and Modern."

23. Joseph S. Nye Jr., "Neorealism and Neoliberalism," *World Politics* 40 (January 1988): 235. The consequences of the Thucydidean image are practical as well as academic. High officials in the U.S. foreign policy establishment, such as George C. Marshall, Louis J. Halle, and Henry Kissinger, have praised the realist insights to be gathered from Thucydides, and even today the U.S. Marine Corps attempts to draw strategic lessons from a realist reading of the *History*. See Doyle, *Ways of War and Peace*; Alexander Kemos, "The Influence of Thucydides in the Modern World: The Father of Political Realism Plays a Key Role in Current Balance of Power Theories," Harvard University, available at http://hcs.harvard.edu/~por/thucydides.html; and Williamson Murray, "War, Theory, Clausewitz, and Thu-

cydides: The Game May Change but the Rules Remain," *Marine Corps Gazette* 81/1 (1997): 62–69.

24. See Morgenthau, *Politics among Nations*; Keohane and Nye, *Power and Interdependence*; Keohane, "Realism, Neorealism, and the Study of World Politics" and "Theory of World Politics: Structural Realism and Beyond," in *Neorealism and Its Critics*, ed. Robert Keohane (New York: Columbia University Press, 1986), 1–26, 158–203; Kenneth N. Waltz, *Man, the State, and War: A Theoretical Analysis* (New York: Columbia University Press, 1959) and *Theory of International Politics*; Robert Gilpin, "The Richness of the Tradition of Political Realism," *International Organization* 38/2 (1984): 287–304; Paul Viotti and Mark Kauppi, *International Relations Theory*; and Michael W. Doyle, "Thucydidean Realism," *Review of International Studies* 16 (1990): 223–237, *Ways of War and Peace*, and "Thucydides: A Realist?" in *Hegemonic Rivalry: From Thucydides to the Nuclear Age*, ed. Richard Ned Lebow and Barry S. Strauss (Boulder, Colo.: Westview, 1991), 169–188.

25. Both classical realists, who explicitly base their theories on a particular reading of human nature, and neorealists, who attempt to explain political outcomes with reference to structural characteristics of the international system, have claimed to find support for their viewpoints in the work of Thucydides. This study is concerned with Thucydides' contribution to the realist view of human nature. Other aspects of his work are beyond its scope. For discussions of Thucydides' potential as a structural realist, see Keohane, "Realism" and "Theory of World Politics"; Laurie Johnson Bagby, "The Use and Abuse of Thucydides in International Relations," *International Organization* 48/1 (1994): 131–153; Kauppi, "Thucydides"; Patrick Coby, "Enlightened Self-Interest in the Peloponnesian War: Thucydidean Speakers on the Right of the Stronger and Inter-State Peace," *Canadian Journal of Political Science* 24/1 (1991): 67–90; Daniel Garst, "Thucydides and Neorealism," *International Studies Quarterly* 33/1 (1989): 3–27; Forde, "International Realism"; and Doyle, "Thucydidean Realism," "Thucydides," and *Ways of War and Peace*. Doyle identifies Thucydides as a "minimalist" or "complex" realist, who realizes that in the anarchic environment of the interstate system human aspirations are likely to clash, but who refrains from deterministic judgments. He distinguishes this view from "structuralist" (Hobbes) and "fundamentalist" (Machiavelli) realism. The latter variant would include fully developed realist motivational assumptions. Johnson Bagby has shown that fundamentalist and structural realists tend to overemphasize, respectively, Thucydides' discussion of human nature and of power relationships as causes of war. See her "Thucydidean Realism: Between Athens and Melos," *Security Studies* 5/2 (1995/1996): 169–193.

26. Laurie M. Johnson, *Thucydides*, xii. See also Paul Rahe, "Thucydides' Critique of Realpolitik," *Security Studies* 5/2 (1995/1996): 105–141.

27. Grene, *Greek Political Theory*, 34.

28. In the next chapter, we shall see how Thomas Hobbes, who translated and greatly admired the *History*, first employed motivational assumptions that he gathered from Thucydides in deductive political theorizing. By basing his theory on the realist view of human nature presented in the Athenian thesis, Hobbes contributed greatly to the realist image of Thucydides. See *Leviathan*.

29. The treatment of motivation plays a large part in the actual text. Mabel Lang points out that Thucydides comments in his narration on the motives of forty-two different individuals, attempting to explain 145 different actions. See her "Participial Motivation in Thucydides," *Mnemosyne* 48/1 (1995): 48–65.

30. This alliance is commonly referred to as the Peloponnesian or Lacedaemonian League.

31. This first period of open hostility between Athens and Sparta is sometimes referred to as the First Peloponnesian War. We are here concerned with the Second Peloponnesian War, which lasted from 431 to 404 B.C.

32. Grene, *Greek Political Theory*, 5.

33. Thuc. 1.23 (*Hobbes's Thucydides*, 42). The term translated here as "fear" is not *deos*, which we will encounter later, but *phobos*, which may also be translated as "panic" or "acute fear." The term used to indicate what Hobbes translates as "necessitated" is a form of the word *ananke*, an expression of determinism that plays a crucial role in realist interpretations of the *History*. See Crane, *The Perseus Project*. For a linguistic discussion of this particular passage and the determinism expressed by the Athenians, see also John D. Noonan, "Thucydides 1.23.6: Dionysius of Halicarnassus and the Scholion," *Greek, Roman, and Byzantine Studies* 33/1 (1992): 37–49. In a study of the concept of "preparedness" (*paraskeue*) in the *History*, June Allison finds that Thucydides uses the word 104 times, compared to the 11 times it appears in the combined works of his contemporaries. She shows that an understanding of the role of *paraskeue*, which includes the dynamic elements of gaining, actualizing, and demonstrating power, plays an important role in Thucydides' explanations for the war. See her *Power and Preparedness in Thucydides* (Baltimore: Johns Hopkins University Press, 1989).

34. See especially Gilpin, "The Theory of Hegemonic War"; and Kugler and Organski, "The Power Transition."

35. Gomme, *A Historical Commentary*, 152. On the distinction between true versus direct causes in Thucydides, see Cornford, *Thucydides Mythistoricus*.

36. See Tellis, "Reconstructing Political Realism"; Kauppi, "Thucydides."

37. Thuc. 1.75 (*Hobbes's Thucydides*, 70).

38. Thuc. 1.76 (*Hobbes's Thucydides*, 70).

39. Crane, *The Perseus Project*.

40. Ibid.

41. Ibid.

42. Tellis, "Reconstructing Political Realism," 20.

43. Henry R. Immerwahr, "Pathology of Power and the Speeches in Thucydides," in *The Speeches in Thucydides*, ed. Philip Staedter (Chapel Hill: University of North Carolina Press, 1973), 20.

44. Steven Forde, "Thucydides on the Causes of Athenian Imperialism," *American Political Science Review* 80/2 (1986): 433.

45. Forde calls these traits "erotic" and "daring impulses" (*tolma*). They are believed to be more visible and, perhaps, more pronounced in the Athenian people, simply because they are allowed to live in greater freedom than the peoples around them. See his "Thucydides."

46. Tellis, "Reconstructing Political Realism," 24, 25.

47. Clifford Orwin, *The Humanity of Thucydides* (Princeton, N.J.: Princeton University Press, 1994), 47. During the latter part of the fifth century B.C., philosophical debate raged over the question of whether human behavior is better explained by *physis* (nature) or *nomos* (civilization). See Silverman, "Generic Revolution." Realism answers unequivocally in favor of physis, arguing that the dictates of nature overwhelm any influence civilization might have. Compare the recent turn to sociobiology in realism, which is discussed in chapter 7.

48. Orwin, *The Humanity of Thucydides*, 47.

49. Ibid., 44.

50. Ibid. The Syracusan Hermocrates, in Book 4 of the *History*, makes an identical argument to motivate the citizens of Syracuse to prepare for the impending war with Athens. See W. Robert Connor, *Thucydides* (Princeton, N.J.: Princeton University Press, 1984).

51. Thuc. 1.76 (*Hobbes's Thucydides*, 70).

52. On the treatment of imperialism in Thucydides, see also Jacqueline de Romilly, *Thucydides and Athenian Imperialism* (Oxford: Blackwell, 1963).

53. Thuc. 1.76 (*Hobbes's Thucydides*, 70–71).

54. Grene, *Greek Political Theory*, 78–79.

55. Thuc. 1.76 (*Hobbes's Thucydides*, 71).

56. James Boyd White, *When Words Lose Their Meaning: Constitutions and Reconstitutions of Language, Character, and Community* (Chicago: University of Chicago Press, 1984).

57. See especially Thomas Johnson, "The Idea of Power Politics: The Sophistic Foundations of Realism," *Security Studies* 5/2 (1995/1996): 194–247. Johnson identifies three principles of sophism: "[F]irst, truth and justice in the world are relatively defined, and there is no one universally knowable or accepted truth; second, an inherently pessimistic view of human nature and its ultimate potentialities; and third, a recognition of the primary role of power . . . in enforcing parochial conceptions of truth" (quoted from Frankel, "Introduction," xv).

58. Johnson, *Thucydides*, 32.

59. See Book 3 of the *History*.

60. Johnson, *Thucydides*, 109.

61. See Rengakos, *Form und Wandel*. In this case, Diodotus uses the Athenian thesis successfully to win moderation. However, this is an untypical result of such rhetorics. See Orwin, *The Humanity of Thucydides*.

62. Johnson, *Thucydides*, 99. It is worthwhile examining how the rhetoric of the Athenians changes during the course of the war. See especially Rengakos, *Form und Wandel*; White, *When Words Lose Their Meaning*.

63. White, *When Words Lose Their Meaning*, 70–71.

64. De Romilly has called that position "objective realism, which, fully recognizing the more unfortunate aspects of Athenian imperialism, excuses them only by relating them to the needs inseparable from any imperialism." See her *Thucydides*, 271.

65. The Athenians' amoral explanation of political reality is so rhetorically persuasive largely because it claims to be based on a scientific view of the world, rather than on mere opinion. To this day, the scientific image of realism feeds the tendency to view realism as a formula for success. See Russell McNeil, "Thucydides as Science," Malaspina University-College (1996), available at http://www.mala.bc.ca/~mcneil/lec18b.htm.

66. Hans Drexler, *Thukydides-Studien* (Hildesheim, Ger.: Georg Olms Verlag, 1976).

67. Christoph Schneider, *Information und Absicht bei Thukydides* (Goettingen, Germany: Vandenhoeck and Ruprecht, 1974).

68. Grene, *Greek Political Theory*, 34.

69. Schneider, *Information und Absicht*, 110. My translation.

70. Schneider, *Information und Absicht*.

71. Drexler, *Thukydides-Studien*, 190. My translation.

72. Rengakos, *Form und Wandel*.

73. Clifford Orwin, "Stasis and Plague: Thucydides on the Dissolution of Society," *Journal of Politics* 50/4 (1988): 845. Peter Ahrensdorf agrees that Thucydides realizes that "the human hopes and moral passions that realism opposes as unreasonable are indelible features of political life." Unlike Orwin's, however, his critique is essentially Hobbesian, in that it

argues that, while realist theory contains unrealistic assumptions, it has prescriptive value. See his "Thucydides' Realistic Critique of Realism," *Polity* 30/2 (1997): 231.

74. Frank Adcock, *Thucydides and His History* (Cambridge: Cambridge University Press, 1963), 52.

75. Ibid., 50, 52.

76. George Abbott, *Thucydides: A Study in Historical Reality* (London: Routledge, 1925), 159.

77. See Grene, *Greek Political Theory*.

78. See Hans-Peter Stahl, *Thukydides: Die Stellung des Menschen im Geschichtlichen Prozess* (Munich: Beck'sche Verlagsbuchhandlung, 1966).

79. Forde finds that "Thucydides' educational project is best conceived of as directed primarily to practical political men." See his *The Ambition to Rule*, 9.

80. Leo Strauss, *Thoughts on Machiavelli* (1958; reprint, Chicago: University of Chicago Press, 1984), 292. This view is shared as well by Arthur Geoffrey Woodhead in *Thucydides on the Nature of Power* (Cambridge: Harvard University Press, 1970).

81. Finley, *Thucydides*, 308.

82. Walter R. M. Lamb, *Clio Enthroned: A Study of Prose-Form in Thucydides* (Cambridge: Cambridge University Press, 1914), 49.

83. Grene, *Greek Political Theory*, 92.

84. Rengakos, *Form und Wandel*. Sara Monoson and Michael Loriaux have recently found that Thucydides' treatment of Pericles betrays both the conviction that political strategy cannot be prudent or successful in defiance of morality and the belief that moral norms need to be defended and enforced. See "The Illusion of Power and the Disruption of Moral Norms: Thucydides' Critique of Periclean Policy," *American Political Science Review* 92/2 (1998): 285–297.

85. By this time, democratic and aristocratic factions, siding with Athens and Sparta, respectively, are dividing many cities of Greece against themselves.

86. Thuc. 3.82 (*Hobbes's Thucydides*, 223).

87. Thuc. 3.84 (*Hobbes's Thucydides*, 224). In a passage whose message is lost in the Hobbesian translation, Thucydides laments that "every form of inequity took root in the Hellenic countries by reason of the troubles. The ancient simplicity into which honor so largely entered was laughed down and disappeared; and society became divided into camps in which no man trusted his fellow" (Thuc. 3.83). Thucydides, *History of the Peloponnesian War*, trans. Richard Crawley (London: J. M. Dent, 1910), 225–226.

88. Nanno Marinatos, *Thucydides and Religion* (Koenigstein/Ts., Ger.: Verlag Anton Hain, 1981), 32. *Arete* is selfless love.

89. Peter R. Pouncey, *The Necessities of War: A Study of Thucydides' Pessimism* (New York: Columbia University Press, 1980).

90. Ibid., 139.

91. On the contrast between Hobbes's and Thucydides' visions of an ideal government, see Johnson, *Thucydides*.

92. On Thucydides' account of the effects of stasis and plague on human behavior, see especially Orwin, "Stasis and Plague."

93. David Cohen, "Justice, Interest, and Political Deliberation in Thucydides," *Quaderni Urbinati* 16/1 (1984): 35–60.

94. Thuc. 5.89 (*Hobbes's Thucydides*, 379).

95. Thuc. 5.105 (*Hobbes's Thucydides*, 381–382).

96. Thuc. 5.113 (*Hobbes's Thucydides*, 384). This passage is the first known direct expression of the realist critique of idealism. After twenty-four hundred years of adversity between the two perspectives, the message as well as the conflict it expresses appear timeless.

97. We find here connections to Hobbesian ideas concerning the disciplinary benefits of fear, as well as to the "diversionary theory of war." See Hobbes, *Leviathan*; and, for example, Jack Levy, "The Diversionary Theory of War," in *Handbook of War Studies*, ed. Manus I. Midlarsky (Boston: Unwin Hyman, 1989), 259–288.

98. Tellis, "Reconstructing Political Realism," 99.

99. See Immerwahr, "Pathology of Power," 31.

100. Orwin, *The Humanity of Thucydides*. Quote from Laurie Johnson Bagby, "The Humanity of a True Realist: Clifford Orwin: The Humanity of Thucydides" (book review), *Review of Politics* 57/2 (1995): 344. This argument is supported by Rahe in "Thucydides' Critique of Realpolitik."

101. See Adcock, *Thucydides*.

102. See Schneider, *Information und Absicht*. On the understanding of justice of Thucydides as opposed to that of Hobbes see Johnson, *Thucydides*.

103. Simon Hornblower, *Thucydides* (Baltimore: Johns Hopkins University Press, 1987), 85.

104. Ibid., 76–77. See also Schneider, *Information und Absicht*.

105. Johnson Bagby, "The Use and Abuse of Thucydides," 133–134.

106. See especially Hartmut Erbse, *Thukydides-Interpretationen* (Berlin: Walter de Gruyter, 1989).

107. See especially Mario Cesa, *La Ragioni della Forza: Tucidide e la Teoria delle Relazioni Internazionali* (Bologna, It.: Il Mulino, 1994).

108. Compare Arnold Wolfers's distinction between a "philosophy of choice" and a "philosophy of necessity" (which he associates with Machiavellian realism) in *Discord and Collaboration: Essays on International Politics* (Baltimore: Johns Hopkins University Press, 1962). On the tragic quality of the *History*, see especially Cornford, *Thucydides Mythistoricus*.

109. Kauppi has emphasized the unresolved contradiction between the power transition argument of the truest cause passage, which he perceives to be deterministic, and the narrative, which stresses the role of human volition. See his "Contemporary International Relations Theory and the Peloponnesian War," in *Hegmonic Rivalry: From Thucydides to the Nuclear Age*, ed. Richard Ned Lebow and Barry S. Strauss (Boulder, Colo: Westview, 1991), 101–124. Johnson Bagby has explained that Thucydidean realism "lies somewhere between Athens and Melos," where "morality and expediency can coincide." See her "Thucydidean Realism,"191.

110. Johnson Bagby, "The Use and Abuse," 153. This argument is supported by White in *When Words Lose Their Meaning*.

111. Of course, this is the political problem addressed by Thomas Hobbes. See chapter 3.

112. The work of Niccolo Machiavelli is the classical realist illustration of the pragmatic instrumentalist view of political science. See chapter 3.

Chapter 3. Realism Goes Modern

1. See, for example, Viotti and Kauppi, *International Relations Theory*.

2. See Michael Loriaux, "The Realists and Saint Augustine: Skepticism, Psychology, and Moral Action in International Relations Thought," *International Studies Quarterly* 36/4 (1992): 401–420; Willis Glover, "Human Nature and the State in Hobbes," *Journal of the*

History of Philosophy 4 (1966): 293–311; Jim George, "Realist Ethics, International Relations, and Postmodernism: Thinking beyond the Egoism–Anarchy Thematic," *Millennium* 24/2 (1995): 195–223. Loriaux argues that the thought of St. Augustine had a particular influence on Reinhold Niebuhr. Glover discusses its impact on Thomas Hobbes. George identifies as the twentieth-century realists most heavily influenced by this tradition Hans Morgenthau, Reinhold Niebuhr, Kenneth Thompson, George Schwarzenberger, George Kennan, Martin Wight, and Herbert Butterfield, "who basically constitute the elite of Cold War power politics Realism in Anglo-American scholarly and policy circles" (200 n.11).

3. George, "Realist Ethics," 200 (n.11).

4. Robert Hariman traces the tradition back to Isocrates' letter "To Nicocles." See his *Political Style: The Artistry of Power* (Chicago: University of Chicago Press, 1995).

5. Gregory Crane, "'Political Style: The Artistry of Power'" (book review), available at http://www.lib.ncsu.edu/stacks/b/bmcr/bmcr-9512-crane-political.txt. It is ironic that realism has become grounded to a considerable extent on the writings and authority of Machiavelli.

6. Ibid.

7. See chapter 10 of Hobbes's "Human Nature: Or the Fundamental Elements of Policy," in *The English Works of Thomas Hobbes of Malmesbury*, vol. 4, ed. Sir William Molesworth (London: Scientia Aalen, 1962), 1–76.

8. See, for example, Viotti and Kauppi, *International Relations Theory*. An exception is Cornelia Navari, who has argued that realism draws on Machiavelli, but completely misreads Hobbes. She attributes this state of affairs largely to Martin Wight's lectures at the London School of Economics in the 1950s, in which he grouped both Machiavelli and Hobbes into what he called the "Realist School." See Navari, "Hobbes and the 'Hobbesian Tradition' in International Thought."

9. Edward H. Carr, *The Twenty Years' Crisis, 1919–1939: An Introduction to the Study of International Relations* (1939; reprint, New York: Harper and Row, 1964), 63. In fact, very similar arguments had been made by much earlier political theorists, as, for example, Mo Tzu in fourth-century B.C. China. However, they had none or only minimal impact on the development of the realist paradigm because their works were not known by those who carried on the tradition in western Europe. See Mo Tzu, *Mo Tzu: Basic Writings*, trans. Burton Watson (New York: Columbia University Press, 1963).

10. Doyle, *Ways of War and Peace*, 109.

11. Markus Fischer, "Machiavelli's Theory of Foreign Politics," *Security Studies* 5/2 (1995/1996): 274. As Fischer points out, the central elements of neorealism—the conception of the interstate system as an anarchic, self-help environment, the security dilemma, and relative-gains concerns—are all addressed in the work of Machiavelli.

12. As Quentin Skinner has emphasized in *Machiavelli* (New York: Hill and Wang, 1981), this evidence is of two types. Doyle explains, "For supporting or contradicting example, he offers his contemporary European experience. . . . For integrated, or definitive and digested, exemplary experience, he offers the glorious experience of Rome, whose successful use as interpreted by Livy validates any procedure" (*Ways of War and Peace*, 94).

13. Doyle identifies Hobbes as a structural realist, but he also states that Hobbes's theory relies on first-image assumptions about human nature. See his *Ways of War and Peace*.

14. As Peter Pouncey points out in *The Necessities of War*, Hobbes never acknowledges any debt to Thucydides for the development of his theory. To what extent he thought himself in agreement with the Greek historian he so admired is unclear.

15. Johnson, *Thucydides*.

16. The parallels between the view of Hobbes and the philosophy underlying the Athenian thesis are stressed by, among others, David Grene in *Greek Political Thought*; Richard Schlatter's Introduction to *Hobbes's Thucydides*, by Thucydides, ed. Richard Schlatter (New Brunswick, N.J.: Rutgers University Press, 1975), xi–xxviii; and Peter Pouncey in *The Necessities of War*.

17. Arnold Green identifies Hobbes as a positivist because he shares the "positivist view that only ignorance and error preclude the seeking of scientific answers in all departments of consciousness." See his *Hobbes and Human Nature* (New Brunswick, N.J.: Transaction Publishers, 1993), 120.

18. Thomas Hobbes, *De Cive* (1647; reprint, Oxford: Clarendon Press, 1983), ch. 3, para. 8, 68.

19. See Donald W. Hanson, "Science, Prudence, and Folly in Hobbes's Political Theory," *Political Theory* 21/4 (1993): 643–664. Hanson argues that Hobbes's hopes for science and philosophy were much less ambitious than is commonly thought.

20. Quentin Skinner, *Reason and Rhetoric in the Philosophy of Hobbes* (Cambridge: Cambridge University Press, 1996).

21. Laurie Johnson Bagby, "The Law of Nations and Other Dimensions in Hobbes' Thought: Understanding the Realist Project" (paper presented at the annual meeting of the International Studies Association, San Diego, Calif., April 1996), 10. See Hobbes, "Human Nature," ch. 13, pt. 4, 73–74. In pre-Socratic philosophy, the distinction is between the *mathematikoi*, who rely on direct study, and the *akousmatikoi*, who rely on hearsay in developing their conclusions.

22. Johnson Bagby, "The Law of Nations."

23. See Victoria Ann Kahn, *Rhetoric, Prudence, and Skepticism in the Renaissance* (Ithaca, N.Y.: Cornell University Press, 1985), 152–181.

24. See Skinner, *Reason and Rhetoric in the Philosophy of Hobbes*.

25. See Ernst Cassirer, *The Myth of the State* (New Haven, Conn.: Yale University Press, 1946); Leo Strauss, "Niccolo Machiavelli," in *History of Political Philosophy*, 2d ed., ed. Leo Strauss and Joseph Cropsey (Chicago: University of Chicago Press, 1982) and *Thoughts on Machiavelli*; Friedrich Meinecke, *Die Idee der Staatsraeson in der Neueren Geschichte* (Munich: R. Oldenbourg, 1924); and Tellis, "Reconstructing Political Realism."

26. Tellis, "Reconstructing Political Realism," 27.

27. The claim that Machiavelli's suggestions are complementary is not without controversy. There exists some considerable scholarly concern over seeming contradictions between Machiavelli's arguments in *The Prince* and the *Discourses*, which have led some scholars to reject the realist interpretation of the latter, or even both works. Jean-Jacques Rousseau claims that we misunderstand *The Prince* unless we see it as written for republicans, not princes, as an exposé of political tyranny. See his "Of The Social Contract," in *The Social Contract and Other Later Political Writings*, ed. and trans. Victor Gourevitch (Cambridge: Cambridge University Press, 1997), bk. 3, ch. 6, sec. 5, fn. Garret Mattingly claims it is to be understood as a political satire. See his "Machiavelli's Prince: Political Science or Political Satire?" *American Scholar* 27 (1958): 482–491. Mary Dietz reads it as a piece of subversive advice, intended to bring down a despised tyrant. See her "Trapping the Prince: Machiavelli and the Politics of Deception," *American Political Science Review* 80/3 (1986): 777–799. Felix Gilbert claims that the two works represent different stages in the evolution of Machiavelli's thought. See his "The Composition and Structure of Machiavelli's Discorsi," *Journal of the History of Ideas* 14 (1953): 136–156. Sheldon Wolin claims that the *Discourses* and *The Prince* deal with different stages in

the political process, a view that is compatible with the interpretation provided here. See his *Politics and Vision: Continuity and Innovation in Western Political Thought* (Boston: Little, Brown, 1960).

28. Niccolo Machiavelli, *Discourses on Livy*, trans. Julia Conaway Bondanella and Peter Bondanella (1513; reprint, Oxford: Oxford University Press, 1997), bk. 3, ch. 43, p. 351.

29. Ibid., bk. 1, ch. 39, p. 105.

30. For an explication of Machiavelli's theory on the workings of the human mind, see Markus Fischer, "Machiavelli's Political Psychology," *Review of Politics* 59/4 (1997): 789–829.

31. Niccolo Machiavelli, *The Prince*, trans. Angelo M. Codevilla (1513; reprint, Cambridge: Cambridge University Press, 1988), ch. 17, p. 62.

32. Ibid., ch. 3, p. 13.

33. Ibid., ch. 6, p. 20, ch. 7, p. 24.

34. Isaiah Berlin, "The Originality of Machiavelli," in *Against the Current: Essays in the History of Ideas* (New York: Viking Press, 1979), 45.

35. See Machiavelli, *The Prince*, ch. 25.

36. Ibid., ch. 25, p. 91.

37. Tellis, "Reconstructing Political Realism," 38.

38. See Machiavelli, *Discourses*, bk. 2, ch. 8.

39. Tellis, "Reconstructing Political Realism," 38.

40. Machiavelli, *The Prince*, ch. 18, p. 67.

41. Ibid., ch. 15, p. 58. Passages like this one are the reason why *The Prince* was placed on the Papal index in its time.

42. Steven Forde, "Classical Realism," in *Traditions of International Ethics*, ed. Terry Nardin and David Mapel (Cambridge: Cambridge University Press, 1992), 3. See Machiavelli, *Discourses*, bk. 2, ch. 2.

43. See Machiavelli, *The Prince*, ch. 8.

44. Ibid., ch. 12, p. 45.

45. This claim is reminiscent of Forde's argument concerning the flourishing of Athenian tolma under conditions of democracy. See his "Thucydides on the Causes."

46. See Machiavelli, *The Prince*, chs. 12 and 13.

47. Doyle, *Ways of War and Peace*, 105.

48. Ibid., 103.

49. Tellis, "Reconstructing Political Realism," 33.

50. Forde, "Classical Realism," 69. Forde has found that, while "Thucydides' realism culminates in the pessimistic or tragic view that there is an inescapable and irresolvable tension between immoral necessity and the ethical possibilities of politics . . . , Machiavelli believes that [this] tension . . . can and should be resolved–in favor of necessity." See his "Varieties of Realism: Thucydides and Machiavelli," *Journal of Politics* 54/2 (1992): 384.

51. John G. A. Pocock, *The Machiavellian Moment: Florentine Political Thought and the Atlantic Republican Tradition* (Princeton, N.J.: Princeton University Press, 1975), viii. Victoria Kahn views the "Machiavellian moment" as a mere rhetorical move to a new argumentative strategy. See her *Machiavellian Rhetoric: From the Counter-Reformation to Milton* (Princeton, N.J.: Princeton University Press, 1994). While the systematic defense of realism that emerges in early modern political theory undoubtedly involves a strong reliance on rhetorical strategies, it is, however, difficult to deny that it involves, above and beyond rhetorics, profound ontological and epistemological commitments. As Piotr Hoffman has recently argued, these commitments can be summarized as the assertion of man's autonomy in the world and his

identification of himself as the locus of perception, the source of agency, the legitimate center of power, and the master over nature. See his *The Quest for Power: Hobbes, Descartes, and the Emergence of Modernity* (Atlantic Highlands, N.J.: Humanities Press, 1996).

52. See Strauss, *Thoughts on Machiavelli.*

53. Albert O. Hirschman, *The Passions and the Interests: Political Arguments for Capitalism before Its Triumph* (Princeton, N.J.: Princeton University Press, 1977), 33.

54. Tellis, "Reconstructing Political Realism," 36.

55. Ibid., 25.

56. Leonardo Olschki, *Machiavelli the Scientist* (Berkeley, Calif.: Gillick, 1945), 47.

57. Ibid.

58. Ibid., 44.

59. Tellis, "Reconstructing Political Realism."

60. Hirschman, *The Passions*, 13. See chapter 15 of *The Prince.* Machiavelli here positions himself in direct opposition to the utopian normativism of Plato, the scientific rationalism of Aristotle, and the metaphysical apologism of St. Augustine.

61. Machiavelli, *The Prince*, ch. 15, p. 57.

62. Doyle, *Ways of War and Peace*, 97–98.

63. Tellis, "Reconstructing Political Realism," 36.

64. Forde, "Classical Realism," 66.

65. Machiavelli, *Discourses*, bk. 1, ch. 9, p. 45.

66. George, "Realist Ethics, International Relations, and Postmodernism," 201.

67. Hirschman, *The Passions*, 33.

68. Meinecke, *Die Idee der Staatsraeson*, 184. P. J. Kain has argued that Machiavelli counsels the prince against the pursuit of his own interest to pursue instead the interests of the state and that he should therefore not be viewed as supportive of the reign of rational self-interest. See his "Machiavelli, Niccolo: Adviser of Princes," *Canadian Journal of Philosophy* 25/1 (1995): 33–55. This is a misleading characterization. In fact, Machiavelli tries to "save" the state by attempting to persuade the prince that what is best for the state is also best for him. He relies on this strategy precisely because he believes that man is inevitably an egoist.

69. Machiavelli was to become influential in the development of this trend in modern philosophy, but only through the reflection of posterity on the relevant consequences of his arguments.

70. While Machiavelli contributes to the realist psychology and epistemology, as well as to the realist view of the purpose of political science, he is less of a determinist than many other realists. This does not only become clear in his treatment of the relationship between *fortuna* and *virtu* but also in his complex views on *necessita* (necessity). According to Kurt Kluxen, Machiavelli identifies constraints to human agency within human nature (predispositions), within power relations (structure), within information processing and decision-making processes (cognitive factors), and within nature itself (environment). However, Machiavelli believes that all these constraints leave man with enough freedom to make mistakes that can be avoided through the imposition of additional, man-made ones. Thus, the state functions as *necessita ordinata dalle leggi* (necessity ordained by law). More important, the goal of *mantenere lo stato* is defined as a necessity for the purpose of supporting Machiavelli's recommendations in a move that alerts us to the ease with which realist rhetoric may make use of deterministic arguments. See Kluxen, *Politik und Menschliche Existenz bei Machiavelli: Dargestellt am Begriff der Necessita* (Stuttgart, Ger.: Kohlhammer, 1967).

71. Tellis, "Reconstructing Political Realism," 28.

72. Christopher McDonald, "Human Nature and the Nature of States: Realism and Political Philosophy" (paper presented at the annual meeting of the International Studies Association, San Diego, Calif., April 1996), 1.

73. Stephen Holmes, Introduction to *Behemoth or The Long Parliament*, by Thomas Hobbes (1682; reprint, Chicago: University of Chicago Press, 1990), xlix.

74. Hobbes, *De Cive*, ch. 1, pt. 2, p. 42.

75. Ibid., ch. 6, pt. 3, p. 93.

76. Ibid., ch. 5, pt. 5, p. 88.

77. Hobbes, *Leviathan*, ch. 13, p. 90.

78. Ibid., 88.

79. Ibid., 90.

80. Hirschman, *The Passions*, 13. On the influence of geometry on Hobbesian thought, see Jeremy Valentine, "Hobbes's Political Geometry," *History of the Human Sciences* 10/2 (1997): 23–40; and Alexander Bird, "Squaring the Circle: Hobbes on Philosophy and Geometry," *Journal of the History of Ideas* 57/2 (1996): 217–231. Hobbes was personally acquainted with both Galileo and the empiricist Francis Bacon.

81. On Hobbes's views concerning the workings of the human mind, see especially Bernard Gert, "Hobbes's Psychology," in *The Cambridge Companion to Hobbes*, ed. Tom Sorell (Cambridge: Cambridge University Press, 1996), 157–174.

82. It should be noted that some analysts have argued that Hobbes leaves man with more autonomy of choice and action than is commonly assumed because he does not prescribe ends or means to actors. See especially David van Mill, "Rationality, Action, and Autonomy in Hobbes's Leviathan," *Polity* 27/2 (1994): 285–306; and George Kateb, "Hobbes and the Irrationality of Politics," *Political Theory* 17/3 (1989): 355–391. Still, Hobbes clearly maintains that all human beings are motivated by the same range of motives and liable to succumb to the same passions in the same situations.

83. Hobbes, *Leviathan*, ch. 13, p. 88.

84. Ibid., 89.

85. Man's natural vulnerability is understood by many international relations theorists to be a structural attribute, caused by the condition of anarchy, rather than by psychological predisposition. As will become more clear in my treatment of structural realism in the next chapter, I disagree with this view for the simple reason that the assumption that anarchy leads to conflict depends on the logically prior assumption that human beings are motivated in such a way that they are likely to harm one another.

86. The laws of nature are rules that man can discover by reason alone (and in which Hobbes's readers should believe because his logic is compelling). Contrary to the common view, Hobbes thus may be viewed as a methodological rationalist as well as an empiricist. He is an empiricist insofar as he believes that science is defined as "evidence of truth from some beginning or principle of sense" (see his "Human Nature," ch. 6, pt. 4, p. 28). He is a rationalist insofar as he relies heavily on theoretical argument to derive prescription from observation. See especially David Johnston, *The Rhetoric of Leviathan: Thomas Hobbes and the Politics of Cultural Transformation* (Princeton, N.J.: Princeton University Press, 1986); Leo Strauss, *The Political Philosophy of Hobbes: Its Basis and Its Genesis* (Chicago: University of Chicago Press, 1952).

87. The Leviathan is a biblical monster, of whom God tells Job in the Book of Job that "there is nothing . . . on earth to be compared with him. He is made so as not to be afraid. He seeth every high thing below him; and is King of all children of pride." See Hobbes, *Leviathan*,

ch. 28, p. 221. Hobbes's choice of title is particularly appropriate, given that it is primarily pride that his Leviathan is designed to suppress.

88. Compare Immanuel Kant, *Ethical Philosophy* (Indianapolis, Ind.: Hackett, 1983).

89. Hobbes, *Leviathan*, ch. 11, p. 70.

90. Ibid.

91. Navari, "Hobbes and the 'Hobbesian Tradition,'" 209.

92. On the instrumental view of reason see also David Hume, *Enquiries Concerning Human Understanding, and Concerning the Principles of Morals* (1777; reprint, Oxford: Clarendon Press, 1975).

93. Hirschman, *The Passions*, 11. In light of the preceding chapter, we should be able to count Thucydides' *History* among those texts.

94. Ibid., 12.

95. Ibid., 20. Hirschman explains that the principle of countervailing passion as well as the doctrine of self-interest, both foreshadowed in the thought of Machiavelli, emerged as answers in the search for means to restrain destructive passions, after key minds had decided that moralizing and religion could not be relied on to do so. Hirschman explains that, in the seventeenth century, the idea of "interest" "comprised the totality of human aspirations, but denoted an element of reflection and calculation with respect to the manner in which these aspirations were to be pursued" (32). The benefits of the reign of interest were, primarily, constancy and predictability.

96. The "possessive individualism," which over time became synonymous with the idea of self-interest, became "harnessed" in the service of capitalism. Illustrative of this interpretive evolution is the narrowing in meaning of the Machiavellian terms of "fortune" and "corruption." Compare also Crawford B. Macpherson, *The Political Theory of Possessive Individualism: Hobbes to Locke* (Oxford: Clarendon Press, 1962), who confirms that Hobbes contributed with his model of man as an atomistic, self-interested being to the development of liberal economic as well as realist and liberal political theory.

97. Hirschman, *The Passions*, 31. Hirschman quotes from chapter 13 of *Leviathan*.

98. On the importance of fear in relation to other passions, particularly pride, see Strauss, *The Political Philosophy of Hobbes*.

99. Hobbes, *Leviathan*, ch. 13, p. 89.

100. Hobbes, *De Cive*, ch. 1, pt. 7, p. 47.

101. Ibid., ch. 1, pt. 2, p. 45. Once again we can see that equality under conditions of anarchy is not by itself a sufficient condition for violent conflict. Instead, realism depends on the additional assumption of a "will of hurting."

102. Ibid., 44.

103. Jan H. Blits, "Hobbesian Fear," *Political Theory* 17/3 (1989): 417. Writing on Thucydides, Forde observes that "a general law of the expansion of power, driven by honor and self-interest as well as fear, makes for a much more virulent realism than one based simply on fear or the structural security dilemma. It makes the possibility of any common good . . . much more remote." See his "Varieties of Realism," 376. For Hobbes, the legitimate "common good" is political stability. It is made possible by the supremacy of fear.

104. Connor, *Thucydides*, 124. Connor is speaking about Hermocrates of Syracuse, who makes a similar argument in Thucydides' *History* (6.33, 6.34).

105. Hobbes, *Leviathan*, ch. 11, p. 70. For a discussion of the concept of power in Hobbes and classical realism, see also Robert F. Litke, "Violence and Power," *International Social Science Journal* 44/2 (1992): 173–183.

106. Hobbes, *Leviathan*, ch. 10, p. 62. On the problems that can arise due to the absence of a sufficient degree of fear, see especially Stephen Holmes, "Political Psychology in Hobbes' Behemoth," in *Thomas Hobbes and Political Theory*, ed. Mary Dietz (Lawrence: University of Kansas Press, 1990), 120–152. The quest for power includes the desires for honor and profit, but is also a function of uncertainty or fear of what the future might bring. According to Blits, writing in "Hobbesian Fear," this "primal, indeterminate fear of the unknown" (418) is likely to be the deepest human fear and the motive underlying even the fear of death.

107. On the tension between the passions in Hobbes, see especially Strauss, *The Political Philosophy of Hobbes*.

108. Hobbes, *Leviathan*, ch. 13, p. 88.

109. Those are the eighth law against "contumely" (provocation), the ninth law against pride itself, and the tenth law against arrogance. See Hobbes, *Leviathan*, ch. 15.

110. Holmes, "Political Psychology in Hobbes's Behemoth," 144.

111. Ibid., 145.

112. Ibid.

113. If anything, Hobbes believes political elites to be worse than the common man because they are in a position to be motivated by vainglory, the most dangerous of all motives. Machiavelli, too, believes that "princes" possess stronger passions than ordinary human beings. However, his admiration for "virtuous" leaders keeps him from condemning strength of passion. Instead, he requires that the leader cultivate his power and reason in proportion to his passions.

114. David P. Gauthier, *The Logic of Leviathan: The Moral and Political Theory of Thomas Hobbes* (Oxford: Clarendon Press, 1969), 20.

115. Johnson, *Thucydides,* 209.

116. Gauthier, *The Logic of Leviathan*, 23.

117. Forde, "Classical Realism," 76.

118. Leslie Mulholland, "Egoism and Morality," *Journal of Philosophy* 86/10 (1989): 542.

119. Dana Chabot, "Thomas Hobbes: Skeptical Moralist," *American Political Science Review* 89/2 (1995): 408.

120. R. E. Ewin, *Virtues and Rights: The Moral Philosophy of Thomas Hobbes* (Boulder, Colo.: Westview, 1991), 4. This is reminiscent of Thucydides' position.

121. Hobbes, *De Cive*, ch. 1, pt. 2, p. 44.

122. Gregory S. Kavka, *Hobbesian Moral and Political Theory* (Princeton, N.J.: Princeton University Press, 1986), 452.

123. Forde, "Classical Realism," 76.

124. Laurence Thomas, "Doing Justice to Egoism," *Journal of Philosophy* 86/10 (1989): 551–552.

125. Navari, "Hobbes and the 'Hobbesian Tradition' in International Thought," 208. Sam Black has pointed out that Hobbes was strongly influenced by the tradition of classical moral skepticism, which he sought to buttress with the arguments of early modern science. See his "Science and Moral Skepticism in Hobbes," *Canadian Journal of Philosophy* 27/2 (1997): 173–207.

126. John Mitchell, "Man as Aggressive, Exploitive, and Selfish," in *Human Nature: Theories, Conjections, and Descriptions*, ed. John Mitchell (Metuchen, N.J.: Scarecrow Press, 1972), 340.

127. Viotti and Kauppi, *International Relations Theory*, 41. In chapter 13 of *Leviathan*, Hobbes indicates that the relations among kings are at least similar to a state of nature. In "De Corpore Politico" he writes, "As for the law of nations, it is the same with the law of nature. For

that which is the law of nature between man and man, before the constitution of the commonwealth, is the law of nations between sovereign and sovereign after" (*The English Works of Thomas Hobbes of Malmesbury*, ed. Sir William Molesworth [London: Scientia Aalen, 1962], vol. 4, pt. 2, ch. 10, sec. 10, p. 228).

128. For a realist explanation of this logic, see Hedley Bull, "Hobbes and the International Anarchy," *Social Research* 48/4 (1981): 717–738. See also the classic, John Herz, "Idealist Internationalism and the Security Dilemma," *World Politics* 2/2 (1950): 157–180.

129. See Michael C. Williams, "Hobbes and International Relations: A Reconsideration," *International Organization* 50/2 (1996): 213–236. Williams argues that neither the realist mainstream nor the "English" interpretation get at the core of the Hobbesian project, which, instead, is concerned with "a series of much more difficult problems concerning epistemology and ethics and their role in the creation of communities" (230).

130. Rousseau writes that "the inequality of men has its limits set by nature, but the inequality of states can grow incessantly, until one of them absorbs all the others." See his "The State of War," in *The Social Contract and Other Later Political Writings*, ed. and trans. Victor Gourevitch (Cambridge: Cambridge University Press, 1997), 162–176. The absence of true equality among nations also leads to a restriction of the autonomy of individual states. As a consequence, they will face different constraints than the individuals in the state of nature, a fact that further complicates the analogy.

131. See Johnson Bagby, "The Law of Nations," in which she points out that the differences between the state of nature and international politics also have the effect that in the latter realm unenforceable covenants are both more likely to be formed and to succeed. This insight, which supports liberal and especially regime theory, is largely ignored by realists.

132. Ibid.

133. Johnson, *Thucydides*, 70–71. In light of this chapter, I disagree with Johnson's judgment on point 6.

134. Navari, "Hobbes and the 'Hobbesian Tradition,' in International Thought," 204.

135. Johnson Bagby, "The Law of Nations," 20.

136. This problem has received particular attention in Johnston's *The Rhetoric of Leviathan* and Strauss's *The Political Philosophy of Hobbes*.

137. Hobbes, *Behemoth*, dialogue 4, p. 188.

138. On the persuasive power of "myths of origin" such as the Hobbesian model of the state of nature, see Robert B. J. Walker, *Inside/Outside: International Relations as Political Theory* (Cambridge: Cambridge University Press, 1993), 27, 88–90.

Chapter 4. Realism Today

1. George, "Realist Ethics," 201.

2. Rousseau, "The State of War," 169.

3. Loriaux, "The Realists and Saint Augustine," 402. The metaphor is found in Rousseau's "A Discourse on the Origin of Inequality," in *The Social Contract and Discourses*, trans. G. D. H. Cole (New York: E. P. Dutton, 1950), 238.

4. See Carl von Clausewitz, *On War*, trans. Michael Howard and Peter Paret (1832–1834; reprint, Princeton, N.J.: Princeton University Press, 1976).

5. Crane, *The Ancient Simplicity*, 15.

6. Ernst-Otto Czempiel, "In der Realismusfalle: Kritik einer Aussenpolitischen Maxime," *Merkur* 52/1 (1998): 15–25.

7. Hirschman, *The Passions*, 14.

8. For an elaboration of this view, see especially Hans Morgenthau, *Scientific Man vs. Power Politics* (Chicago: University of Chicago Press, 1946). Andreas Osiander has recently reexamined the writings of early-twentieth-century idealist scholars of international relations, among them Norman Angell, Alfred Zimmern, and Leonard Woolf. He identifies as "the crucial difference between Idealism and Realism . . . their respective ideas of history," finding that political idealism "relies on the notion of [a] historical process . . . towards ever greater integration of the various subdivisions of humanity." See his "Rereading Early Twentieth-Century IR Theory: Idealism Revisited," *International Studies Quarterly* 42/3 (1998): 409, 429.

9. Brian Schmidt has recently argued that, at least in the United States, the interwar period was not as clearly idealistic as is commonly assumed. See his "Lessons from the Past: Reassessing the Interwar Disciplinary History of International Relations," *International Studies Quarterly* 42/3 (1998): 433–459.

10. George, "Realist Ethics," 201.

11. The official history of the discipline of international relations begins with the endowment of the first dedicated international relations professorship at the University of Wales in 1919.

12. Francis Beer and Robert Hariman, "Realism and Rhetoric in International Relations," in *Post-Realism: The Rhetorical Turn in International Relations*, ed. Francis Beer and Robert Hariman (East Lansing: Michigan State University Press, 1996), 1. In the 1980s, John Vasquez found 90 percent of all hypotheses used in behavioral international relations studies to be realist in conception. See his *The Power of Power Politics*.

13. For a concise summary of the main tenets of contemporary international political realism, see also Czempiel, "In der Realismusfalle."

14. In defense against neoliberals (and other critics), realists continue to emphasize the nation–state as the most important actor in the international system. See, for example, Christopher Layne and Benjamin Schwarz, "No New World Order: America after the Cold War," *Current* 358 (December 1993): 26–33; or Kenneth Waltz, "The Emerging Structure of International Politics," *International Security* 18/2 (1993): 44–79.

15. This logic, which primarily characterizes neorealism but also plays a role in classical realist thought, allows realists to treat states as fundamentally alike. Kenneth Waltz, for example, explicitly posits states to be "like units" (see his *Theory of International Politics*). The logic is further legitimized by traditional realist skepticism concerning the legitimacy of universal value judgments. For example, realists generally hesitate "to discriminate between political societies according to the supposed merits of their domestic constitutional structures and values" (Loriaux, "The Realists and Saint Augustine," 407). This is apparent in realist comments on the "democratic peace proposition." See, for example, John Mearsheimer, "Back to the Future"; or Waltz, "The Emerging Structure of International Politics."

16. For an idealist critique of realist psychological arguments, see Norman Angell, *The Great Illusion: A Study of the Relation of Military Power in Nations to Their Economic and Social Advantage*, 3d ed. (New York: G. P. Putnam's Sons, 1911), 147–329.

17. Realists have worked on developing analogous explanations for ethnic conflict, arguing with Hobbes that the breakdown of authority within a nation can create anarchical conditions under which different factions will be motivated to war for power. See, for example, Barry Posen, "The Security Dilemma and Ethnic Conflict," *Survival* 35/1 (1993): 27–47. The logic is, in principle, transferable to other areas of international competition, such as international economic relations. While in these other issue areas the threat to nations' physical sur-

vival may be less immediate, competition in such fields may well end up triggering military conflicts.

18. As we will see later on in this chapter, game theory can model this dilemma, in which a lack of information about the real intentions of others leads actors to rely on the assumption that those others will rationally pursue their own self-interest. If others' interests are perceived to be contrary to their own, this assumption serves to inhibit trust and cooperation. Interaction under such conditions may lead to suboptimal outcomes for all participants, as it does in the famous "Prisoners' Dilemma." For an overview of game theory see Thomas Schelling, *Choice and Consequence* (Cambridge: Harvard University Press, 1984). For a discussion of the effects of assumptions and expectations on political behavior, see chapter 6.

19. Robert Jervis, Janice Gross Stein, and Richard Ned Lebow, *Psychology and Deterrence* (Baltimore: Johns Hopkins University Press, 1985), viii. Jack Snyder has examined how deterrence policies can become self-defeating by eliciting the very responses they are designed to prevent. Richard Lebow has claimed that deterrence theory is fundamentally flawed because it does not acknowledge that fear is the most common cause of aggression. See Snyder's "Perceptions of the Security Dilemma in 1914," 153–179; and Lebow's "The Deterrence Deadlock: Is There a Way Out?" 180–202, both in Jervis, Gross Stein, and Lebow, *Psychology and Deterrence*. For a forceful defense of the potential of deterrence theory, see Frank Harvey, *The Future's Back* (Toronto: McGill-Queen's University Press, 1997) and "Rigor Mortis, or Rigor, More Tests: Necessity, Sufficiency, and Deterrence Logic," *International Studies Quarterly* 42/4 (1998): 675–707.

20. The only exception would be a situation in which states have practically nothing to lose and everything to gain from such collaboration. Such a situation would most likely be a defensive military alliance.

21. Loriaux, "The Realists and Saint Augustine," 402.

22. On the role of balance-of-power politics in maintaining system stability, see especially Hedley Bull, *The Anarchical Society: A Study of Order in World Politics* (London: Macmillan, 1977).

23. Loriaux, "The Realists and Saint Augustine," 402.

24. The United States is merely the clearest, most visible, and most influential example. See, for example, Ekkehart Krippendorf, *Die Amerikanische Strategie: Entscheidungsprozess und Instrumentarium der Amerikanischen Aussenpolitik* (Frankfurt/Main, Ger.: Suhrkamp, 1970). On the effects of the dominance of realism in post–Cold War western Europe, see Czempiel, "In der Realismusfalle."

25. Thus, Secretary of State George Marshall could say in 1947, "I doubt seriously whether a man can think with full wisdom and with deep convictions regarding certain of the basic international issues today who has not at least reviewed in his mind the period of the Peloponnesian War and the fall of Athens." Quoted in David Ignatius, "They Don't Make Them Like George Marshall Anymore," *Washington Post*, 8 June 1987, p. 25, national edition.

26. See George Marshall, *The Papers of George Catlett Marshall* (Baltimore: Johns Hopkins University Press, 1981). See George Kennan, "Morality and Foreign Policy," *Foreign Affairs* 64/2 (1985/1986): 205–218, the illustrative *American Diplomacy* (1951; reprint, Chicago: University of Chicago Press, 1984), *At a Century's Ending: Reflections, 1982–1995* (New York: Norton, 1996), and the more theoretical *Around the Cragged Hill: A Personal and Political Philosophy* (New York: Norton 1993), in which Kennan sets out to explain how "congenital imperfections in human nature" affect politics (253). See Henry Kissinger, *American Foreign Policy* (1969; reprint, New York: Norton, 1977) and *Diplomacy*.

27. Mary Maxwell, *Morality among Nations: An Evolutionary View* (Albany: State University of New York Press, 1990), 13.

28. John C. Garnett, *Commonsense and the Theory of International Politics* (London: Macmillan, 1984), 72.

29. Stephen Walt, "International Relations." See Mastanduno, "Preserving the Unipolar Moment."

30. Frank W. Wayman and Paul F. Diehl, "Realpolitik: Dead End, Detour, or Road Map?" in *Reconstructing Realpolitik*, ed. Frank W. Wayman and Paul F. Diehl (Ann Arbor: University of Michigan Press, 1994), 263.

31. See, for example, Deputy Secretary of State John C. Whitehead's address to the Hans J. Morgenthau Award Dinner of the National Committee on American Foreign Policy on March 16, 1988, in New York City: "Principled Realism: A Foundation for U.S. Policy," *Department of State Bulletin* 88/2135 (1988): 33–35.

32. Walt, "International Relations," 43.

33. Ibid.

34. See especially Morgenthau, *Scientific Man vs. Power Politics* and *Politics among Nations*; Reinhold Niebuhr, *Moral Man and Immoral Society: A Study in Ethics and Politics* (New York: Scribner, 1932) and *The Structure of Nations and Empires* (New York: Scribner, 1959); Carr, *The Twenty Years' Crisis*; Martin Wight, *Power Politics* (London: Royal Institute of International Affairs, 1949) and "Why Is There No International Theory?" in *Diplomatic Investigations: Essays in the Theory of International Politics*, ed. Herbert Butterfield and Martin Wight (Cambridge: Harvard University Press, 1966), 17–34; Raymond Aron, *Peace and War: A Theory of International Relations* (Garden City, N.Y.: Doubleday, 1966); and John Herz, *Political Realism and Political Idealism: A Study in Theories and Realities* (Chicago: University of Chicago Press, 1951).

35. See, for example, Robert G. Kaufman, "E. H. Carr, Winston Churchill, Reinhold Niebuhr, and Us: The Case for Principled, Prudential, Democratic Realism," *Security Studies* 5/2 (winter 1995/1996): 314–353; Patricia Stein Wrightson, "Morality, Realism, and Foreign Affairs: A Narrative Realist Approach," *Security Studies* 5/2 (winter 1995/1996): 354–386. Kaufman compares Carr and Niebuhr with respect to the degrees of determinism, moral relativism, structuralism, and collectivism apparent in their works. Wrightson claims that, while Niebuhr can legitimately be called a "normative realist," Morgenthau's endeavor to find a role for morality in foreign policy is thwarted by his bleak view of human nature and his separation of the moral from the political sphere.

36. My concentration on the realist elements in the works of the relevant thinkers is not meant to imply that their overall status as realists is clear or undisputed. For example, Herz may be viewed as committed to a position of "realist liberalism," which attempts, by virtue of a normative preference for liberal ideals, to mitigate "power-glorifying force-obsessed Political Realism" (*Political Realism*, v). The characterization of Niebuhr's thought as realist neglects the fact that he continued to express hope that the destructive tendencies of human pride could be kept in check, and that real progress could be achieved through the cultivation of rational modesty. On the complexity of the political thought of Carr see, for example, Charles Jones, "Carr, Mannheim, and a Post-Positivist Science of International Relations," *Political Studies* 45 (1997): 232–246. Jones claims that Carr's thought is properly understood only by recognizing its substantial reliance on Karl Mannheim. Compare Karl Mannheim, *Ideology and Utopia* (New York: Harcourt, Brace, and Company, 1936).

37. Carr, *The Twenty Years' Crisis*, ix.

38. Niebuhr and Morgenthau are perhaps the best examples.

39. Morgenthau, *Politics among Nations*, 4. In this book, Morgenthau identifies six principles of political realism. See 4–13.

40. Morgenthau, *Scientific Man vs. Power Politics*, 204.

41. Morgenthau, *Politics among Nations*, 30. Sociobiological arguments are currently back in fashion in some realist circles. See Bradley Thayer, "Bringing in Darwin: Evolutionary Theory, Realism, and International Relations," *International Security* 25/2 (2000): 124 –151.

42. Tellis, "Reconstructing Political Realism," 40.

43. Morgenthau, *Scientific Man vs. Power Politics*, 192.

44. Morgenthau, *Scientific Man vs. Power Politics*, 193–194.

45. Morgenthau, *Politics among Nations*, 31, and *Scientific Man vs. Power Politics*, 45. Both Morgenthau and Niebuhr believe that man's innate tribalism is another natural source of political conflict. See especially Reinhold Niebuhr, *Man's Nature and His Communities: Essays on the Dynamics and Enigmas of Man's Personal and Social Existence* (New York: Scribner, 1965).

46. Tellis, "Reconstructing Political Realism," 43.

47. See J. E. Hare and Carey B. Joynt, *Ethics and International Affairs* (New York: St. Martin's, 1982).

48. Niebuhr, *Moral Man and Immoral Society*.

49. Reinhold Niebuhr, *Christian Realism* (New York: Charles Scribner's Sons, 1953), 120.

50. Loriaux, "The Realists and Saint Augustine," 406.

51. George, "Realist Ethics," 206. See Fred Halliday, "Theory and Ethics in International Relations: The Contradictions of C. Wright Mills," *Millennium* 23/2 (1994): 377–387.

52. Cited in Michael Nicholson, "The Enigma of Martin Wight," *Review of International Studies* 7/1 (1981): 18.

53. George, "Realist Ethics," 206.

54. Loriaux, "The Realists and Saint Augustine," 406.

55. For another example of neo-Augustinian realism, see Herbert Butterfield, *International Conflict in the Twentieth Century* (New York: Harper, 1960).

56. For a concise statement of the principle differences between political idealism and realism, as perceived by the classical realists, see Hans Morgenthau, "Realism in International Politics," *Naval War College Review* 10/5 (1958): 1–14.

57. Carr, *The Twenty Years' Crisis*, 89. It should be noted that Carr admits that "any sound political thought must be based on elements of both utopia and reality," because "pure realism can offer nothing but a naked struggle for power which makes any kind of international society impossible" (93). Like Herz, Carr attempted in some ways to reconcile a liberal democratic normative persuasion with political realism.

58. The tension between descriptive and prescriptive elements remains pervasive in classical realism. The work of Morgenthau is a good example. According to David Fromkin, Morgenthau grew progressively more skeptical of his own earlier descriptive claims but did not strengthen his prescriptive arguments in response. Perhaps this hesitancy is attributable to his moral convictions. See Fromkin, "Remembering Hans Morgenthau," *World Policy Journal* 10/3 (1993): 81–88. See also Morgenthau's essays in *Truth and Power* (New York: Praeger, 1970).

59. Loriaux, "The Realists and Saint Augustine," 404.

60. Carr, *The Twenty Years' Crisis*, 236.

61. Loriaux, "The Realists and Saint Augustine," 404–405.

62. Ibid., 405. See Carr, *The Twenty Years' Crisis*, esp. chs. 4, 9, and 10. Carr does profess a concern with injustice, as well as a preference for the principles of liberal democracy. However, his position is a typically realist one in that it prioritizes a concern with the

preservation of political order. This tendency is also particularly pronounced in the work of Raymond Aron. A criticism that is levied against realism by reformist approaches is that this concern with the preservation of order adds a tendency to side with the status quo to realist foundational skepticism concerning progressive change, thereby exacerbating the conservatism of realist thought. On the relationship between (continental European) conservatism and political realism, see especially Alfons Soellner, "German Conservatism in America: Morgenthau's Political Realism," *Telos* 72 (summer 1987): 161–172.

63. See the fifth principle of political realism in Morgenthau, *Politics among Nations*, 10. Morgenthau admits more easily than Carr that idealistic aspirations may sometimes be based on universally valid moral norms. Still, like Carr, he bases his theory on a realist skepticism of such aspirations.

64. Johnson Bagby, "The Law of Nations," 20. Twentieth-century realists generally agree with Hobbes on the problem of passions. According to Robert Gilpin, "moral skepticism joined to a hope that reason may one day gain greater control over passions constitutes the essence of realism and unites realists of every generation." See his "The Richness of the Tradition," 304.

65. A wealth of literature deals with the moral relevance and implications of realist international political theory. Some of the more useful texts are Maxwell, *Morality among Nations*; Hare and Joynt, *Ethics and International Affairs*, ch. 2; Forde, "Varieties of Realism"; Kenneth Kipnis and Diana T. Meyers, eds., *Political Realism and International Morality* (Boulder, Colo.: Westview, 1987); and Mervyn Frost, *Ethics in International Relations: A Constitutive Theory* (Cambridge: Cambridge University Press, 1996), ch. 2.

66. See the second principle of political realism in Morgenthau, *Politics among Nations*, 5. The third principle adds that the specific contents of the concepts of interest and power depend on individual circumstances (8–9).

67. Hans Morgenthau, *In Defense of the National Interest* (New York: Knopf, 1951), 242.

68. See Greg Russell, "Hans J. Morgenthau and the National Interest," *Society* 31/2 (1994): 80–84, as well as Michael J. Smith, "Hans Morgenthau and the American National Interest in the Early Cold War," *Social Research* 48/8 (1981): 766–785.

69. Johnson Bagby, "The Law of Nations," 23–24. For example, Morgenthau (who was, after all, trained as a lawyer) takes seriously the role of international law, but holds that, in the end, "international law arises from, and is a function of, the balance of power." See Fromkin, "Remembering Hans Morgenthau," 81.

70. See, for example, Morgenthau, *Politics among Nations*, ch. 16.

71. Morgenthau, *Scientific Man vs. Power Politics*, 203.

72. See the sixth principle of political realism in Morgenthau, *Politics among Nations*, 10–12.

73. Doyle, *Ways of War and Peace*, 106. For a more recent realist attempt to grapple with this issue, see Felix E. Oppenheim, *The Place of Morality in Foreign Policy* (Lexington, Mass.: Lexington Books, 1991).

74. It should be noted that the degree of Morgenthau's skepticism is a matter of considerable debate in the scholarly literature. For example, Loriaux argues that Morgenthau "comes close to a real philosophical skepticism" ("The Realists and Saint Augustine," 405).

75. George, "Realist Ethics," 204. In *Scientific Man vs. Power Politics* (ch. 7), Morgenthau rejects four traditional approaches to the role of morality in politics: a double standard, the argument that ends justify means, an unmediated logic of reason of state, and perfectionist ethics. On the complex relationship between the traditional concept of *raison d'etat* and the

thought of Morgenthau, see Greg Russell, *Hans J. Morgenthau and the Ethics of American Statecraft* (Baton Rouge: Louisiana State University Press, 1990).

76. See the fourth principle of political realism in Morgenthau, *Politics among Nations*, 9–10. See also especially Kenneth W. Thompson and Robert J. Myers, *Truth and Tragedy: A Festschrift for Hans J. Morgenthau* (New Brunswick, N.J.: Transaction Publishers, 1984). It is telling that Morgenthau identifies the roots of realism in Thucydides, while Carr, for example, finds them in Machiavelli. See Morgenthau, *Scientific Man vs. Power Politics*, 42; and Carr, *The Twenty Years' Crisis*, 63–64.

77. Morgenthau, *Politics among Nations*, 7, 9.

78. On the Augustinian influence in the thought of Morgenthau, see also A. J. H. Murray, who comes to the alternative conclusion that Morgenthau does indeed manage to develop a Judeo-Christian nonperfectionist political ethic ("The Moral Politics of Hans Morgenthau," *Review of Politics* 58/1 [1996]: 81–107).

79. Morgenthau, *Scientific Man vs. Power Politics*, esp. ch. 5. Loriaux points out that, ironically, contemporary realism, by combining elements of structural analysis and rational choice theory, has itself taken on the look of a "managerial" approach to statecraft. In contrast to liberal progressivism, however, its advice is strategic, rather than administrative. See his "The Realists and Saint Augustine."

80. Morgenthau, *Politics among Nations*, 4.

81. Forde, "International Realism," 150. By comparison, neorealists tend to judge the scientific standard of their theories by criteria of testability. Morgenthau's idiosyncratic usage of the term notwithstanding, twentieth-century realist theorists generally strive to make their theories "scientific." Thus, Carr entitles the opening chapter of *The Twenty Years' Crisis* "The Science of International Politics," and Herz envisions his *Political Realism* to advance political theory beyond its "pre-scientific stage" (xi).

82. Morgenthau, *Politics among Nations*, 4.

83. As Morgenthau in particular realizes, it is difficult for political theory to inform political practice. See his "Thought and Action in Politics," *Social Research* 38/4 (1971): 611–632.

84. Gilpin, *War and Change in World Politics*, 226.

85. Morgenthau, *Politics among Nations*, 526–530.

86. In *Politics among Nations*, Morgenthau explains that policy is "rational," that is, superior, if it is designed to be both successful and prudent (see 7, 9).

87. Ibid., 4.

88. Robert J. Myers, "Hans J. Morgenthau: On Speaking Truth to Power," *Society* 29/2 (1992): 65. See also Kenneth W. Thompson, "The Cold War: The Legacy of Morgenthau's Approach," *Social Research* 48/4 (1981): 660–676.

89. Forde, "International Realism," 144.

90. Morgenthau, *Politics among Nations*, 6.

91. Ibid. It should be noted that Morgenthau does not claim that motives do not play an important role in foreign policy. Moreover, the fact that they are difficult to know does not have to mean, as he holds, that psychological approaches are futile. The fact that they are frequently distorted may lead us to consider their thorough examination all the more important.

92. Ibid. Morgenthau, like other classical realists, is not consistent in refraining from psychological or sociological explanation. For example, he suggests that the Cold War should be viewed as primarily an ideological conflict.

93. According to Morgenthau, for example, "the [F]irst World War had its origins exclusively in the fear of a disturbance of the European balance of power" (*Politics among Nations*,

173). Of the classical realists, Herz is probably the most structuralist in orientation. On this issue see also Gilpin, "The Richness of the Tradition of Political Realism."

94. For example, Morgenthau was at least somewhat interested in explaining why European nations were afraid of a disturbance of the balance of power and how this fear led to the outbreak of the First World War. See his *Politics among Nations*, 173–175.

95. See J. David Singer, "The Level-of-Analysis Problem in International Relations," in *The International System: Theoretical Essays*, ed. Klaus Knorr and Sidney Verba (Princeton, N.J.: Princeton University Press, 1961), 77–92. For an up-to-date and thorough analysis of the distinctness and advantages of a structuralist approach to the study of international relations, see Patrick James, *International Relations and Scientific Progress: Structural Realism Reconsidered* (Columbus: Ohio State University Press, 2002).

96. Waltz, *Man, the State, and War*, 3.

97. Ibid., 35.

98. See Alexander Wendt, "The Agent-Structure Problem in International Relations Theory," *International Organization* 41 (summer 1987): 335–370.

99. Waltz, *Man, the State, and War*, 35.

100. Keohane, "Realism, Neorealism, and the Study of World Politics," 15.

101. For a contradictory view, see Colin Elman, "Horses for Courses: Why *Not* Neorealist Theories of Foreign Policy?" *Security Studies* 6/1 (1996): 7–53. This issue of *Security Studies* also includes a reaction from Waltz and a reply by Elman.

102. See Waltz, *Theory of International Politics*: "A theory of international politics . . . can describe the range of likely outcomes of the actions and interactions of states within a given system and show how the range of expectations varies as systems change. It can tell us what pressures are exerted and what possibilities are posed by systems of different structure, but it cannot tell us just how, and how effectively, the units of a system will respond to those pressures and possibilities" (71; see also 122).

103. Bruce D. Porter, "External Conflict and External Sovereignty: Towards a Neorealist Theory of the State" (paper presented at the annual meeting of the American Political Science Association, New York City, September 1994), 4.

104. Keohane, "Realism, Neorealism, and the Study of World Politics," 14.

105. Porter, "External Conflict and External Sovereignty," 4.

106. Waltz, *Theory of International Politics*, 18.

107. Waltz, "The Validation," 1. For an explanation of why he judges neorealism to be more "scientific" than classical realism, see also Waltz's "Realist Thought and Neorealist Theory," *Journal of International Affairs* 44/1 (1990): 21–37. For a different view, see Richard Little, "International Relations and the Methodological Turn," *Political Studies* 39 (September 1991): 463–478. Little argues that classical and behavioral approaches cannot properly be distinguished on epistemological or methodological grounds, only by the research questions asked. Compare also Wight's argument that international politics does not lend itself to theorizing at all because the relevant actors are nations, not persons, and because it is a realm in which no real progress can occur. See his "Why Is There No International Theory?"

108. Waltz, *Theory of International Politics*, 81.

109. As we have seen, this assumption appears as a claim in earlier realist arguments. However, the extent of Waltz's reliance on this claim as a theoretical axiom is unprecedented.

110. Some of the better-known scholars developing such theories are J. David Singer, George Modelski and William Thompson, Manus M. Midlarsky, and Charles Doran, as well as Benjamin Most, Harvey Starr, and Randolph Siverson. For summary chapters on their

respective arguments, see Manus Midlarsky, ed., *Handbook of War Studies* (Boston: Unwin Hyman, 1989). See also A. F. K. Organski and Jacek Kugler, *The War Ledger* (Chicago: University of Chicago Press, 1980).

111. Waltz, *Theory of International Politics*, 118.

112. According to Waltz, of all possible balance-of-power configurations, a bipolar system like that of the Cold War is the most stable, as less powerful states tend to ally themselves with either of the two major powers and are less likely to change the overall distribution of power within the system by shifting alliances. In a multipolar system, weak states are more likely to combine forces to balance against stronger states, rather than allying themselves with a hegemon, and are more likely to shift alliances. This leads to a greater degree of unpredictability and volatility in the international system, which poses great danger to international stability and peace. Waltz judges the current system to be unipolar, with the United States as the only superpower, and claims that such a system is inherently unstable and likely to result in the emergence of a multipolar system. See, for example, his "The New-World Order," *Millennium* 22/2 (1993): 187–195. Compare also Christopher Layne, "The Unipolar Illusion: Why New Great Powers Will Rise," in *The Perils of Anarchy: Contemporary Realism and International Security*, ed. Michael E. Brown, Sean M. Lynn-Jones, and Steven E. Miller (Cambridge: MIT Press, 1995), 130–176.

113. To imbue neorealism with more explanatory and predictive power, some scholars have considered complementing Waltz's systemic arguments with hypotheses concerning the impact of second- or first-image factors on state behavior. See especially Patrick James, *Elaborated Structural Realism and Crises in World Politics* (Columbus: Ohio State University Press, 2003); and Jennifer Sterling-Folker "Realist Environment, Liberal Process, and Domestic-Level Variables," *International Studies Quarterly* 41/1 (1997): 1–25. In an effort to introduce an appropriate second-image foundation, Bruce Porter has attempted to complement Waltz's neorealism with a neorealist theory of the state. See his "External Conflict and External Sovereignty." Other scholars have rejected the systemic approach, arguing that, ultimately, "structural change has no other source than unit-level processes" (Keohane, "Realism," 17) or at least that "as to explanation, there seems little doubt that the subsystemic or actor orientation is considerably more fruitful, permitting as it does a more thorough investigation of the processes by which foreign policies are made" (Singer, "The Level-of-Analysis Problem," 89–90).

114. See, for example, Robert Cox, "Social Forces, States, and World Orders," 204–254, and John Gerard Ruggie, "Continuity and Transformation in the World Polity: Toward a Neorealist Synthesis," 131–157, in *Neorealism and Its Critics*, ed. Robert Keohane (New York: Columbia University Press, 1986). For recent attempts to improve realist theory to better account for change, see the essays in Robert Cox, ed., *The New Realism: Perspectives on Multilateralism and World Order* (Tokyo: United Nations University Press, 1997).

115. Waltz explains in *Theory of International Politics*:

> The structure of a system acts as a constraining and disposing force, and because it does so systems theories explain and predict continuity within a system. . . . Within a system a theory explains recurrences and repetitions, not change. . . . A systems theory explains changes across systems, not within them, and yet international life within a given system is by no means all repetition. Important discontinuities occur. If they occur within a system that endures, their causes are found at the unit level. (69, 71)

116. See, for example, the essays in Richard Ned Lebow and Thomas Risse-Kappen, eds., *International Relations Theory and the End of the Cold War* (New York: Columbia University Press, 1995). Within this volume see especially Richard Ned Lebow, "The Long Peace, the

End of the Cold War, and the Failure of Realism," 23–56. See also John Lewis Gaddis, "International Relations Theory and the End of the Cold War," *International Security* 17/3 (winter 1992/1993): 5–58; and Waltz's response to Gaddis: "The Validation of International-Political Theory."

117. As acknowledged by Gilpin, "[N]eorealists . . . adhere to moral values that they seek to promote" (quoted in Keohane, "Realism, Neorealism, and the Study of World Politics," 21). Neorealist theory has tended to defend the Cold War standoff as relatively "safe," which has led some critics to accuse neorealists of advocating Cold War attitudes under the guise of scientific objectivism.

118. Ian Clark, *The Hierarchy of States: Reform and Resistance in the International Order* (Cambridge: Cambridge University Press, 1989), 85. Clark quotes Joseph Nye, "Neorealism and Neoliberalism," 236. His interpretation touches on the potential of neorealist theory to establish reflexive predictions and, in essence, function as a self-fulfilling prophecy. See chapter 6.

119. The most notable exception to the general lack of attention to this problem is the work of Forde. See especially his "International Realism and the Science of Politics."

120. Waltz, *Theory of International Politics*, 122.

121. See especially Peter Ahrensdorf ("Thucydides' Realistic Critique"), who claims that twentieth-century realism accepts the idea of international anarchy as an article of faith.

122. See any textbook on international relations theory; for example, Viotti and Kauppi, *International Relations Theory*.

123. Alexander Wendt, "Collective Identity Formation and the International State," *American Political Science Review* 88/2 (1994): 384.

124. Keohane, "Realism, Neoliberalism, and the Study of World Politics," 20. Richard Ashley's critique of neorealism is particularly sharp. He finds it to be an "'orrery of errors,' a self-enclosed, self-affirming joining of statist, utilitarian, positivist and structuralist commitments" ("The Poverty of Neorealism," 228). For a sympathetic summary of Ashley's arguments, see also Shibashis Chatterjee, "Neo-Realism in International Relations," *International Studies* 34/1 (1997): 39–58. For a neorealist defense, see Gilpin, "The Richness of the Tradition of Political Realism."

125. See especially, Robert Jervis, "Cooperation under the Security Dilemma," *World Politics* 30 (January 1978): 167–214; George H. Quester, *Offense and Defense in the International System* (New York: Wiley, 1977); and Stephen van Evera, "Offense, Defense, and the Causes of War," *International Security* 22/4 (1998): 5–43.

126. See Jervis, "Cooperation under the Security Dilemma."

127. See Walt, "International Relations."

128. See van Evera, "Offense"; and Jack Snyder, *Myths of Empire: Domestic Politics and International Ambition* (Ithaca, N.Y.: Cornell University Press, 1991) and "Myths, Modernization, and the Post-Gorbachev World," in *International Relations Theory and the End of the Cold War*, ed. Richard Ned Lebow and Thomas Risse-Kappen (New York: Columbia University Press, 1995), 109–126. Snyder sheds light on "the recurrent problem of self-defeating aggression among great powers" in his *Myths of Empire: Domestic Politics and International Ambition* (Ithaca: N.Y.: Cornell University Press, 1991), 2. He examines the role of strategic concepts and their function as ideology in domestic politics, arguing that nations "overexpand" because they fall prey to the myth that expansion provides safety. In "Myths" he describes Soviet foreign policy changes under Gorbachev as a shift from offensive to defensive realism.

129. Walt, "International Relations," 37.

130. Ibid.

131. Ibid.

132. For example, defensive realists tend to believe that the United States was fairly secure during the Cold War. As long as both superpowers could credibly extend their protection to their allies, the world was in order, and superpower war was extremely unlikely. As a consequence of such arguments, according to Walt, "by the end of the Cold War, realism had moved away from Morgenthau's dark brooding about human nature and taken on a slightly more optimistic tone" ("International Relations," 32). In their judgment of the potential for interstate cooperation in the absence of supranational authority, defensive realists sometimes approximate a neoliberal institutionalist position. They generally do not grant as much importance to nonstate actors or international norms as do neoliberals. However, their psychological explanations for international cooperation are frequently similar to those of the liberal theorists. Thus, while they would perceive different structural constraints and incentives, their foreign policy logic is usually compatible with liberal arguments. An example for the gray area where liberal institutionalism overlaps with what we might today call "defensive realism" is the work of Keohane. See, for example, his *International Institutions and State Power: Essays in International Relations Theory* (Boulder, Colo.: Westview, 1989). See also the classic Keohane and Nye, *Power and Interdependence.*

133. Randall Schweller, *Deadly Imbalances: Tripolarity and Hitler's Strategy of World Conquest* (New York: Columbia University Press, 1997).

134. See especially Mearsheimer, "Back to the Future" and "The False Promise"; Eric J. Labs, "Beyond Victory: Offensive Realism and the Expansion of War Aims," *Security Studies* 6/4 (1997): 1–49; and Fareed Zakaria, *From Wealth to Power: The Unusual Origins of America's World Role* (Princeton, N.J.: Princeton University Press, 1998).

135. Labs, "Beyond Victory," 5. In a recent analysis, Charles Glaser concludes that the necessary reliance of offensive realism on the empirical claim that states are "greedy" "poses a serious challenge" to its conception of the security dilemma. He also agrees with Jervis that the magnitude of the security dilemma depends in part on a state's knowledge of other states' motives. See Glaser, "The Security Dilemma Revisited," *World Politics* 50/1 (1997): 174. See also Jervis, "Cooperation under the Security Dilemma."

136. Peter Liberman, *Does Conquest Pay? The Exploitation of Occupied Industrial Societies* (Princeton, N.J.: Princeton University Press, 1996). See also his article "The Spoils of Conquest," in *The Perils of Anarchy: Contemporary Realism and International Security*, ed. Michael E. Brown, Sean M. Lynn-Jones, and Steven Miller (Cambridge: MIT Press, 1995), 179–207.

137. Walt, "International Relations," 37.

138. See especially Joseph Grieco, "Anarchy and the Limits of Cooperation: A Realist Critique of the Newest Liberal Institutionalism," *International Organization* 42/3 (1988): 485–507, and *Cooperation among Nations: Europe, America, and Non-Tariff Barriers to Trade* (Ithaca, N.Y.: Cornell University Press, 1990); and Stephen Krasner, *Asymmetries in Japanese–American Trade: The Case for Specific Reciprocity* (Berkeley, Calif.: Institute of International Studies, 1987), and *Defending the National Interest: Raw Materials Investments and U.S. Foreign Policy* (Princeton, N.J.: Princeton University Press, 1978). See also the debate between Grieco, Robert Powell, and Duncan Snidal in "The Relative-Gains Problem for International Cooperation," *American Political Science Review* 87/3 (1993): 729–743.

139. See Keohane's reaction to this view in "Correspondence: Back to the Future, Part II: International Relations Theory and Post Cold War Europe," *International Security* 15/2 (1990): 192–194. See also Keohane and Lisa Martin, "The Promise of Institutionalist Theory," *International Security* 20/1 (1995): 39–51. For an analysis of the debate among different strands

of realist theory over the role of institutions, see Randall Schweller and David Priess, "A Tale of Two Realisms," *Mershon International Studies Review* 41 (suppl. 1; 1997): 1–32.

140. For example, in disagreement with Waltz, Gilpin and Organski and Kugler find that war is more likely to occur when power is distributed relatively equally among the relevant states. See, for example, Gilpin, *War and Change in World Politic*; and Organski and Kugler, *The War Ledger*.

141. See especially John Mueller, *Retreat from Doomsday: The Obsolescence of Major Wars* (New York: Basic Books, 1989). See also Snyder, "Myths, Modernization."

142. Mearsheimer, "The False Promise of International Institutions," 10–11.

143. Stephen Brooks, "Dueling Realisms," *International Organization* 51/3 (1997): 446.

144. Ibid., 447.

145. Stephen van Evera, "Primed for Peace: Europe after the Cold War," *International Security* 15/3 (1990): 7–57. Other defensive realists arrive at similar judgments. See, for example, Jack Snyder, "Averting Anarchy in the New Europe," *International Security* 14/4 (1990): 5–41; and Robert Jervis, "The Future of World Politics: Will It Resemble the Past?" *International Security* 16/3 (winter 1991/1992): 39–73. Keohane, too, sides with van Evera in his judgment of the prospects for a stable peace in a multipolar Europe. See G. Hellmann and R. Wolf, "Systemic Theories after the East–West Conflict," *Oesterreichische Zeitschrift fuer Politikwissenschaft* 22/2 (1993): 153–167.

146. See, for example, John Mearsheimer, "Why We Will Soon Miss the Cold War," *Atlantic* 266/2 (1990): 35–50, "After the Cold War: Will We Miss It?" *Current* 327 (November 1990): 30–40, and "Back to the Future." For critiques of this view, see especially Stanley Hoffman's and Robert Keohane's responses: "Correspondence: Back to the Future, Part II: International Relations Theory and Post Cold War Europe," *International Security* 15/2 (1990): 191–192 and 192–194, respectively.

147. Gauthier, *The Logic of Leviathan*. See chapter 3 of this book.

148. Keohane, "Realism, Neorealism, and the Study of World Politics," 7.

149. Influential examples are Bruce Bueno de Mesquita and David Lalman. See, for example, Bueno de Mesquita, *The War Trap* (New Haven, Conn.: Yale University Press, 1981), and Bueno de Mesquita and Lalman, *War and Reason* (New Haven, Conn.: Yale University Press, 1992). For a useful collection of core texts in rational choice theory published between 1958 and 1988, see Peter Abell, ed., *Rational Choice Theory* (Aldershot, U.K.: Edward Elgar, 1991).

150. Monroe, with Maher, "Psychology," 2.

151. Kristen Renwick Monroe, "The Theory of Rational Action," in *The Economic Approach to Politics: A Critical Reassessment of the Theory of Rational Action*, ed. Kristen Renwick Monroe (New York: HarperCollins, 1991), 1. See this text also on the use of the terms *rational actor theory* and *rational choice theory*. I use them here interchangeably.

152. Ibid.

153. Hirschman, *The Passions*, 32.

154. Ibid.

155. It is worth repeating that the relevant argument in Hobbes is prescriptive, whereas rational choice theory suggests a number of empirical assumptions, to be employed in empirical–analytical theorizing. Thus, Loriaux argues that realism has degenerated in recent decades by seeking, "by embracing the notion of homo oeconomicus, to 'operationalize' a prescriptive political philosophy according to the categories of contemporary social science and to endow it with predictive power" ("The Realists and Saint Augustine," 402).

156. Hirschman, *The Passions*, 42. As all liberal ideology, economic liberalism was inspired by the hope that individuals' pursuit of their private self-interest would bring public benefits by resulting in an advancement of the community as a whole.

157. Similarly, realist political theory implicitly relies on the rationality assumption to predict how political decision makers will respond to political constraints and incentives.

158. Donald Green and Ian Shapiro, *Pathologies of Rational Choice Theory* (New Haven, Conn.: Yale University Press, 1994), 14–17. Compare also James Morrow, *Game Theory for Political Scientists* (Princeton, N.J.: Princeton University Press, 1994), 17–22.

159. Mancur Olson Jr., *The Logic of Collective Action* (1965; reprint, Cambridge: Harvard University Press, 1971), 65.

160. Green and Shapiro, *Pathologies of Rational Choice Theory*, 16.

161. Ibid. In addition, the so-called homogeneity assumption ensures that, in empirical applications of the theory, models are viewed to apply equally to all agents under study.

162. Monroe, with Maher, "Psychology," 2. According to the authors, the limitations of rational actor theory "emanate from the extent to which politics differs from the economic realm for which the theory was originally developed, the extent to which self-interest does not always lead to collective welfare, the fact that humans do not always make decisions as the theory suggests, the theory's overemphasis on goal-directed behavior and a particular conceptualization of choice, and the theory's failure to make allowance for identity's influence on behavior" (19).

163. Allison, *Essence of Decision*, 31.

164. See Herbert A. Simon, *Models of Bounded Rationality* (Cambridge: MIT Press, 1982).

165. John Ferejohn, "Rationality and Interpretation: Parliamentary Elections in Early Stuart England," in *The Economic Approach to Politics: A Critical Reassessment of the Theory of Rational Action*, ed. Kristen Renwick Monroe (New York: HarperCollins, 1991), 282.

166. See Green and Shapiro, *Pathologies of Rational Choice Theory*.

167. James DeNardo, *The Amateur Strategist: Intuitive Deterrence Theories and the Politics of the Nuclear Arms Race* (Cambridge: Cambridge University Press, 1995).

168. Herbert Simon, "Human Nature in Politics: The Dialogue of Psychology with Political Science," *American Political Science Review* 79 (June 1985): 303.

169. John Harsanyi, "Some Social Science Implications of a New Approach to Game Theory," in *Strategic Interaction and Conflict*, ed. Kathleen Archibald (Berkeley, Calif.: Institute of International Studies, 1966), 139. For examples of applications of game theory in political inquiry, see William James Booth, Patrick James, and Hudson Meadwell, *Politics and Rationality* (New York: Cambridge University Press, 1994).

170. Allison, *Essence of Decision*, 29.

171. Ibid., 5.

172. Ibid.

173. Ibid., 30, 29.

174. Morgenthau, *Politics among Nations*, 5. By the time of the fifth edition (1973), Morgenthau had added two paragraphs to the first chapter which indicated his growing interest in complementing his theory with hypotheses on the role of irrationality in international politics.

175. On the problem of defining the self-interest of a nation, see Arthur A. Stein, *Why Nations Cooperate: Circumstance and Choice in International Relations* (Ithaca, N.Y.: Cornell University Press, 1990).

176. A pathbreaking study is Glenn Snyder and Paul Diesing's *Conflict Among Nations: Bargaining, Decision Making, and System Structure in International Crises* (Princeton, N.J.:

Princeton University Press, 1977). The authors apply formal bargaining models to sixteen cases of major-power crisis. For a critical overview of game theoretical approaches to international relations see Robert Jervis, "Realism, Game Theory, and Cooperation," *World Politics* 40/3 (1988): 317–349.

177. Thomas Schelling, *The Strategy of Conflict* (Cambridge: Harvard University Press, 1960), 4.

178. The difficulties of modeling interaction force game theorists in practice to radically simplify such scenarios.

179. Allison, *Essence of Decision*, 15.

180. Duncan Snidal, "The Game Theory of International Politics," in *Cooperation under Anarchy*, ed. Kenneth Oye (Princeton, N.J.: Princeton University Press, 1986), 36.

181. Holmes, "Introduction," xv.

182. See especially Robert M. Axelrod, *The Evolution of Cooperation* (New York: Basic Books, 1984).

183. Snidal, "The Game Theory," 25. Compare also Axelrod, *The Evolution of Cooperation* and Robert Axelrod and Douglas Dion, "The Further Evolution of Cooperation," *Science* 242/4884 (1988): 1385–1390. Game theory could, in principle, be useful to realists in another way as well: It could explain how employing restrictive motivational assumptions diminishes the number of ways in which the moves of other actors can reasonably be interpreted, how it thereby narrows the range of policy options available, and what the consequences may be. See chapter 6 of this book.

184. For an overview of some of the relevant literature, see the essays in Keith Dowding and Desmond King, eds., *Preferences, Institutions, and Rational Choice* (Oxford: Clarendon Press, 1995). The editors distinguish institutional rational choice theory from so-called historical institutionalism by the condition that, while the latter may employ supplemental models to examine the formation of preferences, actors' preferences must be exogenous in the decision-making models of rational choice theory (see their "Introduction"). For an overview of historical institutionalism, which is a theoretical approach primarily employed in the field of comparative politics, see the essays in Sven Steinmo, Kathleen Thelen, and Frank Longstreth, eds., *Structuring Politics: Historical Institutionalism in Comparative Analysis* (Cambridge: Cambridge University Press, 1992).

185. James Morrow, *Game Theory for Political Scientists* (Princtone, N.J.: Princton University Press, 1994), 17.

186. Dowding and King, "Introduction," 1.

187. Ibid., 2.

188. See, for example, Michael Laver, *Private Desires, Political Action: An Invitation to the Politics of Rational Choice* (London: Sage, 1997).

189. Ibid., 16.

190. See Verba, "Assumptions of Rationality."

191. Petracca, "The Rational Actor Approach to Politics," 178.

192. Ibid.

193. Simon, "Human Nature in Politics."

194. Dowding and King, "Introduction," 14. The authors also confirm that this conception of the individual may have its roots in deontological liberalism, in which, as John Rawls has put it, the "self is prior to the ends which are affirmed by it" (*A Theory of Justice* [Oxford: Oxford University Press, 1971], 560).

195. Petracca, "The Rational Actor Approach to Politics," 180.

196. Jane Mansbridge, "Rational Choice Gains by Losing," *Political Psychology* 16/1 (1995): 137.

197. Ibid. Mansbridge identifies the following gains: First, "versions of game theory that reduce motives to self-interest help us to understand that one's self-interest is dynamic and interactive" (138). Second, they can reveal "social interaction as difficult and achieved rather than easy and natural" (139). Third, they can, through an understanding of their limitations, "eventually allow us to understand better the role in social interaction of non self-interested motivation" (140). Fourth, they can help advance our understanding of the relationship between altruistic and self-interested motivation. The losses involved in simplifying motivation in this manner are the following: First, the models require the (unrealistic) conception that individuals are fundamentally separate from and, in significant ways, independent of one another. Second, they require that all relevant behavior be understood as in some way contributing to the actor's self-interest. Third, this has the consequence that unselfish motivation becomes increasingly difficult to identify. Its relevance may even be denied in defense of the requirements of modeling. Fourth, such theorizing and modeling creates a temptation to expect the real world to comply with the expectations created by the models and even has the potential of serving to legitimize selfishness.

198. Ibid., 137. Mansbridge warns that rational choice and game theory usually tend to

> marginalize altruism through underemphasis and distortion. Underemphasis occurs when a disciplinary decision to use self-interest for parsimony in modeling becomes a substantive conviction that most real world forms of action . . . can be explained by narrow self-interest. Then both the language of utility theory and the evolved predilections of its practitioners lead some of those practitioners actively to shun altruistic motivations. Distortion occurs when, trying to incorporate altruistic motivations in their models, theorists find they must express those motivations through a metric of utils which intrinsically implies hedonic satisfaction,

that is, in a language that stresses, "sometimes with conscious delight, the surface pleasures accruing to the actor rather than the actor's renunciation of his or her pleasure for the good of another or of a principle" (152).

199. Ibid., 138.

200. Laver, *Private Desires, Political Action*, 4.

201. According to Laver, "the purpose of rational choice theory is the search for interesting and non-trivial tautological arguments" (ibid., 6). See also Robert H. Bates, Jean-Laurent Rosenthal, Margaret Levi, Barry R. Weingast, and Avner Greif, *Analytic Narratives* (Princeton, N.J.: Princeton University Press, 1998). Bates and his colleagues consider rational choice models as "narratives," which must be evaluated by, among other criteria, examining whether their assumptions fit the facts inasmuch as they are known.

202. Laver, *Private Desires, Political Action*, 11.

203. Ibid.

204. Ibid., 7.

205. Gordon Tullock, *The Vote Motive* (London: Institute of Economic Affairs, 1976), 5.

206. Mansbridge, "Rational Choice Gains by Losing," 149. Mansbridge cites as one example Anthony Downs, *An Economic Theory of Democracy* (New York: Harper and Row, 1957). She claims that the early Downs is typical among rational choice theorists, who, while they "grant a place for non-self-interested motivations, . . . make that place relatively small and analytically uninteresting" (150).

207. It must be noted that this last characteristic does not apply to so-called defensive realism, as it was defined above. Indeed, according to the image of realism presented in this study, it is unlikely that defensive realism is still part of the paradigm proper and, thus, that it is legitimately a target of my critique. See especially Legro and Moravcsik, "Is Anybody Still a Realist?" The authors worry that neoclassical and defensive realists, in an effort to address anomalies faced by realist research, have instead undermined the theoretical core of realism itself.

208. Verba, "Assumptions of Rationality."

209. G. Thomas Goodnight has examined Morgenthau's *In Defense of the National Interest* as a rhetorical masterpiece designed to inculcate international policy making with the ideals of civic humanism. See Goodnight's "Hans J. Morgenthau In Defense of the National Interest: On Rhetoric, Realism, and the Public Sphere," in *Post Realism: The Rhetorical Turn in International Relations*, ed. Francis Beer and Robert Hariman (East Lansing: Michigan State University Press, 1996), 143–170.

210. Carr, *The Twenty Years' Crisis*, 10, 89. Reinhold Niebuhr, *The Children of Light and the Children of Darkness* (New York: Scribner's, 1944), 126.

211. Once again, Waltz makes himself the easiest target, most notably by deriving from his theory the rather counterintuitive proposition that nuclear proliferation might make the world a safer place. See his *Theory of International Politics*.

212. See, for example, Waltz, *Theory of International Politics*.

213. See Vasquez, "The Realist Paradigm."

Chapter 5. Realist Man through the Ages: A Synopsis

1. See Hobbes, *De Cive*.

2. Thuc. 1.75 and 1.76 (*Hobbes's Thucydides*, 70).

3. It should be noted that the cautious and rational human being is presented by Machiavelli as a cowardly opportunist (see *The Prince*). Machiavelli, while counseling *Realpolitik* and establishing a modern view of the use of political science, does not share in prescriptive realist rationalism.

4. Johnson, *Thucydides*, 208. Compare Morgenthau, *Scientific Man* and *Dilemmas of Politics* (Chicago: University of Chicago Press, 1958).

5. See Waltz, *Man, the State and War* and *Theory of International Politics*.

6. Johnson points out that "the assumptions that classical realists make about statesmen are the very assumptions neorealists have to make about the 'motivations' of states" (*Thucydides*, 204).

7. Ibid., 208.

8. Waltz, *Theory of International Politics*, 16.

9. See Machiavelli, *The Prince*; and Hobbes, *Leviathan*.

10. On realist versus idealist views on the possibility of progress, see especially Osiander, "Rereading Early Twentieth-Century IR Theory."

11. It should be noted that Waltz has argued that theories should be judged by the usefulness of their explanations, rather than by their ability to deliver accurate predictions. This, of course, raises the question how we may judge the usefulness of explanations. See his *Theory of International Politics*.

12. Forde, "International Realism and the Science of Politics," 158.

13. Ibid., 152.

14. See Morgenthau, *Scientific Man vs. Power Politics* and *Politics among Nations.*

15. See Rousseau, "The State of War."

16. It is possible to interpret the evolution of the European Union in this way, at least with respect to the cooperation among its core powers.

Chapter 6. What Is Wrong with the Realist Psychology?

1. See Henry A. Murray, *Explorations in Personality* (New York: Oxford University Press, 1938); and McClelland, *Human Motivation.* McClelland makes a distinction between "approach motives," such as power, achievement, and affiliative motives on the one hand, and "avoidance motives," such as fears, on the other hand.

2. See, for example, McClelland and Steele, eds., *Human Motivation.* On the motive of power, see especially David Winter, *The Power Motive* (New York: Free Press, 1973); and David C. McClelland, *Power: The Inner Experience* (New York: Irvington, 1975). On the motive of achievement, see especially David C. McClelland, John W. Atkinson, Russell E. Clark, and Edgar L. Lowell, *The Achievement Motive* (New York: Appleton-Century-Crofts, 1953); and John Atkinson, *A Theory of Achievement Motivation* (New York: Wiley, 1966).

3. Abraham H. Maslow, *Motivation and Personality* (New York: Harper and Row, 1952).

4. Wolfers, "The Goals of Foreign Policy," in *Discord and Collaboration.*

5. Richard W. Cottam, *Foreign Policy Motivation: A General Theory and a Case Study* (Pittsburgh, Pa.: University of Pittsburgh Press, 1977).

6. Graham Allison and Gregory Treverton, eds., *Rethinking America's Security: Beyond Cold War to New World Order* (New York: Norton, 1992), 20.

7. William O. Chittick, Keith Billingsley, and Rick Travis, "A Three-Dimensional Model of American Foreign Policy Beliefs," *International Studies Quarterly* 39/3 (1995): 313–331.

8. William O. Chittick and Annette Freyberg-Inan, "The Impact of Basic Motivation on Foreign Policy Opinions concerning the Use of Force: A Three-Dimensional Framework," in *When the Going Gets Tough: Democracy, Public Opinion, and the International Use of Force*, ed. Philip Everts and Pierangelo Isernia (London: Routledge, 2000).

9. McClelland, *Power.* See especially chapter 9: "Love and Power: The Psychological Basis of War," 314–359.

10. Winter, *The Power Motive.*

11. Winter, "Power, Affiliation, and War."

12. Peterson, Winter, and Doty, "Laboratory Tests." See also Mark Schafer, "Cooperative and Conflictual Policy Preferences: The Effect of Identity, Security, and Image of the Other," *Political Psychology* 20/4 (1999): 829–844. In Schafer's experiments, increased feelings of security are found to correspond to more cooperative behavior, even while image of the other appears to have no significant effect.

13. Ahrensdorf, "Thucydides' Realistic Critique of Realism," 262.

14. Ibid., 262–263. See also Orwin, *The Humanity of Thucydides*, 204. Orwin points out that, "for reasons that are wholly rationalistic, Thucydides rejects 'rationalism in politics.'"

15. Holmes, "Introduction," xx.

16. Johnson Bagby, "The Law of Nations," 23.

17. For a comprehensive critique, see Michael Argyle, "A Critique of Cognitive Approaches to Social Judgment and Social Behavior," in *Emotion and Social Judgments*, ed. Joseph Forgas (Oxford: Pergamon, 1991), 161–178.

18. Vertzberger, *The World in Their Minds.* According to Joseph de Rivera, the psychological dimension of an actor's definition of his situation includes his perception (his "construction" of "reality"), his thought and expectations, his decision-making characteristics, and his personality. See his *The Psychological Dimension of Foreign Policy* (Columbus, Ohio: Merrill, 1968).

19. Simon, "Human Nature in Politics," 293.

20. Allison, *Essence of Decision*, 36.

21. Ibid., 37.

22. On the role of altruism, see, for example, Monroe, with Maher, "Psychology and Rational Actor Theory."

23. See, for example, George Akerlof, "Loyalty Filters," *American Economic Review* 73/1 (1983): 54–63; Jack Hirshleifer, "On the Emotions as Guarantors of Threats and Promises," in *The Latest and the Best: Essays on Evolution and Optimality*, ed. John Dupre (Cambridge: MIT Press, 1987), 307–326; Jane Mansbridge, ed., *Beyond Self-Interest* (Chicago: University of Chicago Press, 1990); Robert H. Frank, *Passions within Reason* (New York: Norton, 1988); and the classic Axelrod, *The Evolution of Cooperation.*

24. Remember also the arguments employed in early liberal economic and utilitarian thought, which affirm the pacifying effects of the pursuit of economic interests.

25. See the essays in David C. McClelland, ed., *Studies in Motivation* (New York: Appleton-Century-Crofts, 1955), for a vista of the breadth and depth of studies of human motivation.

26. See, for example, Carl Jung, *The Integration of the Personality* (New York: Farrar and Rinehart, 1939); and Alfred Adler, *Understanding Human Nature* (London: G. Allen and Unwin, 1928).

27. See, for example, Alfred Adler, *Social Interest: A Challenge to Mankind* (London: Faber and Faber, 1938).

28. See, for example, Angell, "The Human Nature of the Case," in *The Great Illusion.*

29. Inasmuch as realism argues back and forth between the level of individual psychology and the level of nation–states, empirical analyses based on realist theoretical arguments that do not solve this issue through clear specification may face the threat of "ecological fallacy," which is the error of interpreting results that are based on aggregate-level data as if they applied to individuals. Vice versa, they may suffer from what James Richards Jr. has referred to as the "individual differences fallacy," which involves the interpretation of results based on individual-level data as if they applied to aggregates. See his "Units of Analysis and the Individual Differences Fallacy in Environmental Assessment," *Environment and Behavior* 22/3 (1990): 307–319. On problems of cross-level inference, see also Sharon Schwartz, "The Fallacy of the Ecological Fallacy," *American Journal of Public Health* 84 (May 1994): 819–824.

30. See Singer, "The Level-of-Analysis Problem"; and Barry Buzan, "The Level of Analysis Problem in International Relations Reconsidered," in *International Relations Theory Today*, ed. Ken Booth and Steve Smith (Cambridge: Polity Press, 1995), 198–216.

31. As Winter points out, the convergence between the operation of motivation at an individual and at a collective level can ultimately only be demonstrated by empirical testing. See his "Power, Affiliation, and War."

32. For a discussion of the merits of Niebuhr's thesis on the psychological egoism of groups see Hare and Joint, *Ethics and International Affairs*, ch. 2.

33. Once again, we may also counter such an argument by noting that realist theory traditionally relies on the structural analogy between the situation of individuals in a "state of nature" and that of nation–states in an anarchic interstate system. At least with respect to the

constraint of anarchy, which is of primary importance in realist theory, the analogy between the individual and the nation–state level of analysis is difficult to deny.

34. Or, as Alexandre Dumas has written, "[A]ll generalizations are dangerous, even this one." Dumas (the younger) quoted in William Poundstone, *Labyrinths of Reason* (1988; reprint, New York: Anchor Books/Doubleday, 1990), 128.

35. This judgment is shared by psychologist Lawrence Wrightsman, who has drawn attention to the fact that research in psychology and sociology has actively promoted some motivational assumptions and ignored others, while neglecting the study of their role in and implications for social scientific research. Wrightsman also confirms that, largely owing to the origins of positivist science in early Greek philosophy, "assumptions of determinism and other physical-science assumptions are the basis for contemporary behavioristic and psychoanalytic assumptions about human nature" (*Assumptions about Human Nature: Implications for Researchers and Practitioners*, 2d ed. [Newbury Park, Calif.: Sage, 1992], 44). See also his earlier work *Assumptions about Human Nature: A Social-Psychological Approach* (Monterey, Calif.: Brooks/Cole, 1974).

Chapter 7. The Effects of the Realist Bias

1. Thomas S. Kuhn, "Reflections on My Critics," in *Criticism and the Growth of Knowledge*, ed. Imre Lakatos and Alan Musgrave (Cambridge: Cambridge University Press, 1970), 276.

2. Graham Allison, "Conceptual Models and the Cuban Missile Crisis," *American Political Science Review* 63/3 (1969): 689.

3. For a thorough explanation of this problem, see especially Ronald A. Fisher, *Statistical Methods and Scientific Inference* (New York: Hafner, 1956).

4. Alan C. Lamborn, "Theory and the Politics in World Politics," *International Studies Quarterly* 41/2 (1997): 188.

5. Ibid., 187.

6. Robert Jervis, "Models and Cases in the Study of International Conflict," *Journal of International Affairs* 44/1 (1990): 94–95.

7. Petracca, "The Rational Actor Approach to Politics," 181.

8. Robert Jervis, "Hans Morgenthau, Realism, and the Scientific Study of International Politics," *Social Research* 61/4 (1994): 859.

9. Loriaux, "The Realists and Saint Augustine," 418.

10. Charles Beitz, "Recent International Thought," *International Journal* 43/2 (1988): 202 (Kennan quoted on p. 202). According to Beitz, Robert Gilpin maintains a similar position.

11. George, "Realist Ethics," 196. George cites as a prime example of the "realist ethic of (non)responsibility" (204) Robert Tucker's *The Inequality of Nations* (New York: Basic Books, 1977).

12. Steven Forde, "International Realism," 158. Forde's work is especially useful in elucidating the moral (or immoral) implications of realist theory. See also his "Classical Realism."

13. Steven Forde, "International Realism and the Science of Politics," 158.

14. Ibid., 156

15. Ibid., 158.

16. See Frost, *Ethics in International Relations*.

17. Loriaux, "The Realists and Saint Augustine," 418.

18. See Carr, *The Twenty Years' Crisis*, ch. 6.

19. Forde, "Classical Realism," 81.

20. As Forde has put it, Machiavelli solves this problem "by resorting to public deceptions and by removing morality from the foundation of the political community" ("Classical Realism," 82). Hobbes and Benedict de Spinoza "follow Machiavelli in reducing the basis of community to self-interest" (ibid.).

21. Kurt Taylor Gaubatz, "The Hobbesian Problem and the Microfoundations of International Relations Theory or: If Politics Stops at the Water's Edge, How Did Everyone Get to Be So Wet?" (paper presented at the annual meeting of the American Political Science Association, New York City, September 1994). Gaubatz compares national security communities and argues that successful ones are "built around the institutionalization of decision making and accountability and around associative norms" (abstract).

22. Forde, "Classical Realism," 82.

23. Forde, "Varieties of Realism," 389.

24. White, *When Words Lose Their Meaning*, 79.

25. Forde, "International Realism and the Science of Politics," 156.

26. Ibid., 158.

27. Ibid.

28. Forde, "Classical Realism," 82.

29. Forde, "International Realism and the Science of Politics," 158.

30. Ibid., 156.

31. See Hans Morgenthau, "Another 'Great Debate': The National Interest of the United States," *American Political Science Review* 46/4 (1952): 961–988, and "Defining the National Interest—Again: Old Superstitions, New Realities," *The New Republic*, 22 January 1977, 50–55.

32. Axelrod, *The Evolution of Cooperation.*

33. Forde, "International Realism and the Science of Politics," 157.

34. Michael Argyle, *Cooperation: The Basis of Sociability* (London: Routledge, 1991).

35. Jervis, "Realism, Game Theory, and Cooperation," 348.

36. Ibid.

37. Ibid., 349. On the problems realism encounters in attempting to employ game theoretical models, see Robert Axelrod, "The Emergence of Cooperation among Egoists," *American Political Science Review* 75/2 (1981): 306–318; and Duncan Snidal, "Relative Gains and the Pattern of International Cooperation," *American Political Science Review* 85/3 (1991): 701–726.

38. Loriaux, "The Realists and Saint Augustine," 417.

39. Vertzberger, *The World in Their Minds*, 123.

40. Cottam, *Foreign Policy Motivation*. He cites as another example the Vietnam policy debate in the United States in 1968.

41. James F. Voss and Ellen Dorsey, "Perceptions and International Relations: An Overview," in *Political Psychology and Foreign Policy*, eds. Eric Singer and Valerie Hudson (Boulder, Colo.: Westview, 1992), 8.

42. Ibid. The perceptual perspective seems to imply an interpretivist ontology. However, it does not require the use of interpretivist methods. Expected utility theory, for example, is interested in how decision makers perceive the reality of the decision-making process, yet assumes the "objective" observational stance, which is characteristic of positivist science.

43. See Richard C. Snyder, H. W. Bruck, and Burton Sapin, *Decision-Making as an Approach to the Study of International Politics* (Princeton, N.J.: Princeton University Press, 1954), and *Foreign Policy Decisionmaking* (Glencoe, Ill.: Free Press, 1962); and Harold Sprout and Margaret Sprout, *Man-Milieu Relationship Hypotheses in the Context of International Politics* (Prince-

ton, N.J.: Center of International Studies, 1956), and "Environmental Factors in the Study of International Politics," *Journal of Conflict Resolution* 1 (1957): 309–328.

44. See, for example, Bueno de Mesquita, *The War Trap*.

45. See de Rivera, *The Psychological Dimension*; and the essays in Lawrence S. Falkowski, ed., *Psychological Models of International Politics* (Boulder, Colo.: Westview, 1979).

46. See, for example, Robert Jervis, *Perception and Misperception in International Politics* (Princeton, N.J.: Princeton University Press, 1976); or Robert Mandel, "Psychological Approaches to International Relations," in *Political Psychology*, ed. Margaret G. Hermann (San Francisco: Jossey-Bass, 1986), 251–278.

47. Voss and Dorsey, "Perceptions and International Relations," 24.

48. Ibid., 6–7.

49. Ibid., 8.

50. An example would be Vertzberger, *The World in Their Minds*.

51. See Allen Newell and Herbert A. Simon, *Human Problem Solving* (Englewood Cliffs, N.J.: Prentice-Hall, 1972); and Dean G. Pruitt, "Definition of the Situation as a Determinant of International Interaction," in *International Behavior: A Social–Psychological Analysis*, ed. Herbert C. Kelman (New York: Holt, Rinehart, and Winston, 1965), 393–432.

52. Voss and Dorsey, "Perceptions," 6. See Leon Festinger, *A Theory of Cognitive Dissonance* (Stanford, Calif.: Stanford University Press, 1957); and Fritz Heider, *The Psychology of Interpersonal Relations* (Hillside, N.J.: Erlbaum, 1958).

53. Robert Art and Robert Jervis, "Perspectives on Decisionmaking," in *International Politics: Enduring Concepts and Contemporary Issues*, 3d ed., ed. Robert Art and Robert Jervis (New York: HarperCollins, 1992), 394.

54. Jervis, *Perception and Misperception in International Politics*, 9–10.

55. Art and Jervis, "Perspectives on Decisionmaking," 394–395.

56. Voss and Dorsey, "Perceptions and International Relations," 8.

57. See, respectively, Cottam, *Foreign Policy Motivation*; Robert Axelrod, "How a Schema Is Used to Interpret Information," in *Thought and Action in Foreign Policy*, ed. G. M. Bonham and Michael J. Shapiro (Basel: Birkhauser Verlag, 1977), 226–241; Roger C. Schank and Robert P. Abelson, *Scripts, Plans, Goals, and Understanding* (Hillsdale, N.J.: Erlbaum, 1977); and Philip N. Johnson-Laird, *Mental Models: Towards a Cognitive Science of Language, Inference, and Consciousness* (Cambridge: Harvard University Press, 1983).

58. Kenneth Boulding, "National Images and International Systems," *Journal of Conflict Resolution* 3 (June 1959): 120. See also his *The Image* (Ann Arbor: University of Michigan Press, 1956).

59. Boulding, "National Images and International Systems," 121.

60. Voss and Dorsey, "Perceptions and International Relations," 9.

61. See, for example, Ole R. Holsti, "The Belief System and National Images: A Case Study," *Conflict Resolution* 6/3 (1962): 244–252; Cottam, *Foreign Policy Motivation*; and David J. Finlay, Ole R. Holsti, and Richard R. Fragen, *Enemies in Politics* (Chicago: Rand McNally, 1967).

62. Voss and Dorsey, "Perceptions and International Relations," 9.

63. Holsti, "The Belief System," 244. According to Quincy Wright, conflict can be understood as taking place between distorted images of states, rather than the states themselves. See his "Design for a Research Project on International Conflict and the Factors Causing Their Aggravation or Amelioration," *Western Political Quarterly* 10 (1957): 263–275.

64. Boulding, "National Images and International Systems," 130.

65. Holsti, "The Belief System and National Images," 251.

66. Urie Bronfenbrenner, "The Mirror Image in Soviet–American Relations: A Social Psychologist's Report," *Journal of Social Issues* 17/3 (1961): 51.

67. Cottam, *Foreign Policy Motivation*; and Philip E. Tetlock, "Integrative Complexity of American and Soviet Foreign Policy Rhetoric: A Time Series Analysis," *Journal of Personality and Social Psychology* 49 (1985): 565–585.

68. Voss and Dorsey, "Perceptions and International Relations," 17.

69. Ole Holsti, *Crisis, Escalation, War* (Montreal: McGill-Queen's University Press, 1972).

70. Richard E. Petty and John T. Cacioppo, *Attitudes and Persuasion: Classic and Contemporary Approaches* (Dubuque, Iowa: Brown, 1981), 7.

71. Voss and Dorsey, "Perceptions and International Relations," 11.

72. Holsti, "The Belief System," 245. Holsti quotes George A. Miller, Eugene Galantoer, and Karl Pribram, *Plans and the Structure of Behavior* (New York: Holt, 1960), 16. For examples of the operation of belief systems, see Michael Brecher's case study *The Foreign Policy System of Israel: Settings, Images, Process* (New Haven, Conn.: Yale University Press, 1972).

73. Holsti, "The Belief System and National Images," 244.

74. See Milton Rokeach, *The Open and Closed Mind* (New York: Basic Books, 1960), on the distinction between "open" and "closed" belief system structure and personality types.

75. Anatol Rapoport, *Fights, Games, and Debates* (Ann Arbor: University of Michigan Press, 1960), 258.

76. See, for example, Raymond A. Bauer, "Problems of Perception and the Relation between the United States and the Soviet Union," *Journal of Conflict Resolution* 5 (1961): 223–229; Harvey Wheeler, "The Role of Myth System in American–Soviet Relations," *Journal of Conflict Resolution* 4 (1960): 179–184; and Douglas W. Blum, "The Soviet Foreign Policy Belief System: Beliefs, Politics, and Foreign Policy Outcomes," *International Studies Quarterly* 37/4 (1993): 373–394.

77. See especially Rokeach, *The Open and Closed Mind*; and Wheeler, "The Role of Myth System." Looking at such findings, it seems possible that the ultimate causes for the "democratic peace" lie in the flexibility and pluralism of the "open society," as envisioned by Karl Popper and, more currently, George Soros.

78. See, for example, M. Brewster Smith, Jerome S. Bruner, and Robert W. White, *Opinions and Personality* (New York: Wiley, 1956); Rokeach, *The Open and Closed Mind;* and Robert E. Lane, *Political Ideology: Why the American Common Man Believes What He Does* (Glencoe, Ill.: Free Press, 1962). Lane examines beliefs in the context of ideologies.

79. Voss and Dorsey, "Perceptions and International Relations," 11.

80. Ibid., 12. See, for example, Ernest R. May, *"Lessons" of the Past: The Use and Misuse of History in American Foreign Policy* (New York: Oxford, 1973); Richard E. Neustadt and Ernest R. May, *Thinking in Time: The Uses of History for Decision-Makers* (New York: Free Press, 1986); or Yuen Foong Khong, *Analogies at War: Korea, Munich, Dien Bien Phu, and the Vietnam Decisions of 1965* (Princeton, N.J.: Princeton University Press, 1992).

81. See especially Jervis, *Perception and Misperception*. The concept of an "operational code" refers to those beliefs that are presumed to influence a decision maker's interpretation of an event and his subsequent reaction to it.

82. See Jervis, *Perception and Misperception*, and "War and Misperception," *Journal of Interdisciplinary History* 18/4 (1988): 675–700. See also William A. Gamson and Andre Modigliani, *Untangling the Cold War* (Boston: Little, Brown, 1971), in which they find that the discrepancy between an actor's self-perception and the perceptions others have of it can play a major role in international relations.

83. Jervis, *Perception and Misperception*, 10.

84. Ibid.

85. Jervis, "War and Misperception."

86. See Vertzberger, *The World in Their Minds*.

87. Ibid., 190.

88. Ibid., 360.

89. Ibid., 190.

90. See, for example, Robert L. Ivie, "Realism Masking Fear: George F. Kennan's Political Rhetoric," in *Post-Realism: The Rhetorical Turn in International Relations*, ed. Francis Beer and Robert Hariman (East Lansing: Michigan State University Press, 1996), 55–74, in which he explores the impact of motivational biases inspired by fear and of the employment of distorted imagery on Kennan's political judgment and rhetoric.

91. Vertzberger, *The World in Their Minds*, 360.

92. Art and Jervis, "Perspectives on Decisionmaking," 395.

93. Jervis, *Perception and Misperception*, 10.

94. See, for example, Richard K. Herrmann, James F. Voss, Tonya Y. E. Schooler, and Joseph Ciarrochi, "Images in International Relations: An Experimental Test of Cognitive Schemata," *International Studies Quarterly* 41/3 (1997): 403–433.

95. Charles F. Hermann, "Changing Course: When Governments Plan to Redirect Foreign Policy," *International Studies Quarterly* 34/1 (1990): 3–21. Margaret Hermann and Joe D. Hagan confirm that "leadership matters" more under the present conditions of a shifting world order. See their "International Decision Making: Leadership Matters," *Foreign Policy* 110 (1998): 124–137.

96. See White, *Fearful Warriors*.

97. Ibid., ix.

98. Keith L. Shimko, *Images and Arms Control: Perceptions of the Soviet Union in the Reagan Administration* (Ann Arbor: University of Michigan Press, 1991).

99. See Richard Ned Lebow, *Nuclear Crisis Management: A Dangerous Illusion* (Ithaca, N.Y.: Cornell University Press, 1987), in which he examines three possible sequences that could lead to the escalation of a nuclear crisis. See also Richard Ned Lebow and Janice Gross Stein, "Beyond Deterrence," *Journal of Social Issues* 43/4 (1987): 5–71, and *We All Lost the Cold War* (Princeton, N.J.: Princeton University Press, 1995) for case studies of the Cuban Missile Crisis of 1963 and the confrontations arising out of the Arab–Israeli War of 1973; see also Leon V. Sigal, *Disarming Strangers* (Princeton, N.J.: Princeton University Press, 1999) for a case study of the 1994 crisis between the United States and North Korea.

100. See the essays in Robert Jervis, Janice Gross Stein, and Richard Ned Lebow, *Psychology and Deterrence*, on how deterrence may fail to work in practice; and Harvey, *The Future's Back*, and "Rigor Mortis" for a realist response.

101. Jervis, Gross Stein, and Lebow, *Psychology and Deterrence*, ix; and Lebow, "The Deterrence Deadlock."

102. White, *Fearful Warriors*, 111.

103. Ibid., 112.

104. Ibid.

105. Compare Sigmund Freud, *The Problem of Anxiety* (Albany, N.Y.: The Psychoanalytic Quarterly Press, 1936).

106. White, *Fearful Warriors*, 114. See also Charles A. Kupchan, *The Vulnerability of Empire* (Ithaca, N.Y.: Cornell University Press, 1994). Kupchan has examined the effects of the

belief that one's state is vulnerable. He finds that a strong sense of vulnerability encourages leaders of declining powers to appease those they perceive to be rising powers, while it leads rising powers to act in overly competitive ways.

107. White, *Fearful Warriors*, 120.

108. Ibid., 123.

109. Ross Stagner, *Psychological Aspects of International Conflict* (Belmont, Calif.: Brooks/Cole, 1967). See also Richard Hofstadter, "The Paranoid Style in American Politics," in *The Paranoid Style in American Politics, and Other Essays* (New York: Knopf, 1965), 3–40, in which he draws his examples from U.S. domestic policy making but emphasizes that his observations hold true for the international arena as well.

110. White, *Fearful Warriors*, 168.

111. Robert B. McCalla, *Uncertain Perceptions: U.S. Cold War Crisis Decision Making* (Ann Arbor: University of Michigan Press, 1992). McCalla uses the terms *situational* and *dispositional* misperceptions to refer to unmotivated and motivated misperceptions.

112. White, *Fearful Warriors*, 161.

113. Ibid., 161–162.

114. Ibid., 165.

115. Ibid., 162–163.

116. Quoted in Roderick M. Kramer and Alice M. Isen, "Trust and Distrust: Its Psychological and Social Dimensions," *Motivation and Emotion* 18/2 (1991): 107.

117. Miller and Ratner, "The Disparity." See also the essays in Mansbridge, ed., *Beyond Self-Interest* on the relevance of other motivational factors.

118. Compare Vertzberger, *The World in Their Minds*.

119. Jervis, *Perception and Misperception*, 117–315.

120. Festinger, *A Theory of Cognitive Dissonance*.

121. Heider, *The Psychology of Interpersonal Relations*.

122. White, *Fearful Warriors*, 168.

123. Ibid., 169.

124. Ibid., 173.

125. White, *Fearful Warriors*, 175. See Edward E. Jones and Richard E. Nisbett, *The Actor and the Observer: Divergent Perceptions of the Causes of Behavior* (New York: General Learning Press, 1971).

126. White, *Fearful Warriors*, 176.

127. Ibid., 178.

128. Ibid., 175.

129. Vertzberger, *The World in Their Minds*, 191.

130. A significant part of the challenge faced by cognitive approaches today is to develop ways to test their hypotheses. See, for example, Chaim D. Kaufmann, "Out of the Lab and into the Archives: A Method for Testing Psychological Explanations for Political Decision Making," *International Studies Quarterly* 38/4 (1994): 557–586.

131. Margaret Hermann and Hagan, "International Decision Making," 126.

132. Ibid. See John Vasquez, *The War Puzzle*.

133. Snyder, *Myths of Empire*, 2, 1.

134. Czempiel, "In der Realismusfalle," 17; my translation.

135. Ibid.; my translation.

136. Ibid., 18; my translation.

137. This suggestion is a typical component of most contemporary critiques of realism, especially of those developed within liberal international relations theory.

138. Osiander, "Rereading Early Twentieth-Century IR Theory," 409. Osiander bases his judgment on a close reading of the works of Norman Angell, Alfred Zimmern, and Leonard Woolf, among others.

139. Ibid., 430.

140. Hedley Bull, "The Theory of International Politics: 1919–1969," in *The Aberystwyth Papers: International Politics, 1919–1969*, ed. Brian Porter (London: Oxford University Press, 1972), 36.

141. Osiander, "Rereading Early Twentieth-Century IR Theory," 430.

142. Forde, "Classical Realism," 80.

143. Ibid.

144. Ibid., 81.

145. Czempiel, "In der Realismusfalle," 18; my translation.

146. Ibid., 15.

147. Ibid.; my translation.

148. Ibid., 22; my translation.

Chapter 8. A Self-Fulfilling Prophesy?

1. Petracca, "The Rational Actor Approach to Politics," 181.

2. Miller and Ratner, "The Disparity."

3. Robert H. Frank, Thomas Gilovich, and Dennis Regan, "Does Studying Economics Inhibit Cooperation?" *Journal of Economic Perspectives* 7/2 (1993): 159.

4. For example, it was unclear whether particularly uncooperative persons are drawn to the field of economics or whether the study of economics turns them into such persons. However, these studies could show that economists are more likely than others to expect other actors to act selfishly. See especially Gerard Marwell and Ruth Ames, "Economists Free Ride, Does Anyone Else?" *Journal of Public Economics* 15 (1981): 295–310; and John Carter and Michael Irons, "Are Economists Different, and If So, Why?" *Journal of Economic Perspectives* 5 (1991): 171–177.

5. Frank, Gilovich, and Regan, "Does Studying Economics Inhibit Cooperation?"

6. Robert Frank, Thomas Gilovich, and Dennis Regan, "Do Economists Make Bad Citizens?" *Journal of Economic Perspectives* 10/1 (1996): 192.

7. Petracca, "The Rational Actor Approach to Politics," 187.

8. Czempiel, "Governance and Democratization," 270.

9. Johnson, *Thucydides*.

10. Roger C. Buck, "Reflexive Predictions," in *Readings in the Philosophy of the Social Sciences*, ed. May Brodbeck (London: Macmillan, 1968), 436. According to Buck, a prediction is truly reflexive if

> 1. Its truth-value would have been different had its dissemination status been different. 2. The dissemination status it actually had was causally necessary for the social actors involved to hold relevant and causally efficacious beliefs. 3. The prediction was, or if disseminated, would have been believed and acted upon, and finally 4. Something about the dissemination status or its causal consequences was abnormal, or at the very least unexpected by the predictor, by whoever calls it reflexive, or by those to whose attention its reflexive character is called. (439–440)

11. The claim that realist motivational assumptions are generally unrealistic is compatible with this criticism, since the self-fulfilling prophecy is expected to affect perceptions, expectations, and behavior, but not basic human nature.

12. Viotti and Kauppi, *International Relations Theory*, 61.

13. Ibid.

14. Ibid., 61–62.

15. Ibid., 61.

16. Ibid., 66.

17. Beer and Hariman, "Realism and Rhetoric in International Relations," 4. The authors draw on Kenneth Burke, *A Grammar of Motives* (Berkeley and Los Angeles: University of California Press, 1969).

18. Hans Blumenberg, "An Anthropological Approach to the Contemporary Significance of Rhetoric," in *After Philosophy: End or Transformation?* ed. Kenneth Baynes, Thomas McCarthy, and James Bohman (Cambridge: MIT Press, 1987), 454.

19. Beer and Hariman, "Realism and Rhetoric in International Relations," 6. The rhetorical success of realism is also affected positively by the fact that related worldviews dominate in related issue areas. As we have earlier observed, the premises of realism are, for example, largely compatible with those of economic liberalism, and the vast rhetorical success of the market metaphor has contributed to the entrenchment of those premises that are shared by the two paradigms. Perhaps partly as a consequence of the success of the relevant ontological assumptions, across disciplinary subdivisions, all types of political behavior are frequently conceptualized as struggles for power or control over resources. For example, Harold Lasswell's definition of politics as the struggle over "who gets what, when, and how" enjoys great popularity in the discipline of political science. See his *Politics: Who Gets What, When, How* (New York: McGraw-Hill, 1938).

20. See Kuhn, *The Structure of Scientific Revolutions*.

21. See Imre Lakatos, "Falsification and the Methodology of Scientific Research Programmes," in *Criticism and the Growth of Knowledge*, ed. Imre Lakatos and Alan Musgrave (Cambridge: Cambridge University Press, 1970), 91–196.

22. See, for example, Mearsheimer, "Back to the Future." For a summary critique, see Stanley Hoffmann, "Correspondence."

23. This is argued by Vasquez in "The Realist Paradigm." A prime example for the kinds of ad hoc theoretical adjustments employed by realists to save their grand theory from empirical contradiction is found in Kenneth Waltz's reaction to the end of the Cold War (see his "The Validation of International-Political Theory").

24. Popper, *Conjectures and Refutations*, 37.

25. Popper, *The Logic of Scientific Discovery*.

26. David Hume, for example, argues that theories can be verified only by an infinite number of confirming results. See his *Enquiries*. Popper formulates his arguments partly to distance himself from Hume's understanding of the consequences of this claim.

27. For a critical interpretation of Popper's logic, see Gary King, Robert O. Keohane, and Sidney Verba, *Designing Social Inquiry: Scientific Inference in Qualitative Research* (Princeton, N.J.: Princeton University Press, 1994). King and his colleagues, in my opinion, misunderstand Popper's rationale and thus misrepresent the strategy of "falsificationism."

28. Popper, *Conjectures and Refutations*, 35.

29. Popper, *The Logic of Scientific Discovery*.

30. Popper, *Conjectures and Refutations*, 37.

31. See Popper, *Conjectures and Refutations.*

32. See Popper, *Realism and the Aim of Science.*

33. Kuhn, *The Structure of Scientific Revolutions.*

34. Lakatos, "Falsification," 132.

35. Vasquez, "The Realist Paradigm." Vasquez relies on Lakatos, "Falsification."

36. Ibid., 900, 902. Vasquez cites Martin Hollis and Steve Smith, *Explaining and Understanding International Relations* (Oxford: Clarendon Press, 1990), and Frank Wayman and Paul Diehl, eds., *Reconstructing Realpolitik* (Ann Arbor: University of Michigan Press, 1994), in defense of the scientific status of realism.

37. Vasquez, "The Realist Paradigm," 900.

38. Ibid., 899.

39. Colin Elman and Miriam Fendius Elman hold that Vasquez misrepresents Lakatos's criteria for evaluating scientific research programs. See their "Lakatos and Neorealism: A Reply to Vasquez," *American Political Science Review* 91/4 (1997): 923–926. See also Elman and Elman, eds., *Bridges and Boundaries* (Cambridge: MIT Press, 2001), for alternative applications of Lakatosian criteria to various international relations research programs. For another critique of Vasquez, see Stephen M. Walt, "The Progressive Power of Realism," *American Political Science Review* 91/4 (1997): 931–935.

40. Vasquez, "The Realist Paradigm," 900.

41. Ibid., 901.

42. Ibid.

43. Ibid.

44. Ibid., 902.

45. Ibid., 910. In response, Waltz faults Vasquez for failing to consider "the puzzles posed by the interdependence of theory and facts." He holds that "explanation, not prediction, is the ultimate criterion of good theory, that a theory can be validated only by working back and forth between its implications and an uncertain state of affairs that we take to be the reality against which theory is tested, and that the results of tests are always problematic" ("Evaluating Theories," *American Political Science Review* 91/4 [1997]: 913).

46. Bahman Fozouni, "Confutation of Political Realism," *International Studies Quarterly* 39/4 (1995): 479. It should be noted that Fozouni believes that the reasons for the epistemological problems of realism are found in the deductive–nomological structure of the theory. He claims that the logic of realism could not depend on realist assumptions about human nature, because these assumptions do not possess the status of an established uniformity or law and thus cannot serve as an acceptable explanans. While I would agree with this observation, I disagree with Fozouni's judgment that realist theory does not vitally depend on such assumptions, acceptable or not.

47. See, for example, Keohane, "Theory of World Politics."

48. See Ernst B. Haas, "The Balance of Power Prescription, Context, or Propaganda?" *World Politics* 5/4 (1953): 442–477.

49. See, for example, Hare and Joint, *Ethics and International Affairs*, ch. 2.

50. This practice seems particularly common in statistical studies of conflict behavior. A survey of relevant studies suggests that a large part of the discrepancy of tests results may be attributed to rival operationalizations of the variable of state power. Test results are doomed to remain inconclusive as long as such operationalizations are not placed on a solid theoretical footing. For an overview of some of the relevant theoretical disagreements, compare the essays in Midlarsky, ed., *Handbook of War Studies.*

51. Jack Donnelly, "Twentieth-Century Realism," in *Traditions of International Ethics*, ed. Terry Nardin and David Mapel (Cambridge: Cambridge University Press, 1992), 97.

52. Ibid., 96. Donnelly cites as examples, besides Morgenthau, Carr, and Kennan, Georg Schwarzenberger's *Power Politics: A Study of International Society* (New York: Praeger, 1951) and Kenneth Thompson's *Moralism and Morality in Politics and Diplomacy* (Lanham, Md.: University Press of America, 1985).

53. Donnelly, "Twentieth-Century Realism," 97.

54. George, "Realist Ethics," 199, 204.

55. Waltz, *Theory of International Politics*, 124.

56. Karl R. Popper, "Normal Science and Its Dangers," in *Criticism and the Growth of Knowledge*, ed. Imre Lakatos and Alan Musgrave (Cambridge: Cambridge University Press, 1970), 52–53.

57. Ibid., 56.

58. Tellis, "Reconstructing Political Realism," 89–90.

59. See Popper, *The Open Universe*.

60. Karl R. Popper, "The Logic of the Social Sciences," in *The Positivist Dispute in German Sociology*, ed. Theodor W. Adorno, Hans Albert, Ralf Dahrendorf, Jürgen Habermas, Harold Pilot, and Karl R. Popper (London: Heinemann, 1976), 90.

61. Popper, *Conjectures and Refutations*, 373.

62. Popper, *Conjectures and Refutations*. It should be noted again that Waltz, for one, directly contradicts this view (see chapter 4).

63. Forde, "International Realism and the Science of Politics," 141.

64. Jean Bethke Elshtain, "International Politics and Political Theory," in *International Relations Theory Today*, ed. Ken Booth and Steve Smith (Cambridge: Polity Press, 1995), 275.

65. See Johnston, *The Rhetoric of Leviathan*.

66. Robert B. J. Walker, "International Relations and the Concept of the Political," in *International Relations Theory Today*, ed. Ken Booth and Steve Smith (Cambridge: Polity Press, 1995), 318.

67. Ibid., 317.

68. See Robyn Dawes, "The Nature of Human Nature: An Empirical Case for Withholding Judgment—Perhaps Indefinitely," *Political Psychology* 16/1 (1995): 81–97.

69. Jervis, *Perception and Misperception*, 10.

70. Herrmann, Voss, Schooler, and Ciarrochi, "Images in International Relations," 423–424.

Chapter 9. Conclusion: Great Debates and Small Suggestions

1. At least it would not be difficult to argue that other paradigms, such as liberalism, suffer from a similar lack of refutability.

2. Brooks, "Dueling Realisms," 473.

3. Fozouni, "Confutation of Political Realism," 507. Fozouni suggests that the post–Cold War transition opens possibilities for a "Gestalt switch" during which realism might be divested of a degree of parsimony to create a new and more useful approach to the study of international politics.

4. Frank Wayman and Paul Diehl agree that realist theory needs to make its assumptions explicit and establish propositions that can be tested to identify the empirical limitations of the theory. See their "Realpolitik: Dead End, Detour, or Road Map?"

5. Andrew Bard Schmookler, *Parable of the Tribes: The Problem of Power in Social Evolution*, 2d ed. (Albany: State University of New York Press, 1994).

6. Thayer, "Bringing in Darwin."

7. See the survey by Daniel M. Hausman and Michael S. McPherson, "Taking Ethics Seriously: Economics and Contemporary Moral Philosophy," *Journal of Economic Literature* 31/2 (1993): 671–731.

8. See Carr, *The Twenty Years' Crisis*, 10, 89; and Niebuhr, *The Children of Light*, 126.

9. Wayman and Diehl, "Realpolitik: Dead End, Detour, or Road Map?"

10. Ibid., 263.

11. Among the clearest examples of research employing insights created by applications of realist theory to transcend the limitations of the paradigm are the works of Robert Keohane and of John Ruggie. See also John Mercer, "Anarchy and Identity," *International Organization* 49/2 (1995): 229–252.

12. Ken Booth, "Dare Not to Know: International Relations Theory versus the Future," in *International Relations Theory Today*, ed. Ken Booth and Steve Smith (Cambridge: Polity Press, 1995), 328–350.

13. Joseph S. Nye, "Conflicts after the Cold War," *Washington Quarterly* 19/1 (1996): 5–24.

14. Robert Jervis, "Leadership, Post–Cold-War Politics, and Psychology," *Political Psychology* 15/4 (1994): 769–777.

15. "Small" states are less powerful states. On the difficulties of defining this category see, for example, John Scott Masker, *Small States and Security Regimes: The International Politics of Nuclear Non-Proliferation in Nordic Europe and the South Pacific* (Lanham, Md.: University Press of America, 1995); and Peter J. Katzenstein, *Small States in World Markets* (Ithaca, N.Y.: Cornell University Press, 1985).

16. Miriam Fendius Elman, "The Foreign Policies of Small States: Challenging Neorealism in Its Own Backyard," *British Journal of Political Science* 25/2 (1995): 171–217.

17. Efraim Inbar and Gabriel Sheffer, eds., *The National Security of Small States in a Changing World* (London: Frank Cass, 1997).

18. Gabriel Sheffer, "The Security of Small Ethnic States: A Counter Neo-Realist Argument," in *The National Security of Small States in a Changing World*, ed. Efraim Inbar and Gabriel Sheffer (London: Frank Cass, 1997), 38.

19. Masker, *Small States*. See also Mark Hong, "Small States in the United Nations," *International Social Science Journal* 47 (1995): 277–287.

20. Richard Ned Lebow, "Small States and Big Alliances" (bk. review), *American Political Science Review* 91 (September 1997): 705–709.

21. For an overview of the three approaches from a realist perspective, see Walt, "International Relations." For an overview sympathetic to postmodernist critical theory, see Steve Smith, "The Self-Images of a Discipline: A Genealogy of International Relations Theory," in *International Relations Theory Today*, ed. Ken Booth and Steve Smith (Cambridge: Polity Press, 1995), 1–37.

22. For a general overview of primarily neoliberal challenges to realism today, see the essays in Charles Kegley Jr., ed., *Controversies in International Relations Theory: Realism and the Neoliberal Challenge* (New York: St. Martin's, 1995). For a selection of essays more representative

of the general breadth of spectrum of international relations theory, see Booth and Smith, eds., *International Relations Theory*.

23. For an overview, see Andrew Moravcsik, "Taking Preferences Seriously: A Liberal Theory of International Politics," *International Organization* 51/4 (1997): 513–554; and David Baldwin, ed., *Neorealism and Neoliberalism: The Contemporary Debate* (New York: Columbia University Press, 1993).

24. It should be noted that some, such as, notably, Keohane and Nye, distinguish between liberal and institutionalist theory, emphasizing that institutionalism draws on both the realist and the liberal tradition. See Robert O. Keohane and Joseph S. Nye Jr., "Introduction: The End of the Cold War in Europe," in *After the Cold War: International Institutions and State Strategies in Europe, 1989–1991*, ed. Robert Keohane, Joseph Nye, and Stanley Hoffman (Cambridge: Harvard University Press, 1993), 1–22. However, given the general compatibility of realist and liberal thought and the variety of approaches within either of the stipulated categories, such distinctions have limited use for the present purpose.

25. To mention a few seminal works, the research of Karl Deutsch on the development of pluralistic security communities, Ernst Haas's observations on regional integration in Europe, and Keohane and Nye's study of the growing extent of international interdependence all have contributed significantly to the growing strength of liberal approaches to the study of international politics. See Deutsch, *Political Community and the North Atlantic Area* (Princeton, N.J.: Princeton University Press, 1957); Haas, *The Uniting of Europe: Political, Social, and Economic Forces, 1950–1957* (Stanford, Calif.: Stanford University Press, 1958); and Keohane and Nye, *Power and Interdependence*, and "Power and Interdependence Revisited, *International Organization* 41/4 (1987): 725–753.

26. Peter J. Katzenstein, "Introduction: Alternative Perspectives on National Security," in *The Culture of National Security: Norms and Identity in World Politics*, ed. Peter J. Katzenstein (New York: Columbia University Press, 1996), 19.

27. As Andreas Hasenclever, Peter Mayer, and Volker Rittberger have shown, the study of regimes can profit from all three of the major approaches: "interest-based neoliberalism, power-based realism, and knowledge-based cognitivism." See their thorough overview "Interests, Power, Knowledge: The Study of International Regimes," *Mershon International Studies Review* 40 (October 1996): 177.

28. See, for example, Oran R. Young, *International Cooperation: Building Regimes for Natural Resources and the Environment* (Ithaca, N.Y.: Cornell University Press, 1989), in which he examines the role of regimes in overcoming collective action problems by institutionalizing cooperation.

29. See, for example, Susan Strange, *The Retreat of the State: The Diffusion of Power in the World Economy* (Cambridge: Cambridge University Press, 1996).

30. See, for example, Allison, *Essence of Decision*.

31. See, for example, the essays in Keohane, Nye, and Hoffman, eds., *After the Cold War*.

32. Keohane and Nye, "Introduction," 7. See also Keohane and Martin, "The Promise of Institutionalist Theory."

33. John Gerard Ruggie, "The False Premise of Realism," *International Security* 20/1 (1995): 62, 70.

34. Ibid., 70.

35. See Alfie Kohn, "Cooperation: What It Means and Doesn't Mean," in *Cooperation: Beyond the Age of Competition*, ed. Allan Combs (Philadelphia: Gordon and Breach, 1995),

3–11. Kohn insists that cooperation should be defined not as the opposite of conflict but as positive interdependence, in which the success of one actor's pursuit depends on the success of the other's.

36. In the words of liberal philosopher John Locke, the natural rights of citizens include the rights to "life, liberty, and property." Thomas Jefferson, in framing the U.S. Declaration of Independence, changed the term *property* to the more general *pursuit of happiness*.

37. See Charles Kegley Jr, "The Neoidealist Moment in International Studies? Realist Myths and the New International Realities," *International Studies Quarterly* 37/2 (1993): 131–146. In an attempt to systematically assess the roles ideas may play in foreign policy making, Judith Goldstein and Robert Keohane have recently distinguished between three types of beliefs—worldviews, normative beliefs, and causal beliefs—and three types of "causal pathways," by which they may exert their influence: They may be used as "road maps" to reduce uncertainty, employed as "focal points" to solve coordination problems, or they may become institutionalized. See Goldstein and Keohane, eds., *Ideas and Foreign Policy: Beliefs, Institutions, and Political Change* (Ithaca, N.Y.: Cornell University Press, 1993). While this study is unusual in that it is conceived as complementary and not contradictory to realist assumptions, most of the work done within the third cluster of theories distances itself from realist theory and betrays a greater affinity for complementing liberal arguments, or distances itself from both of the other approaches.

38. My interpretation of the contructivist contribution may be contested. For a different view, see, for example, Jennifer Sterling-Folker, "Competing Paradigms or Birds of a Feather? Constructivism and Neoliberal Institutionalism Compared," *International Studies Quarterly* 44/1 (2000): 97–119, and "Realism and the Constructivist Challenge: Rejecting, Reconstructing or Rereading," *International Studies Review* 4/1 (spring 2002): 73–97.

39. Richard Ned Lebow and Thomas Risse-Kappen, "Introduction: International Relations Theory and the End of the Cold War," in *International Relations Theory and the End of the Cold War*, ed. Richard Ned Lebow and Thomas Risse-Kappen (New York: Columbia University Press, 1995), 17.

40. See, for example, the essays in Lebow and Risse-Kappen, eds., *International Relations Theory*. For instance, constructivist theorists Rey Koslowski and Friedrich V. Kratochwil argue that changes in beliefs and practices help cause changes in foreign policies and international politics ("Understanding Change in International Politics," 127–166). Snyder holds that Mikhail Gorbachev's foreign policy reform can be understood as a shift from aggressive to defensive realism ("Myths," 109–126). Risse-Kappen argues that the post–Cold War transition cannot be properly understood without taking into account leaders' changing ideas ("Ideas Do Not Float Freely: Transnational Coalitions, Domestic Structures, and the End of the Cold War," 187–222). Janice Gross Stein suggests that theories of political learning are helpful in elucidating such changes of ideas ("Political Learning by Doing: Gorbachev as Uncommitted Thinker and Motivated Learner," 223–258).

41. Lebow and Risse-Kappen, "Introduction," 17. See also Richard K. Herrmann, "Conclusions: The End of the Cold War—What Have We Learned?" in *International Relations Theory and the End of the Cold War*, ed. Richard Ned Lebow and Thomas Risse-Kappan (New York: Columbia University Press, 1995), 259–284.

42. Czempiel, "Governance and Democratization," 271.

43. Ronald Jepperson, Alexander Wendt, and Peter Katzenstein, "Norms, Identity, and Culture in National Security," in *The Culture of National Security: Norms and Identity in World Politics*, ed. Peter Katzenstein (New York: Columbia University Press, 1996), 60.

44. For an overview of constructivist international relations theory compare, for example, Peter Katzenstein, ed., *The Culture: Norms and Identity in World Politics* (New York: Columbia University Press, 1996); Yosef Lapid and Friedrich Kratochwil, eds., *The Return of Culture and Identity in IR Theory* (Boulder, Colo.: Lynne Rienner, 1996); or Alexander Wendt, "Anarchy Is What States Make of It: The Social Construction of Power Policy," *International Organization* 46/2 (1992): 391–425.

45. Frost, *Ethics*, 63. See also Cathal J. Nolan, ed., *Ethics and Statecraft: The Moral Dimension of International Affairs* (Westport, Conn.: Praeger, 1995). Among the essays in this volume, one finds contemporary constructivist studies of the processes by which interests are created out of considerations of both power and morality, or capabilities and norms.

46. Wendt, "Constructing International Politics."

47. See especially Ernst B. Haas, *Beyond the Nation State* (Stanford, Calif.: Stanford University Press, 1964); and John Gerard Ruggie, "International Responses to Technology," *International Organization* 29 (summer 1975): 557–584.

48. Emanuel Adler and Peter M. Haas, "Conclusion: Epistemic Communities, World Order, and the Creation of a Reflective Research Program," *International Organization* 46/1 (1992): 367. Epistemic communities may affect national policies in ways similar to regimes.

49. See, for example, James Kennedy, "Thinking Is Social: Experiments with the Adaptive Culture Model," *Journal of Conflict Resolution* 42/1 (1998): 56–76. Building on Robert Axelrod's model of the spread of culture ("The Dissemination of Culture: A Model with Local Convergence and Global Polarization," *Journal of Conflict Resolution* 41/2 [1997]: 203–226), Kennedy shows how "social interaction can function as an algorithm for optimizing cognition" (56).

50. See, for example, Patricia Doyle Corner, Angelo Kinicki, and Barbara Keats, "Integrating Organizational and Individual Information-Processing Perspectives on Choice," *Organizational Science* 5/3 (1994): 294–308. Such research should inform, more thoroughly than it does now, political scientific studies of group dynamics, bureaucratic politics, and coalition building. For an overview of these areas of research, see Hermann and Hagan, "International Decision Making."

51. See Clark, *The Hierarchy of States*.

52. Wendt, "Collective Identity Formation," 384.

53. Lebow and Risse-Kappen, "Introduction," 15. See also Richard Ned Lebow, "The Search for Accommodation: Gorbachev in Comparative Perspective" (167–186), and Koslowski and Kratochwil, "Understanding Change" (127–166), in *International Relations Theory and the End of the Cold War*, ed. Richard Ned Lebow and Thomas Risse-Kappen (New York: Columbia University Press, 1995).

54. Katzenstein, "Introduction," 6.

55. Martha Finnemore, *National Interests in International Society* (Ithaca, N.Y.: Cornell University Press, 1996), 22. Finnemore examines how international organizations help shape national interests.

56. Jepperson, Wendt, and Katzenstein, "Norms, Identity," 59. See also Marysia Zalewski and Cynthia Enloe, "Questions about Identity in International Relations," in *International Relations Theory Today*, ed. Ken Booth and Steve Smith (Cambridge: Polity Press, 1995), 279–305. See also Charles A. Kupchan and Clifford A. Kupchan, "The Promise of Collective Security," *International Security* 20/1 (1995): 52–61, on the role of self-identification for the establishment and stability of security communities.

57. See Galen V. Bodenhausen, "Identity and Cooperative Social Behavior: Pseudospeciation or Human Integration?" in *Cooperation: Beyond the Age of Competition*, ed. Allan Combs

(Philadelphia: Gordon and Breach, 1992), 12–23. Bodenhausen draws on Eric Erikson's "The Concept of Identity in Race Relations: Notes and Queries," *Daedalus* 95/1 (1966): 145–171. Erikson created the term *pseudospeciation* for the identification with a subset of human beings rather than the human species as a whole. Pseudospeciation leads to ingroup–outgroup effects, which may increase cohesion and cooperation within the group while inhibiting cohesion and cooperation across groups. Constructivists also make the interesting point that conflicts which rest on contradictory fundamental assumptions may be overcome by establishing shared meanings through shared praxis. By acting together, actors can create shared meanings where they did not previously exist, thus creating the possibilities for communication and identification that can create community and decrease the likelihood of conflict.

58. For example, the essays in Lebow and Risse-Kappen, eds., *International Relations Theory*, collectively create the impression that the end of the Cold War can only be explained through the combined efforts of all three approaches and with reference to all three motivational categories.

59. Lamborn, "Theory and the Politics in World Politics."

60. See, for example, Charles Kegley Jr., "The Neoliberal Challenge to Realist Theories of World Politics: An Introduction" (1–24), and James Lee Ray, "Promise or Peril: Neorealism, Neoliberalism, and the Future of International Politics" (335–353), in *Controversies in International Relations Theory: Realism and the Neoliberal Challenge*, ed. Charles W. Kegler Jr. (New York: St. Martin's, 1995).

61. See, for example, Eric Heginbotham and Richard J. Samuels, "Mercantile Realism and Japanese Foreign Policy," *International Security* 22/4 (1998): 171–203.

62. Jerome D. Frank, *Sanity and Survival: Psychological Aspects of War and Peace* (New York: Random House, 1967), 287.

63. Morgenthau, *Politics among Nations*.

64. Alexander L. George, *Bridging the Gap: Theory and Practice in Foreign Policy* (Washington, D.C.: United States Institute of Peace, 1993).

65. William Chittick and I have suggested a framework for employing the three basic motives discussed here in the study of foreign policy. See "The Impact of Basic Motivation on Foreign Policy Opinions." We have also demonstrated the usefulness of such a framework by applying it to a case study of foreign policy decisions in the Peloponnesian War. See "'Chiefly for Fear, Next for Honor, and Lastly for Profit': An Analysis of Foreign Policy Motivation in the Peloponnesian War," *Review of International Studies* 27 (spring 2001): 69–90.

66. See, for example, Michael Nicholson, *Causes and Consequences in International Relations: A Conceptual Study* (New York: Cassell Academic, 1996).

67. Peter Winch, *The Idea of a Social Science and Its Relation to Philosophy* (1958; reprint, London: Routledge 1988).

68. Mark A. Neufeld, *The Restructuring of IR Theory* (New York: Cambridge University Press, 1995).

69. Yale H. Ferguson and Richard W. Mansbach, "Between Celebration and Despair: Constructive Suggestions for Future International Theory," *International Studies Quarterly* 35/4 (1991): 369. See Yosef Lapid, "Without Any Guarantees: The 'Third Way' (in the 'Third Debate') to International Theory" (paper presented at the Northeastern Political Science Association meeting, Philadelphia, Pa., November 1989). See also his "The Third Debate: On the Prospects of International Theory in a Post–Positivist Era," *International Studies Quarterly* 33/3 (1989): 235–254. Lapid associates the positivist approach with the position of despair and the postpositivist approach with the position of celebration. This is reminiscent of Ian Clark's

identification of realism as "the tradition of despair" and idealism as "the tradition of optimism" (*The Hierarchy of States*).

70. Ferguson and Mansbach, "Between Celebration and Despair."

71. John A. Vasquez, "The Post-Positivist Debate: Reconstructing Scientific Enquiry and International Relations Theory after Enlightenment's Fall," in *International Relations Theory Today*, ed. Ken Booth and Steve Smith (Cambridge: Polity Press, 1995), 238.

72. Ibid., 239.

73. Nicholson, *Causes and Consequences in International Relations.*

74. On the preferability of a problem-solving orientation, see also Booth, "Dare Not to Know."

75. Karl R. Popper, *Objective Knowledge: An Evolutionary Approach* (Oxford: Clarendon Press, 1972).

76. For examples of theorizing that places international relations theory in the wider context of social and political thought, see Walker, *Inside/Outside*; V. Spike Peterson, "Transgressing Boundaries: Theories of Knowledge, Gender, and IR," *Millennium* 21/2 (1992): 183–206; and Pauline Rosenau, "Once Again into the Fray: IR Confronts the Humanities," *Millennium* 19/1 (1990): 83–110.

77. According to Quincy Wright, psychology belongs at the "core" of our discipline. See his *The Study of International Relations* (New York: Appleton-Century-Crofts, 1955), 506.

78. Lebow and Risse-Kappen, "Introduction," 17.

79. See, for example, Reeve, *Understanding Motivation and Emotion.*

80. Wrightsman, *Assumptions about Human Nature*, 44.

81. Valerie M. Hudson and Christopher S. Vore, "Foreign Policy Analysis Yesterday, Today, and Tomorrow," *Mershon International Studies Review* 39 (suppl. 2; 1995): 209–238.

82. Academic divisions between the study of domestic politics and foreign policy need to be met with similar disrespect, if our research questions demand it.

83. Stanley Hoffmann, "Notes on the Limits of 'Realism,'" *Social Research* 48/4 (1981): 659.

84. See, for example, Roger D. Spegele, *Political Realism in International Theory* (Cambridge: Cambridge University Press, 1996).

Bibliography

Abbott, George F. *Thucydides: A Study in Historical Reality*. London: Routledge, 1925.

Abell, Peter, ed. *Rational Choice Theory*. Aldershot, U.K.: Edward Elgar, 1991.

Adcock, Frank E. *Thucydides and His History*. Cambridge: Cambridge University Press, 1963.

Adler, Alfred. *Understanding Human Nature*. London: G. Allen and Unwin, 1928.

———. *Social Interest: A Challenge to Mankind*. London: Faber and Faber, 1938.

Adler, Emanuel, and Peter M. Haas. "Conclusion: Epistemic Communities, World Order, and the Creation of a Reflective Research Program." *International Organization* 46/1 (1992): 367–390.

Adorno, Theodor W., Hans Albert, Ralf Dahrendorf, Jürgen Habermas, Harold Pilot, and Karl R. Popper. *The Positivist Dispute in German Sociology*. London: Heinemann, 1976.

Ahrensdorf, Peter J. "Thucydides' Realistic Critique of Realism." *Polity* 30/2 (1997): 231–265.

Akerlof, George. "Loyalty Filters." *American Economic Review* 73/1 (1983): 54–63.

Allison, Graham T. "Conceptual Models and the Cuban Missile Crisis." *American Political Science Review* 63/3 (1969): 689–718.

———. *Essence of Decision: Explaining the Cuban Missile Crisis*. Boston: Little, Brown, 1971.

Allison, Graham T., and Gregory F. Treverton, eds. *Rethinking America's Security: Beyond Cold War to New World Order*. New York: Norton, 1992.

Allison, June W. *Power and Preparedness in Thucydides*. Baltimore: Johns Hopkins University Press, 1989.

Angell, Norman. *The Great Illusion: A Study of the Relation of Military Power in Nations to Their Economic and Social Advantage*, 3rd ed. New York: G. P. Putnam's Sons, 1911.

Archibald, Kathleen, ed. *Strategic Interaction and Conflict*. Berkeley, Calif.: Institute of International Studies, 1966.

Argyle, Michael. *Cooperation: The Basis of Sociability*. London: Routledge, 1991.

———. "A Critique of Cognitive Approaches to Social Judgments and Social Behavior." In *Emotion and Social Judgments*, edited by Joseph P. Forgas, 161–178. Oxford: Pergamon, 1991.

Aron, Raymond. *Peace and War: A Theory of International Relations*. Garden City, N.Y.: Doubleday, 1966.

Art, Robert J., and Robert Jervis. "Perspectives on Decisionmaking." In *International Politics: Enduring Concepts and Contemporary Issues*, 3rd ed., edited by Robert J. Art and Robert Jervis, 391–395. New York: HarperCollins, 1992.

———, eds. *International Politics: Enduring Concepts and Contemporary Issues*, 3rd ed. New York: HarperCollins, 1992.

Ashley, Richard K. "The Poverty of Neorealism." *International Organization* 38/2 (1984): 225–286.

Atkinson, John W. *A Theory of Achievement Motivation*. New York: Wiley, 1966.

Axelrod, Robert M. "How a Schema Is Used to Interpret Information." In *Thought and Action in Foreign Policy*, edited by G. M. Bonham and Michael J. Shapiro, 226–241. Basel: Birkhauser Verlag, 1977.

———. "The Emergence of Cooperation among Egoists." *American Political Science Review* 75/2 (1981): 306–318.

———. *The Evolution of Cooperation*. New York: Basic Books, 1984.

———. "The Dissemination of Culture: A Model with Local Convergence and Global Polarization." *Journal of Conflict Resolution* 41/2 (1997): 203–226.

Axelrod, Robert M., and Douglas Dion. "The Further Evolution of Cooperation." *Science* 242/4884 (1988): 1385–1390.

Baldwin, David, ed. *Neorealism and Neoliberalism: The Contemporary Debate*. New York: Columbia University Press, 1993.

Bates, Robert H., Jean-Laurent Rosenthal, Margaret Levi, Barry R. Weingast, and Avner Greif. *Analytic Narratives*. Princeton, N.J.: Princeton University Press, 1998.

Bauer, Raymond A. "Problems of Perception and the Relation between the United States and the Soviet Union." *Journal of Conflict Resolution* 5 (1961): 223–229.

Baynes, Kenneth, Thomas McCarthy, and James Bohman. *After Philosophy: End or Transformation?* Cambridge: MIT Press, 1987.

Beer, Francis A., and Robert Hariman. "Realism and Rhetoric in International Relations." In *Post-Realism: The Rhetorical Turn in International Relations*, edited by Francis A. Beer and Robert Hariman, 1–30. East Lansing: Michigan State University Press, 1996.

———, eds. *Post-Realism: The Rhetorical Turn in International Relations*. East Lansing: Michigan State University Press, 1996.

Beitz, Charles. "Recent International Thought." *International Journal* 43/2 (1988): 183–204.

Berlin, Isaiah. "The Originality of Machiavelli." In *Against the Current: Essays in the History of Ideas*. New York: Viking, 1979.

Bird, Alexander. "Squaring the Circle: Hobbes on Philosophy and Geometry." *Journal of the History of Ideas* 57/2 (1996): 217–231.

Black, Sam. "Science and Moral Skepticism in Hobbes." *Canadian Journal of Philosophy* 27/2 (1997): 173–207.

Blits, Jan H. "Hobbesian Fear." *Political Theory* 17/3 (1989): 417–431.

Blum, Douglas W. "The Soviet Foreign Policy Belief System: Beliefs, Politics, and Foreign Policy Outcomes." *International Studies Quarterly* 37/4 (1993): 373–394.

Blumenberg, Hans. "An Anthropological Approach to the Contemporary Significance of Rhetoric." In *After Philosophy: End or Transformation?* edited by Kenneth Baynes, Thomas McCarthy, and James Bohman, 429–458. Cambridge: MIT Press, 1987.

Bodenhausen, Galen V. "Identity and Cooperative Social Behavior: Pseudospeciation or Human Integration?" In *Cooperation: Beyond the Age of Competition*, edited by Allan Combs, 12–23. Philadelphia: Gordon and Breach, 1992.

Bonham, G. M., and Michael J. Shapiro, eds. *Thought and Action in Foreign Policy*. Basel: Birkhauser Verlag, 1977.

Booth, Ken. "Dare Not to Know: International Relations Theory versus the Future." In *International Relations Theory Today*, edited by Ken Booth and Steve Smith, 328–350. Cambridge: Polity Press, 1995.

Booth Ken, and Steve Smith, eds. *International Relations Theory Today*. Cambridge: Polity Press, 1995.

Booth, William James, Patrick James, and Hudson Meadwell. *Politics and Rationality*. New York: Cambridge University Press, 1994.

Boulding, Kenneth. *The Image*. Ann Arbor: University of Michigan Press, 1956.

———. "National Images and International Systems." *Journal of Conflict Resolution* 3 (June 1959): 120–131.

Brecher, Michael. *The Foreign Policy System of Israel: Settings, Images, Process*. New Haven, Conn.: Yale University Press, 1972.

Brodbeck, May. "Models, Meaning, and Theories." In *Readings in the Philosophy of the Social Sciences*, edited by May Brodbeck, 579–600. London: Macmillan, 1968.

——, ed. *Readings in the Philosophy of the Social Sciences*. London: Macmillan, 1968.

Bronfenbrenner, Urie. "The Mirror Image in Soviet–American Relations: A Social Psychologist's Report." *Journal of Social Issues* 17/3 (1961): 45–56.

Brooks, Stephen G. "Dueling Realisms." *International Organization* 51/3 (1997): 445–477.

Brown, Michael E., Sean M. Lynn-Jones, and Steven E. Miller. *The Perils of Anarchy: Contemporary Realism and International Security*. Cambridge: MIT Press, 1995.

Brunt, P. A. Introduction to *The Peloponnesian Wars*, by Thucydides, translated by Benjamin Jowett. London: New English Library, 1966.

Buck, Roger C. "Reflexive Predictions." In *Readings in the Philosophy of the Social Sciences*, edited by Mary Brodbeck, 436–447. London: Macmillan, 1968.

Bueno de Mesquita, Bruce. *The War Trap*. New Haven, Conn.: Yale University Press, 1981.

Bueno de Mesquita, Bruce, and David Lalman. *War and Reason*. New Haven, Conn.: Yale University Press, 1992.

Bull, Hedley. "The Theory of International Politics: 1919–1969." In *The Aberystwyth Papers: International Politics, 1919–1969*, edited by Brian Porter, 30–55. London: Oxford University Press, 1972.

——. *The Anarchical Society: A Study of Order in World Politics*. London: Macmillan, 1977.

——. "Hobbes and the International Anarchy." *Social Research* 48/4 (1981): 717–738.

Burke, Kenneth. *A Grammar of Motives*. Berkeley and Los Angeles: University of California Press, 1969.

Butterfield, Herbert. *International Conflict in the Twentieth Century*. New York: Harper, 1960.

Butterfield, Herbert, and Martin Wight, eds. *Diplomatic Investigations*. Cambridge: Harvard University Press, 1966.

Buzan, Barry. "The Level of Analysis Problem in International Relations Reconsidered." In *International Relations Theory Today*, edited by Ken Booth and Steve Smith, 198–216. Cambridge: Polity Press, 1995.

Carr, Edward H. *The Twenty Years' Crisis, 1919–1939: An Introduction to the Study of International Relations*. 1939. Reprint, New York: Harper and Row, 1964.

Carter, John, and Michael Irons. "Are Economists Different, and If So, Why?" *Journal of Economic Perspectives* 5 (spring 1991): 171–177.

Cassirer, Ernst. *The Myth of the State*. New Haven, Conn.: Yale University Press, 1946.

Cesa, Mario. *Le Ragioni della Forza: Tucidide e la Teoria delle Relazioni Internazionali*. Bologna, It.: Il Mulino, 1994.

Chabot, Dana. "Thomas Hobbes: Skeptical Moralist." *American Political Science Review* 89/2 (1995): 401–410.

Chatterjee, Shibashis. "Neo-Realism in International Relations." *International Studies* 34/1 (1997): 39–58.

Chittick, William O., Keith Billingsley, and Rick Travis. "A Three-Dimensional Model of American Foreign Policy Beliefs." *International Studies Quarterly* 39/3 (1995): 313–331.

Chittick, William O., and Annette Freyberg-Inan. "The Impact of Basic Motivation on Foreign Policy Opinions concerning the Use of Force: A Three-Dimensional Framework." In *When the Going Gets Tough: Democracy, Public Opinion, and the International Use of Force*, edited by Philip Everts and Pierangelo Isernia. London: Routledge, 2000.

———. "'Chiefly for Fear, Next for Honor, and Lastly for Profit': An Analysis of Foreign Policy Motivation in the Peloponnesian War." *Review of International Studies* 27 (spring 2001): 69–90.

Clark, Ian. *The Hierarchy of States: Reform and Resistance in the International Order*. Cambridge: Cambridge University Press, 1989.

Clark, Michael T. "Realism Ancient and Modern: Thucydides and International Relations." *PS: Political Science and Politics* 26/3 (1993): 491–494.

Coby, Patrick. "Enlightened Self-Interest in the Peloponnesian War: Thucydidean Speakers on the Right of the Stronger and Inter-State Peace." *Canadian Journal of Political Science* 24/1 (1991): 67–90.

Cochrane, Charles Norris. *Thucydides and the Science of History*. New York: Russell and Russell, 1965.

Cogan, Marc. *The Human Thing: The Speeches and Principles of Thucydides' History*. Chicago: University of Chicago Press, 1981.

Cohen, David. "Justice, Interest, and Political Deliberation in Thucydides." *Quaderni Urbinati* 16/1 (1984): 35–60.

Combs, Allan, ed. *Cooperation: Beyond the Age of Competition*. Philadelphia: Gordon and Breach, 1992.

Connor, W. Robert. *Thucydides*. Princeton, N.J.: Princeton University Press, 1984.

Cornford, Francis Macdonald. *Thucydides Mythistoricus*. London: Routledge and Kegan Paul, 1965.

Cottam, Richard W. *Foreign Policy Motivation: A General Theory and a Case Study*. Pittsburgh, Pa.: University of Pittsburgh Press, 1977.

Cox, Robert W. "Social Forces, States, and World Orders: Beyond International Relations Theory." In *Neorealism and Its Critics*, edited by Robert O. Keohane, 204–254. New York: Columbia University Press, 1986.

———, ed. *The New Realism: Perspectives on Multilateralism and World Order*. Tokyo: United Nations University Press, 1997.

Crane, Gregory R. *The Ancient Simplicity: Thucydides and the Limits of Political Realism*. Berkeley and Los Angeles: University of California Press, 1998.

———. "'Political Style: The Artistry of Power'" (book review). Available at http://www.lib.ncsu.edu/stacks/b/bmcr/bmcr-9512-crane-political.txt. Accessed June 25, 1998.

———, ed. *The Perseus Project*. Available at http://www.perseus.tufts.edu. Accessed June 17, 1998.

Czempiel, Ernst-Otto. "Governance and Democratization." In *Governance without Government: Order and Change in World Politics*, edited by James N. Rosenau and Ernst-Otto Czempiel, 250–271. New York: Cambridge University Press, 1992.

———. "In der Realismusfalle: Kritik einer Aussenpolitischen Maxime." *Merkur* 52/1 (1998): 15–25.

Dawes, Robyn M. "The Nature of Human Nature: An Empirical Case for Withholding Judgment—Perhaps Indefinitely." *Political Psychology* 16/1 (1995): 81–97.

DeBell, Daryl. "The Pernicious Paranoia of the Realist Theory of International Relations and Its Unrealistic Basis." Paper presented at the annual scientific meeting of the International Society for Political Psychology, Amsterdam, The Netherlands, July 1999.

DeNardo, James. *The Amateur Strategist: Intuitive Deterrence Theories and the Politics of the Nuclear Arms Race*. Cambridge: Cambridge University Press, 1995.

de Rivera, Joseph. *The Psychological Dimension of Foreign Policy*. Columbus, Ohio: Merrill, 1968.

Deutsch, Karl. *Political Community and the North Atlantic Area*. Princeton, N.J.: Princeton University Press, 1957.

Dietz, Mary. "Trapping the Prince: Machiavelli and the Politics of Deception." *American Political Science Review* 80/3 (1986): 777–799.

———, ed. *Thomas Hobbes and Political Theory*. Lawrence: University of Kansas Press, 1990.

Donnelly, Jack. "Twentieth-Century Realism." In *Traditions of International Ethics*, edited by Terry Nardin and David R. Mapel, 85–111. Cambridge: Cambridge University Press, 1992.

———. *Realism and International Relations*. Cambridge: Cambridge University Press, 2000.

Dowding, Keith, and Desmond King. Introduction to *Preferences, Institutions, and Rational Choice*, edited by Keith Dowding and Desmond King, 1–19. Oxford: Clarendon Press, 1995.

———, eds. *Preferences, Institutions, and Rational Choice*. Oxford: Clarendon Press, 1995.

Downs, Anthony. *An Economic Theory of Democracy*. New York: Harper and Row, 1957.

Doyle, Michael W. "Thucydidean Realism." *Review of International Studies* 16 (July 1990): 223–237.

———. "Thucydides: A Realist?" In *Hegemonic Rivalry: From Thucydides to the Nuclear Age*, edited by Richard Ned Lebow and Barry S. Strauss, 169–188. Boulder, Colo.: Westview, 1991.

———. *Ways of War and Peace: Realism, Liberalism, and Socialism*. New York: Norton, 1997.

Doyle Corner, Patricia, Angelo Kinicki, and Barbara Keats. "Integrating Organizational and Individual Information-Processing Perspectives on Choice." *Organizational Science* 5/3 (1994): 294–308.

Drexler, Hans. *Thukydides-Studien*. Hildesheim, Ger.: Georg Olms Verlag, 1976.

Dupre, John, ed. *The Latest and the Best: Essays on Evolution and Optimality*. Cambridge: MIT Press, 1987.

Elman, Colin. "Horses for Courses: Why *Not* Neorealist Theories of Foreign Policy?" *Security Studies* 6/1 (1996): 7–53.

Elman, Colin, and Miriam Fendius Elman. "Lakatos and Neorealism: A Reply to Vasquez." *American Political Science Review* 91/4 (1997): 923–926.

———, eds. *Bridges and Boundaries*. Cambridge: MIT Press, 2001.

Elman, Miriam Fendius. "The Foreign Policies of Small States: Challenging Neorealism in Its Own Backyard." *British Journal of Political Science* 25/2 (1995): 171–217.

Elshtain, Jean Bethke. "International Politics and Political Theory." In *International Relations Theory Today*, edited by Ken Booth and Steve Smith, 263–278. Cambridge: Polity Press, 1995.

Erbse, Hartmut. *Thukydides-Interpretationen*. Berlin: Walter de Gruyter, 1989.

Erikson, Eric H. "The Concept of Identity in Race Relations: Notes and Queries." *Daedalus* 95/1 (1966): 145–171.

Ewin, R. E. *Virtues and Rights: The Moral Philosophy of Thomas Hobbes*. Boulder, Colo.: Westview, 1991.

Falkowski, Lawrence S., ed. *Psychological Models in International Politics*. Boulder, Colo.: Westview, 1979.

Ferejohn, John. "Rationality and Interpretation: Parliamentary Elections in Early Stuart England." In *The Economic Approach to Politics: A Critical Reassessment of the Theory of*

Rational Action, edited by K. Renwick Monroe, 279–305. New York: HarperCollins, 1991.

Ferguson, Yale H., and Richard W. Mansbach. "Between Celebration and Despair: Constructive Suggestions for Future International Theory." *International Studies Quarterly* 35/4 (1991): 363–386.

Festinger, Leon. *A Theory of Cognitive Dissonance*. Stanford, Calif.: Stanford University Press, 1957.

Finlay, David J., Ole R. Holsti, and Richard R. Fragen. *Enemies in Politics*. Chicago: Rand McNally, 1967.

Finley, John Huston. *Thucydides*. Ann Arbor: University of Michigan Press, 1963.

Finnemore, Martha. *National Interests in International Society*. Ithaca, N.Y.: Cornell University Press, 1996.

Fischer, Markus. "Machiavelli's Theory of Foreign Politics." *Security Studies* 5/2 (winter 1995/1996): 248–279.

——. "Machiavelli's Political Psychology." *Review of Politics* 59/4 (1997): 789–829.

Fisher, Ronald A. *Statistical Methods and Scientific Inference*. New York: Hafner, 1956.

Forde, Steven. "Thucydides on the Causes of Athenian Imperialism." *American Political Science Review* 80/2 (1986): 433–448.

——. *The Ambition to Rule: Alcibiades and the Politics of Imperialism in Thucydides*. Ithaca, N.Y.: Cornell University Press, 1989.

——. "Classical Realism." In *Traditions of International Ethics*, edited by Terry Nardin and David R. Mapel, 62–84. Cambridge: Cambridge University Press, 1992.

——. "Varieties of Realism: Thucydides and Machiavelli." *Journal of Politics* 54/2 (1992): 372–393.

——. "International Realism and the Science of Politics: Thucydides, Machiavelli, and Neorealism." *International Studies Quarterly* 39/2 (1995): 141–160.

Forgas, Joseph P., ed. *Emotion and Social Judgments*. Oxford: Pergamon Press, 1991.

Fozouni, Bahman. "Confutation of Political Realism." *International Studies Quarterly* 39/4 (1995): 479–510.

Frank, Jerome D. *Sanity and Survival: Psychological Aspects of War and Peace*. New York: Random House, 1967.

Frank, Robert H. *Passions within Reason*. New York: Norton, 1988.

Frank, Robert H., Thomas Gilovich, and Dennis Regan. "Does Studying Economics Inhibit Cooperation?" *Journal of Economic Perspectives* 7/2 (1993): 159–171.

——. "Do Economists Make Bad Citizens?" *Journal of Economic Perspectives* 10/1 (1996): 187–192.

Frankel, Benjamin. "Introduction." *Security Studies* 5/2 (1995/1996): ix–xxiii.

Freud, Sigmund. *The Problem of Anxiety*. Albany, N.Y.: The Psychoanalytic Quarterly Press, 1936.

Fromkin, David. "Remembering Hans Morgenthau." *World Policy Journal* 10/3 (1993): 81–88.

Frost, Mervyn. *Ethics in International Relations: A Constitutive Theory*. Cambridge: Cambridge University Press, 1996.

Gaddis, John Lewis. "International Relations Theory and the End of the Cold War." *International Security* 17/3 (winter 1992/1993): 5–58.

Gamson, William A., and Andre Modigliani. *Untangling the Cold War*. Boston: Little, Brown, 1971.

Garnett, John C. *Commonsense and the Theory of International Politics*. London: Macmillan, 1984.

Garst, Daniel. "Thucydides and Neorealism." *International Studies Quarterly* 33/1 (1989): 3–27.

Gaubatz, Kurt Taylor. "The Hobbesian Problem and the Microfoundations of International Relations Theory or: If Politics Stops at the Water's Edge, How Did Everyone Get to Be So Wet?" Paper presented at the annual meeting of the American Political Science Association, New York City, September 1994.

Gauthier, David P. *The Logic of Leviathan: The Moral and Political Theory of Thomas Hobbes*. Oxford: Clarendon Press, 1969.

Geen, Russell G. *Human Motivation: A Social Psychological Approach*. Pacific Grove, Calif.: Brooks/Cole, 1995.

George, Alexander L. *Bridging the Gap: Theory and Practice in Foreign Policy*. Washington, D.C.: United States Institute of Peace, 1993.

George, Jim. "Realist Ethics, International Relations, and Postmodernism: Thinking beyond the Egoism–Anarchy Thematic." *Millennium* 24/2 (1995): 195–223.

Gert, Bernard. "Hobbes's Psychology." In *The Cambridge Companion to Hobbes*, edited by Tom Sorell, 157–174. Cambridge: Cambridge University Press, 1996.

Gilbert, Felix. "The Composition and Structure of Machiavelli's Discorsi." *Journal of the History of Ideas* 14 (1953): 136–156.

Gilpin, Robert. *War and Change in World Politics*. New York: Cambridge University Press, 1981.

——. "The Richness of the Tradition of Political Realism." *International Organization* 38/2 (1984): 287–304.

——. "The Theory of Hegemonic War." In *The Origin and Prevention of Major Wars*, edited by Robert I. Rotberg and Theodore K. Rabb, 15–37. Cambridge: Cambridge University Press, 1989.

Glaser, Charles L. "The Security Dilemma Revisited." *World Politics* 50/1 (1997): 171–201.

Glover, Willis. "Human Nature and the State in Hobbes." *Journal of the History of Philosophy* 4 (1966): 293–311.

Goldstein, Judith, and Robert O. Keohane, eds. *Ideas and Foreign Policy: Beliefs, Institutions, and Political Change*. Ithaca, N.Y.: Cornell University Press, 1993.

Gomme, Arnold W. *A Historical Commentary on Thucydides*. Oxford: Clarendon Press, 1945.

Gommel, Juergen. *Rhetorisches Argumentieren bei Thukydides*. Hildesheim, Ger.: Georg Olms Verlag, 1966.

Goodnight, G. Thomas. "Hans J. Morgenthau In Defense of the National Interest: On Rhetoric, Realism and the Public Sphere." In *Post-Realism: The Rhetorical Turn in International Relations*, edited by Francis Beer and Robert Hariman, 143–165. East Lansing: Michigan State University Press, 1996.

Green, Arnold W. *Hobbes and Human Nature*. New Brunswick, N.J.: Transaction Publishers, 1993.

Green, Donald P., and Ian Shapiro. *Pathologies of Rational Choice Theory: A Critique of Applications in Political Science*. New Haven, Conn.: Yale University Press, 1994.

Grene, David. *Greek Political Theory: The Image of Man in Thucydides and Plato*. Chicago: University of Chicago Press, 1965.

Grieco, Joseph M. "Anarchy and the Limits of Cooperation: A Realist Critique of the Newest Liberal Institutionalism." *International Organization* 42/3 (1988): 485–507.

———. *Cooperation among Nations: Europe, America, and Non-Tariff Barriers to Trade*. Ithaca, N.Y.: Cornell University Press, 1990.

Grieco, Joseph M., Robert Powell, and Duncan Snidal. "The Relative-Gains Problem for International Cooperation." *American Political Science Review* 87/3 (1993): 729–743.

Guzzini, Stefano. *Realism in International Relations and International Political Economy: The Continuing Story of a Death Foretold*. London: Routledge, 1998.

Haas, Ernst B. "The Balance of Power Prescription, Context, or Propaganda?" *World Politics* 5/4 (1953): 442–477.

———. *The Uniting of Europe: Political, Social, and Economic Forces, 1950–1957*. Stanford, Calif.: Stanford University Press, 1958.

———. *Beyond the Nation State*. Stanford, Calif.: Stanford University Press, 1964.

Halliday, Fred. "Theory and Ethics in International Relations: The Contradictions of C. Wright Mills." *Millennium* 23/2 (1994): 377–387.

Hanson, Donald W. "Science, Prudence, and Folly in Hobbes's Political Theory." *Political Theory* 21/4 (1993): 643–664.

Hare, J. E., and Carey B. Joynt. *Ethics and International Affairs*. New York: St. Martin's, 1982.

Hariman, Robert. *Political Style: The Artistry of Power*. Chicago: University of Chicago Press, 1995.

Harsanyi, John C. "Some Social Science Implications of a New Approach to Game Theory." In *Strategic Interaction and Conflict*, edited by Kathleen Archibald, 1–18. Berkeley, Calif.: Institute of International Studies, 1966.

Harvey, Frank P. *The Future's Back*. Toronto: McGill-Queen's University Press, 1997.

———. "Rigor Mortis, or Rigor, More Tests: Necessity, Sufficiency, and Deterrence Logic." *International Studies Quarterly* 42/4 (1998): 675–707.

Hasenclever, Andreas, Peter Mayer, and Volker Rittberger. "Interests, Power, Knowledge: The Study of International Regimes." *Mershon International Studies Review* 40 (October 1996): 177–228.

Hausman, Daniel M., and Michael S. McPherson. "Taking Ethics Seriously: Economics and Contemporary Moral Philosophy." *Journal of Economic Literature* 31/2 (1993): 671–731.

Heckhausen, Heinz. *Motivation and Action*. New York: Springer, 1991.

Heginbotham, Eric, and Richard J. Samuels. "Mercantile Realism and Japanese Foreign Policy." *International Security* 22/4 (1998): 171–203.

Heider, Fritz. *The Psychology of Interpersonal Relations*. Hillside, N.J.: Erlbaum, 1958.

Hellmann, G., and R. Wolf. "Systemic Theories After the East-West Conflict: Outcomes and Perspectives of the Neo-Realism–Institutionalism Debate." *Oesterreichische Zeitschrift fuer Politikwissenschaft* 22/2 (1993): 153–167.

Hermann, Charles F. "Changing Course: When Governments Plan to Redirect Foreign Policy." *International Studies Quarterly* 34/1 (1990): 3–21.

Hermann, Margaret G., ed. *Political Psychology*. San Francisco: Jossey-Bass, 1986.

Hermann, Margaret G., and Joe D. Hagan. "International Decision Making: Leadership Matters." *Foreign Policy* 110 (1998): 124–137.

Herrmann, Richard K. "Conclusions: The End of the Cold War—What Have We Learned?" In *International Relations Theory and the End of the Cold War*, edited by Richard Ned Lebow and Thomas Risse-Kappen, 259–284. New York: Columbia University Press, 1995.

Herrmann, Richard K., James F. Voss, Tonya Y. E. Schooler, and Joseph Ciarrochi. "Images in International Relations: An Experimental Test of Cognitive Schemata." *International Studies Quarterly* 41/3 (1997): 403–433.

Herz, John. "Idealist Internationalism and the Security Dilemma," *World Politics* 2/2 (1950): 157–180.

——. *Political Realism and Political Idealism: A Study in Theories and Realities*. Chicago: University of Chicago Press, 1951.

Hirschman, Albert O. *The Passions and the Interests: Political Arguments for Capitalism before Its Triumph*. Princeton, N.J.: Princeton University Press, 1977.

Hirshleifer, Jack. "On the Emotions as Guarantors of Threats and Promises." In *The Latest and the Best: Essays on Evolution and Optimality*, edited by John Dupre, 307–326. Cambridge: MIT Press, 1987.

Hobbes, Thomas. "Notes, Book 1, 19." In Thucydides, *Hobbes' Thucydides*, edited by Richard Schlatter. New Brunswick, N.J.: Rutgers University Press, 1975.

——. *De Cive*. 1647. Reprint, Oxford: Clarendon Press, 1983.

——. *Leviathan*. 1651. Reprint, Cambridge: Cambridge University Press, 1991.

——. *Behemoth or The Long Parliament*. 1682. Reprint, Chicago: University of Chicago Press, 1990.

——. "Human Nature: Or the Fundamental Elements of Policy." In *The English Works of Thomas Hobbes of Malmesbury*, vol. 4, edited by Sir William Molesworth, 1–76. London: Scientia Aalen, 1962.

——. "De Corpore Politico: Or the Elements of Law, Moral, and Politic." In *The English Works of Thomas Hobbes of Malmesbury*, vol. 4, edited by Sir William Molesworth, 77–228. London: Scientia Aalen, 1962.

Hoffman, Piotr. *The Quest for Power: Hobbes, Descartes, and the Emergence of Modernity*. Atlantic Highlands, N.J.: Humanities Press, 1996.

Hoffman, Stanley. "Notes on the Limits of 'Realism.'" *Social Research* 48/4 (1981): 653–659.

——. "Correspondence: Back to the Future, Part II: International Relations Theory and Post Cold War Europe." *International Security* 15/2 (1990): 191–192.

Hofstadter, Richard. "The Paranoid Style in American Politics." In *The Paranoid Style in American Politics, and Other Essays*. New York: Knopf, 1965.

Holborn, Hajo. "Greek and Modern Concepts of History." *Journal of the History of Ideas* 10 (1949).

Hollis, Martin, and Steve Smith. *Explaining and Understanding International Relations*. Oxford: Clarendon Press, 1990.

Holmes, Stephen. Introduction to *Behemoth or The Long Parliament*, by Thomas Hobbes, vii–l. 1682. Reprint, Chicago: University of Chicago Press, 1990.

——. "Political Psychology in Hobbes' Behemoth." In *Thomas Hobbes and Political Theory*, edited by Mary Dietz, 120–152. Lawrence: University of Kansas Press, 1990.

Holsti, Ole R. "The Belief System and National Images: A Case Study." *Conflict Resolution* 6/3 (1962): 244–252.

——. *Crisis, Escalation, War*. Montreal: McGill-Queen's University Press, 1972.

Hong, Mark. "Small States in the United Nations." *International Social Science Journal* 47 (June 1995): 277–287.

Hoover, Kenneth R. *The Elements of Social Scientific Thinking*, 5th ed. New York: St. Martin's, 1992.

Hornblower, Simon. *Thucydides*. Baltimore: Johns Hopkins University Press, 1987.

——. *A Commentary on Thucydides*. Oxford: Clarendon Press, 1991.

Hudson, Valerie M. and Christopher S. Vore. "Foreign Policy Analysis Yesterday, Today, and Tomorrow." *Mershon International Studies Review* 39 (suppl. 2; 1995): 209–238.

Hume, David. *Enquiries Concerning Human Understanding, and Concerning the Principles of Morals*. 1777. Reprint, Oxford: Clarendon Press, 1975.

Ignatius, David. "They Don't Make Them Like George Marshall Anymore." *Washington Post*, 8 June 1987, p. 25, national edition.

Immerwahr, Henry R. "Pathology of Power and the Speeches in Thucydides." In *The Speeches in Thucydides*, edited by Philip A. Staedter. Chapel Hill: University of North Carolina Press, 1973.

Inbar, Efraim, and Gabriel Sheffer, eds. *The National Security of Small States in a Changing World*. London: Frank Cass, 1997.

Ivie, Robert L. "Realism Masking Fear: George F. Kennan's Political Rhetoric." In *Post-Realism: The Rhetorical Turn in International Relations*, edited by Francis Beer and Robert Hariman, 55–74. East Lansing: Michigan State University Press, 1996.

James, Alan. "The realism [*sic*] of Realism." *Review of International Studies* 15 (1989): 215–229.

James, Patrick. *International Relations and Scientific Progress: Structural Realism Reconsidered*. Columbus: Ohio State University Press, 2002.

——. *Elaborated Structural Realism and Crises in World Politics*. Columbus: Ohio State University Press, 2003.

Jepperson, Ronald L., Alexander Wendt, and Peter J. Katzenstein. "Norms, Identity, and Culture in National Security." In *The Culture of National Secutiry: Norms and Identity in World Politics*, edited by Peter J. Katzenstein, 33–75. New York: Columbia University Press, 1996.

Jervis, Robert. *Perception and Misperception in International Politics*. Princeton, N.J.: Princeton University Press, 1976.

——. "War and Misperception." *Journal of Interdisciplinary History* 18/4 (1988): 675–700.

——. "Cooperation under the Security Dilemma." *World Politics* 30 (January 1978): 167–214.

——. "Realism, Game Theory, and Cooperation." *World Politics* 40/3 (April 1988): 317–349.

——. "Models and Cases in the Study of International Conflict." *Journal of International Affairs* 44/1 (1990): 81–101.

——. "The Future of World Politics: Will It Resemble the Past?" *International Security* 16/3 (winter 1991/1992): 39–73.

——. "Hans Morgenthau, Realism, and the Scientific Study of International Politics." *Social Research* 61/4 (1994): 853–876.

——. "Leadership, Post-Cold-War Politics, and Psychology." *Political Psychology* 15/4 (1994): 769–777.

Jervis, Robert, Janice Gross Stein, and Richard Ned Lebrow. *Psychology and Deterrence*. Baltimore: Johns Hopkins University Press, 1985.

Johnson, Laurie M. *Thucydides, Hobbes, and the Interpretation of Realism*. Dekalb: Northern Illinois University Press, 1993.

Johnson, Thomas. "The Idea of Power Politics: The Sophistic Foundations of Realism." *Security Studies* 5/2 (winter 1995/1996): 194–247.

Johnson Bagby, Laurie M. "The Use and Abuse of Thucydides in International Relations." *International Organization* 48/1 (1994): 131–153.

——. "The Humanity of a True Realist: Clifford Orwin: The Humanity of Thucydides" (book review). *Review of Politics* 57/2 (1995): 342–344.

——. "Thucydidean Realism: Between Athens and Melos." *Security Studies* 5/2 (winter 1995/1996): 169–193.

——. "The Law of Nations and Other Dimensions in Hobbes' Thought: Understanding the Realist Project." Paper presented at the annual meeting of the International Studies Association, San Diego, California, April 1996.

Johnson-Laird, Philip N. *Mental Models: Towards a Cognitive Science of Language, Inference, and Consciousness*. Cambridge: Harvard University Press, 1983.

Johnston, David. *The Rhetoric of Leviathan: Thomas Hobbes and the Politics of Cultural Transformation*. Princeton, N.J.: Princeton University Press, 1986.

Jones, Charles. "Carr, Mannheim, and a Post-Positivist Science of International Relations." *Political Studies* 45 (June 1997): 232–246.

Jones, Edward E., and Richard E. Nisbett. *The Actor and the Observer: Divergent Perceptions of the Causes of Behavior*. New York: General Learning Press, 1971.

Jung, Carl G. *The Integration of the Personality*. New York: Farrar and Rinehart, 1939.

Kahn, Victoria Ann. *Rhetoric, Prudence, and Skepticism in the Renaissance*. Ithaca, N.Y.: Cornell University Press, 1985.

——. *Machiavellian Rhetoric: From the Counter-Reformation to Milton*. Princeton, N.J.: Princeton University Press, 1994.

Kain, P. J. "Machiavelli, Niccolo: Adviser of Princes." *Canadian Journal of Philosophy* 25/1 (1995): 33–55.

Kant, Immanuel. *Ethical Philosophy*. Indianapolis, Ind.: Hackett, 1983.

Kateb, George. "Hobbes and the Irrationality of Politics." *Political Theory* 17/3 (1989): 355–391.

Katzenstein, Peter J. *Small States in World Markets*. Ithaca, N.Y.: Cornell University Press, 1985.

——. "Introduction: Alternative Perspectives on National Security." In *The Culture of National Security: Norms and Identity in World Politics*, edited by Peter J. Katzenstein, 1–32. New York: Columbia University Press, 1996.

——, ed. *The Culture of National Security: Norms and Identity in World Politics*. New York: Columbia University Press, 1996.

Kaufman, Robert G. "E. H. Carr, Winston Churchill, Reinhold Niebuhr, and Us: The Case for Principled, Prudential, Democratic Realism." *Security Studies* 5/2 (winter 1995/1996): 314–353.

Kaufmann, Chaim D. "Out of the Lab and into the Archives: A Method for Testing Psychological Explanations for Political Decision Making." *International Studies Quarterly* 38/4 (1994): 557–586.

Kauppi, Mark V. "Contemporary International Relations Theory and the Peloponnesian War." In *Hegemonic Rivalry: From Thucydides to the Nuclear Age*, edited by Richard Ned Lebow and Barry S. Strauss, 101–124. Boulder, Colo.: Westview, 1991.

——. "Thucydides: Character and Capabilities." *Security Studies* 5/2 (winter 1995/1996): 142–168.

Kavka, Gregory S. *Hobbesian Moral and Political Theory*. Princeton, N.J.: Princeton University Press, 1986.

Kegley, Charles W. Jr. "The Neoidealist Moment in International Studies? Realist Myths and the New International Realities." *International Studies Quarterly* 37/2 (1993): 131–146.

——. "The Neoliberal Challenge to Realist Theories of World Politics: An Introduction." In *Controversies in International Relations Theory: Realism and the Neoliberal Challenge*, edited by Charles W. Kegley Jr., 1–24. New York: St. Martin's, 1995.

——, ed. *Controversies in International Relations Theory: Realism and the Neoliberal Challenge.* New York: St. Martin's, 1995.

Kelman, Herbert C., ed. *International Behavior: A Social–Psychological Analysis.* New York: Holt, Rinehart, and Winston, 1965.

Kemos, Alexander. "The Influence of Thucydides in the Modern World: The Father of Political Realism Plays a Key Role in Current Balance of Power Theories." Harvard University. Available at http://hcs.harvard.edu/~por/thucydides.html. Accessed May 26, 1998.

Kennan, George F. *American Diplomacy.* 1951. Reprint, Chicago: University of Chicago Press, 1984.

——. "Morality and Foreign Policy." *Foreign Affairs* 64/2 (1985/1986): 205–218.

——. *Around the Cragged Hill: A Personal and Political Philosophy.* New York: Norton 1993.

——. *At a Century's Ending: Reflections, 1982–1995.* New York: Norton, 1996.

Kennedy, James. "Thinking Is Social: Experiments with the Adaptive Culture Model." *Journal of Conflict Resolution* 42/1 (1998): 56–76.

Keohane, Robert O. "Realism, Neorealism, and the Study of World Politics." In *Neorealism and Its Critics*, edited by Robert O. Keohane, 1–26. New York: Columbia University Press, 1986.

——. "Theory of World Politics: Structural Realism and Beyond." In *Neorealism and Its Critics*, edited by Robert O. Keohane, 158–203. New York: Columbia University Press, 1986.

——. *International Institutions and State Power: Essays in International Relations Theory.* Boulder, Colo.: Westview, 1989.

——. "Correspondence: Back to the Future, Part II: International Relations Theory and Post Cold War Europe." *International Security* 15/2 (1990): 192–194.

——, ed. *Neorealism and Its Critics.* New York: Columbia University Press, 1986.

Keohane, Robert O., and Lisa L. Martin. "The Promise of Institutionalist Theory." *International Security* 20/1 (1995): 39–51

Keohane, Robert O., and Joseph S. Nye Jr. "Power and Interdependence Revisited." *International Organization* 41/4 (1987): 725–753.

——. *Power and Interdependence*, 2nd ed. Glenview, Ill.: Scott, Foresman, 1989.

——. "Introduction: The End of the Cold War in Europe." In *After the Cold War: International Institutions and State Strategies in Europe, 1989–1991*, edited by Robert O. Keohane, Joseph Nye, and Stanley Hoffman, 1–22. Cambridge: Harvard University Press, 1993.

Keohane, Robert O., Joseph Nye, and Stanley Hoffman, eds. *After the Cold War: International Institutions and State Strategies in Europe, 1989–1991.* Cambridge: Harvard University Press, 1993.

Khong, Yuen Foong. *Analogies at War: Korea, Munich, Dien Bien Phu, and the Vietnam Decisions of 1965.* Princeton, N.J.: Princeton University Press, 1992.

King, Gary, Robert O. Keohane, and Sidney Verba. *Designing Social Inquiry: Scientific Inference in Qualitative Research.* Princteton, N.J.: Princeton University Press, 1994.

Kipnis, Kenneth, and Diana T. Meyers, eds. *Political Realism and International Morality.* Boulder, Colo.: Westview, 1987.

Kissinger, Henry. *American Foreign Policy.* 1969. Reprint, New York: Norton, 1977.

——. *Diplomacy.* New York: Simon and Schuster, 1994.

Kluxen, Kurt. *Politik und Menschliche Existenz bei Machiavelli: Dargestellt am Begriff der Necessita.* Stuttgart, Ger.: Kohlhammer, 1967.

Knorr, Klaus, and Sidney Verba, eds. *The International System: Theoretical Essays.* Princeton, N.J.: Princeton University Press, 1961.

Kohn, Alfie. "Cooperation: What It Means and Doesn't Mean." In *Cooperation: Beyond the Age of Competition*, edited by Allan Combs, 3–11. Philadelphia: Gordon and Breach, 1995.

Koslowski, Rey, and Friedrich V. Kratochwil. "Understanding Change in International Politics: The Soviet Empire's Demise and the International System." In *International Relations Theory and the End of the Cold War*, edited by Richard Ned Lebow and Thomas Risse-Kappen, 127–166. New York: Columbia University Press, 1995.

Kramer, Roderick M., and Alice M. Isen. "Trust and Distrust: Its Psychological and Social Dimensions." *Motivation and Emotion* 18/2 (1991): 105–107.

Krasner, Stephen D. *Defending the National Interest: Raw Materials Investments and U.S. Foreign Policy.* Princeton, N.J.: Princeton University Press, 1978.

———. *Asymmetries in Japanese–American Trade: The Case for Specific Reciprocity.* Berkeley, Calif.: Institute of International Studies, 1987.

Krippendorf, Ekkehart. *Die Amerikanische Strategie: Entscheidungsprozess und Instrumentarium der Amerikanischen Aussenpolitik.* Frankfurt/Main, Ger.: Suhrkamp, 1970.

Kugler, Jacek, and A. F. K. Organski. "The Power Transition: A Retrospective and Prospective Evaluation." In *Handbook of War Studies*, edited by Manus I. Midlarsky, 171–194. Boston: Unwin Hyman, 1989.

Kuhn, Thomas. "Reflections on My Critics." In *Criticism and the Growth of Knowledge*, edited by Imre Lakatos and Alan Musgrave, 231–278. Cambridge: Cambridge University Press, 1970.

———. *The Structure of Scientific Revolutions*, 3rd ed. Chicago: University of Chicago Press, 1996.

Kupchan, Charles A. *The Vulnerability of Empire.* Ithaca, N.Y.: Cornell University Press, 1994.

Kupchan, Charles A., and Clifford A. Kupchan. "The Promise of Collective Security." *International Security* 20/1 (1995): 52–61.

Labs, Eric J. "Beyond Victory: Offensive Realism and the Expansion of War Aims." *Security Studies* 6/4 (1997): 1–49.

Lakatos, Imre. "Falsification and the Methodology of Scientific Research Programmes." In *Criticism and the Growth of Knowledge*, edited by Imre Lakatos and Alan Musgrave, 91–196. Cambridge: Cambridge University Press, 1970.

———. *The Methodology of Scientific Research Programmes.* Cambridge: Cambridge University Press, 1978.

Lakatos, Imre, and Alan Musgrave, eds. *Criticism and the Growth of Knowledge.* Cambridge: Cambridge University Press, 1970.

Lamb, Walter R. M. *Clio Enthroned: A Study of Prose-Form in Thucydides.* Cambridge: Cambridge University Press, 1914.

Lamborn, Alan C. "Theory and the Politics in World Politics." *International Studies Quarterly* 41/2 (1997): 187–214.

Lane, Robert E. *Political Ideology: Why the American Common Man Believes What He Does.* Glencoe, Ill.: Free Press, 1962.

Lang, Mabel L. "Participial Motivation in Thucydides." *Mnemosyne* 48/1 (1995): 48–65.

Lapid, Yosef. "Without Any Guarantees: The 'Third Way' (in the 'Third Debate') to International Theory." Paper presented at the Northeastern Political Science Association meeting, Philadelphia, Pa., November 1989.

———. "The Third Debate: On the Prospects of International Theory in a Post-Positivist Era." *International Studies Quarterly* 33/3 (1989): 235–254.

Lapid, Yosef, and Friedrich Kratochwil, eds. *The Return of Culture and Identity in IR Theory.* Boulder, Colo.: Lynne Rienner, 1996.

Lasswell, Harold D. *Politics: Who Gets What, When, How.* New York: McGraw-Hill, 1938.

Laver, Michael. *Private Desires, Political Action: An Invitation to the Politics of Rational Choice.* London: Sage, 1997.

Layne, Christopher. "The Unipolar Illusion: Why New Great Powers Will Rise." In *The Perils of Anarchy: Contemporary Realism and International Security,* edited by Michael E. Brown, Sean M. Lynn-Jones, and Steven E. Miller, 130–176. Cambridge: MIT Press, 1995.

Layne, Christopher, and Benjamin Schwarz. "No New World Order: America after the Cold War." *Current* 358 (December 1993): 26–33.

Lebow, Richard Ned. "The Deterrence Deadlock: Is There a Way Out?" In *Psychology and Deterrence,* edited by Robert Jervis, Janice Gross Stein, and Richard Ned Lebow, 180–202. Baltimore: Johns Hopkins University Press, 1985.

——. *Nuclear Crisis Management: A Dangerous Illusion.* Ithaca, N.Y.: Cornell University Press, 1987.

——. "Thucydides, Power Transition Theory, and the Causes of War." In *Hegemonic Rivalry: From Thucydides to the Nuclear Age,* edited by Richard Ned Lebow and Barry S. Strauss, 125–168. Boulder, Colo.: Westview, 1991.

——. "The Long Peace, the End of the Cold War, and the Failure of Realism." In *International Relations Theory and the End of the Cold War,* edited by Richard Ned Lebow and Thomas Risse-Kappen, 23–56. New York: Columbia University Press, 1995.

——. "The Search for Accommodation: Gorbachev in Comparative Perspective." In *International Relations Theory and the End of the Cold War,* edited by Richard Ned Lebow and Thomas Risse-Kappen, 167–186. New York: Columbia University Press, 1995.

——. "Small States and Big Alliances" (book review). *American Political Science Review* 91 (September 1997): 705–709.

Lebow, Richard Ned, and Janice Gross Stein. "Beyond Deterrence." *Journal of Social Issues* 43/4 (1987): 5–71.

——. *We All Lost the Cold War.* Princeton, N.J.: Princeton University Press, 1995.

Lebow, Richard Ned, and Thomas Risse-Kappen. "Introduction: International Relations Theory and the End of the Cold War." In *International Relations Theory and the End of the Cold War,* edited by Richard Ned Lebow and Thomas Risse-Kappen, 1–22. New York: Columbia University Press, 1995.

——, eds. *International Relations Theory and the End of the Cold War.* New York: Columbia University Press, 1995.

Lebow, Richard Ned, and Barry S. Strauss, eds. *Hegemonic Rivalry: From Thucydides to the Nuclear Age.* Boulder, Colo.: Westview, 1991.

Legro, Jeffrey W., and Andrew Moravcsik. "Is Anybody Still a Realist?" *International Security* 24/2 (1999): 5–55.

Levy, Jack S. "The Diversionary Theory of War: A Critique." In *Handbook of War Studies,* edited by Manus I. Miklarsky, 259–288. Boston: Unwin Hyman, 1989.

Liberman, Peter. "The Spoils of Conquest." In *The Perils of Anarchy: Contemporary Realism and International Security,* edited by Michael E. Brown, Sean M. Lynn-Jones, and Steven E. Miller, 179–207. Cambridge: MIT Press, 1995.

——. *Does Conquest Pay? The Exploitation of Occupied Industrial Societies.* Princeton, N.J.: Princeton University Press, 1996.

Litke, Robert F. "Violence and Power." *International Social Science Journal* 44/2 (1992): 173–183.
Little, Richard. "International Relations and the Methodological Turn." *Political Studies* 39 (September 1991): 463–478.
Lord, Luis E. *Thucydides and the World War*. New York: Russell and Russell, 1945.
Loriaux, Michael. "The Realists and Saint Augustine: Skepticism, Psychology, and Moral Action in International Relations Thought." *International Studies Quarterly* 36/4 (1992): 401–420.
Machiavelli, Niccolo. *The Prince*. Translated by Angelo M. Codevilla. 1513. Reprint, Cambridge: Cambridge University Press, 1988.
——. *Discourses on Livy*. Translated by Julia Conaway Bondanella and Peter Bondanella. 1513. Reprint, Oxford: Oxford University Press, 1997.
Macpherson, Crawford B. *The Political Theory of Possessive Individualism: Hobbes to Locke*. Oxford: Clarendon Press, 1962.
Madsen, K. B. *Modern Theories of Motivation: A Comparative Metascientific Study*. New York: Wiley, 1974.
Mandel, Robert. "Psychological Approaches to International Relations." In *Political Psychology*, edited by Margaret G. Hermann, 251–278. San Franciso: Jossey-Bass, 1986.
Mannheim, Karl. *Ideology and Utopia*. New York: Harcourt, Brace, and Company, 1936.
Mansbridge, Jane. "Rational Choice Gains by Losing." *Political Psychology* 16/1 (1995): 137–155.
——, ed. *Beyond Self-Interest*. Chicago: University of Chicago Press, 1990.
Marinatos, Nanno. *Thucydides and Religion*. Koenigstein/Ts., Ger.: Verlag Anton Hain, 1981.
Marshall, George C. *The Papers of George Catlett Marshall*. Baltimore: Johns Hopkins University Press, 1981.
Marwell, Gerard, and Ruth Ames. "Economists Free Ride, Does Anyone Else?" *Journal of Public Economics* 15 (June 1981): 295–310.
Masker, John Scott. *Small States and Security Regimes: The International Politics of Nuclear Non-Proliferation in Nordic Europe and the South Pacific*. Lanham, Md.: University Press of America, 1995.
Maslow, Abraham H. *Motivation and Personality*. New York: Harper and Row, 1952.
Mastanduno, Michael. "Preserving the Unipolar Moment: Realist Theories and U.S. Grand Strategy after the Cold War." *International Security* 21/4 (1997): 49–88.
Mattingly, Garret. "Machiavelli's Prince: Political Science or Political Satire?" *American Scholar* 27 (1958): 482–491.
Maxwell, Mary. *Morality among Nations: An Evolutionary View*. Albany: State University of New York Press, 1990.
May, Ernest R. *"Lessons" of the Past: The Use and Misuse of History in American Foreign Policy*. New York: Oxford University Press, 1973.
McCalla, Robert B. *Uncertain Perceptions: U.S. Cold War Crisis Decision Making*. Ann Arbor: University of Michigan Press, 1992.
McClelland, David C. *Power: The Inner Experience*. New York: Irvington, 1975.
——. *Human Motivation*. Cambridge: Cambridge University Press, 1987.
——, ed. *Studies in Motivation*. New York: Appleton-Century-Crofts, 1955.
McClelland, David C., John W. Atkinson, Russell A. Clark, and Edgar L. Lowell. *The Achievement Motive*. New York: Appleton-Century-Crofts, 1953.
McClelland, David C., and Robert S. Steele. Introduction to *Human Motivation: A Book of Readings*, edited by David C. McClelland and Robert S. Steele, vii–x. Cambridge: Cambridge University Press, 1987.

——, eds. *Human Motivation: A Book of Readings*. Morristown, N.J.: General Learning Press, 1973.

McDonald, Christopher. "Human Nature and the Nature of States: Realism and Political Philosophy." Paper presented at the annual meeting of the International Studies Association, San Diego, California, April 1996.

McNeil, Russell. "Thucydides as Science." Malaspina University-College (1996). Available at http://www.mala.bc.ca/~mcneil/lec18b.htm. Accessed May 26, 1998.

Mearsheimer, John J. "Why We Will Soon Miss the Cold War." *Atlantic* 266/2 (1990): 35–50.

——. "After the Cold War: Will We Miss It?" *Current* 327 (November 1990): 30–40.

——. "Back to the Future: Instability in Europe after the Cold War." *International Security* 15/1 (1990): 5–56.

——. "The False Promise of International Institutions." *International Security* 19/3 (winter 1994/1995): 5–49.

Meinecke, Friedrich. *Die Idee der Staatsraeson in der Neueren Geschichte*. Munich: R. Oldenbourg, 1924.

Mercer, John. "Anarchy and Identity," *International Organization* 49/2 (1995): 229–252.

Midlarsky, Manus I., ed. *Handbook of War Studies*. Boston: Unwin Hyman, 1989.

Miller, Dale T., and Rebecca K. Ratner. "The Disparity between the Actual and Assumed Power of Self-Interest." *Journal of Personality and Social Psychology* 74/1 (1998): 53–62.

Miller, George A., Eugene Galante, and Karl H. Pribram. *Plans and the Structure of Behavior*. New York: Holt, 1960.

Mitchell, John J. "Man as Aggressive, Exploitive, and Selfish: Overview." In *Human Nature: Theories, Conjection, and Descriptions*, edited by John J. Mitchell, 339–349. Metuchen, N.J.: Scarecrow Press, 1972.

——, ed. *Human Nature: Theories, Conjections, and Descriptions*. Metuchen, N.J.: Scarecrow Press, 1972.

Monroe, Kristen Renwick. "The Theory of Rational Action: Origins and Usefulness for Political Science" in *The Economic Approach to Politics: A Critical Reassessment of the Theory of Rational Action*, edited by Kristen Renwick Monroe, 1–31. New York: HarperCollins, 1991.

——, ed. *The Economic Approach to Politics: A Critical Reassessment of the Theory of Rational Action*. New York: HarperCollins, 1991.

Monroe, Renwick, Kristen, with Kristen Hill Maher. "Psychology and Rational Actor Theory." *Political Psychology* 16/1 (1995): 1–21.

Monoson, S. Sara and Michael Loriaux. "The Illusion of Power and the Disruption of Moral Norms: Thucydides' Critique of Periclean Policy." *American Political Science Review* 92/2 (1998): 285–297.

Moravcsik, Andrew. "Taking Preferences Seriously: A Liberal Theory of International Politics." *International Organization* 51/4 (1997): 513–554.

Morgenthau, Hans J. *Scientific Man vs. Power Politics*. Chicago: University of Chicago Press, 1946.

——. *In Defense of the National Interest*. New York: Knopf, 1951.

——. "Another 'Great Debate:' The National Interest of the United States." *American Political Science Review* 46/4 (1952): 961–988.

——. *Politics among Nations: The Struggle for Power and Peace*, 2nd ed. New York: Knopf, 1955.

——. *Dilemmas of Politics*. Chicago: University of Chicago Press, 1958.

——. "Realism in International Politics." *Naval War College Review* 10/5 (1958): 1–14.

——. *Truth and Power*. New York: Praeger, 1970.

——. "Thought and Action in Politics." *Social Research* 38/4 (1971): 611–632.

——. "Defining the National Interest—Again: Old Superstitions, New Realities." *The New Republic*, 22 January 1977, 50–55.

Morrow, James D. *Game Theory for Political Scientists*. Princeton, N.J.: Princeton University Press, 1994.

Mo Tzu. *Mo Tzu: Basic Writings*. Translated by Burton Watson. New York: Columbia University Press, 1963.

Mueller, John. *Retreat from Doomsday: The Obsolescence of Major Wars*. New York: Basic Books, 1989.

Mulholland, Leslie. "Egoism and Morality." *Journal of Philosophy* 86/10 (1989): 542–550.

Murray, A. J. H. "The Moral Politics of Hans Morgenthau." *Review of Politics* 58/1 (1996): 81–107.

Murray, Henry A. *Explorations in Personality*. New York: Oxford University Press, 1938.

Murray, Williamson. "War, Theory, Clausewitz, and Thucydides: The Game May Change but the Rules Remain." *Marine Corps Gazette* 81/1 (1997): 62–69.

Myers, Robert J. "Hans J. Morgenthau: On Speaking Truth to Power." *Society* 29/2 (1992): 65–71.

Nardin, Terry, and David R. Mapel, eds. *Traditions of International Ethics*. Cambridge: Cambridge University Press, 1992.

Navari, Cornelia. "Hobbes and the 'Hobbesian Tradition' in International Thought." *Millennium* 11/3 (1982): 203–222.

Neufeld, Mark A. *The Restructuring of IR Theory*. New York: Cambridge University Press, 1995.

Neustadt, Richard E., and Ernest R. May. *Thinking in Time: The Uses of History for Decision-Makers*. New York: Free Press, 1986.

Newell, Allen, and Herbert A. Simon. *Human Problem Solving*. Englewood Cliffs, N.J.: Prentice-Hall, 1972.

Nicholson, Michael. "The Enigma of Martin Wight." *Review of International Studies* 7/1 (1981): 15–22.

——. *Formal Theories in International Relations*. New York: Cambridge University Press, 1992.

——. *Causes and Consequences in International Relations: A Conceptual Study*. New York: Cassell Academic, 1996.

Niebuhr, Reinhold. *Moral Man and Immoral Society: A Study in Ethics and Politics*. New York: Scribner, 1932.

——. *The Children of Light and the Children of Darkness*. New York: Scribner, 1944.

——. *Christian Realism*. New York: Scribner, 1953.

——. *The Structure of Nations and Empires*. New York: Scribner, 1959.

——. *Man's Nature and His Communities: Essays on the Dynamics and Enigmas of Man's Personal and Social Existence*. New York: Scribner, 1965.

Nolan, Cathal J., ed. *Ethics and Statecraft: The Moral Dimension of International Affairs*. Westport, Conn.: Praeger, 1995.

Noonan, John D. "Thucydides 1.23.6: Dionysius of Halicarnassus and the Scholion." *Greek, Roman, and Byzantine Studies* 33/1 (1992): 37–49.

Nye, Joseph S. Jr. "Ethics and Foreign Policy." *An Occasional Paper*. Queenstown, Md.: Aspen Institute, 1985.

——. "Neorealism and Neoliberalism." *World Politics* 40 (January 1988): 235–251.

——. "Conflicts after the Cold War." *Washington Quarterly* 19/1 (1996): 5–24.

Olschki, Leonardo. *Machiavelli the Scientist*. Berkeley, Calif.: Gillick, 1945.

Olson, Mancur Jr. *The Logic of Collective Action*. 1965. Reprint, Cambridge: Harvard University Press, 1971.

Oppenheim, Felix E. *The Place of Morality in Foreign Policy*. Lexington, Mass.: Lexington Books, 1991.

Organski, A. F. K., and Jacek Kugler. *The War Ledger*. Chicago: University of Chicago Press, 1980.

Orwin, Clifford. "Stasis and Plague: Thucydides on the Dissolution of Society." *Journal of Politics* 50/4 (1988): 831–847.

——. *The Humanity of Thucydides*. Princeton, N.J.: Princeton University Press, 1994.

Osiander, Andreas. "Rereading Early Twentieth-Century IR Theory: Idealism Revisited." *International Studies Quarterly* 42/3 (1998): 409–432.

Oye, Kenneth A., ed. *Cooperation under Anarchy*. Princeton, N.J.: Princeton University Press, 1986.

Peterson, Bill E, David Winter, and Richard Doty. "Laboratory Tests of a Motivational–Perceptual Model of Conflict Escalation." *Journal of Conflict Resolution* 38/4 (1994): 719–748.

Peterson, V. Spike. "Transgressing Boundaries: Theories of Knowledge, Gender, and IR." *Millennium* 21/2 (1992): 183–206.

Petracca, Mark P. "The Rational Actor Approach to Politics: Science, Self-Interest, and Normative Democratic Theory." In *The Economic Approach to Politics: A Critical Reassessment of the Theory of Rational Action*, edited by Kristen Renwick Monroe, 171–203. New York: HarperCollins, 1991.

Petty, Richard E., and John T. Cacioppo. *Attitudes and Persuasion: Classic and Contemporary Approaches*. Dubuque, Iowa: Brown, 1981.

Pocock, John G. A. *The Machiavellian Moment: Florentine Political Thought and the Atlantic Republican Tradition*. Princeton, N.J.: Princeton University Press, 1975.

Popper, Karl R. *The Logic of Scientific Discovery*. 1934. Reprint, New York: Basic Books, 1959.

——. *Conjectures and Refutations: The Growth of Scientific Knowledge*. New York: Basic Books, 1962.

——. "Normal Science and Its Dangers." In *Criticism and the Growth of Knowledge*, edited by Imre Lakatos and Alan Musgrave, 51–58. Cambridge: Cambridge University Press, 1970.

——. *Objective Knowledge: An Evolutionary Approach*. Oxford: Clarendon Press, 1972.

——. "The Logic of the Social Sciences." In *The Positivist Dispute in German Sociology*, edited by Theodor W. Adorno, Hans Albert, Ralf Dahrendorf, Jürgen Habermas, Harold Pilot, and Karl R. Popper, 87–104. London: Heinemann, 1976.

——. *The Open Universe: An Argument for Indeterminism*. Totowa, N.J.: Rowman and Littlefield, 1982.

——. *Realism and the Aim of Science*. Totowa, N.J.: Rowman and Littlefield, 1983.

Porter, Brian, ed. *The Aberystwyth Papers: International Politics, 1919–1969*. London: Oxford University Press, 1972.

Porter, Bruce D. "External Conflict and External Sovereignty: Towards a Neorealist Theory of the State." Paper presented at the annual meeting of the American Political Science Association, New York City, September 1994.

Posen, Barry. "The Security Dilemma and Ethnic Conflict." *Survival* 35/1 (1993): 27–47.

Pouncey, Peter R. *The Necessities of War: A Study of Thucydides' Pessimism*. New York: Columbia University Press, 1980.

Poundstone, William. *Labyrinths of Reason*. 1988. Reprint, New York: Anchor Books/Doubleday, 1990.

Pruitt, Dean G. "Definition of the Situation as a Determinant of International Interaction." In *International Behavior: A Social–Psychological Analysis*, edited by Herbert C. Kelman, 393–432. New York: Holt, Rinehart, and Winston, 1965.

Quester, George H. *Offense and Defense in the International System*. New York: Wiley, 1977.

Rahe, Paul. "Thucydides' Critique of Realpolitik." *Security Studies* 5/2 (winter 1995/1996): 105–141.

Rapoport, Anatol. *Fights, Games, and Debates*. Ann Arbor: University of Michigan Press, 1960.

Rawls, John. *A Theory of Justice*. Oxford: Oxford University Press, 1971.

Ray, James Lee. "Promise or Peril: Neorealism, Neoliberalism, and the Future of International Politics." In *Controversies in International Relations Theory: Realism and the Neoliberal Challenge*, edited by Charles W. Kegley Jr., 335–335. New York: St. Martin's, 1995.

Reeve, Johnmarshall. *Understanding Motivation and Emotion*. San Diego, Calif.: Harcourt Brace Jovanovich, 1992.

Rengakos, Antonios. *Form und Wandel des Machtdenkens der Athener bei Thukydides*. Stuttgart, Ger.: F. Steiner Wiesbaden, 1984.

Richards, James M. Jr. "Units of Analysis and the Individual Differences Fallacy in Environmental Assessment." *Environment and Behavior* 22/3 (1990): 307–319.

Risse-Kappen, Thomas. "Ideas Do Not Float Freely: Transnational Coalitions, Domestic Structures, and the End of the Cold War." In *International Relations Theory and the End of the Cold War*, edited by Richard Ned Lebow and Thomas Risse-Kappen, 187–222. New York: Columbia University Press, 1995.

Rokeach, Milton. *The Open and Closed Mind*. New York: Basic Books, 1960.

Romilly, Jacqueline de. *Thucydides and Athenian Imperialism*. Oxford: Blackwell, 1963.

Rosenau, James N. *Turbulence in World Politics*. Princeton, N.J.: Princeton University Press, 1990.

Rosenau, James N., and Ernst-Otto Czempiel, eds. *Governance without Government: Order and Change in World Politics*. New York: Cambridge University Press, 1992.

Rosenau, Pauline. "Once Again into the Fray: IR Confronts the Humanities." *Millennium* 19/1 (1990): 83–110.

Rotberg, Robert I., and Theodore K. Rabb, eds. *The Origin and Prevention of Major Wars*. Cambridge: Cambridge University Press, 1989.

Rousseau, Jean-Jacques. "A Discourse on the Origin of Inequality." In *The Social Contract and Discourses*, translated by G. D. H. Cole, 175–282. New York: E. P. Dutton, 1950.

———."Of The Social Contract." In *The Social Contract and Other Later Political Writings*, edited and translated by Victor Gourevitch, 39–152. Cambridge: Cambridge University Press, 1997.

———. "The State of War." In *The Social Contract and Other Later Political Writings*, edited and translated by Victor Gourevitch, 162–176. Cambridge: Cambridge University Press, 1967.

Ruggie, John Gerard. "International Responses to Technology." *International Organization* 29 (summer 1975): 557–584.

——. "Continuity and Transformation in the World Polity: Toward a Neorealist Synthesis." In *Neorealism and Its Critics*, edited by Robert O. Keohane, 131–157. New York: Columbia University Press, 1986.

——. "The False Premise of Realism." *International Security* 20/1 (1995): 62–70.

Russell, Greg. *Hans J. Morgenthau and the Ethics of American Statecraft*. Baton Rouge: Louisiana State University Press, 1990.

——. "Hans J. Morgenthau and the National Interest." *Society* 31/2 (1994): 80–84.

Schafer, Mark. "Cooperative and Conflictual Policy Preferences: The Effect of Identity, Security, and Image of the Other." *Political Psychology* 20/4 (1999): 829–844.

Schank, Roger C., and Robert P. Abelson. *Scripts, Plans, Goals, and Understanding*. Hillsdale, N.J.: Erlbaum, 1977.

Schelling, Thomas. *The Strategy of Conflict*. Cambridge: Harvard University Press, 1960.

——. *Choice and Consequence*. Cambridge: Harvard University Press, 1984.

Schlatter, Richard. Introduction to *Hobbes's Thucydides*, by Thucydides, edited by Richard Schlatter, xi–xxviii. New Brunswick, N.J.: Rutgers University Press, 1975.

Schmidt, Brian C. "Lessons from the Past: Reassessing the Interwar Disciplinary History of International Relations." *International Studies Quarterly* 42/3 (1998): 433–459.

Schmookler, Andrew Bard. *Parable of the Tribes: The Problem of Power in Social Evolution*, 2nd ed. Albany: State University of New York Press, 1994.

Schneider, Christoph. *Information und Absicht bei Thukydides*. Goettingen, Ger.: Vandenhoeck and Ruprecht, 1974.

Schwartz, Sharon. "The Fallacy of the Ecological Fallacy: The Potential Misuse of a Concept and the Consequences." *American Journal of Public Health* 84 (1994): 819–824.

Schwarzenberger, Georg. *Power Politics: A Study of International Society*. New York: Praeger, 1951.

Schweller, Randall L. *Deadly Imbalances: Tripolarity and Hitler's Strategy of World Conquest*. New York: Columbia University Press, 1997.

Schweller, Randall L., and David Priess. "A Tale of Two Realisms: Expanding the Institutions Debate." *Mershon International Studies Review* 41 (suppl. 1; 1997): 1–32.

Sheffer, Gabriel. "The Security of Small Ethnic States: A Counter Neo-Realist Argument." In *The National Security of Small States in a Changing World*, edited by Efraim Inbar and Gabriel Sheffer, 9–40. London: Frank Cass, 1997.

Shimko, Keith L. *Images and Arms Control: Perceptions of the Soviet Union in the Reagan Administration*. Ann Arbor: University of Michigan Press, 1991.

Sigal, Leon V. *Disarming Strangers*. Princeton, N.J.: Princeton University Press, 1999.

Silverman, David L. "Generic Revolution." Available at http://web.reed.edu/academic/departments/Humanities/Hum110/ThucLecture95.html. Accessed May 26, 1998.

Simon, Herbert A. *Models of Bounded Rationality*. Cambridge: MIT Press, 1982.

——. "Human Nature in Politics: The Dialogue of Psychology with Political Science." *American Political Science Review* 79 (June 1985): 293–304.

Singer, David J. "The Level-of-Analysis Problem in International Relations." In *The International System: Theoretical Essays*, edited by Klaus Knorr and Sidney Verba, 77–92. Princeton, N.J.: Princeton University Press, 1961.

Singer, Eric, and Valerie Hudson, eds. *Political Psychology and Foreign Policy*. Boulder, Colo.: Westview, 1992.

Skinner, Quentin. *Machiavelli*. New York: Hill and Wang, 1981.

——. *Reason and Rhetoric in the Philosophy of Hobbes*. Cambridge: Cambridge University Press, 1996.

Smith, M. Brewster, Jerome S. Bruner, and Robert W. White. *Opinions and Personality*. New York: Wiley, 1956.

Smith, Michael J. "Hans Morgenthau and the American National Interest in the Early Cold War." *Social Research* 48/8 (1981): 766–785.

———. *Realism from Weber to Kissinger*. Baton Rouge: Louisiana State University Press, 1986.

Smith, Steve. "The Self-Images of a Discipline: A Genealogy of International Relations Theory." In *International Relations Theory Today*, edited by Ken Booth and Steve Smith, 1–37. Cambridge: Polity Press, 1995.

Snidal, Duncan. "The Game Theory of International Politics." In *Cooperation under Anarchy*, edited by Kenneth A. Oye, 25–57. Princeton, N.J.: Princeton University Press, 1986.

———. "Relative Gains and the Pattern of International Cooperation." *American Political Science Review* 85/3 (1991): 701–726.

Snyder, Glenn H., and Paul Diesing. *Conflict among Nations: Bargaining, Decision Making, and System Structure in International Crises*. Princeton, N.J.: Princeton University Press, 1977.

Snyder, Jack. "Perceptions of the Security Dilemma in 1914." In *Psychology and Deterrence*, edited by Robert Jervis, Janice Gross Stein, and Richard Ned Lebow, 153–179. Baltimore: Johns Hopkins University Press, 1985.

———. "Averting Anarchy in the New Europe." *International Security* 14/4 (1990): 5–41.

———. *Myths of Empire: Domestic Politics and International Ambition*. Ithaca, N.Y.: Cornell University Press, 1991.

———. "Myths, Modernization, and the Post-Gorbachev World." In *International Relations Theory and the End of the Cold War*, edited by Richard Ned Lebow and Thomas Risse-Kappen, 109–126. New York: Columbia University Press, 1995.

Snyder, Richard C., H. W. Bruck, and Burton Sapin. *Decision-Making as an Approach to the Study of International Politics*. Princeton, N.J.: Princeton University Press, 1954.

———. *Foreign Policy Decisionmaking*. Glencoe, Ill.: Free Press, 1962.

Soellner, Alfons. "German Conservatism in America: Morgenthau's Political Realism." *Telos* 72 (summer 1987): 161–172.

Sorell, Tom, ed. *The Cambridge Companion to Hobbes*. Cambridge: Cambridge University Press, 1996.

Spegele, Roger D. *Political Realism in International Theory*. Cambridge: Cambridge University Press, 1996.

Sprout, Harold, and Margaret Sprout. *Man–Milieu Relationship Hypotheses in the Context of International Politics*. Princeton, N.J.: Center of International Studies, 1956.

———. "Environmental Factors in the Study of International Politics." *Journal of Conflict Resolution* 1 (1957): 309–328.

Staedter, Philip A., ed. *The Speeches in Thucydides*. Chapel Hill: University of North Carolina Press, 1973.

Stagner, Ross. *Psychological Aspects of International Conflict*. Belmont, Calif.: Brooks/Cole, 1967.

Stahl, Hans-Peter. *Thukydides: Die Stellung des Menschen im Geschichtlichen Prozess*. Munich: Beck'sche Verlagsbuchhandlung, 1966.

Stein, Arthur A. *Why Nations Cooperate: Circumstance and Choice in International Relations*. Ithaca, N.Y.: Cornell University Press, 1990.

Stein, Janice Gross. "Political Learning by Doing: Gorbachev as Uncommitted Thinker and Motivated Learner." In *International Relations Theory and the End of the Cold War*, edited by Richard Ned Lebow and Thomas Risse-Kappen, 223–258. New York: Columbia University Press, 1995.

Steinmo, Sven, Kathleen Thelen, and Frank Longstreth, eds. *Structuring Politics: Historical Institutionalism in Comparative Analysis*. Cambridge: Cambridge University Press, 1992.

Sterling-Folker, Jennifer. "Realist Environment, Liberal Process, and Domestic-Level Variables." *International Studies Quarterly* 41/1 (1997): 1–25.

——. "Competing Paradigms or Birds of a Feather? Constructivism and Neoliberal Institutionalism Compared." *International Studies Quarterly* 44/1 (2000): 97–119.

——. "Realism and the Constructivist Challenge: Rejecting, Reconstructing or Rereading." *International Studies Review* 4/1 (2002): 73–97.

Strange, Susan. *The Retreat of the State: The Diffusion of Power in the World Economy*. Cambridge: Cambridge University Press, 1996.

Strauss, Leo. "Niccolo Machiavelli." In *History of Political Philosophy*, 2nd ed., edited by Leo Strauss and Joseph Cropsey, 271–291. Chicago: University of Chicago Press, 1982.

——. *Thoughts on Machiavelli*. 1958. Reprint, Chicago: University of Chicago Press, 1984.

——. *The Political Philosophy of Hobbes: Its Basis and Its Genesis*. Chicago: University of Chicago Press, 1952.

Tellis, Ashley J. "Reconstructing Political Realism: The Long March to Scientific Theory." *Security Studies* 5/2 (winter 1995/1996): 3–101.

Tetlock, Philip E. "Integrative Complexity of American and Soviet Foreign Policy Rhetoric: A Time Series Analysis." *Journal of Personality and Social Psychology* 49 (1985): 565–585.

Thayer, Bradley. "Bringing in Darwin: Evolutionary Theory, Realism, and International Relations." *International Security* 25/2 (2000): 124 –151.

Thomas, Laurence. "Doing Justice to Egoism." *The Journal of Philosophy* 86/10 (1989): 551–552.

Thompson, John B. "Hermeneutics." In *The Social Science Encyclopedia*, 2nd ed., edited by Adam Kuper and Jessica Kuper, 360–361. London: Routledge, 1996.

Thompson, Kenneth W. "The Cold War: The Legacy of Morgenthau's Approach." *Social Research* 48/4 (1981): 660–676.

——. *Moralism and Morality in Politics and Diplomacy*. Lanham, Md.: University Press of America, 1985.

Thompson, Kenneth W., and Robert J. Myers. *Truth and Tragedy: A Festschrift for Hans J. Morgenthau*. New Brunswick, N.J.: Transaction Publishers, 1984.

Thucydides. *History of the Peloponnesian War*. Translated by Richard Crawley. London: J. M. Dent, 1910.

——. *The Peloponnesian Wars*. Translated by Benjamin Jowett. London: New English Library, 1966.

——. *History of the Peloponnesian War*. Translated by Rex Warner. Harmondsworth, U.K.: Penguin Books, 1972.

——. *Hobbes's Thucydides*. Edited by Richard Schlatter. New Brunswick, N.J.: Rutgers University Press, 1975.

Tucker, Robert. *The Inequality of Nations*. New York: Basic Books, 1977.

Tullock, Gordon. *The Vote Motive*. London: Institute of Economic Affairs, 1976.

Valentine, Jeremy. "Hobbes's Political Geometry." *History of the Human Sciences* 10/2 (1997): 23–40.

van Evera, Stephen. "Primed for Peace: Europe after the Cold War." *International Security* 15/3 (1990): 7–57.

———. "Offense, Defense, and the Causes of War." *International Security* 22/4 (1998): 5–43.

van Mill, David. "Rationality, Action, and Autonomy in Hobbes's Leviathan." *Polity* 27/2 (1994): 285–306.

Vasquez, John A. *The Power of Power Politics: An Empirical Evaluation of the Scientific Study of International Relations.* New Brunswick, N.J.: Rutgers University Press, 1983.

———. *The War Puzzle.* New York: Cambridge University Press, 1993.

———. "The Post-Positivist Debate: Reconstructing Scientific Enquiry and International Relations Theory After Enlightenment's Fall." In *International Relations Theory Today*, edited by Ken Booth and Steve Smith, 217–240. Cambridge: Polity Press, 1995.

———. "The Realist Paradigm and Degenerative versus Progressive Research Programs: An Appraisal of Neotraditional Research on Waltz's Balancing Proposition." *American Political Science Review* 91/4 (1997): 899–912.

———. *The Power of Power Politics: From Classical Realism to Neotraditionalism.* Cambridge: Cambridge University Press, 1998.

Verba, Sidney. "Assumptions of Rationality and Non-Rationality in Models of the International System." In *The International System: Theoretical Essays*, edited by Klaus Knorr and Sidney Verba, 93–117. Princeton, N.J.: Princeton University Press, 1961.

Vertzberger, Yaacov Y. I. *The World in Their Minds: Information Processing, Cognition, and Perception in Foreign Policy Decisionmaking.* Stanford, Calif.: Stanford University Press, 1990.

Viotti, Paul R., and Mark V. Kauppi. *International Relations Theory: Realism, Pluralism, Globalism.* New York: Macmillan, 1987.

Voeglin, Eric. *Order and History.* Vol. 2, *The World of the Polis.* Baton Rouge: Louisiana State University Press, 1957.

von Clausewitz, Carl. *On War.* Translated by Michael Howard and Peter Paret. 1832–1834. Reprint, Princeton, N.J.: Princeton University Press, 1976.

Voss, James F., and Ellen Dorsey. "Perceptions and International Relations: An Overview." In *Political Psychology and Foreign Policy*, edited by Eric Singer and Valerie Hudson, 3–30. Boulder, Colo.: Westview, 1992.

Walker, Robert B. J. "Realism, Change, and International Political Theory," *International Studies Quarterly* 31/1 (1987): 65–86.

———. *Inside/Outside: International Relations as Political Theory.* Cambridge: Cambridge University Press, 1993.

———. "International Relations and the Concept of the Political." In *International Relations Theory Today*, edited by Ken Booth and Steve Smith, 306–327. Cambridge: Polity Press, 1995.

Walt, Stephen M. "The Progressive Power of Realism." *American Political Science Review* 91/4 (1997): 931–935.

———. "International Relations: One World, Many Theories." *Foreign Policy* 110 (1998): 29–46.

Waltz, Kenneth N. *Man, the State, and War: A Theoretical Analysis.* New York: Columbia University Press, 1959.

———. *Theory of International Politics.* New York: McGraw-Hill, 1979.

———. "Realist Thought and Neorealist Theory." *Journal of International Affairs* 44/1 (1990): 21–37.

———. "The New-World Order." *Millennium* 22/2 (1993): 187–195.

———. "The Emerging Structure of International Politics." *International Security* 18/2 (1993): 44–79.

———. "The Validation of International-Political Theory." Paper presented at the annual meeting of the American Political Science Association, New York City, September 1994.

———. "Evaluating Theories." *American Political Science Review* 91/4 (1997): 913–917.

Wayman, Frank W., and Paul F. Diehl. "Realpolitik: Dead End, Detour, or Road Map?" In *Reconstructing Realpolitik*, edited by Frank W. Wayman and Paul F. Diehl, 247–265. Ann Arbor: University of Michigan Press, 1994.

Wayman, Frank W., and Paul F. Diehl, eds. *Reconstructing Realpolitik*. Ann Arbor: University of Michigan Press, 1994.

Wendt, Alexander. "The Agent-Structure Problem in International Relations Theory." *International Organization* 41 (summer 1987): 335–370.

———. "Anarchy Is What States Make of It: The Social Construction of Power Politics." *International Organization* 46/2 (1992): 391–425.

———. "Collective Identity Formation and the International State." *American Political Science Review* 88/2 (1994): 384–396.

———. "Constructing International Politics." *International Security* 20/1 (1995): 71–81.

Wheeler, Harvey. "The Role of Myth System in American–Soviet Relations." *Journal of Conflict Resolution* 4 (1960): 179–184.

White, James Boyd. *When Words Lose Their Meaning: Constitutions and Reconstitutions of Language, Character, and Community*. Chicago: University of Chicago Press, 1984.

White, Ralph K. *Fearful Warriors: A Psychological Profile of U.S.–Soviet Relations*. New York: Free Press, 1984.

Whitehead, John C. "Principled Realism: A Foundation for U.S. Policy." *Department of State Bulletin* 88/2135 (1988): 33–35.

Wight, Martin. *Power Politics*. London: Royal Institute of International Affairs, 1949.

———. "Why Is There No International Theory?" In *Diplomatic Investigations: Essays in the Theory of International Politics*, edited by Herbert Butterfield and Martin Wight, 17–34. Cambridge: Harvard University Press, 1966.

Williams, Michael C. "Hobbes and International Relations: A Reconsideration." *International Organization* 50/2 (1996): 213–236.

Winch, Peter. *The Idea of a Social Science and Its Relation to Philosophy*. 1958. Reprint, London: Routledge 1988.

Winter, David G. *The Power Motive*. New York: Free Press, 1973.

———. "Power, Affiliation, and War: Three Tests of a Motivational Model." *Journal of Personality and Social Psychology* 65/3 (1993): 532–545.

Wolfers, Arnold. *Discord and Collaboration: Essays on International Politics*. Baltimore: Johns Hopkins University Press, 1962.

Wolin, Sheldon S. *Politics and Vision: Continuity and Innovation in Western Political Thought*. Boston: Little, Brown, 1960.

Woodhead, Arthur Geoffrey. *Thucydides on the Nature of Power*. Cambridge: Harvard University Press, 1970.

Wright, Quincy. *The Study of International Relations*. New York: Appleton-Century-Crofts, 1955.

———. "Design for a Research Project on International Conflict and the Factors Causing Their Aggravation or Amelioration." *Western Political Quarterly* 10 (1957): 263–275.

Wrightsman, Lawrence S. *Assumptions about Human Nature: A Social–Psychological Approach*. Monterey, Calif.: Books/Cole, 1974.

——. *Assumptions about Human Nature: Implications for Researchers and Practitioners*, 2nd ed. Newbury Park, Calif.: Sage, 1992.

Wrightson, Patricia Stein. "Morality, Realism, and Foreign Affairs: A Normative Realist Approach." *Security Studies* 5/2 (winter 1995/1996): 354–386.

Young, Oran R. *International Cooperation: Building Regimes for Natural Resources and the Environment*. Ithaca, N.Y.: Cornell University Press, 1989.

Zakaria, Fareed. *From Wealth to Power: The Unusual Origins of America's World Role*. Princeton, N.J.: Princeton University Press, 1998.

Zalewski, Marysia, and Cynthia Enloe. "Questions about Identity in International Relations." In *International Relations Theory Today*, edited by Ken Booth and Steve Smith, 279–305. Cambridge: Polity Press, 1995.

Index

Suny series in Global Politics
James N. Rosenau, editor

American Patriotism in a Global Society—Betty Jean Craige

The Political Discourse of Anarchy: A Disciplinary History of International Relations—Brian C. Schmidt

From Pirates to Drug Lords: The Post–Cold War Caribbean Security Environment—Michael C. Desch, Jorge I. Dominguez, and Andres Serbin, editors

Collective Conflict Management and Changing World Politics—Joseph Lepgold and Thomas G. Weiss, editors

Zones of Peace in the Third World: South America and West Africa in Comparative Perspective—Arie M. Kacowicz

Private Authority and International Affairs—A. Claire Cutler, Virginia Haufler, and Tony Porter, editors

Harmonizing Europe: Nation–States within the Common Market—Francesco G. Duina

Economic Interdependence in Ukrainian–Russian Relations—Paul J. D'Anieri

Leapfrogging Development? The Political Economy of Telecommunication Restructuring—J. P. Singh

States, Firms, and Power: Successful Sanctions in United States Foreign Policy—George E. Shambaugh

Approaches to Global Governance Theory—Martin Hewson and Timothy J. Sinclair, editors

After Authority: War, Peace, and Global Politics in the Twenty-First Century—Ronnie D. Lipschutz

Pondering Postinternationalism: A Paradigm for the Twenty-First Century?—Heidi H. Hobbs, editor

Beyond Boundaries? Disciplines, Paradigms, and Theoretical Integration in International Studies—Rudra Sil and Eileen M. Doherty, editors

Why Movements Matter: The West German Peace Movement and U.S. Arms Control Policy—Steve Breyman

International Relations—Still an American Social Science? Toward Diversity in International Thought—Robert M. A. Crawford and Darryl S. L. Jarvis, editors

Which Lessons Matter? American Foreign Policy Decision Making in the Middle East, 1979–1987—Christopher Hemmer, editor

Hierarchy Amidst Anarchy: Transaction Costs and Institutional Choice—Katja Weber

Counter-Hegemony and Foreign Policy: The Dialectics of Marginalized and Global Forces in Jamaica—Randolph B. Persaud

Global Limits: Immanuel Kant, International Relations, and Critique of World Politics—Mark F. N. Franke

Power and Ideas: North–South Politics of Intellectual Property and Antitrust—Susan K. Sell

Money and Power in Europe: The Political Economy of European Monetary Cooperation—Matthias Kaelberer

Agency and Ethics: The Politics of Military Intervention—Anthony F. Lang Jr

Life After the Soviet Union: The Newly Independent Republics of the Transcaucasus and Central Asia—Nozar Alaolmolki

Theories of International Cooperation and the Primacy of Anarchy: Explaining U.S. International Monetary Policy-Making After Bretton Woods—Jennifer Sterling-Folker

Information Technologies and Global Politics: The Changing Scope of Power and Governance—James N. Rosenau and J. P. Singh, editors

Technology, Democracy, and Development: International Conflict and Cooperation in the Information Age—Juliann Emmons Allison, editor

The Arab–Israeli Conflict Transformed: Fifty Years of Interstate and Ethnic Crises—Hemda Ben-Yehuda and Shmuel Sandler

Systems of Violence: The Political Economy of War and Peace in Colombia—Nazih Richani

Debating the Global Financial Architecture—Leslie Elliot Armijo

Political Space: Frontiers of Change and Governance in a Globalizing World—Yale Ferguson and R. J. Barry Jones, editors

Crisis Theory and World Order: Heideggerian Reflections—Norman K. Swazo

Political Identity and Social Change: The Remaking of the South African Social Order—Jamie Frueh

Social Construction and the Logic of Money: Financial Predominance and International Economic Leadership—J. Samuel Barkin

What Moves Man: The Realist Theory of International Relations and Its Judgment of Human Nature—Annette Freyberg-Inan